The First Book of

the Mac

Second Edition

The First Book of

the Mac

Second Edition

Jay and Carla Rose

alpha books

A Division of Prentice Hall Computer Publishing

11711 North College, Carmel, Indiana 46032 USA

To Harpo

International Standard Book Number: 0-672-27418-3
Library of Congress Catalog Card Number: 92-73173

95 94 93 92 8 7 6 5 4 3 2

Interpretation of the printing code: the rightmost number of the first series of numbers is the year of the book's printing; the rightmost number of the second series of numbers is the number of the book's printing. For example, a printing code of 92-2 shows that the second printing of the book occurred in 1992.

Printed in the United States of America

Publisher
Marie Butler-Knight

Managing Editor
Elizabeth Keaffaber

Acquisitions Manager
Steve Poland

Product Development Manager
Lisa Bucki

Production Editor
Annalise N. Di Paolo

Copy Editor
San Dee Phillips

Cover Illustrator
Polly McNeal

Designer
Michele Laseau

Indexer
Jeanne Clark

Production Team
Terri Edwards
Tim Groeling
Dennis Clay Hager
John Kane
Carrie Keesling
Carla Hall-Batton
Roger Morgan
Linda Quigley
Michelle Self
Greg Simsic
Angie Trzepacz
Julie Walker
Alyssa Yesh

Special thanks to Steve Poland
for assuring the technical accuracy of this book.

Contents

Introduction

A few short years ago, Steve Jobs introduced the Mac at an Apple annual meeting. Or, more correctly, the Mac introduced itself. Jobs put a small beige box on the podium and it said, "Hello, I am Macintosh." The voice was mechanical, but it thrilled the audience. So did its next line: "I'd like to share with you a maxim I thought of the first time I met an IBM mainframe—never trust a computer you can't lift."

Along with the laughter and amazement, there were glints of recognition and delight in the auditorium. Here was a machine with personality, even with charisma. Clearly, this was a different kind of computer. In the years since then, the Mac has grown smarter, faster, more versatile, and more colorful. Its wise-guy attitude has also matured, making it an energetic and creative partner in many businesses.

But the Mac can still cause laughter and amazement, not only among sophisticated experts but also among people who think they hate computers. We hope, in teaching you how to use this handy machine effectively, we'll be able to share some of the laughter and amazement also.

Introduction to the Second Edition

In mid-1991, we hit Save for the last time. We had combined the distilled knowledge of seven years of Mac ownership, along with the expertise of countless consultants, software gurus, and usergroup members we'd met along the way.

But *the more things change, the more you've got a computer.* After we finished the first edition of this book, Apple introduced a new operating system and a slew of new machines. Software companies came out with radically new programs and radically improved some old favorites. Even the two competing giants of desktop computing—Apple and IBM—agreed to work together.

So, we rewrote most of the book to reflect the changes. And while we were at it, we revised a few sections to make them easier to use.

If you're thinking about buying a Mac, this book will help you choose a good new or used one (and show you some secrets Apple doesn't want you to know).

If you already own a Mac, it'll help you get the most out of it.

And if you just want to see what the fuss is all about, this book will tell you why—after almost a decade—we still love our favorite computer.

Conventions Used in This Book

As you read through *The First Book of the Mac, Second Edition,* you'll notice certain conventions we've used to make the book easier for you to use.

Any choices you should select from a Mac menu appear in color.

Text you type in appears in **`bold, color computer font`**. Text that appears on-screen appears in `computer font`.

The Mac allows you to enter commands via menus or keystrokes. Keystrokes to be made in combination are separated by a hyphen (-) and in this book are represented by small key cap illustrations meant to replicate the common keyboard key appearance. For example, ⌘-Space bar indicates you should press the ⌘ and the Space bar simultaneously.

TIPS: offer hints and shortcuts for using your Mac more effectively.

CAUTIONS: alert you to potential pitfalls and help solve common problems.

NOTES: point out additional features and provide background information you need to understand special terms.

FYIdeas describe practical ways you can use your Mac at work or at home, to create projects and documents you may not have even thought of!

Interesting history, additional information, or miscellaneous comments.

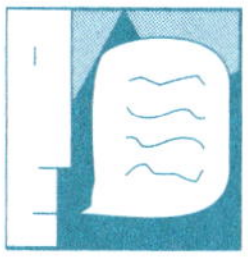

System Icons inform you of any particularities concerning which system you are running.

Acknowledgments

First of all, we'd like to thank all the people at Prentice Hall who made both editions possible, especially Steve Poland and Lisa Bucki (and Dan Derrick, who started the ball rolling by introducing us to Steve).

We'd like to express our gratitude to the many vendors of software and hardware who were generous with help and review copies of their products, and to the on-line services who let us come and play in their backyards.

Thanks are also due to the Boston Computer Society Macintosh Bulletin Board members, who helped us find answers to all kinds of questions. Their collective expertise is astounding!

Last, but never least, thanks to Josh and Dan for being good critics, highly skilled Mac users, and patient children of a sometimes-overworked pair of authors.

Trademark Acknowledgments

1

The Rest of Us

This short chapter represents the "gosh, golly" part of this book. It talks about a few of the things ordinary Macintosh owners are doing with ordinary software and recalls a little bit of Macintosh's early history (it's not what you think). If you want to get right down to learning how to use the Macintosh, skip ahead to Chapter 2.

Mac at Work and Play

Friday morning. Jeff Johnson, director of product development at Granpappy's Cookies, Inc., just received a challenge. The concession buyers from Harry Hamster's Holiday Park have just called. They're in town for just one day, and they'd like to drop by—say, around noon—to discuss a possible contract for five years' worth of rodent-shaped munchies. Jeff's boss, Granpappy, wants to give them a full presentation . . . in an hour and a half.

> Jeff is fictitious. So are Granpappy and Harry Hamster. Product development, deadlines, and presentations are unfortunately very real.

In an earlier age, this situation would have been cause for panic, but not now. Jeff turns to a small computer screen, nudges a little plastic box around on his desk, and activates an outliner to help organize the job. He starts jotting down ideas, and filling in details. Jeff then calls Granpappy's computer. The boss sees his message, makes a few changes on the outline, and sends it back. Meanwhile, Jeff delegates parts of the job to other departments.

- In purchasing, Patty connects to an on-line commodity investment service. She looks up long-term predictions for flour, sugar, and chocolate chips.
- Dave, in design, sketches a full-color, three-dimensional "Hungry Hamster" box on his screen.
- Mickey of marketing checks the database. He's gathering information that will graph Granpappy's popularity among twelve-year-olds.
- And Charlotte the comptroller is examining the potential effects of each cookie sold on the company's bottom line. She's smiling.

Each department's contribution streams into Jeff's computer, as he puts the finishing touches on the text. He uses an electronic thesaurus and grammar checker to polish his writing, while Sam (his secretary) calls their ad agency for an electronic version of the logo.

You know how it's all going to end. A few minutes before noon, the first pages of a beautifully typeset presentation start streaming out of Sam's laser printer. She hands them to Jeff as he marches triumphantly into the meeting. Applause and fade out.

> In the real world, the buyers would probably want the presentation sent to their offices instead. That's no problem. Sam's computer can also send an instant fax of the whole thing to Hamster HQ.

The story may be fiction, but it's not science fiction. All of the computers in Granpappy's offices are Macintoshes, with standard off-the-shelf software. Some of the machines in the network cost less than a thousand dollars each, and most of the programs cost only a few hundred.

The people who run Granpappy's company are cookie experts, not engineers. But they even wired the network themselves, using telephone cords from a discount store. To paraphrase an ad, these people are just like "the rest of us"—ordinary folks solving everyday problems with an incredibly easy-to-use computer. In fact, the same kind of computer and software are just as applicable to a grammar school project.

The Play's the Thing . . .

Jeff's wife, Judy, is president of the parents' organization at their child's school. A free-lance writer who works at home, she's always being "volunteered" to help out. This month, Judy and her Mac have been drafted to organize the school play. In addition to the usual posters, programs, and tickets, Judy will prepare diagrams of the stage layout for the director and lighting designer, news releases for the local media, and even a special newsletter to be printed at a local service bureau.

She has volunteers' names and phone numbers listed in HyperCard, so it's easy to have her computer speed-dial potential scenery builders and painters. She keeps track of ticket sales in a different database. The day before the play, she'll send a message to Jeff's computer at work, reminding him to bring home cartons of Granpappy's best for the refreshment table.

Judy's Mac even goes to the show. In the lobby, it displays an automated, animated presentation on the benefits of parent organization membership . . . until the music teacher borrows it to control his all-synthesizer band.

Afterward, she'll run expenses through the family bookkeeping program to see how much money was made, and then graph each classroom's ticket sales in a spreadsheet. (The winning class gets a pizza party instead of school lunch.) Finally, she'll use her word processor's "merge" function to create custom thank-you letters for everyone who helped.

The Point of It All

Judy and Jeff never thought they'd own computers, and certainly never expected to use them every day. They're not scientists figuring prime numbers to a thousand digits, or computer hackers programming in binary for pleasure (these people would probably want a different kind of computer, anyway). Jeff and Judy just want to get through their lives with a minimum of complication. They're a lot like the rest of us. That's why they use a Mac.

Process versus Product

Some computer systems are process oriented. You have to pay attention to the software and constantly make mental adjustments between what you're doing, what you did last, and what you'll end up with. Running the machine becomes more complicated than running the project.

The Macintosh was designed as a response to these machines and is product oriented. It's easy to learn, gives you instant feedback, and lets you concentrate on what your finished product will be like. Besides, it's fun.

Working Together

People think in many modes at once to generate a product. Jeff needed to pass information between outlining, networking, charting, financial forecasting, and design functions. Judy's project used a mix of clip art, budgeting, databases, animation, and music. Each used word processing and desktop publishing, but in different ways.

From the start, Apple insisted that all Macintosh programs support this kind of jumping around. At the heart of Mac's usefulness is the way it exchanges data from one program to another, even between programs from different publishers. A sketch from

Claris' MacPaint II can become part of an essay in Microsoft Word, integrated with a chart from Ashton-Tate's Full Impact, and then arranged graphically with Aldus PageMaker. Other programs could be added to the mix just as easily.

And learning these programs isn't difficult. Apple insisted that all its programs be based on how ordinary people work in the ordinary, noncomputer world. The Scrapbook and Folder concepts aren't just cute marketing gimmicks: they were carefully developed for people who have better things to do than learn about "data libraries" and "subdirectories."

The Opposite of Serious Isn't Frivolous

When Apple introduced the Macintosh in 1984, the biggest criticism was that it "wasn't a serious computer." People (primarily partisans of IBM's Personal Computer) called it a silly toy, of no use to button-down business people. Tools aren't supposed to be serious, they're supposed to be handy. Nobody ever complained that a typewriter or adding machine was too easy to work.

The Mac isn't serious about computing the way IBM is, because it (and its predecessor machines) redefined computing its own way. It is, however, a lot handier for most people than a similarly equipped PC. In fact, the two features IBM people made most fun of—the mouse and windows—have finally been adopted by the IBM PC and its clones. Apple and IBM are now working together to create the next major computing revolution.

Not a Way of Life, Just a Computer

By now, we've all heard the stories about the early days at Apple—how Steve Jobs and Steve Wozniak, boy geniuses, single-handedly pioneered a computer revolution in an old garage. It's a tale of true grit, single-minded devotion, and the American way. It's also a tale brought to you by the Apple Corporation public relations department.

In reality, Jobs' and Woz's first enterprise was the manufacture of blue boxes: little electronic signal generators, with absolutely no purpose except to defraud the telephone company. These gadgets would inject tones into the phone line, convincing Ma Bell's computers—back when there was a Ma Bell—that a long distance call had been properly paid for. Woz designed and built the boxes. Jobs marketed them. This was an important distinction, because Steve Jobs' contribution to computing (and ultimately to the Macintosh) wasn't based on any skills as an engineer. Jobs was the ultimate visionary: someone who could latch onto an idea and convince others to share his enthusiasm.

While the two Steves were building their blue boxes and enjoying life in San Francisco in the late 1960s, no less a corporate giant than Xerox was building a scientist's dream of a laboratory nearby, the Palo Alto Research Center (PARC). Xerox's intention was to develop their own computer technology, surpassing that of industry leader IBM, and to create a new computer individual researchers or engineers could use at their own desks. Until then, computers were either hulking monsters, requiring armies of technicians to operate, or inflated adding machines that couldn't do much more than solve equations.

PARC's first computer was the ALTO, a true personal computer that combined a mouse (invented earlier at Stanford Research Institute) and a high-resolution screen (developed largely at the University of Utah). Alan Kay, one of the PARC programmers, developed an operating system that included icons, windows, and a revolutionary "What You See Is What You Get" screen display. These eventually became the Macintosh user interface, which is discussed in Chapters 2 through 4 of this book.

Meanwhile, Jobs and Wozniak had gotten caught up in the San Francisco-based computer community and decided to revive their partnership by building a simple hobby computer. Their Apple (named after nothing more remarkable than an orchard where one of the Steves had spent some time) eventually caught on, largely because of an incredibly useful new program called a *spreadsheet* that Dan Bricklin had written (see Chapter 8). Like good entrepreneurs everywhere, Jobs and Woz started selling stock. Xerox's management, knowing a good thing when they saw it (and not having much luck marketing computers on their own), decided to invest.

The rest, as they say, is history. As part of their investment, Xerox let Jobs prowl through the PARC. He saw what they were doing with the ALTO and heard about Alan Kay's ideas for Dynabook: a simple, powerful computer that people could use in their everyday lives. Jobs got caught up in these ideas, and with evangelistic zeal started developing a new computer, Apple's *Lisa,* which soon became the Macintosh we know today.

And That's How Mac Was Born

The point is, a lot of very smart people—more than could ever be mentioned in this book—worked at a lot of different institutions to create the computer we now take for granted. (A few of them, who worked directly for Jobs, had their names engraved inside the box of the original Mac.)

Don't be amazed that this revolutionary gadget sprang out of Steve Jobs' or any other inventor's mind, because it didn't. If you want to be amazed about anything at all, consider that this entire story took place within the past dozen years or so.

Now that you're properly impressed, read the rest of this book. The Macintosh is handy, easy to use, and mostly fun. You can make it work for you.

In This Chapter

How to Turn on the Mac

•

Taking Control

•

The Desktop

One of the things that makes the Mac friendly is its *operating system*, the "super-program" that controls how other programs like a word processor or spreadsheet will work. Apple made its operating system resemble a standard office desk. Once you learn the Mac's *Desktop*, you'll be ready to use any other program easily. Before you can become a "power user" (computerese for those people who really know their way around the Mac), you've got to power it up. If your Mac isn't all set up and ready to go, jump ahead to Chapter 16 for help putting it together.

2

Finding Your Way Around

The first step in becoming a *Power User*—someone who can make their Mac work efficiently with a minimum of fuss—is turning on the Power. Turning on the program starts the *operating system* for your Mac. The operating system is the master program that controls your Mac's operations and lets you work with other applications. There are two operating systems currently in use on most Macs System 6.0.X and System 7. Both look and operate basically the same, but when System 7 was introduced in late 1991, it added several neat capabilities for Macs. New machines come with System 7. We'll highlight the differences between System 6 and System 7 throughout this book. Finding the power switch depends on which Mac you're using. *Compact Macs*—the ones with a classic "Mac" shape (including the Mac Classic)—have a black switch on the rear panel, right next to the power cord. If you're sitting in front of the computer, just reach your left hand around to the back, and you'll feel it about four inches up from the bottom. *Mac II* models—those with a separate monitor—have an unlabeled keyboard button with a triangle on it (as in Figure 2.1). This turns on both the computer and the monitor. *PowerBooks* have a little power button on their back panels. You might have to open an access door to see it.

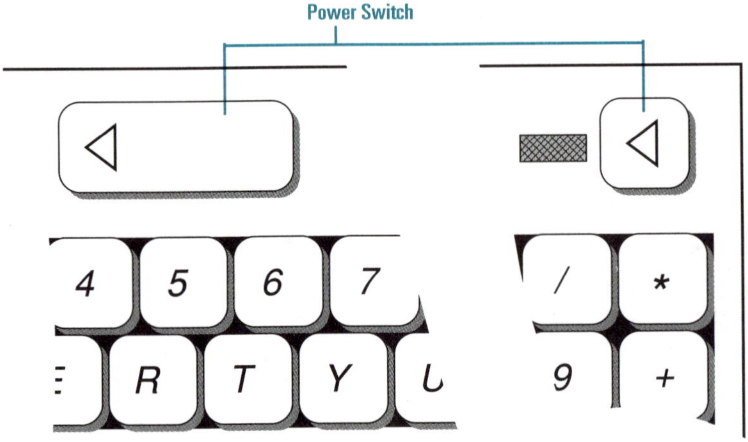

Figure 2.1

The power switch on two different model keyboards.

Non-Mac-II models may also have a "triangle" key. Push it all you want. It doesn't do anything.

Turn the computer on. (If you have an external hard disk, turn it on *first,* and wait about ten seconds for it to reach its running speed.) You'll hear a beep, or possibly a boing, chime, or harp glissando, to let you know the Mac is ready to go to work. If this is the first time anyone's turned on the Mac, a piece of plastic will pop out of the disk drive(s). Keep these drive protectors with your packing materials. Use them to protect the drives from damage if you have to pack your Mac for shipping.

If your computer has a built-in hard disk, just wait a few moments, and you'll see a "Happy Mac" icon, and then Finder, shown in Figure 2.2 appears.

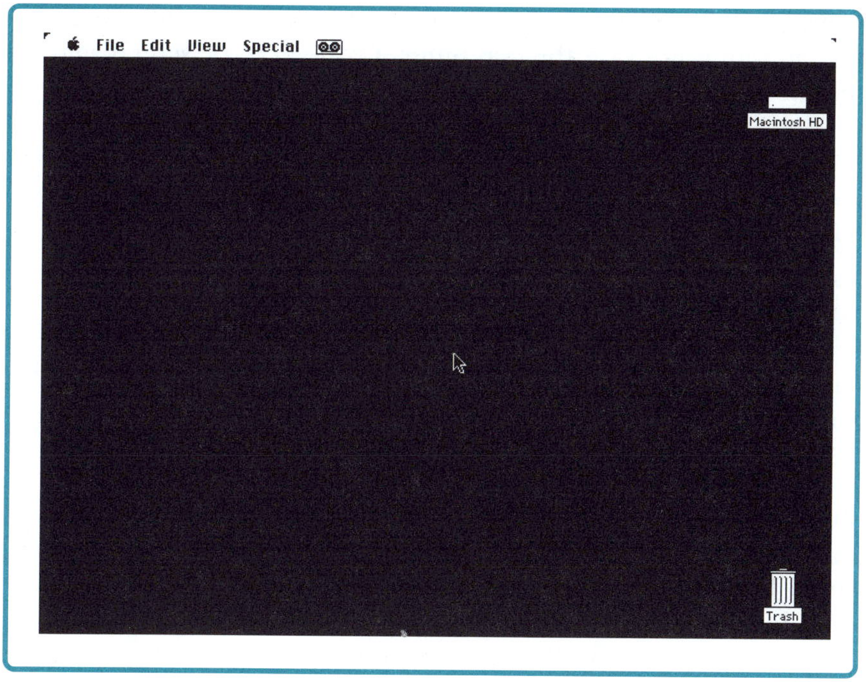

Figure 2.2
The Finder.

If your Mac doesn't have a hard drive, take a look at the screen. You'll see an icon. (An *icon* is a small picture which represents a computer function.) In this case, it's a disk with a question mark on it, as shown in Figure 2.3. This means that the Mac is asking which disk to use. find the floppy disk marked *System* or *System Tools*, or any other disk which has the System and Finder files on it.

Figure 2.3
The Disk Icon.

If you don't see anything at all, or if you see only dim images, try adjusting the screen contrast. On Macs with built-in screens, it's a little thumbwheel under the overhanging edge of the Mac, just under the Apple logo. On Powerbooks, look for a sliding control under the screen. If you're using a Mac II with a separate monitor, see the instructions for your monitor. By the way, your eyes will be happier through long hours at the computer if you keep the screen slightly dimmed.

Inserting a System Disk (or Any Other Disk, for That Matter)

Even though Macintosh disks are actually quite rigid, they're called *floppy disks* or *floppies.* Figure 2.4 shows the front and back of a floppy disk. (There are also *hard disks,* which a later chapter will explain.) Hold the floppy disk so that the label faces upward and the metal shutter points toward the Mac. Push it into the slot. Once it's almost in, the computer will pull it the rest of the way. You'll hear a "clunk" and a hum as the Mac opens the metal shutter and starts the disk spinning to read it. Now, the screen should show a "Happy Mac" face, as shown in Figure 2.5. (If you're inserting a data disk, not starting up, a disk icon appears on the desktop.)

Figure 2.4

A floppy disk.

As long as Mac looks happy, all is well. In another few seconds, he'll disappear and you'll see a dialog box, welcoming you to Macintosh. Finally, you'll see the *Finder,* shown in Figure 2.2. If your screen looks something like this figure, skip ahead to the beginning of the next section. If not, please keep reading.

Figure 2.5

The Happy Mac face.

> Please come back and read the next section later. There might be a time when the Finder doesn't pop up as it should. You ought to know what to do when that happens, right?

No Happy Faces

If, instead of a happy face, the computer ejects your disk and shows you the icon in Figure 2.6, it's telling you that the disk you're using isn't a system disk. Try a different disk. (Look for a disk marked system that came with your Mac.) If the Mac face looks sad, as shown in Figure 2.7, and has a string of letters and numbers below it, there's a hardware problem or a serious software problem. On newer Macs, you'll also hear an arpeggio instead of the nice major chord (that's musician for "separated notes") when there's a problem. See Chapter 14 for information and suggestions.

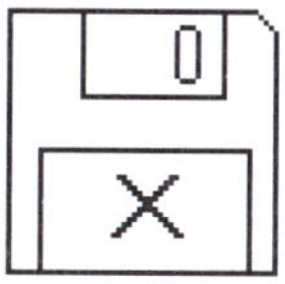

Figure 2.6

The No System icon.

If you get a Sad Mac icon, you may need to eject the defective disk manually. Do this by pressing and holding the mouse button while you switch the computer off, and then on again. Don't be alarmed if you hear a squeal as the disk ejects.

Figure 2.7

The Sad Mac icon.

> Don't jump if you hear a "woof" when you eject a disk. If you have a dog, it may (like ours) learn to associate the disk-eject squeal with the end of the work day and expect to go for a walk.

Taking Control

There are basically two ways to communicate with your Macintosh: the *keyboard* and the *mouse*. The keyboard looks like an ordinary typewriter keyboard, but with some extra keys. Different Mac models use slightly different keyboard layouts (see Figure 2.8).

The earliest Mac keyboards do not have the *calculator* keypad later models have. Neither does the PowerBook's keyboard. The Plus has a ten-key pad but no function keys, and the SE and Mac II keyboards come in "standard" and "extended" models. But the essentials are the same for all.

The first nontypewriter key you'll use is the *command key*, also called the *Apple key* or the *clover key*. It has the Apple logo and a clover symbol on it: ⌘. Use the command key with another key, usually a single letter or number key, to tell the Mac to do more than type that letter. Some Mac keyboards include Esc (escape) and Ctrl, which may be used in advanced applications.

Figure 2.8

The standard Apple keyboard (top) and the Apple Extended keyboard (bottom).

You also can use the mouse to tell the Mac what to do. The mouse is a little box with a ball underneath and a button on top, as shown in Figure 2.9. Computer mice don't like cheese, and they never squeak unless they need cleaning. To use a mouse, position it so the heel of your hand is on the table and your thumb and fingers grip the sides of the box lightly. Your index finger should rest on the button on top. The cord (tail?) of the mouse is closest to your fingertips. As you move the mouse, the rolling ball tells the computer what direction the mouse is moving. Watch the screen while you move the mouse around on the table. The arrow or *pointer* moves in the same direction and speed as the mouse.

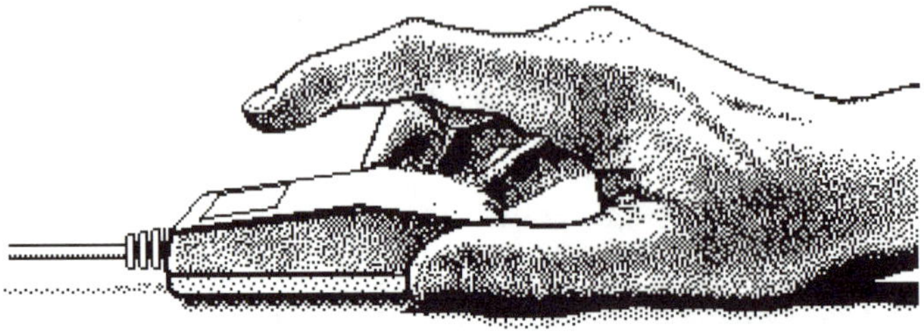

Figure 2.9
Hold that Mouse!

NOTE: Instead of a mouse, you could use a trackball controller. It looks something like a billiard ball in a box, but handles like a mouse. There are sophisticated optical mice(which give extremely precise control), wireless mice and more. We'll explain the differences in Chapter 13.

TIP: If you run out of desk space to move the mouse, just lift the mouse off the surface and reposition it. The pointer remains in the same place as long as the ball isn't moving.

Incidentally, mice like clean surfaces. Dust the desk frequently, and don't drag the mouse through spilled liquids. You may want to invest in a mouse pad (also described in Chapter 13), or you can roll your mouse on a pad of clean paper.

That arrow you see on the screen is a *pointer*, and it may take on a different shape during different applications, as shown in Figure 2.10. The pointer becomes an *I-beam* when you're entering text, and turns into a *wristwatch* when the Mac is doing something that takes time, like opening an application.

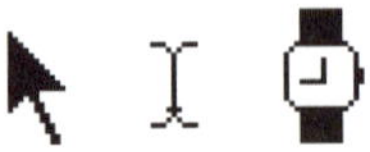

Figure 2.10
Pointers.

Mouse Techniques

Move the pointer to an on-screen object, then click the button on the mouse once to select the object. Point and double-click to open or activate an object. Double-clicking means pressing the mouse button twice in quick succession without moving the mouse. (Just a very quick tap-tap does it.) Place the arrow on the trash can. Click once. The trash can changes color, as shown in Figure 2.11. Now double-click the button. You've opened the trash window, shown in Figure 2.12.

The official Apple term for selecting is *highlighting*, even though the selected item turns black on black-and-white Macs. But it's your computer. Call it whatever you want.

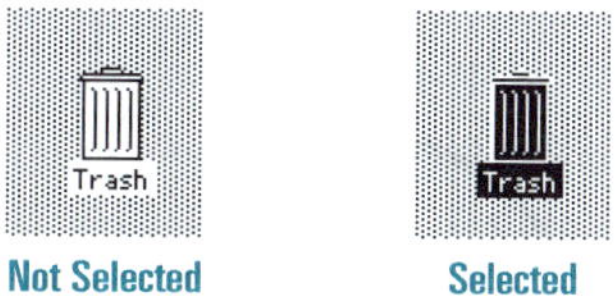

Figure 2.11
The Trash can icon.

Figure 2.12
The Trash window.

To close the trash window again, place the pointer in the little white square (a close box) at the upper-left corner of the window. Click once. The window closes.

Moving something by holding the mouse button down and rolling the mouse is called *dragging*. Try dragging the trash can icon around. Select it again, leaving the pointer on top of the trash icon. Hold the mouse button down and move the pointer around the screen. The trash can moves, too!

> Right now, you probably don't have anything in the trash. Later, you'll learn how to throw things away.

Understanding Your Desktop

By the way, your Mac may be on top of your desk or under it, but the screen you're looking at now is also called the *Desktop*. There are *files* to work with, just like paper files, and they can be kept neatly sorted in *folders*. Just like your old-fashioned desk may have a note pad or a calculator, your Mac Desktop has a selection of *desk accessories* you can customize to suit your needs and taste. Many Mac users keep a selection of toys on their desks, too. A few gadgets on your Mac desk don't appear on ordinary desks, such as a Control Panel. We'll discuss these items in more detail in Chapter 3.

What's on the Menu?

The strip across the top of the screen contains the names of several pull-down menus. To choose a command or option from a menu, you have to open it. Place the pointer on the menu name and hold the mouse button down. You'll see the list of things that menu enables you to do.

The first menu, marked by the Apple logo at the left side of the menu, is (logically) called the Apple menu. It's where you'll find your desk accessories. Use the File menu, shown in Figure 2.13, to create new folders; open or close a folder, application, or document; print; create a new folder or duplicate any existing file or folder; print a catalog of the files in a folder; find out about a file or folder; or quit what you're doing.

Figure 2.13

Opening a pull-down menu.

To select any of a pull-down menu's items, move the pointer down the list to the item you want, keeping the button down. When you let go of the mouse button, the selected activity occurs. You'll notice that some of the menu choices are in black type—nice and easy to read. Others look gray or patterned. That's because these choices are *disabled* (dimmed) at the moment. When you first pull down the File menu, you have only a few choices available. You can Open the selected icon. (In this case it's the disk icon called *System Tools.*) You can Get Information about it. You can put a New Folder on the desktop. You can't Print, Close, or Duplicate, because no file or window is open to perform those activities on.

Your menu might look slightly different: some of the choices appear only if you're running System 7.

SYSTEM

The Edit menu has different choices for making changes to an open document. You'll learn how to use these commands in the next chapter. Some of the Edit commands will be disabled on the desktop screen, or when there's nothing selected to cut or copy, or nothing in the clipboard to paste. And you obviously can't undo what you haven't yet done. Almost all programs have File and Edit menus.

The View menu, shown in Figure 2.14, enables you to decide how you want to find out about the items on your desktop. Would you like to see them appear as Icons, as a list alphabetically by Name, by the Date they were last used, by the amount of information in each file (Size), or by Kind of file? You can use full size icons or small (space-saving) icons.

System 7 users can turn on an additional View option, by Label, discussed in the next chapter. The Special menu helps you keep your desktop clean, and lets you shut down and restart the Mac.

Figure 2.14

The View menu with small icon and regular icon.

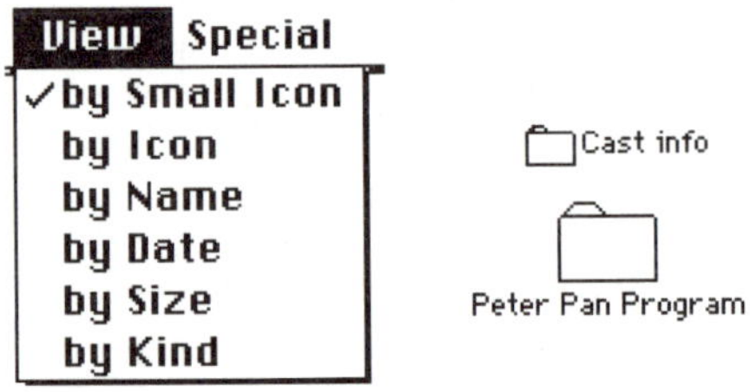

As you get further into using your Mac, you'll discover that each application has its own set of menus. But the conventions stay the same. If a menu choice has an ellipsis (...) after it, it brings up a *dialog box* to ask for more instructions—such as, how you want a page printed. If a menu choice has a triangle beside it, it displays a *submenu* with additional choices. You'll even find *pop-up menus* in some dialog boxes: they appear as shadowed rectangles, until you open them. Figure 2.15 shows submenus and menus with dialog boxes; Figure 2.16 shows a pop-up menu.

The important thing to remember about menus is that they all work the same way. You *open* a menu by pointing to it and holding down the mouse button. You *select* a menu item by sliding the pointer down until you highlight the item you want. When you release the mouse button, the computer does whatever you've selected.

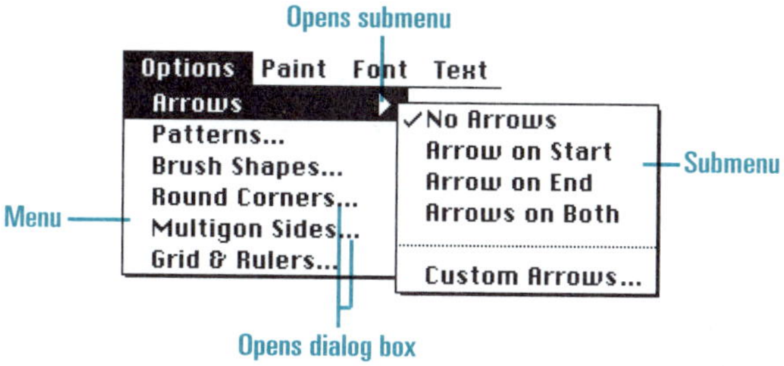

Figure 2.15

Submenu.

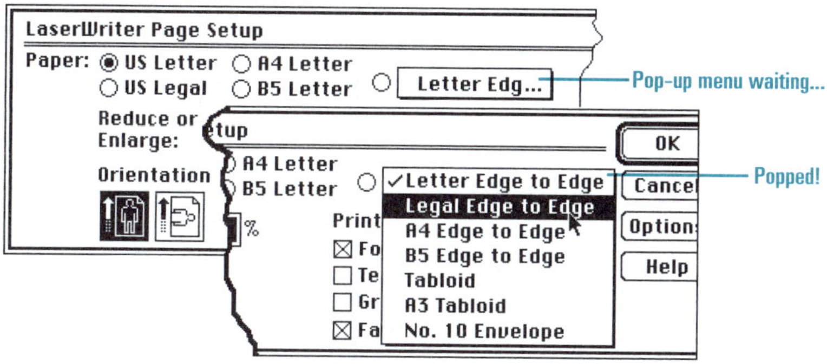

Figure 2.16

Pop-up menu.

> **TIP:** If you don't want to do a menu selection that you've highlighted, just slide the pointer off it before you let go of the mouse. If you slide all the way back to the desktop before you let go, absolutely nothing will happen. This also works for just about every other kind of on-screen choice in the Mac world.

Doing Windows

Right now, there's nothing on the desktop screen except a disk icon and a trash can. Depending on what kind of a disk you're using, the icon might look like the one in Figure 2.17. Floppy disks almost always look like the icon on the left. A hard disk may look like the Apple HD icon, depending on the whim of the disk designer. Even though different disks have different icons, they all work the same. To open a disk, click on its icon once to select it. It will change color. Then open the disk by choosing Open on the File menu. Or, just double-click the selected icon. Figure 2.18 shows the open System Tools disk. Later on, we'll teach you some shortcuts for selecting some menu choices.

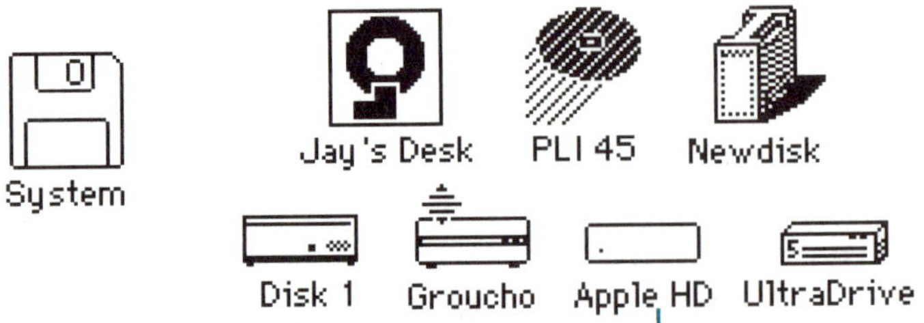

Figure 2.17

Various types of disk icons.

This is the hard drive icon you'll see on most new Macs.

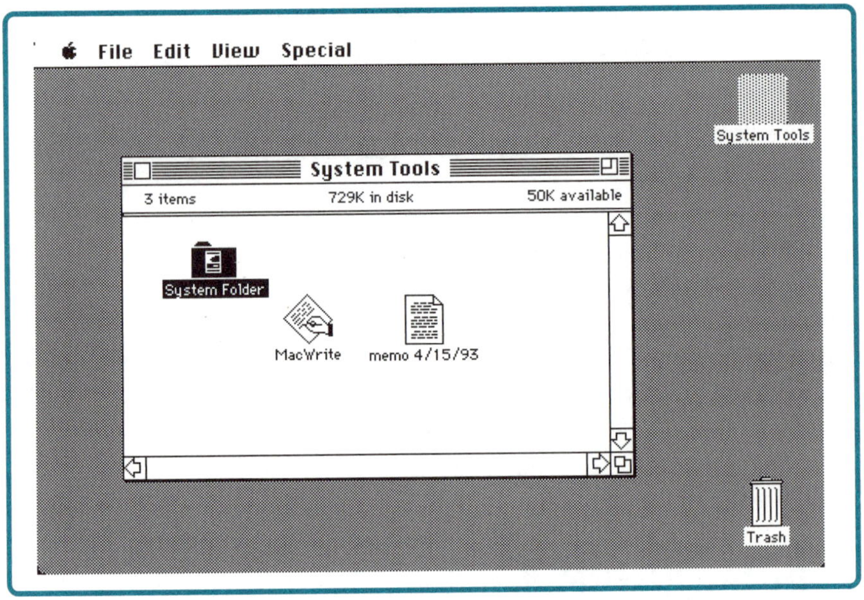

Figure 2.18

The open System Tools window.

What you've opened is called a *window.* The window shows you what's in the System Tools Disk. On our sample disk, there's a folder called *System Folder*, an application called *MacWrite*, and a document called *Memo 4/15/91.*

The *system folder* contains the instructions which tell the Mac how to operate. If you think of your disk as a file cabinet, the first item in it is Mac's operating system. (It's a good idea to keep all the system files in the system folder.) *Applications* are specialized instructions for doing a particular job, such as word processing or playing a game. *MacWrite* is an application. *Documents* are the things you create using the applications. The *Memo* is filed as a separate document.

Just as you would with a filing cabinet, you can organize your files any way you like. You may want to keep your documents and applications in separate file folders. Figure 2.19 is an example of a typical desktop.

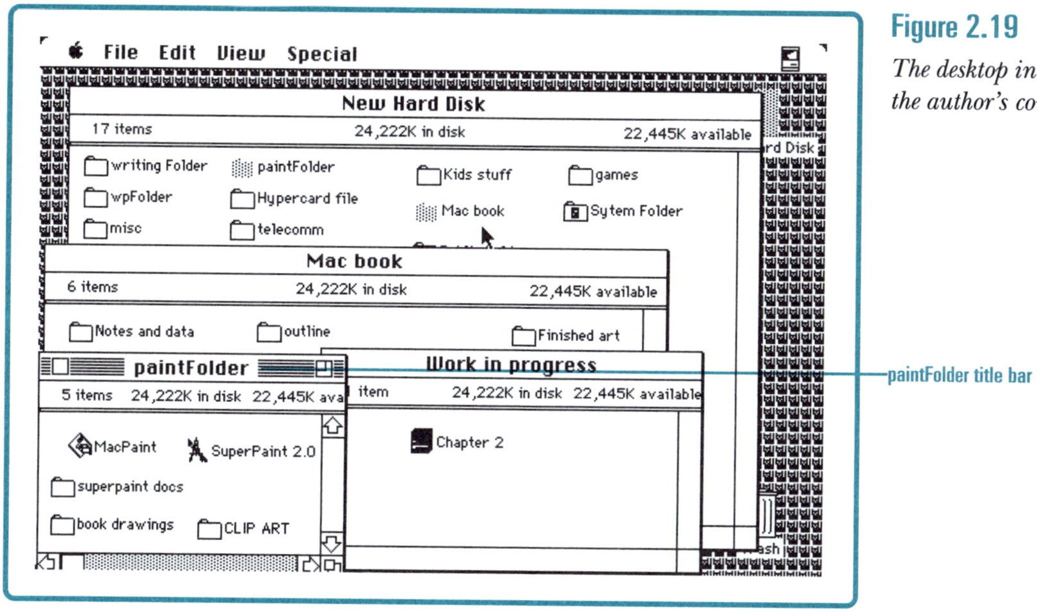

Figure 2.19

The desktop in one of the author's computers.

Notice that there are several windows open. The underlying window, called *New Hard Disk*, shows all the folders in the hard disk. The *Mac book*, *Work in progress*, and *PaintFolder* are open, and their icons have changed color in the underlying window to show that fact. The PaintFolder is *active*; we've clicked inside it, so we can get to the documents in that folder. You can tell the folder is active because its title bar is striped.

TIP: If a window gets hidden behind another, you can bring it forward by double-clicking on its icon, even though the icon appears disabled, or by clicking on a corner of the window, if one is sticking out.

Window Boxes

You can have as many as a dozen windows open on the desktop at the same time. You can also change the size of the open window, so that you can see several at once. To see more of what's in a window, use the *size box* at the bottom right corner of the window, shown in Figure 2.20. Just drag the corner to where you want it, and the window will shrink or grow accordingly. The contents of the window don't change when you change the size. You just see more or less of it. To expand a window to fill the screen, click the *zoom box* at the upper right corner, also shown in Figure 2.20. To return the window to its former size, click the zoom box again. To move a window to another location on the screen, position the pointer on the striped *title bar* at the top of the window. Drag the window to the desired spot and release the mouse button.

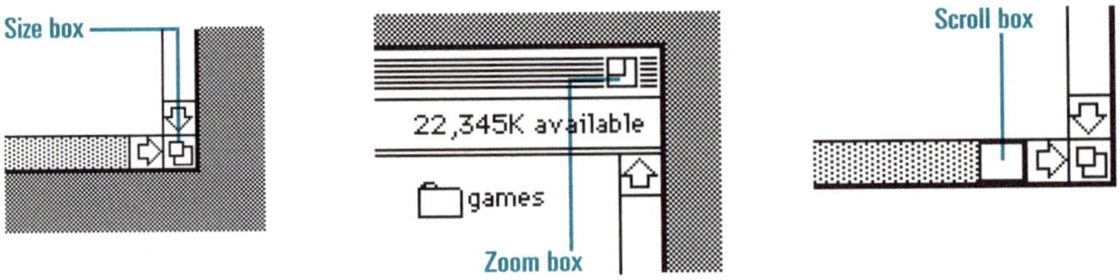

Figure 2.20

The size box, title bar, zoom box, and scroll box.

If there's more in the window that can be seen, the *scroll bar* turns gray, as in the third illustration of Figure 2.20. Drag the white box in the scroll bar to move the other parts of the document into view. To close a window, click the *close box* in the upper left corner (see Figure 2.21).

Dialog boxes appear on your screen whenever there's a physical action that you must perform for the Mac, a question to be answered, or a warning given. A dialog box may ask you to insert a particular disk, or may ask, for example, if you're sure you meant to put the application "PicassoPaint" in the trash . Figure 2.16, referred to earlier, shows a typical dialog box—the one you see if you select Page Setup... and have a laser printer. The little circles, squares, icons, or rounded rectangles are *buttons*; click on them to designate your choices. The button with the heavy line around it (OK, in our example) is a *default*. The Mac will close the dialog box and do whatever this button says when you click on it or hit Return on the keyboard. Most dialog boxes have a Cancel button, which you can click on if you change your mind.

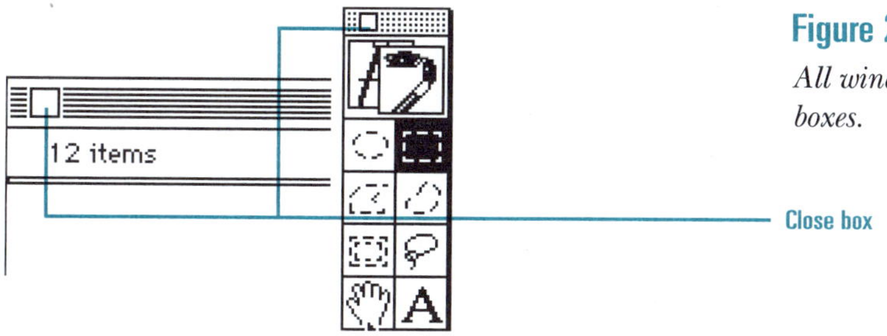

Figure 2.21

All windows have close boxes.

The different button shapes aren't there just to make the dialog box look pretty. Squares are *check boxes*: click as many of these options as you want. Circles are *radio buttons*, and are always found in groups: selecting one option will cancel the others (like the buttons on a car radio). Rounded rectangles carry out an action as soon as you click them. *Icons* usually work like radio buttons, but are there to make the dialog box look pretty.

Application icons usually look something like their "real-world" functions. Paint programs tend to have paintbrushes, HyperCard stacks are represented by stacks of cards, game icons look like the game, and so on. Document icons carry information about which program created them. Normally in a program, you can only open documents saved by itself or another version of the same program. Figure 2.22 shows an assortment of typical icons.

You can change the name of an icon on your desktop by selecting it, and then positioning the pointer over the name. The pointer then turns into an I-beam, indicating that you may type. Use the Delete key to erase the old name and put in a new one. It's not a good idea to rename applications or system files. You'll confuse the Mac (and yourself) if you do.

Figure 2.22

Typical icons.

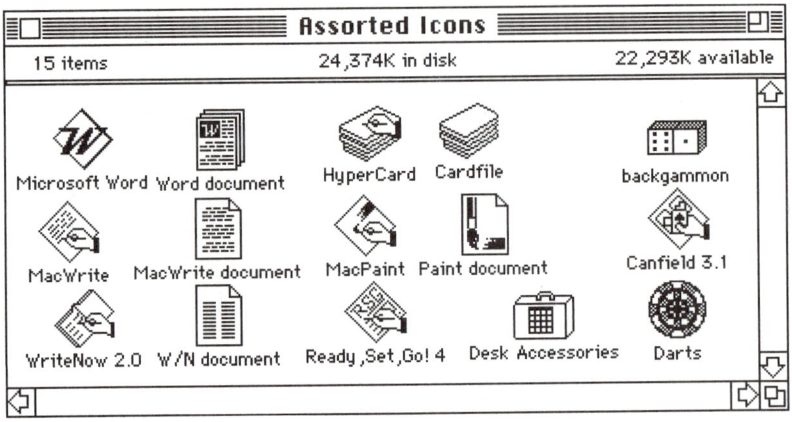

You may open applications such as MacWrite and MacPaint either by selecting them and pressing ⌘, by clicking down the Open... command in the File menu, or by double-clicking the icon. You can also open a document created in one of these applications in the same way, so long as the application is also available to the computer.

If you see a *generic document*—a blank, dog-eared page—it doesn't have any application information attached to it. You may be able to open it from within a word processing or paint program, or see Chapter 14 for some other ways to deal with it.

A Brief Discourse on Disks

The Mac uses hard disks and/or floppy disks. Floppy disks are like single drawers of a file cabinet, able to hold a certain amount of information. A hard disk could be considered more like a row of large file cabinets, able to hold a great deal of information. Even if your Macintosh has a hard disk, you'll want to make backup copies of important data and applications on floppy disks. Floppy disks, by the way, are generally just called *floppies*, even though they're relatively firm. Bending any kind of floppy will probably damage it.

If you're not using a hard disk, you'll soon have more data than can fit on one floppy, just as you might have more files than would fit in one file cabinet. When this happens, you'll need to *format* more floppies. Insert a blank disk into the disk drive. (If your Mac has only one disk slot and no hard drive, first eject the system disk by pressing ⌘-e.) You'll get a dialog box which will look like Figure 2.23, if you've inserted a standard disk, or one similar to it if you're using a high-density disk. Unless you're formatting for a very early Mac, click the Two-Sided button.

CAUTION: Initializing a disk permanently erases anything already on it! If you're reusing a disk, be sure there's nothing on it you'll ever want to see again.

Figure 2.23

Dialog box asking if you want to initialize (format) a floppy disk.

After you tell the Mac to initialize a disk, it will confirm that you really want to erase what's already on it. Then it'll ask you to name the disk. Give it any name you like, up to 28 letters.

TIP: The Mac also uses numbers, punctuation, and symbols in its names. You could call a disk Ÿ, or 42, or !@#*&$. The only symbol you can't use is the colon (:). The Mac reserves that one for its own use.

Locking a Disk

When a disk is locked, the Mac can read it but not erase anything from it or write on it. You can lock a disk manually by sliding the lock tab on the back of the disk (Figure 2.24) to uncover the square hole. (High-density disks have two holes, but only one of them has a sliding tab.) Covering the locking hole unlocks the disk. But if you can see through the hole, the Mac won't write on it.

Figure 2.24

Locking a disk.

Whenever you buy software, lock the original disks and make back-up "working" copies of them. This will help protect the originals against inadvertent damage and will guarantee that you'll be able to make another clean copy when you need one. Some obsolete copy-protection schemes won't let you copy disks, or require the disk to be unlocked when you make a copy. If you come across disks like that, follow their instructions (and consider buying your software from other sources).

Recycling Disk Space—the Trash

When you need more room in your file cabinets, you might go through the files and throw away papers you don't need any more. You can do the same thing with the Mac, by dragging the documents you don't want to keep into the trash. What can you throw away? Anything that's not in use. The section on disk management in Chapter 14 may be helpful.

In general, even if you have a large hard disk, it's pointless to keep documents you never need to look at again, like old correspondence. Transfer these items to floppy disks, and keep them in a safe place. Once you've copied something onto another disk, you can throw away the original. Select the trash and drag whatever you're throwing away to it. The trash icon expands to let you know there's something inside, as shown in Figure 2.25.

Figure 2.25

The full and empty Trash icon.

If you put something in the trash, it's not immediately and necessarily gone forever. If you think you may have thrown out something you meant to keep, open the trash by double-clicking. As long as you can still see the icon for whatever you want to rescue, you can drag it out again. Empty the trash by selecting Empty Trash from the Special menu.

System 6 also empties the trash automatically when you eject the disk that originally had the file, shut down, or start an application. System 7 waits for you to make the menu selection.

Can you ever rescue a trashed file once the trash is empty? Yes. There are recovery programs that may be able to do this, if nothing has been written over the area on the disk that stored the trashed file. See the section on recovery programs in Chapter 14 for more information.

In This Chapter

The Apple Menu

•

System 7 . . . and Should You Use It?

•

The View and Special Menus

•

Shutting Down

One of the features that made the Mac unique among personal computers was the menu bar—since adopted by other systems—where you could find all of the necessary commands conveniently arranged. These commands change slightly depending on whether you're using System 6 or System 7. This chapter introduces you to the Mac's menus and will help you choose the most efficient system for the way you work.

3

Of Mice and Menus

The Apple menu (Figure 3.1) contains *desk accessories* of all kinds: useful ones, vital ones, and some that are just for fun. Desk accessories (DAs for short), like the ones on your real-world desk, include such items as an Alarm Clock, a Note Pad, and a Calculator. Other desk accessories help you use your Mac: the Control Panel, Key Caps, and Chooser. There are game and puzzle DAs, and utilities like a mini-word processor or spreadsheet. You add or delete DAs using *Font/DA Mover* or the System folder, depending on the System number you're running.

Figure 3.1

The Apple menu.

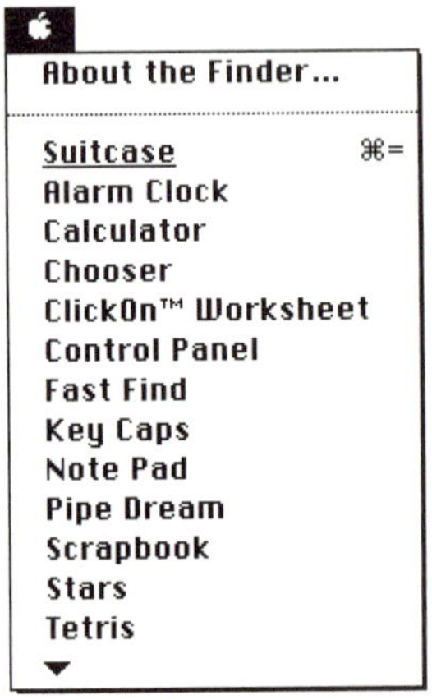

SYSTEM

If you have System 7, you can also add *Aliases*—quick Apple-menu shortcuts to any other application or document in your computer.

DAs are always available to you and stay open while you're using most applications. Just like you can pick up a pocket calculator and check your math while typing, you can open and use Calculator while you're word processing. DAs may disappear under the document you're working on (just as pocket calculators often get buried on a real desk) but they're still there, waiting for you to close the document. Now, let's look at some common DAs supplied by Apple with their system disks. If they don't appear in your Apple menu, it just means somebody's changed them using techniques described later in this chapter. They're probably still on your original system disks.

Getting Alarmed

Choose Alarm Clock from the Apple menu to see the digital clock shown in Figure 3.2. You can open the clock, as shown in Figure 3.3, by clicking the lever. The Alarm Clock expands and enables you to set the time, date, or alarm by selecting your choice from the bottom of the panel. Simply click the icon for the time, date, or alarm and then click the digits you want to change. A pair of arrows then appears next to the M. Click the up arrow to advance numbers and the down arrow to back up.

Figure 3.2

Opening the clock.

Figure 3.3

Setting the clock.

When you click the Alarm Clock, a switch appears to the left of the alarm time. Move the switch up to activate the alarm. If your Mac is on when it's time for the alarm to ring, it beeps, and the Apple icon on the menu bar changes to a little Alarm Clock. Open the Alarm Clock to turn it off or to reset the alarm. Turn off the alarm by clicking the switch down. Figure 3.4 shows the Alarm Clock, set to beep at 7 a.m.

Figure 3.4

The alarm will ring at 7 a.m.

All Macs have a battery to keep the clock running when the computer's turned off. If the battery wears down, the Mac won't know what time or day it is. Dead batteries should be replaced following the procedures described in Chapter 14.

Numbers and Notes

The Calculator DA, shown in Figure 3.5, works like a real one. You can enter numbers and signs either by clicking on them or by typing them from the keyboard or keypad. You can also paste numbers to the calculator and copy the answers. Chapter 4 explains editing techniques like cutting and pasting. The Note Pad, shown in Figure 3.6, lets you make up to eight pages of notes. Click on the upturned corner of the page to go to the next. Click on the exposed page beneath to go back. The next chapter describes text entry in detail.

Figure 3.5
The Calculator.

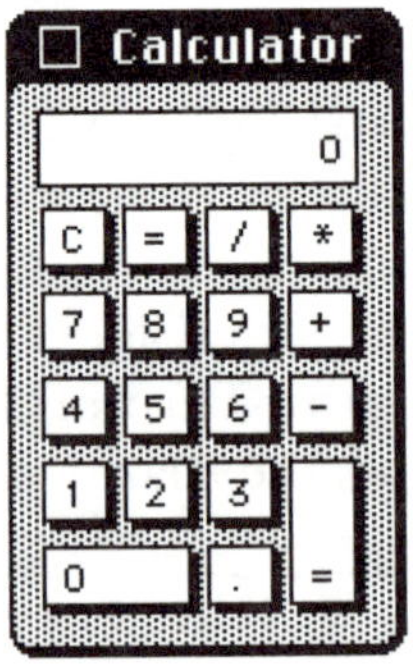

Figure 3.6
The Note Pad.

Saving Scraps

The Scrapbook lets you store drawings and text to paste into your documents. You may want to keep things like logos, letterheads, signatures, text boilerplates, or other frequently used items in the Scrapbook. You can copy and paste images and text to the Scrapbook. Each time you cut and paste an image, it adds a new page to the Scrapbook with just that image or text. To turn pages, use the scroll box on the bottom. The contents of the Scrapbook are stored in a Scrapbook File on the system disk (in the System Folder, if you have a hard drive).

It's possible and maybe even helpful to have customized Scrapbooks for different applications. You might keep a Scrapbook of letterheads and custom stationery with your word processor, and another Scrapbook of drawings to use with a paint program or desktop publishing application. The system only reads the Scrapbook named *Scrapbook File.* To start a new one, change the name of the old one to something like *old scrapbook.* The system opens a new one automatically. To reactivate the old Scrapbook, rename it *Scrapbook File* and change the name of the new Scrapbook.

Don't be alarmed if you attempt to paste an image into the Scrapbook and don't see all of it on the Scrapbook page, as in Figure 3.7. The full image is really there (but the Scrapbook can't hold an image larger than the maximum size of a MacPaint document). Use the scroll bar at the bottom of the Scrapbook window to change pages. The fraction below the scroll bar tells you what page you're on and how many pages there are in all. In our sample Scrapbook, the 6/18 means the pussycat is on page 6 of 18. In Chapter 4, we'll discuss in detail how you can cut, copy, and paste into your Scrapbook.

Figure 3.7

What you see, as opposed to what you get.

The Key to Key Caps

The Key Caps DA, shown in Figure 3.8, helps you take advantage of the hidden characters in Macintosh typefaces. It also lets you see what a type style looks like without actually using it. When you open Key Caps, a diagram of the Mac keyboard appears on-screen, and the words `Key Caps` appear as the last item on the menu bar. This Key Caps menu lists all the fonts installed in your system. Select the font you want to examine by dragging the highlight bar down to it. The letters and characters on the keyboard change accordingly. If you hold the Shift key down, Key Caps displays capitals. If you hold the Option—or Shift and Option—keys down, Key Caps shows the *optional characters* in whatever font you've selected. The optional characters vary from one font to another.

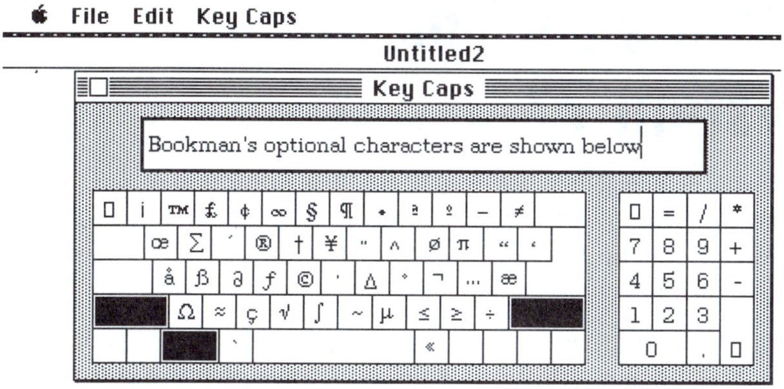

Figure 3.8
Using Key Caps.

Anything you type appears in the window above the keyboard diagram. You can copy and paste this text into any other DA or into a document, but you might have to change the font when you do. (These techniques are discussed in the next two chapters.) You can also type optional characters directly in a document. Just hold down the Option key or Shift and Option as you type the appropriate letter or character. (If you forget what you need to type, open Key Caps to locate the ones you need.) After a short time, it will become instinctive to press combinations such as Option-8 for a bullet (•), or Shift-Option-8 for a degree symbol (°).

Accents, those little marks you need in other languages, are also hiding in the optional character set. To use accents, first press the option key and then the letter to be accented. Available accent marks in most fonts include å, é, ø, ç, ü, and ñ. The grave accent used in French (è) is produced by typing the following combination: Option, \ (it's the same key as the tilde ~, but the location varies on different keyboards), and e. Pressing Option, u, and o gives you ö.

What's All This About System 7?

So far, everything we've described works pretty much the same in all versions of Macintosh software. But from time to time, we've had to refer to differences in "System 7."

In mid-1991, Apple introduced a major revision to the Macintosh Operating System—those thousands of lines of computer programming that control the familiar menus and windows, and let individual applications communicate with each other and the outside world. Apple's goal was to make Macs more powerful in business applications, while at the same time, making them easier for non-computer types. They reached their goal, but not perfectly: while many users love System 7, others refuse to run it. Some current applications work badly—if at all—under System 7, and some basic functions seem to be a lot slower.

Apple's *System 7 Tune-Up*, released a few months later, addresses some of these problems. (System 7.0.1 is intended to support just a few specific Mac models.) System 7 is more powerful than previous Mac operating systems; but as we write this—more than a year after its introduction—it's still not right for every Mac user. The rest of this section discusses its pros and cons, to help existing Mac owners decide whether or not to make the switch. The choice is yours; except for a few cases, System 7 is not an absolute requirement (and don't let any dealers or advertisements tell you otherwise).

Being at Sixes and Sevens

Choosing between System 6 and System 7 shouldn't give you nightmares. You can decide based on the kind of Mac you own and the way you use it. There are *utilities*—short separate programs—available to help you preview the switch. And the decision isn't final; you can always switch back.

Before you go much further, verify which software you already have. While you're in the Finder (see the previous chapter, if you're not sure), select the first item in the Apple menu. It'll be either About The Finder... or About This Macintosh..., depending on the version. In the window that appears, look for `System` or `System Software` and the version number will follow: most likely, either 6.0.7, 6.0.8, 7.0.0, or 7.0.1. (Don't be confused by the Finder version; it's not the same thing.)

> If you're running a software version earlier than 6, you definitely should upgrade to at least 6.0.7. This upgrade is free from most user groups and dealers, and most of today's software won't work without it. Also, most of the advice in this book isn't valid for earlier, now-obsolete systems.

What's Your Mac?

If you own a Classic II, PowerBook, or Quadra, the question of whether to use System 6 or System 7 is moot; System 7 was shipped with your computer, and you *must* run it. These machines simply won't operate with earlier systems. You can skip this section, or skim through it to pick up insights on the operating system you have to use.

If you have a floppy-disk-only Plus or SE, it's also no contest: the new software is so big that a hard disk is mandatory. In floppy-disk-only computers, you should run System 6.0.7 or 6.0.8. (The differences between two versions are minimal. If you're on a network with other computers and a laser printer, use 6.0.8. Otherwise, it doesn't matter.)

The majority of Mac owners, with other compact Macs including the original Classic, as well as Portables, LCs, or any of the Mac II versions, should choose the system that's best for their needs. Apple recommends system 7.0.1, and ships it with all new Macs, but many experts disagree. If System 7 came with your brand-new LC or Mac II, you can still switch to System 6.

It's possible to run a PowerBook with System 6.0.8, but we don't recommend it. You'll lose some critical functions like the Screen Brightness control.

Connectivity versus Cosmetics

The major functions of System 7 can be grouped into two categories: minor and major. Some of the most advertised features, such as *Balloon Help*, *Aliasing*, and the new System folder structure, are really minor revisions and not great computer breakthroughs. More revolutionary is the way System 7 breaks down barriers between other programs and other Macs. *Publish and Subscribe* and *Apple Events* coordinate how multiple applications use information. *File Sharing* lets network users open files on each others' desks without additional software. (Unfortunately, very few applications take advantage of the new coordinating features. And Apple's File Sharing isn't as powerful as the third-party versions you can get in any computer store.)

A third kind of System 7 function, *Virtual Memory*, lets you simulate tens of megabytes of additional computer memory so you can have many programs running at the same time. System 6 versions of this have been available from third-party suppliers for years.

System 7 Advantages

Some of System 7's features might be just right for the way you compute. Here's a discussion of the most visible ones.

Balloon Help

If you click the little comic-strip balloon on the upper-right corner of a System 7 screen, the Mac becomes its own guided tour. As you move the pointer over different menus and buttons, captions appear to tell you how they work. We combined a bunch of them in Figure 3.9. New users often find balloons helpful, especially in programs with many obscure icons. (Balloons won't put authors like us out of business: the ones in the Finder are too simplified to be much use, and the function isn't supported in many current programs.)

> **TIP:** After a day or so, most users turn balloons off. Otherwise, random rectangles keep popping up on-screen whenever they move their mice.

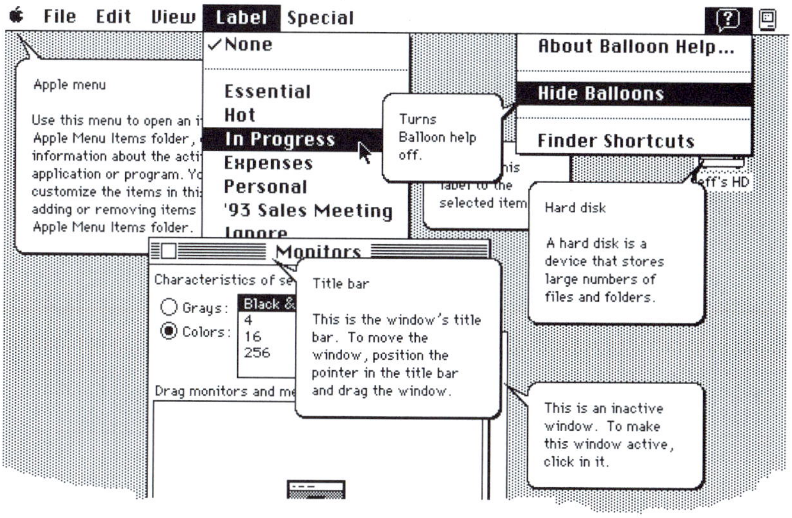

Figure 3.9

A bunch of balloons. You'll never see more than one at a time.

Aliasing

This feature can be wonderful, especially as your hard disk becomes cluttered with multiple files and folders. *Aliasing* creates instant shortcuts to anything on your desktop. Select any item—an application or file, a folder, or even a whole disk—and choose Make Alias from the File menu. Another icon instantly appears, marked as that item's *alias.* Now you can bury the original in whatever folder you want. When you double-click the alias, the Mac automatically finds and opens the original, no matter where it's gone. (If you've aliased a file on a floppy, the Mac will ask you to insert the proper disk.) You can make as many aliases as you want for any item on the desktop.

FYI Idea

Aliases in Action

- Some complicated programs need lots of supporting files for dictionary or help functions, internal databases, or "plug-ins." Keeping documents in the same folder with these files can create confusing windows. If you make an alias for the program, however, you can throw all of its files into a single folder, throw all of these folders into a massive one (called something like "Stuffed Closet"), and never open it again!
- If you work with project folders—one for "Memos," for example, and a different one for "1993 Sales Meeting"—you can keep aliases for applications in each one. The programs you need will always be at your fingertips.
- Aliases can be created for documents, too. Frequently used files, like a HyperCard Address stack, can appear in every folder.
- Aliases can be dropped into the Apple Menu Items folder in your System folder. Once you do that, it'll appear in the list whenever you click the Apple menu icon. Imagine opening your favorite drawing program without leaving your word processor!
- Aliases for Control Panel and Chooser extensions can also be dropped into the Apple Items Folder, for a quick shortcut to frequently used system functions.

Each alias uses 1K disk space, so you can have a thousand of them without noticeably crowding your hard disk.

> **TIP:** System 6 users can also bury their programs in folders, if they open the application first and save a blank page in it. Give the page a name like "Opens MacWrite," and move it wherever you want. When you double-click the blank page, the Mac finds the proper application.

Labels

System 7 lets you assign different categories to desktop items and then sort them by these categories. Select Control Panels in the Apple menu, and open the Labels... icon. You'll see a dialog box like the one on the left in Figure 3.10. Give each category a useful name and close the dialog box. Now select any file or folder, and pull down the Labels menu in the desktop. It looks like the right half of Figure 3.10. When you click on one of the categories you've typed, it'll be attached to the selected file or folder. You can sort a folder by these categories by simply selecting By Label in the View menu. The results look like Figure 3.11.

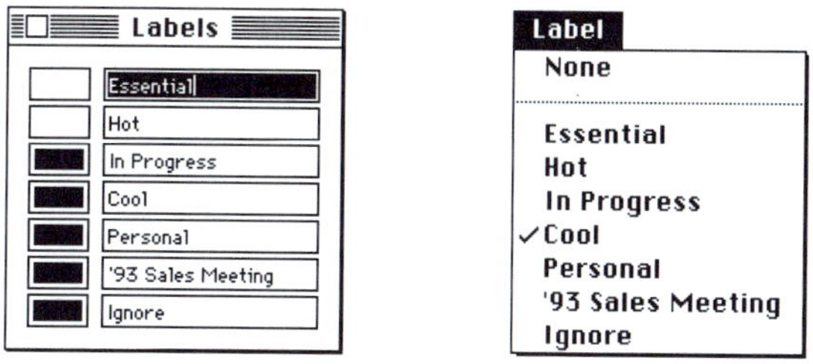

Figure 3.10
Naming and assigning labels.

Figure 3.11

Viewing by Label.

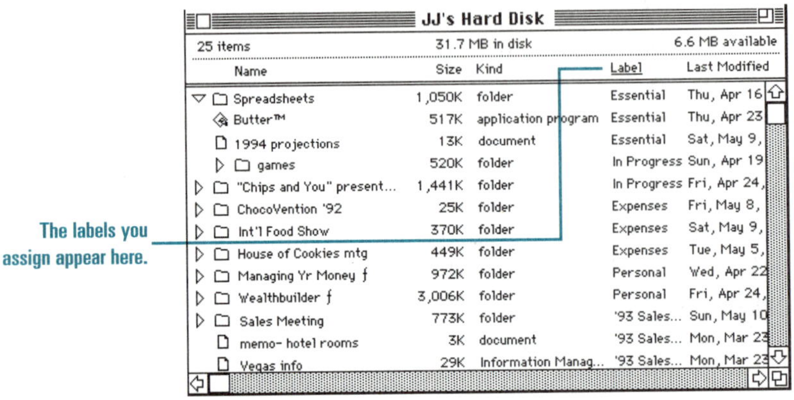

> The Mac keeps track of labels with an internal number, not by the name you assign. If you decide to rename the "1993 Vacation" label to plan the "1994 Sales Meeting," the number stays the same. All your old travel files will be attached to the new name (and probably show up when the boss is checking sales meeting plans). To remove a label, you have to assign a different one to the file.

File Sharing

If two or more System 7 machines are connected on an AppleTalk network, they can open files on each others' desktops and share documents. Central databases and reports can be kept on a central machine, and read or changed by people throughout a company. (Security isn't a problem; you can limit accessibility to certain users, require passwords, or keep some files absolutely private.) File sharing is discussed as part of Networking in Chapter 16.

Publish and Subscribe

Macintosh users have always had the ability to transfer information easily from one application to another. Even the first machines would let you draw a figure in MacPaint and *paste* it into a memo in MacWrite. All Mac programs support this feature—Apple vigorously insists on it—so you can integrate spreadsheets, databases, scanned photos, and just about anything else you want.

Unfortunately, pasting is static. If you go back to MacPaint and edit your original figure, the changes won't show up in your memo unless you paste it in again. System 7 takes the process a major step forward. You can *publish* a painting, graph, or section of text in one program, and *subscribe* to it in another. The data is transferred into the new program, but with a constant link to the published version. If you change the published data, the new program reflects the change also.

With this feature, a graph from a spreadsheet can be dynamically integrated in a report. Change the numbers on the spreadsheet, and the report changes to match when you print it. This feature, combined with File Sharing, lets groups work on the same project easily. People can create graphics, text, and charts at their own desks, while an artist simultaneously designs the pages. The techniques for Publish and Subscribe are simple extensions of Copy and Paste, discussed in the next chapter.

A similar feature has existed for years in such professional page-layout programs as Aldus *PageMaker*. As of this writing, many simpler programs don't support the System 7 version of Publish and Subscribe. Check carefully: you might have to buy new software to use this.

System 7 Limitations

We don't want to call this section "disadvantages," because so many people swear by System 7. However, a lot of folks swear *at* the new software: some of its most promising new features work awkwardly, if at all, and some of the most-loved features of System 6—particularly its speed—work poorly in the new version.

System 7 Is a Memory Hog

All these new features require lots of memory. A 2M SE can run a small word processor and graphics program simultaneously with 6.0.7. But with 7.0.1, there's hardly enough room left for one program. Virtual memory doesn't help too much. Because it lives on your hard disk, "virtual" is much slower than "real" memory. Chapter 13 tells you why and how to add more memory to your Mac.

> System 7's memory requirements are notorious. Some cynics have suggested Apple requires it in new Classic IIs so they can sell more memory chips.

System 7 Is Slow

Even without virtual memory, System 7 appears to run more slowly than previous versions. Apple insists 7 is faster, overall. But user groups and bulletin boards are full of complaints about its slowness, especially when starting up or opening the Finder. Two of the authors' Macs have identical brains but different operating systems. When we turn them on in the morning, System 6 is already word processing while System 7 is still waking up.

System 7 Can Be Expensive

Be prepared to pay $99 for Apple's Personal Upgrade Kit, if you want the official manuals and registration cards. (You can get the software alone from large user groups and bulletin boards, for a modest distribution or connect fee.) No matter how you get the system, you'll probably have to buy more memory. And you may have to buy new applications.

Apple changed so much of the system basics that many popular programs and utilities don't work under 7 at all. Publishers have scrambled to come out with "System 7-ready updates," available for fees ranging from about $25 to $75. Some brand new programs don't use most of System 7's advanced features.

Even some hardware isn't compatible. A popular monitor and a top-rated text scanner both require upgrades that aren't even available as this book goes to press. One third-party printer works exactly like an ImageWriter under System 6 but is dead under 7, and no upgrade is planned. If you already own hardware, check before you switch.

System 7 May Be Unreliable

Apple is notorious for releasing software that doesn't work as well as their sales staff would have us believe. (They're also famous for issuing "upgrades" a few months later, to correct the problems.) In Apple's defense, computer operating systems are complicated. It's impossible to anticipate all the problems. Even so, many experienced users are reluctant to buy the first version of *any* Apple product.

Even with System 7 Tune-up, users have reported problems with File Sharing, file selection, and disappearing or randomly locked folders. These things don't happen all the time, and may result from undiscovered conflicts with other utilities. Apple isn't acknowledging serious problems, but their history certainly suggests a more reliable "System 7.1" will be released soon. Until then, many folks prefer to stick with their trusty old 6.0.7 or 6.0.8.

System 7 Simulators

Apple's stack, *Before You Install System 7,* is available from user groups and shipped with the Upgrade Kit. It uses HyperCard, a program shipped with every Mac for the past four years, to graphically simulate some of the new system's features. A companion stack, *Compatibility Checker,* scans your disk and prints recommendations about upgrading. Teknosys' *HELP!* software does the same thing, and it also compiles suggestions about other problems you might be having with software or hardware. Both of these utilities are only as current as their databases, however. As new versions of programs come out, the databases must be updated. A trial copy of *HELP!*, fresh out of the box, listed non-existent problems on our System 6 machine and failed to spot two well-documented incompatibilities. (Teknosys has promised frequent updates on a subscription basis.)

System 7 Summary

Imagine a powerful, new computing system with exciting new features: part of it works well, and part of it just suggests a direction for the future. That describes System 7, and it also describes the original Macintosh in 1984. People bought Macs back then—the authors included—and put up with its peculiarities in order to enjoy its advantages. Others waited and bought more powerful models later for the same money.

In a few years, the choice between Systems 6 and 7 won't be an issue: all software will be compatible, and System 6 will be as obsolete as the original Mac. But for now, you should look carefully before you switch.

Authors' Note: The rest of this book applies equally to both systems. In the few cases where they diverge, we'll point out the differences.

Setup Functions

The items we've discussed so far in the Apple menu are Desk Accessories: mini-programs, designed to manipulate data or handle specific functions like calculating (or playing games). Other items in the Apple menu let you take control of your Mac on a system level and customize its operating parameters. Despite their power, they're as easy to use as any other part of the Mac.

The Control Panel

Use the Control Panel, shown in Figure 3.12, to customize your Mac. Once you select a Control Panel icon, you'll be able to make changes in *CDEVs* (pronounced "see-devs"). The term is (very) short for *Control Panel Devices.* We'll look at some Apple CDEVs. Others control, and are supplied with, specific programs and utilities. Select Control Panel from the Apple menu. Click the General icon if it isn't already selected.

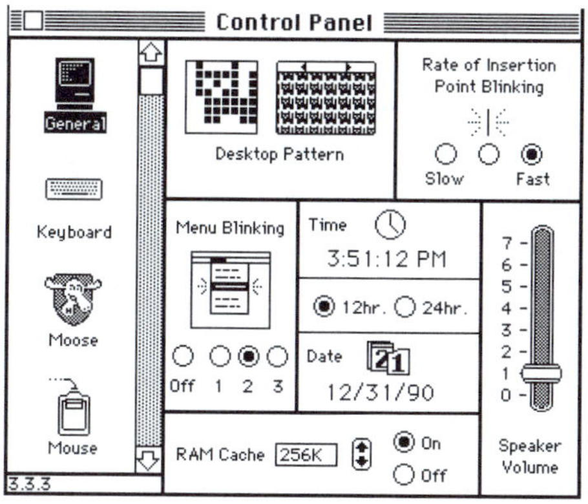

Figure 3.12

The General Controls.

The General Control Panel

Use General to select a fancier pattern on your desktop. You can select from a dozen existing patterns by clicking the arrows over the sample desktop as shown in Figure 3.13. (This Mac is obviously owned by a cat lover.) The arrows scroll through built-in pattern choices. You can modify a built-in pattern or design your own on the magnified square on the left. Just click individual dots—called *pixels*—to turn them on or off, and watch your pattern develop on the sample screen. When you're satisfied with your design, click inside the sample screen on the right to set the pattern.

Color Macs let you select one of eight colors for each dot on your desktop. On these machines, eight colored boxes appear below the sample desktop. Click inside a box to pick up a color, then click on a pixel to assign that color.

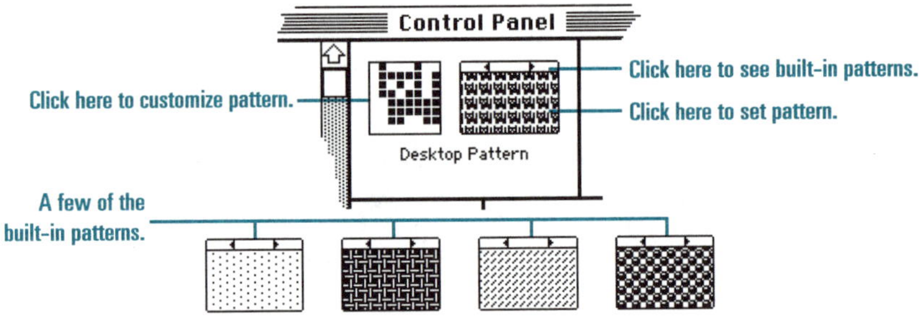

Figure 3.13

Redesigning your desktop.

The rest of the General Control Panel is self-explanatory. The *Menu Blinking Device* lets you tell the Mac how many times to blink its menu bar (when you click on a menu item, the Menu bar blinks to acknowledge the choice). Choosing `Off` means the Menu item doesn't blink at all.

The *RAM Cache* choice enables the Mac to reserve some of its memory as an accessory to the disk. Doing so lets the computer work much faster, because it doesn't have to use the relatively slow disk each time. Many programs bypass the RAM Cache, and some types of hard disks make it unnecessary. If you're running programs one at a time from floppy disks, try setting RAM Cache to somewhere between 128K and 256K for optimum speed.

Macs "beep" to get your attention when they've got a question or you've done something wrong. The *Speaker Volume control* works like the one on a hi fi, with a couple of exceptions. Click on the knob with your mouse, and while you're holding it down, you can slide to a different level. When you let go, you'll hear a sample beep at that volume. If you're hearing-disabled (or don't want to disturb your roommates) set a volume of 0. The menu bar will flash, instead, when the Mac wants you.

Other Control Devices

Apple supplies a number of CDEVs with its system disks, and many programs and utilities give you others. To install a CDEV, simply drag it from the desktop into the System folder. The following two control panels appear on most Macs.

If you're using System 7, drop it into the *closed* folder icon rather than into an open System Folder window.

When you press and hold a Macintosh key, the character repeats. If you're not an expert typist, you may need to adjust its response time with the *Keyboard* control panel. Adjust here if you start getting unintended repeating characters, likeeeeeee thissssss.

If your "real-world" desk has limited room, or if you don't want to move your mouse too far to traverse the screen, use the *Mouse* control panel shown in Figure 3.14. Experienced users sometimes change the mouse speed for different applications. A fast mouse feels more responsive, but a slow mouse might be easier to manipulate and more precise when doing delicate drawing. Click the Very Slow button if you're using a graphics tablet. The Very Slow button assures a constant speed for the pointer.

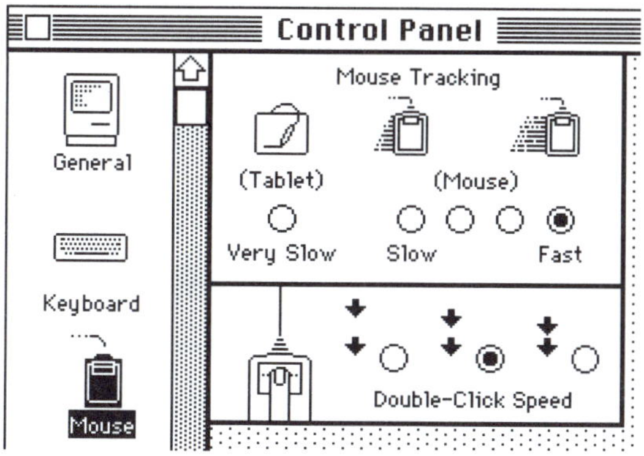

Figure 3.14
Adjusting mouse control.

You can also adjust the double-click speed to suit your preference. The left button in the Double-Click Speed area lets the Mac interpret two fairly slow clicks as a double-click. The right button lets you tap very quickly, and the center button, for most people, is a happy medium.

Choose Chooser

The other important "setup" DA is called the *Chooser* (Figure 3.15). If you're running a simple system with one computer and one printer, you won't ever have to think about the Chooser. But if you acquire a second printer, or set your Mac up in an office with several others and a shared printer or modem, the Chooser enables you to do some remarkable things. You can tell the Mac which printer to print on or find out which of your co-workers is tying up the laser printer. You can even pass files back and forth to another computer on the network and send notes which pop up in dialog boxes on someone else's screen.

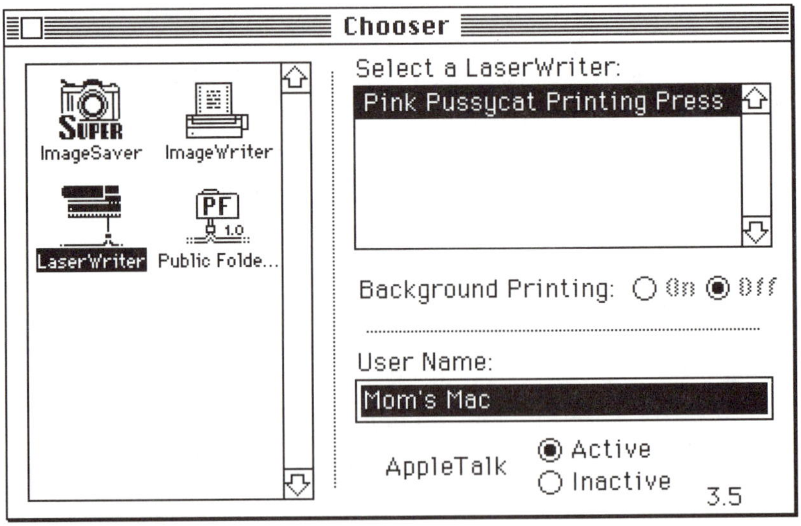

Figure 3.15

The Chooser.

In Figure 3.15, Mom's Mac is choosing a laser writer called Pink Pussycat Printing Press. (You can assign any name you like to your printer and Mac. Computing doesn't have to be serious all the time.) This *AppleTalk network* could include other printers, and more than one computer can use the same printer. Printing is discussed in Chapter 5, and sharing information through a network is discussed in Chapter 16.

Typical DA Games

So far, we've looked at some of the serious DAs. There are also many which are strictly for fun, such as the games in Figure 3.16.

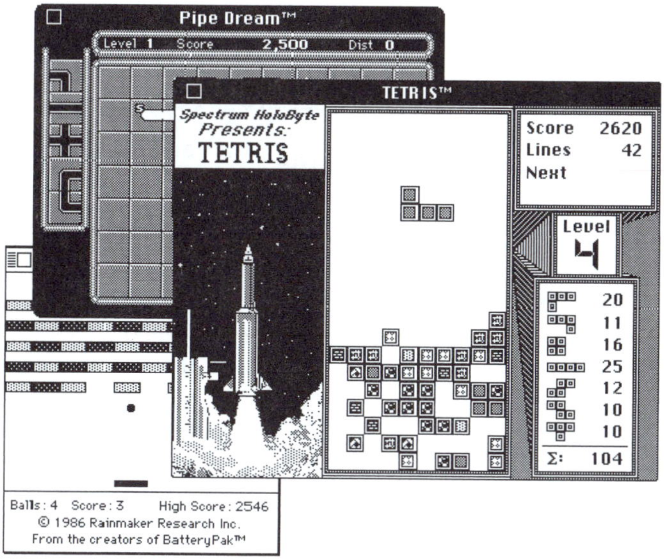

Figure 3.16

Typical DA games.

Screen savers protect your Mac from image "burn-in," a real possibility if the machine is left on and unused for long periods. Besides, screen savers are fun to watch. There are screen savers of all kinds, including some that resemble aquariums with swimming fish, a trip through outer space, or a fireworks display. You can add your own DAs through techniques discussed in the next section. You can fit up to 15 DAs on the Apple menu, and even more with Suitcase II.

Moving Day

Use *Font/DA Mover* (Figure 3.17) to add or remove desk accessories in your system file. Your Macintosh comes with some desk accessories and fonts. To find out where you can get other DAs, see the information on shareware in Chapter 12. The Font/DA Mover lets you copy DAs from one disk to another, or install and remove them from your system.

SYSTEM

Font/DA Mover is obsolete with System 7. Just grab the desk accessory on the desktop, and drop it into your System Folder.

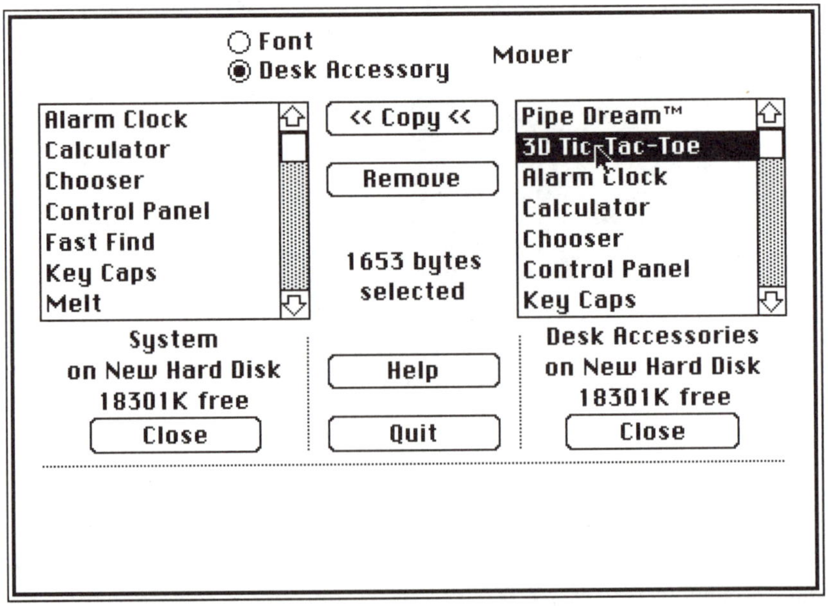

Figure 3.17
Font/DA Mover.

Open the Font/DA Mover by double-clicking its icon, which is a little drawing of a moving van. You'll find it on the *Utilities* disk, or in the *Utilities* file on the hard disk. The dialog box has two buttons at the top. Click the Desk Accessory button. You'll see, on the left, a list of the DAs presently in place. To remove one, select it, and click the Remove button. If you need to install a DA from another disk, or want to see what other DAs are available on your disks, click Open on the right-hand window. A dialog box directory opens to let you locate the DAs you want by using the Drive, Open, and Eject Files buttons. When you find the file you want, select it and click Open. This action lists the DAs in the file in the right window. Select the one you want and click Copy. Figure 3.17 shows us moving the DA *3D Tic Tac Toe* into our Apple menu. When you finish moving DAs, click the Quit button to go back to the desktop.

DAs, just like the accessories on a real desk, take up room. In this case, it's not desk surface area, but memory. If your system uses floppy disks, you may not want to go overboard with DA toys. Or, if you like to play, you might want to make up a special system disk with a lot of the neat DA games and toys that are on the market, either as shareware or commercially. See Chapter 11 for more information on games.

Making Copies

There are many reasons why you might want to copy documents and applications. When you buy software, the first thing you're told to do is to make a copy to work with (or play with), while you keep the original disk in a safe place. You can copy a document, folder, or disk to another disk, as long as both disk icons are present on the desktop. To copy a document onto another disk, drag its icon to the location where you want to place the copy, and the Mac will copy it.

You can copy to a disk or to a specific folder within the disk. If you drag the icon of the item being copied to the icon of the destination disk, the copy will appear on the desktop. If you open the destination disk and copy into a folder, the copy appears in the folder. If the folder is open, you'll see the copy. If you're copying to a closed disk or folder, you'll have to open it to locate the copy.

Single Drive Copying

Even if you have only one disk drive, you can still make copies. You'll just have to remove disks and replace them as a dialog box directs. Make sure you have a formatted disk to copy onto. If not, put a new disk into the drive and format it according to your Mac's needs (one-sided, two-sided, or high density). Put the disk you want to copy to into the drive, and look for its icon on-screen. Now eject that disk, and put the original disk back in the drive. Select the material you want to copy, and drag it to the icon for the destination disk, even though the icon is *disabled.*

> Disabled icons are gray, instead of black. A disabled icon represents something that the Mac can't do at that moment, such as access a disk not currently in the drive.

After the Mac reads some data from the original disk, it ejects the disk and asks you to insert the destination disk. The number of disk swaps you'll need to make depends on how much memory the Mac has available. It may take two, three, or many more swaps if you're copying a whole disk. The point is, it's possible. (If it gets too frustrating, you can plug a second floppy drive into most Macs. See chapter 13.)

> **TIP:** If you've got a system with a hard drive and one floppy, it may be faster to copy an entire disk into a folder on your hard drive, eject the disk, and then copy the folder back to a blank floppy.

Whenever you make a copy of something, the Mac leaves the original behind. If your intention was to move the item, rather than duplicate it, just throw the original in the trash after you've made the copy. To reclaim the space immediately, select Empty Trash from the Special menu.

You can copy or move your own documents with no trouble. You can also copy most applications without problems. However, there are a few exceptions: some applications are *copy-protected* and can't be duplicated. The next section explains why.

Free the Software: A Fable for Our Time

Once upon a time, when computers were new, there weren't very many programs (or programmers). When new software was created, copies were immediately passed around. An application written at MIT could work its way to Berkeley in a matter of days and then come right back to Cambridge revised and enhanced. Many people spent a lot of time developing software for free, just because it was fun. It was a form of art.

Eventually, some of the people writing programs realized that there was rent to pay and new computers to buy, and it would take more than a simple "thanks for the neat program" to do the job. They formed companies to develop even more interesting and useful applications . . . and to collect money for them . This system seemed fine, until the companies noticed they were selling far fewer programs than people seemed to be using.

Obviously, people were passing around the commercial software just as they had the free stuff. The companies were losing money. So they invented *copy protection,* a scheme for making disks that could not be copied, by burying codes that could not be duplicated, that bypassed the normal operating system. You could buy a copy of Butter—the High-Price Spreadsheet—and use the floppy disk as much as you wanted. But you couldn't put it on your more efficient hard drive. If you wanted to let your friends try it, you'd have to give them your disk. And if a disk were damaged, you were out of luck. You could write to the publisher for a replacement, but getting one often took weeks.

So the software companies came up with alternatives to protect themselves and the users. But every scheme created hassles. Today, most software companies have decided that copy protection isn't worth the effort, but they ask you to return a registration card when you buy a program. This often entitles you to telephone support, free or low-cost upgrades when new features are released, and discounts on copyrights, which stand up in court.

So the real point of this history lesson is: UNAUTHORIZED COPYING OF SOFTWARE IS NOT ONLY IMMORAL. IT'S ALSO ILLEGAL.

We should point out that there are ways to copy protect disks, using a copying program made just for that purpose. In certain circumstances—particularly when making protection copies in case a disk gets damaged—this is both legal and advisable. You just shouldn't let the copies get away from you.

The View Menu

Under the *View* menu, you can select any of several ways to organize your desktop and folders. Your first options are to view by Small Icon or by Icon. Small icons obviously take up less room on-screen, while still letting you tell at a glance whether you're looking at a folder, an application, or a single document. Large icons are easier to see, but on a busy desktop or in a full folder, they may make things too crowded.

Viewing by Name puts everything into alphabetical order. *Viewing by Date* puts the most recently used items at the head of the list, and even tells you, to the minute, when you last used them. This is especially helpful if you have two versions of a document and you want to see which one you worked on last. *Viewing by Size* lets you see how much memory is used by specific documents or applications. *Viewing by Kind* sorts your desktop or folder into applications and types of documents. If you've forgotten what you called a particular file, viewing in this way may help you locate it more easily. *Viewing by Label*, a System 7 feature, is discussed earlier in this chapter.

Special Cases—The Special Menu

The last menu is the *Special* menu. Those of us who live with perennially messy real-world desks appreciate the ease of cleaning up our Mac desktops. All you need to do in order to have a neatly arranged desktop is to open the disk icon and select Clean up from the Special menu. Like magic, the files arrange themselves in neat rows. Figure 3.18 shows an example desktop, with varying levels of neatness.

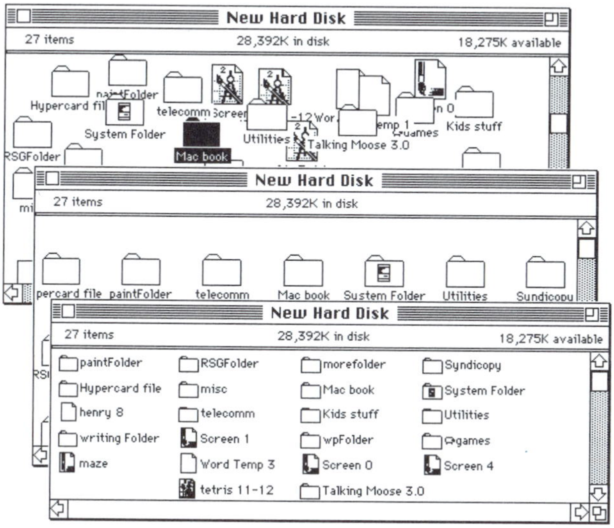

Figure 3.18

Messy desktop, neat desktop with regular icons and with small icons.

If you select one file or document, the Mac straightens it. If you select several, they'll march in an orderly procession to their places, leaving the rest of the files as they were. Of course, Clean up only works when you're viewing by icon or by small icon.

We've already discussed emptying the trash. Remember, as long as the trash can bulges, you can retrieve your files simply by opening the trash can and removing your files. Empty trash throws them away for good. The following paragraphs describe the other commands on the Special menu.

Erase Disk is almost as traumatic as it sounds. If you want to reuse a disk, insert it, and select it. Then select Erase Disk. Before the Mac erases, though, you get a chance to reconsider. A dialog box asks `Completely erase disk named...`. Depending on your system and the type of floppy you've inserted, you may then be asked to select the format: one-sided or two-sided. Once the disk is erased, everything on it is gone. The good news is you can't erase the Startup disk that's running your Mac. It needs the information on it in order to erase.

Set Startup tells your Mac how to dress for work. You can turn on your Mac and go directly into an application without going through the Finder. To do this, select your application on the desktop. Don't open it, just select it and then select `Set Startup`. A dialog box verifies your choice. If you are not using System 7, you can choose `Multifinder` under `Set Startup`, if it's in your system folder. Multifinder lets you open a variety of applications and switch back and forth among them. It does, however, require a lot of memory to use.

Restart does exactly that. It shuts down the Mac and immediately restarts it. This is handy when you have just installed a startup application and want to see if it works, or for a variety of other possible reasons, which you'll discover as you need to.

Shut Down gets your Mac ready for bed. When you're through using the computer, select Shut Down, and it ejects any disks in use and darken the screen. Mac IIs turn themselves off completely when you select `Shut Down`. You need to turn other Macs off manually. The power switch location varies, but it's usually near the power cord. Turn off the computer first, and then the hard disk. Don't forget to turn off the printer, too!

In This Chapter

Why Mac Programs Are So Easy to Learn

•

Keeping Software Up-to-Date

•

Cutting, Pasting, Dragging, and Undoing

•

Editing Text in Any Mac Program

•

Saving Your Work

The Mac makes it easy to do many different tasks on the same computer. Once you've learned one program, you can go ahead and use just about any other. The basics, such as editing text, using command keys, and saving or retrieving files, stay the same.

4

Mac Editing Techniques

Before the Mac, computer companies made computers—the keyboard, screen, and brains of the system—and sold only a few programs (applications) to go with them. Software companies were practically left alone to write useful applications any way they wanted.

While the software companies wrote many programs, the effect of having separate hardware and software makers was chaotic. There was no consistency from one program to the next. You'd learn a command that meant one thing in the *WordSmith* program (such as pressing [T] to set a Tab stop), only to find it meant something else in *WordChopper* (press [T] to type the page), and something totally disastrous in *HemingWay* (press [T] to trash this file). These examples are fictitious, but the situation was very real. With most computers, you had to learn a new program *and* unlearn the old program.

The same situation is true today for non-Macintosh users; they frequently end up using only one program. Typists become experts with a word processor, but don't learn how to use the computer to balance a checkbook. Accountants know their spreadsheet software insideout, but need someone else to type word processing documents.

User Interface

Apple's vision for the Macintosh, on the other hand, included a *consistent user interface*; the same commands do the same job, no matter which Macintosh program you use. Things you learned about MacWrite last year apply to Microsoft Word today (and to Aldus PageMaker next week). The Macintosh user interface also defines consistent ways to store and transfer information, making it easy for programs to share text, numbers, or pictures.

The point is, once you learn how to use one Macintosh program, you're almost ready to use them all. Most Macintosh owners are equally at home with at least two programs. Publishers sometimes sell combinations of Mac word processing, spreadsheet, database, and graphics programs—all in one package, at a reduced price.

MacWrite: The First

Apple did more than just give us standards. The company gave us the programs that set the standards. For the first few years of Macintosh's life, every system sold included *MacWrite* and *MacPaint.* These were good programs (and for a while, the *only* programs). They were powerful for their time, easy to learn, and available to every Mac owner. Users quickly became familiar with Apple's way of doing things.

As other companies developed competing programs, their programmers stuck to the *MacWrite* conventions and interface. Their goal was to keep the transition as easy as possible for prospective customers. So, even though today's *MacWrite II* is just one of many Mac word processors, the original techniques still apply. Changing and formatting text are the same in almost every Macintosh text program, and manipulating files is the same in virtually *every* program.

New Tricks for Old Software

We mentioned "today's *MacWrite II*" in the preceding paragraph. That's because computer software is one of the few products a manufacturer continues to reinvent even after it's successful. Programmers continually think up new features, and publishers respond to suggestions from users. Besides, minor programming mistakes (*bugs*) are hard to find until many people have used a program. For these reasons, software manufacturers often release new versions of an existing program.

> The term "bug" dates from the earliest days of computing, when programs were carried on miles of cotton-covered wire rather than floppy disks. These room-sized machines had to be rewired for each new task. Errors were frequently blamed on live, cotton-chomping insects, who'd snack on the insulation and cause short circuits!

Version Numbers

You can tell which revision of a program you have by checking the *version number*. To do so, choose About this program, the first entry in the menu, or choose Get Info on the desktop. Manufacturers frequently add the version number to the program name. Most software companies adhere to the following convention for numbering versions:

- ▲ The first commercial release of a program usually carries the number 1.0 after it, as in *WordMasher 1.0* or *WordMasher Version 1.0*.

- Program versions with major changes incorporating powerful, new features get a new number (*WordMasher 2.0*, rather than *New Improved WordMasher*).
- The number for versions with minor changes (primarily to correct programming mistakes and enhance existing features) increases by tenths (*WordMasher 2.1*).
- Versions with very minor changes get a second decimal point or a letter (*2.1.11* or *2.1b*).
- A program with a version number less than one (as in *BetterLetter 0.99*) is almost always a Beta version, written to test the program and be distributed to selected users who actively search for bugs. It's unlikely you'll come across a Beta version of a program; but if you do, expect to find bugs also.

Sometimes a software company completely rewrites a program but wants to hang on to a good reputation earned by the original version. In these cases, the company usually adds Roman numerals to the program name. For example, the current rewrite of the original Mac word processor (as of this writing) is *MacWrite II Version 1.1.*

Should You Upgrade?

Most software publishers have liberal upgrade policies, once you've registered yourself as a legitimate program owner (by sending in the reply card packed with the software). If a program isn't working well because of a bug, check with the publisher. If they've issued a new release to fix the bug, they'll probably send you a free copy.

Major upgrades aren't free, but are frequently offered at one tenth to one quarter of the retail cost. For the upgrade price, you often get everything a new customer would get (the complete retail package, including new instruction manuals). You can learn the most recent version numbers for your software by calling the publisher, checking the chart in *MacWorld* magazine, by (electronically) checking America Online, or asking a dealer.

A good dealer won't consciously try to mislead you about version numbers. But most store employees will naturally assume that the box on the shelf is the one they should sell, especially if it's been on the shelf for a while. Be sure to ask for the most current version.

> New software versions often have powerful new features. But they might also require more memory and new System files (see Chapter 13). If you're totally happy with the way a program works now, there may be no reason to upgrade. Software doesn't wear out, and no law says you have to have the latest version to do the job. Be warned, however. The rest of this book will tempt you with the features *today's* software offers.

Selecting, Cutting, Copying, and Pasting

Even if you never process one word on your Mac, read this section. The principles it describes apply to virtually every type of Macintosh program: graphics, accounting, database, music, animation, and even games.

As we pointed out, MacWrite II is just one of many excellent word processing applications you can buy for the Macintosh today. (It's no longer given away free with new computers.) Even so, almost all Mac word processing programs have basic features and operations in common. The differences are in speed, features, and flexibility. Usually the most powerful programs aren't the fastest.

We illustrate most of the examples in this chapter using Microsoft Word. Your software may differ slightly. But even if our examples don't look exactly like yours, most of the details will be the same. Try things we suggest. They'll probably work. If they don't, try experimenting. Your software may be very similar. Or (horrors!) read the manual.

> Microsoft Word has been the best-selling Macintosh word processor for more than three years, as of this writing. We don't believe it's the ideal choice for every user, but there sure are a lot of copies of it out there.

Word Processing, Jigsaw-Puzzle Style

The basic Macintosh text editing operations resemble those you'd do with scissors, glue, and a typewritten page. The Mac's much faster (and less messy). In fact, taking a moment to think about this earliest form of word processing will make it easier to learn how Mac does it.

If you wanted to move the word "penetration," you'd first cut it out, as shown in the middle image in Figure 4.1. Then, with a few extra cuts and some tape and glue, you'd paste it where it belongs, as in the bottom image. Not very pretty, but it does the job.

Word Processing, Macintosh Style

Using a Mac, you do the same cutting and pasting—but faster and cleaner. The computer takes care of retyping and closing up the gaps. On a Mac screen, the sample memo looks like Figure 4.2.

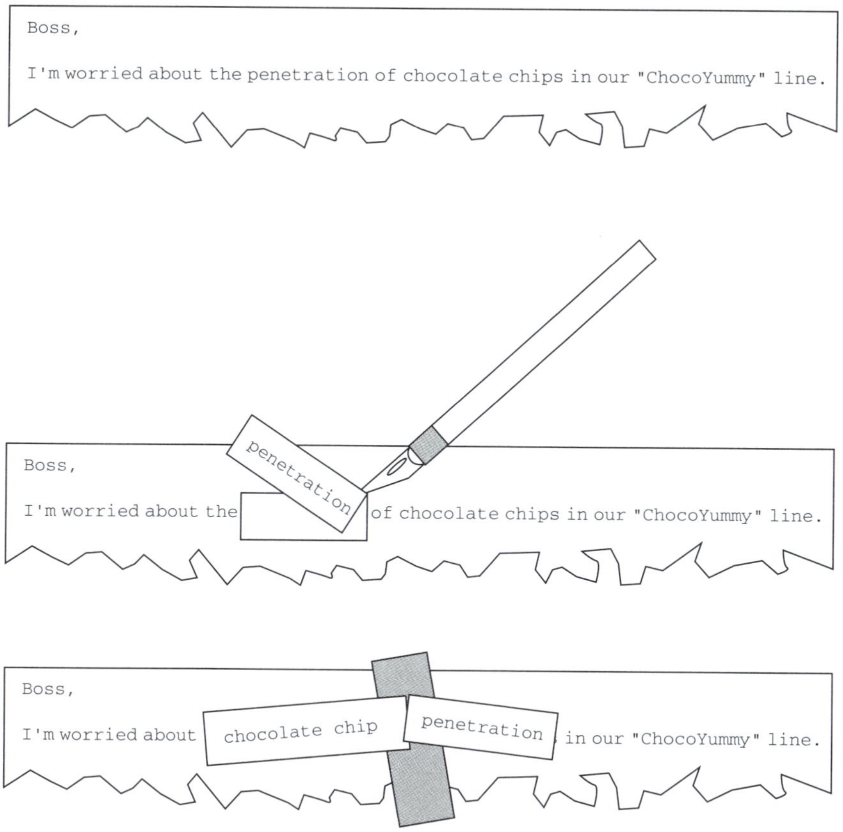

Figure 4.1

Memo on paper (top), cutting (middle), and pasting.

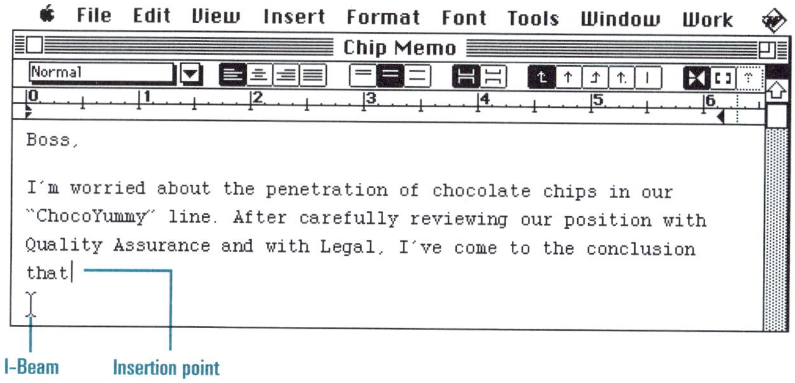

Figure 4.2

Original memo, Macintosh style.

For these examples, it may help to have a machine in front of you, but it isn't necessary. If you are near a Mac, open a word processing document (see Chapter 3), or start a word processing application and type some text into the new document that automatically appears. A few programs don't automatically start you out with a new document. To start a new document in any program, click the word New in the File menu.

The Insertion Point

The *I-beam* pointer in Figure 4.2 shows that the mouse is over text you can edit. If you click, the I-beam changes to an *insertion point*: the vertical line after the word "that." The insertion point flashes to call attention to itself (as do some demented city dwellers). Anything you now type appears at the insertion point location. Anything after the insertion point slides to make room for the text you type.

If your Mac has arrow keys (the early models don't), you can also use them to move the insertion point, one letter horizontally or one line vertically at a time. You can also press Delete to eliminate letters, one at a time, moving left from the insertion point. Delete works like the correction key on a self-correcting typewriter. (Extended keyboards also have a *Del* key, which deletes the character to the right of the insertion point.)

> On early Macs, the Delete key was called the Backspace key. Starting with Macintosh SE, Apple renamed the key Delete. Go figure.

Selecting Text

Macintosh programs can do much more than merely emulate a typewriter. If you *select* text (highlight it), you can manipulate it in a variety of interesting ways. Depending on the program, you can change type (lettering) style, capitalize initial letters, sort or number the lines, reorganize the text as an outline, and do a bunch of other nifty things. With every program, you can copy or replace the selected text.

To select a single word, move the I-beam to a word and *double-click* (see Chapter 2). The Mac highlights the nearest whole word to show it's selected. (Highlighting means that a Mac outlines a selection with a contrasting color. A black and white Mac inverts selected text to highlight it, as shown in Figure 4.3.)

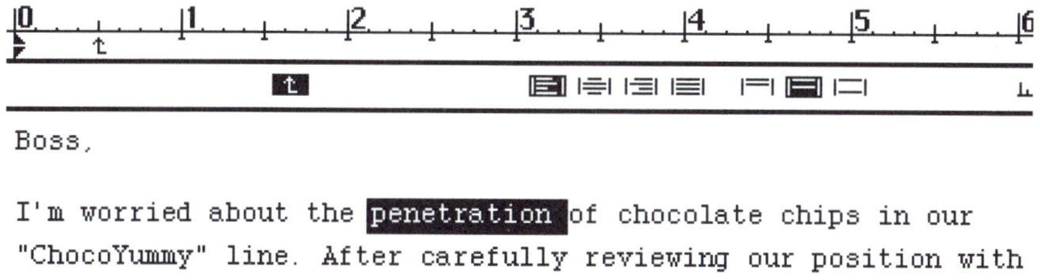

Figure 4.3
A highlighted word.

You can select anything, from a single letter to a group of words or paragraphs, by holding down the mouse button and dragging across the desired text, as shown in Figure 4.4. When you release the button, the Mac selects everything you dragged over. Other programs may give you additional ways to select text by searching for a particular word, using the Tab key, using the numeric keypad, or whatever struck the programmer's fancy. But double-clicking and dragging always works in every program, in every situation where you can edit text. You're now ready to process the words you've selected.

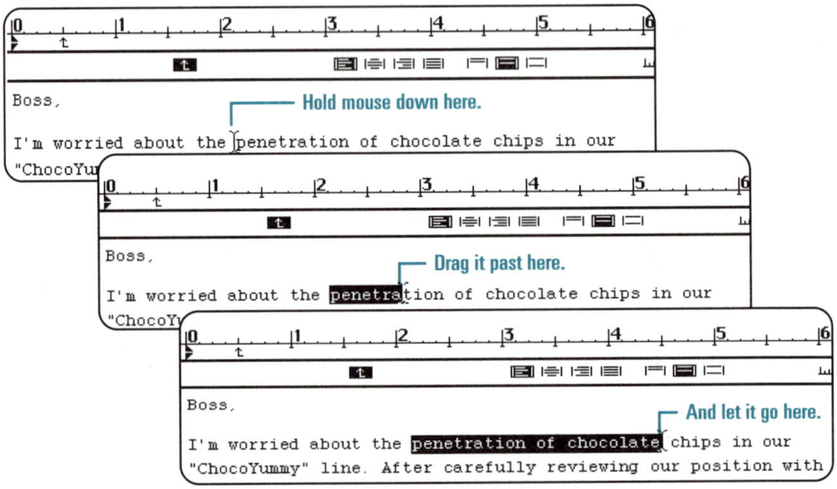

Figure 4.4
Selecting by dragging.

Cutting and Pasting

Before you could move a word on a paper memo, you had to cut that piece of the paper out (as in Figure 4.1). Use a similar procedure to *cut* on-screen text with a Mac. Begin by selecting the desired word, as shown in the top image of Figure 4.5. Then, pull down the Edit menu and choose the Cut command, as shown in the middle image in Figure 4.5. The selection promptly disappears from the screen, as in the bottom image of Figure 4.5.

If you had cut the word out of a piece of paper, you could put that little scrap aside for later use. Similarly, Macintosh holds the cut out word in computer memory, in the *Clipboard.* The Clipboard holds the last thing you cut: a word, a paragraph, or even a whole story. It can also hold graphics or numbers if you cut them from appropriate programs. When you cut something new, the Clipboard throws away what it had been holding to make room for the new material.

TIP: Many programs let you choose the Show Clipboard command to check what the clipboard's holding.

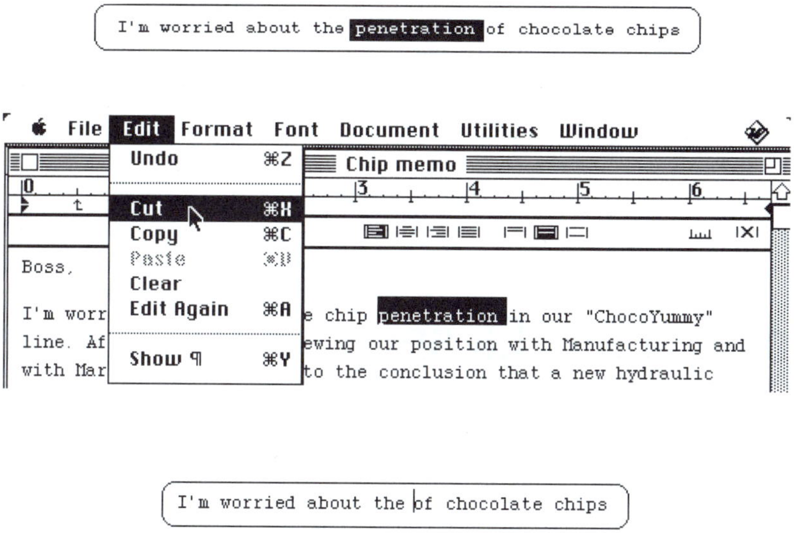

Figure 4.5

Selecting a word (top). Choosing the Cut command (middle). Remaining text (bottom).

Now that we've put something into the Clipboard (the word "penetrate") by cutting it from a document, we can *paste* the Clipboard contents into a new location on the document. To put the insertion point where you want the word to appear, pull down the Edit menu, and choose Paste. The Mac pastes the word from the Clipboard into place, as shown in Figure 4.6.

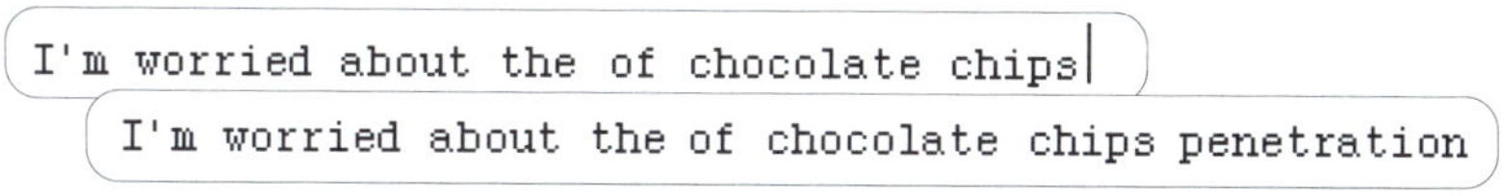

Figure 4.6

Before and after pasting at the insertion point.

If you select text before you paste, the material from the Clipboard replaces the highlighted text, as shown in Figure 4.7. Delete any extraneous words or letters (or select them and cut), and your memo is finished, as shown in Figure 4.8. Later, this chapter explains how to print your memo.

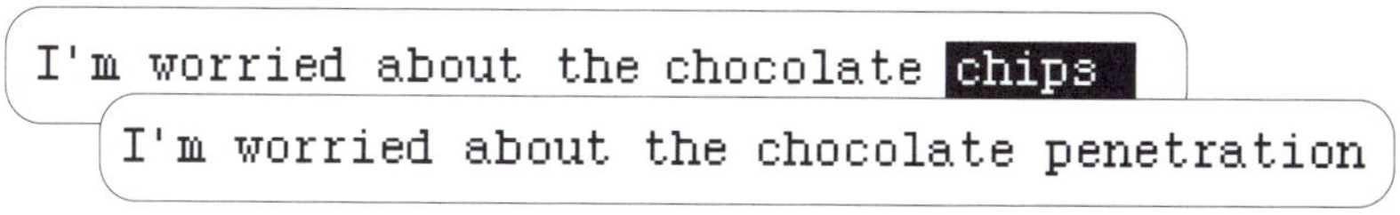

Figure 4.7

Before and after pasting over selected text.

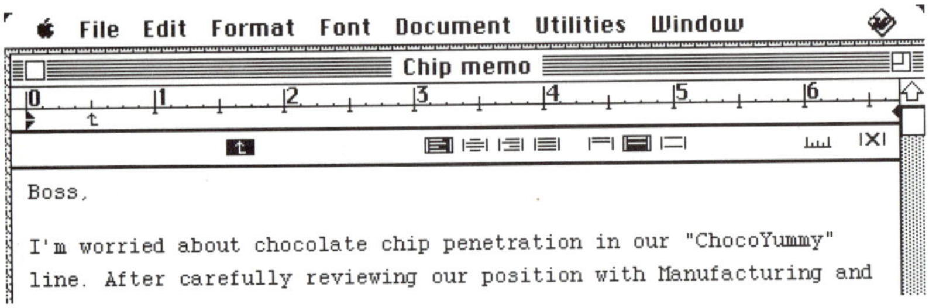

Figure 4.8

The edited memo, ready to print.

Copying and Clearing

Two other commands on the Edit menu help you work with text. The Copy command works almost exactly like Cut. Select text, choose Copy, and the Mac puts the selected text in the Clipboard. But the selected text won't disappear from the page. As the name Copy suggests, the Mac places a copy of the selected text on the Clipboard. You can insert the text copy by clicking the mouse where you want to place the text, and then selecting the Paste command.

The Clear command deletes selected text without affecting the Clipboard. You can accomplish the same operation by selecting text and pressing Delete. Clear appears in most, but not all, Macintosh programs. If you clear something you really wanted to keep, choose Undo, described in the following paragraphs.

The Magic Undo

The command at the top of the Edit menu is one of those design breakthroughs the Mac is known for: something simple and obvious, but never appeared earlier on practical computers. The Undo command does exactly what it says. Select it, and your last operation goes away. If you've cut or deleted something, Undo puts it back. If you've pasted something, Undo removes it. The Undo command has some limitations, as follows:

You can only undo the last operation. If you choose another command, or type something else, Undo forgets the previous operation. (Some programs, including the highly rated Nisus word processor, don't have this limitation.)

Depending on the program, you can't undo some changes. You'll always be able to undo cut, paste, or delete operations (subject to the rule above).

You can't undo something after you've quit and restarted a program. With many programs, you can't undo after you've saved a document.

Changes involving very large selections might not be undoable. That's because the Mac needs enough memory to keep both versions. If memory isn't sufficient, the system will warn you the operation can't be undone (and your friendly local dealer will recommend you buy more memory).

If you can't undo an operation for any reason, the command name appears dimmed. Some programs add additional words to the Undo menu command to tell you exactly what will be undone. For example, Microsoft Word messages include `Undo Cut`, `Undo Formatting`, `Undo Typing`, and so on.

> **TIP:** Undo itself is undoable! If you've undone something, you can redo it by clicking **Undo** again. You can undo the redo, by clicking a third time. And re-redo the undo, by clicking a fourth time. If you don't type or edit anything else, you can keep on un-undoing and re-redoing until your mouse finger wears out.

All of these menu selections have command-key shortcuts, and they're the same in virtually every Macintosh program. Hold the ⌘ key down while you press the indicated letter, and the effect will be the same as if you clicked on the menu selection. Table 4.1 lists the command-key shortcuts available for Edit menu commands. Because the four commands in Table 4.1 are the ones you'll use most often with Mac programs, their four shortcut key letters are the ones closest to the key.

Table 4.1
Command-key shortcuts for the Edit menu.

Shortcut	Menu Selection
⌘-X	Cut
⌘-C	Copy
⌘-V	Paste
⌘-Z	Undo

FYI Idea

That's all there is to it. Now you know how to edit text on the Macintosh. These operations apply to every popular word processing program, and to the text-entry functions in drawing programs, desktop publishing, spreadsheets, and databases. You can also use them with the Note Pad DA (described in Chapter 3). Furthermore, the basics of cutting, copying, and pasting apply to using graphics, as well. While different programs have different ways of selecting pictures, most use these same Edit menu commands and the Clipboard. You also can cut, copy, or paste graphics or text to the Scrapbook DA.

Saving Your Document

Most Macintosh programs keep your current work in electronic memory. ("Current" work. "Electronic" memory. Get it? Never mind.) When you take away the memory by quitting the program or turning off the power, the work disappears. Work you've stored on magnetic disk (either removable floppy disks or the computer's hard disk) is relatively permanent. Barring a magnetic catastrophe like those described in Chapter 14, you can recover the work anytime.

To save your work, choose Save from the File menu, or use the shortcut, ⌘-S. This procedure works in every standard Macintosh program. The disk whirls or the hard disk light blinks for a few moments, and the Mac writes the document to disk. If the proper disk isn't in the machine, Mac will ask for it. A few programs, most notably *HyperCard*, don't have a save command. These programs automatically save every change you make.

> **TIP:** You can save anytime. Each time you save a document without changing its name, you replace the previously saved version. (If you *do* want to change the name, choose Save As... instead of Save. . . .) It's a good idea to save frequently, rather than just when you're ready to quit. Experienced Macintosh users press ⌘-S every five minutes or so while they're working.

Save is not undoable. Once you've saved a version of a document, you can't go back to the previously saved one. (One word processor, *WriteNow*, lets you revert to an earlier version. You *can* undo a save with this program.) Macintosh saves documents with names you give them. The first time you try to save a new document, it doesn't have a name, and the Mac displays a dialog box like the one shown in Figure 4.9. Type the name you'd like in the box. (The insertion point will already be flashing there.) When you enter the file name, you can use the same selecting and deleting techniques you've already learned. Later, this chapter discusses the few limitations to entering file names.

Click on the disk name to see other folders on that disk. Click Drive to see other disks that might be in your machine, and click Eject to remove a floppy disk so you can put a different one in. (This last command is dimmed in Figure 4.9. You can't eject Jeff's—or anyone else's—hard disk. The system can only eject floppy disks.) The list of existing files will help you avoid typing in a file name that's already taken. If you type a name that's already in a folder, Macintosh will ask if you want to replace the original file with the new material. Doing so will erase the file that originally had that name.

When you're ready to save, click the Save button or press the Return key. Needless to say, you should save before you close a file or quit an application. Most Macintosh programs automatically remind you to save if you try to close a file or quit. If you've made any changes since the last time you saved your file, the Mac presents the dialog box shown in Figure 4.10 when you try to quit. Yes saves your changes. No preserves the previously saved version. Cancel calls off the whole quitting or closing operation.

Figure 4.9
The Save As dialog box.

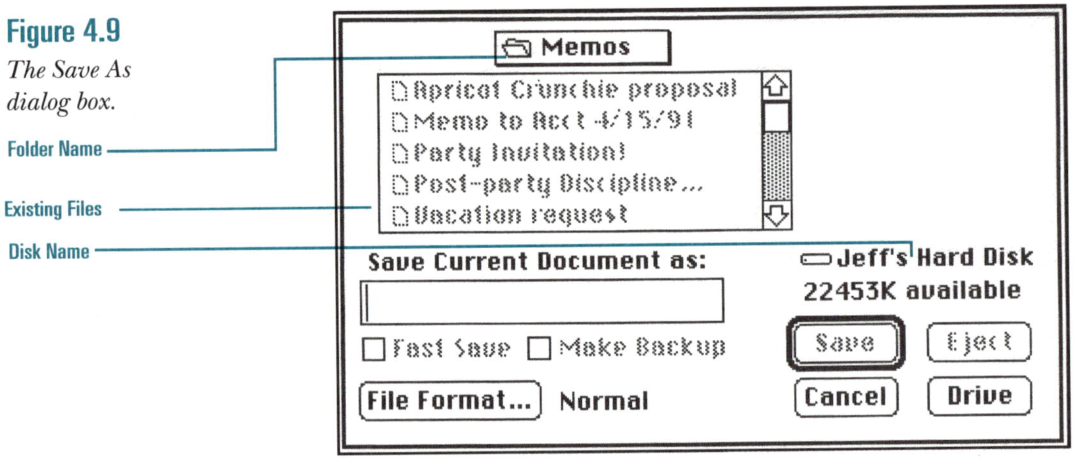

Figure 4.10
Dialog box reminding you to save your changes.

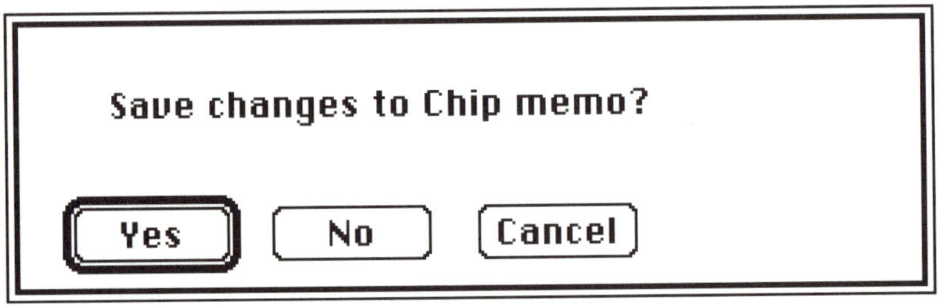

Macintosh File Names

If you've worked with other personal computers, you've probably seen (and been perplexed by) file names like the following:

MEMO_APR.DOC

MEMO_ACT.DOC

PARTY.TXT

MS-DOS (the operating system on IBM and IBM PC clones) restricts you to eight letters in a file name, followed by a period and a three-letter identifier (usually dictated by the application). You can't use spaces or most punctuation characters in MS-DOS file names. If you have a lot of files in your disk directory (and it's hard to imagine working *without* a lot of files), these names can get confusing very quickly.

Macintosh users, on the other hand, can be more explicit. The following are all valid Mac file names:

Steve's vacation plans, 12/20/92

Cookie & Cake Recipes

"Oh Calcutta!" review

You can use spaces, upper- or lowercase letters, and any punctuation or special characters on the keyboard in Mac file names. The only character you can't use is the colon (:), which is reserved by the system to specify folder paths.

> Upper- and lowercase letters are just cosmetic and are ignored by the Macintosh system. "Steve's Vacation" and "steve's vacation" would be the same file name.

Don't waste space on the date or time in a file name, unless you'll need to refer to the dates often. The Mac automatically records when you save a file anyway, and you can tell when any file was saved by using Get Info in the Finder. The maximum length of a name is 31 characters or spaces. (*Steve's vacation* . . . , in the list given earlier, pushes the limit.) However, most applications can display only the first 24 characters of the file name, as shown in Figure 4.11. The two Steve's Vacation Plans file names in the figure aren't really the same, but you'd never know it from the listing. (The files are for different years. Steve likes to plan ahead.)

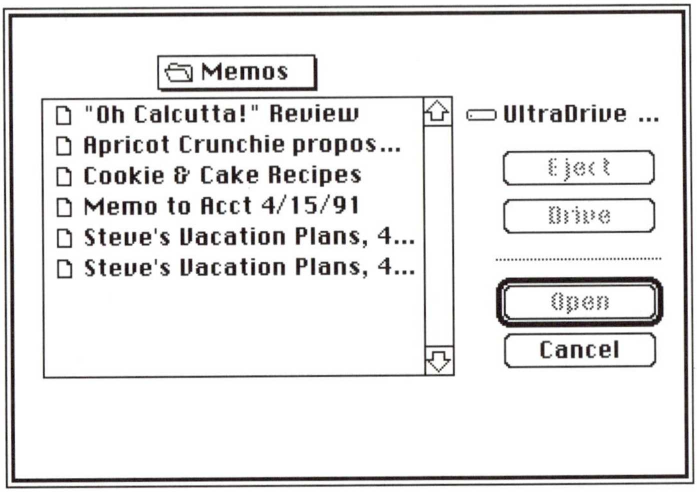

Figure 4.11
Open dialog box, showing abbreviated file names.

TIP: To make a file easier to find, put unique parts of its name towards the front. Dialog boxes automatically alphabetize, so you can force a file to the top of the list by putting a *non*-alphabetical character (a number or punctuation) in front of its name.

Other File Menu Commands

Click Close or the window's close box to clear a document off the screen. Closing a document frees up memory for the next document (and keeps your screen from getting too cluttered). The Close command frequently has the non-intuitive shortcut ⌘-W (for "Close Window," we suppose).

The Save As... command lets you keep multiple versions of a file. Selecting this command brings up the dialog box shown in Figure 4.9, so you can give the new version a name. When you click the Save button, the Mac closes the old version and opens a copy of it, with the new name.

Open... brings up the dialog box shown in Figure 4.11, so you can choose an existing document to work on. The dialog box displays only the documents in the current folder. If you don't see the file you want, click on the disk name to change folders (it works just like the Save As... dialog box). When you see the file you want to open, select it by clicking on its name, and then click the Open button to open it. You also can double-click on the document name to open it. Or select a name and press the Return key. Open... has a shortcut key combination, ⌘-O.

> One of the nice things about Macintosh is that there are usually two or three ways to do anything. Take your pick.

Most applications let you have multiple documents open at the same time. Each document appears in its own window, and you can work on whichever window you click in. To open multiple files, just keep hitting ⌘-O.

Some Macintosh programs also give you a Delete... command to erase files. Use it with caution. There's no good way to recover a file once you've deleted it. It's a lot better to get rid of unwanted files by throwing them away in the trash can. That way, you have the chance to rescue the documents.

The last command in the File menu is always Quit. Click it when you're finished working, and the Mac takes you back to the desktop so you can work with another program. Quit usually has the shortcut ⌘-Q.

> **CAUTION:** When you finish working with your Mac, Quit the application and Shut Down from the desktop. Don't just turn off the power.

Many programs do a "clean up" routine when you quit. If you turn off the computer without using this command, the program might not work properly the next time (and in rare cases, your system disk might get damaged). Table 4.2 summarizes the command-key shortcuts for the File menu.

Table 4.2
Command-key shortcuts for the File menu.

Shortcut	Menu Selection
⌘-N	New
⌘-O	Open...
⌘-W*	Close
⌘-S	Save
⌘-Q*	Quit

*Shortcut might not work in all programs.

In This Chapter

WYSIWYG: What You See Is What You Get

•

Looking Your Best with Rulers and Styles

•

How to Use Type Fonts

•

Putting Charts and Drawings in any Document

•

Finishing Touches

•

How to Create Custom Mailings with Mail Merge

•

Getting the Best Results from Apple's ImageWriter or StyleWriter

When you type a memo on a piece of paper, you're pretty much stuck with the way it looks. When you write a memo on the Macintosh, you can alter its appearance anytime—even after you've finished typing. You can change type styles or sizes for emphasis (or even change the typeface); move columns and margins; put boxes around text; add headers, footers, footnotes, or endnotes; and even paste in graphics. Then you can change them again (or undo the changes) until you're satisfied.

5

Dressing up Your Words

Creating all types of text styles is so easy on the Macintosh because of something its designers liked to call WYSIWYG: What You See Is What You Get. (If you're reading this book aloud, don't make rude noises. It's usually pronounced "Wizzy-wig.")

Formatting Codes

Some early word processors—including most sold for the early PC and its clones—made you put codes on the screen to indicate how the printed page should look. You'd have to learn the codes (or mess up your keyboard with notes and cardboard templates), and then use the right ones while you were typing. A typical word processor could make you type `/c/d/b/ Memo /n/` on-screen, just to get the headline *Memo* on the printed page. All these extra characters can detract from efficient writing and editing.

When the Mac was introduced, it was the first desktop computer that could let you select styling options from on-screen menus and instantly see the special formatting in front of you. You didn't have to memorize codes, because the menu let you see all the available choices. And you didn't have to wait for a printout to see the effects of your choices on your text, so it was easier to experiment with different ways to make your words more effective. Now, WYSIWYG word processing is available for almost all computers.

Actually, what you see isn't *exactly* what you get. Most printers are capable of much finer resolution than the Mac screen, so the system has to compromise slightly. But the screen version is a good approximation of the printed page. Figure 5.1 shows both a screen and its final printout. They're certainly so close that JJ could experiment with different ways to present his hard-hitting interoffice memo.

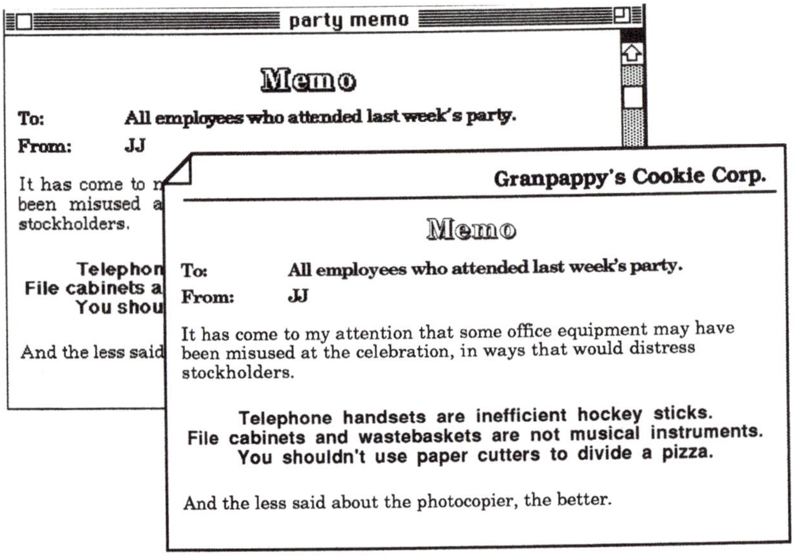

Figure 5.1

What you see is, well, close to what you get.

Margins and Tabs

Macintosh word processing programs let you determine how text will fall on a page by putting a picture of a *ruler* at the top of the screen. You set margins and tabs by moving little icons on the ruler, and the text conforms to the ruler icons. Figure 5.2 shows a sample ruler from Microsoft Word.

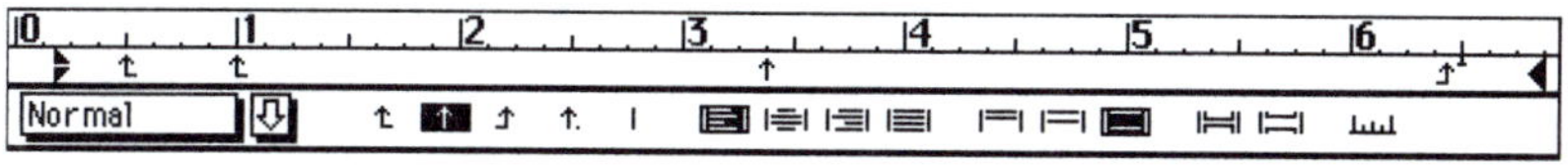

Figure 5.2
The Microsoft Word ruler.

The markings across the bottom are inches, and appear about an inch apart on-screen (reduced for printing). You also can change the measurements to centimeters or *picas* (a pica is one-sixth of an inch). The row of icons across the top control type styles and are a unique feature in Microsoft Word. But the icons across the middle are a direct descendent of those in MacWrite and appear in almost every Macintosh word processor. Slide them around with the mouse; when you do, the text moves to match. Table 5.1 explains what each one does.

Table 5.1
Ruler icons.

Icon	What It Does
	This sets the left margin. The top half sets the first line of a paragraph; the bottom sets all the other lines. Grab them with the mouse and slide them to set. If you put the halves in different places, paragraphs automatically indent.
	Controls the right margin.
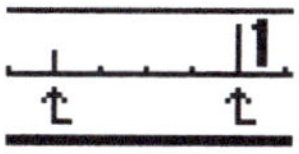	These are standard tabs, like on a typewriter.
	This is the tab stop supply. Each icon sets a different kind of tab (see Figure 5.3). To use one, select an icon and then click directly below the inch marking where you want it to appear.
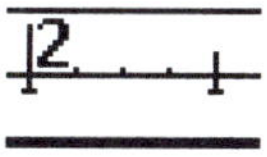	These are default tab stops. They appear automatically every half inch after any tabs you've specified.
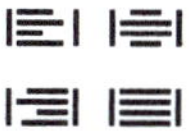	These are justification controls. Click to set flush left, centered, flush right, or evenly justified.

continues

Table 5.1
continued

Icon	What It Does
	These set line spacing. The more space between the horizontal lines on the icon, the more space between the lines on your page.
	These insert extra spaces between paragraphs.
	These appear only in Microsoft Word, to set up page boundaries or tables.

Each of the tab symbols has a different effect. Figure 5.3 shows the wide range of tab options in Word. Other programs use similar symbols for the tabs offered.

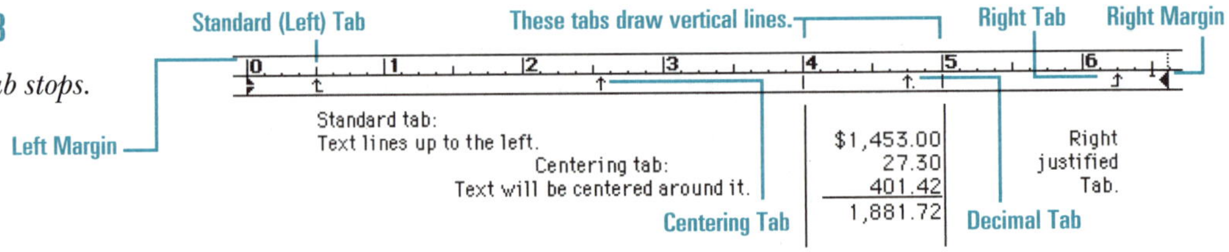

Figure 5.3
Types of tab stops.

A Short "Wrap" About Paragraphs

Ruler settings apply to whole paragraphs, rather than individual lines. A paragraph is anything you type from one *Return* to the next. "Return," of course, is a carryover from the days of mechanical typewriters. You'd press the carriage return, and the paper (or type element) would slam over to the margin for a new line. All Mac keyboards have a Return key over the right-hand ⇧Shift key. In word processing programs, it acts like a carriage return.

> Newer keyboards also have a separate Enter key on the extreme right. In most word processors, these two keys have the same effect.

Experienced typists will usually ask the following questions:

- If you press Return to start a new paragraph, how do you start each new line within a paragraph?
- What do you do when you get close to the right-hand margin?

You don't have to do *anything* with the Return key while you're typing a paragraph. The program does it for you.

Wrapping and Breaking

Word processors have a feature called *word wrap.* When a line has too many characters to fit between the margins, the offending word jumps (or *wraps around the screen*) to the next line. You type continuously, and the computer breaks the text into proper line-length chunks. Using automatic word wrap means breaking a habit. If you learned to type on one of those old-fashioned clacking things, you'll want to press Return when you near the edge of the line. It's worth changing your style, since word wrapping makes typing faster and means you don't have to look at the screen (or listen for the bell). It also lets your computer do some neat tricks:

- If you add or delete text, all the subsequent text moves up or down automatically and rewraps.
- If you change the margins, the text rearranges itself to fit.

Most programs let you use many rulers in the same document so you can format each paragraph differently. Good programs also give you a way to automate this formatting, using *style sheets.*

Style Sheets

The pop-up menu on the left of the ruler (see Figure 5.4) controls the *style sheet* feature, an easy way to format text throughout a document. You define a style by setting up text the way you want it, selecting it, and naming the format with the Define Styles... command. For example, the *style sheet* we used to create this chapter is shown in Figure 5.5. By clicking a style name, we could attach that style's type font and size, margins, and tabs to the current paragraph. If we change a style later, every paragraph with that style will change to match. (The style, brown fox, in Figure 5.5 applies to some examples in Chapter 14. Macintosh names are frequently fanciful.)

Figure 5.4

The Style pop-up menu.

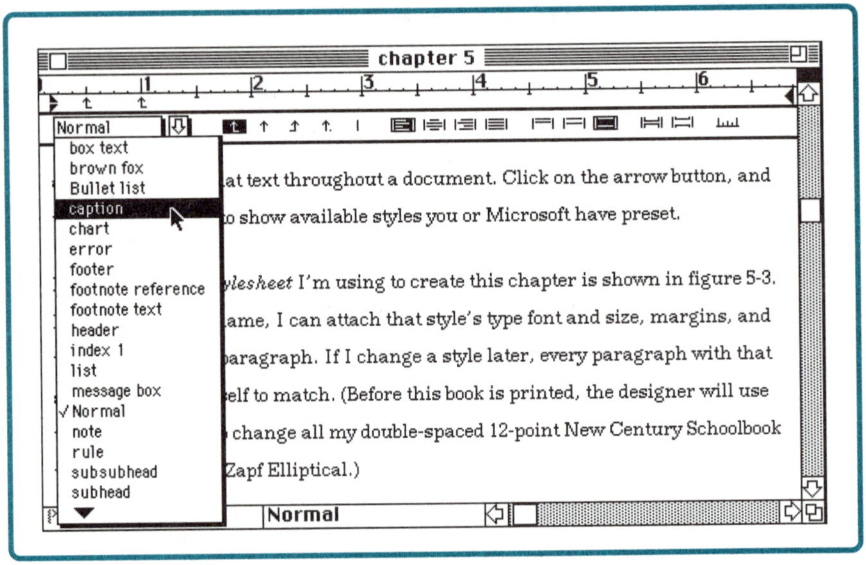

Figure 5.5

A style menu from Word.

You can have different style sheets for each document, style sheets that apply to groups of similar documents, or a single style sheet for everything you create. Other good word processors and desktop publishing programs either use a very similar feature, or offer some other way to keep a consistent look to your word-processed documents. Of course, too many styles in the same document can lead to visual chaos.

Putting on Your Best (Type) Face

When the Mac was first introduced, one of its more revolutionary features was the ability to mix type fonts, styles, and sizes freely in a page or on-screen. Unfortunately, people sometimes got carried away (as in Figure 5.6). Now that the system is more mature—as well as the font-happy users—there's an even greater selection of type styles, sizes, and effects. Many programs give you separate menus for each, as shown in Figure 5.7.

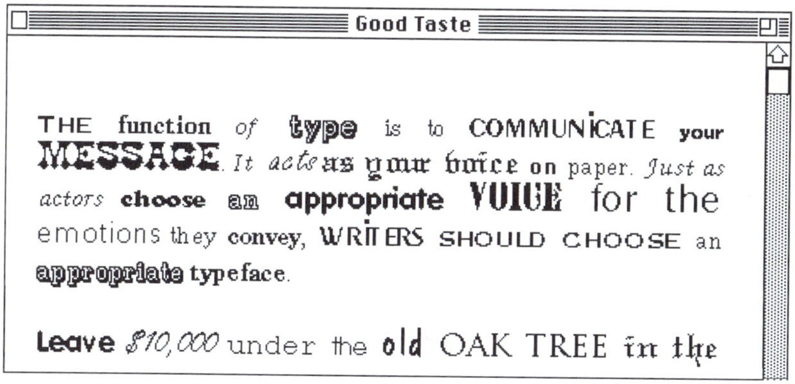

Figure 5.6

An early Macintosh composition.

The menus in Figure 5.7 are from the authors' copy of *WriteNow*, a popular word processing application with advanced typographic features. I say "authors' copy" because our particular list of type fonts probably doesn't appear on any other machine (not even our other machines). Apple supplies five basic fonts with the system. It's up to users to install more if they want. The type sizes that appear outlined on the menu are those available to your system (non-outlined sizes might not look as good on-screen or with an ImageWriter printer). You can add or delete fonts and sizes by using the techniques described in Chapter 3.

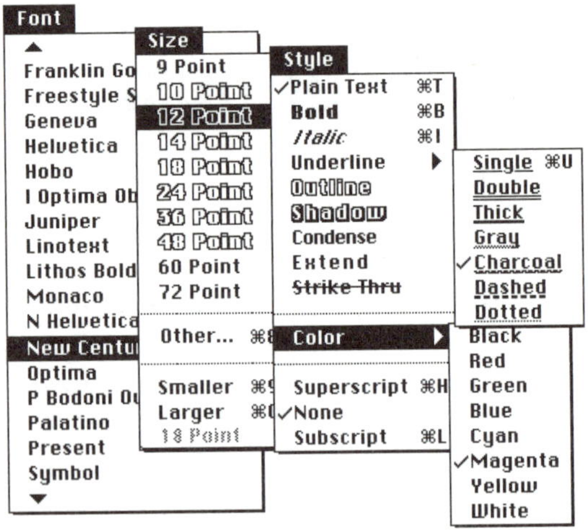

Figure 5.7

Type selection menus.

Use the following steps to change a type font, size, or style:

1. Select the text you want to change.
2. While the text remains highlighted, open the appropriate menu and choose a font, size, or style.
3. Your selected text changed to the new style. If you continue typing within the selection, the new text will also be in that style. To set a style for new typing, simply choose the new styles from the menu after setting the insertion point.

Finishing Your Work

Every Mac word processor enables you to add headers or footers, insert footnotes that renumber themselves as you edit, or add correct page numbers automatically as the document prints. The problem is that the original *MacWrite* barely implemented these features, so programmers didn't inherit a standard way to use them. Check the program manual for instructions. Or, if you're the type of person who prefers hands-on learning, just click and experiment—you'll usually find the functions under a Format or Document menu. Save your work first, just in case an experiment doesn't pan out as desired.

A Thousand Words

Even the earliest versions of MacWrite had the revolutionary ability to easily mix text and pictures. A user could insert drawings and graphs at will and see the effect on-screen instantly. All Macintosh word processors have inherited MacWrite's technique for pasting pictures. You can prepare illustrations in any graphics program, generate graphs with a spreadsheet, use commercial *clip art*, or even digitize existing pictures or video images (other chapters of this book explain how to accomplish such operations).

To put a graphic in your document, first place the insertion point where you want the image to appear (as shown in Figure 5.8). Go to the Scrapbook or any program that creates graphics, and select and copy the image. If you're using the Scrapbook, it selects the entire image as soon as you scroll to the appropriate page (see Figure 5.9).

Return to the document and select Paste from the Edit menu. The picture will appear at the insertion point (see Figure 5.10). If you select text (or another graphic), the pasted picture will replace the selected material. You can now select the picture and use Cut or Copy as you would for text. Most word processors also let you change spacing around the picture by treating it as a separate paragraph, or change its size by grabbing the rectangular *handles* (as in Figure 5.10) and dragging.

Be wary when resizing a graphic. If you resize something originally created in the "paint" layer of a graphics program (see Chapter 6), the graphic may become horribly distorted. For the graphic to remain undistorted, resizing has to follow the resolution ratios of the screen and output device, something that's impossible to control in most word processors.

Figure 5.8

Document ready for graphic.

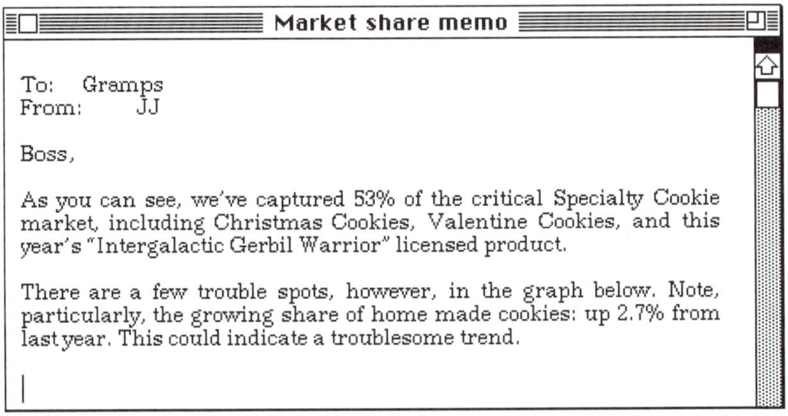

Figure 5.9

Selected scrapbook image.

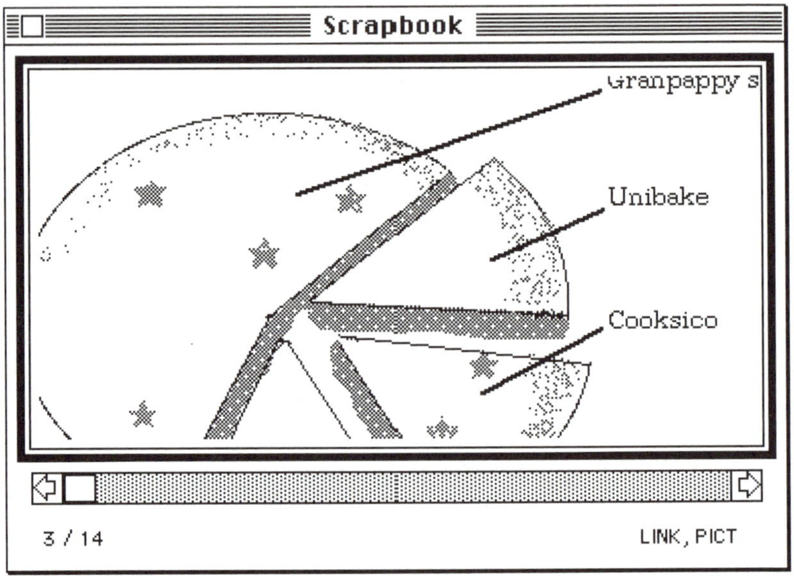

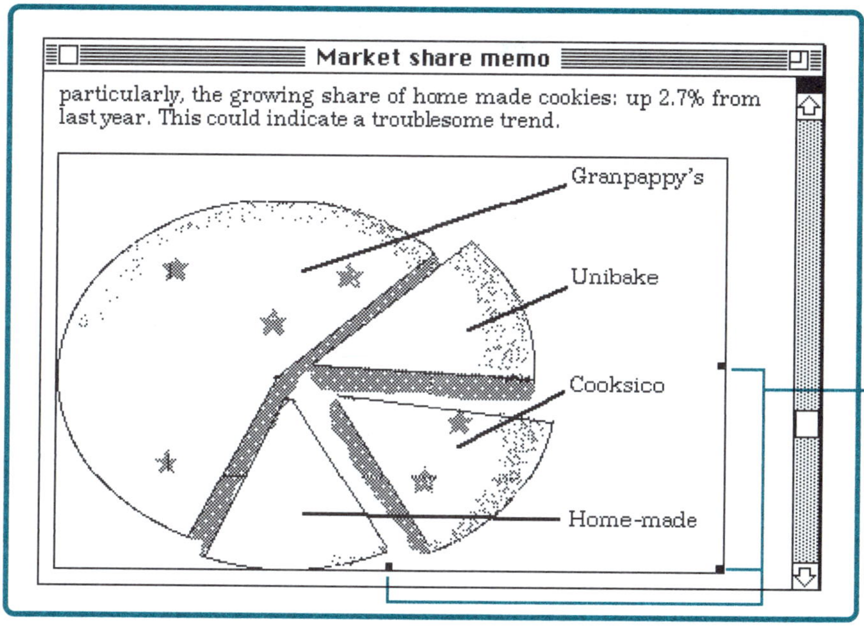

Handles

Figure 5.10

Document with graphic selected. Note the handles for resizing.

TIP: If you're resizing a graphic in a program that lets you set the enlargement or reduction ratio, always use multiples of the formula 72/*pr*, where *pr* is your printer's resolution in dots per inch.

pr should equal 144 for ImageWriters in Best mode, 360 for StyleWriters in Best mode, and 300 for laser printers with Precision Bitmap Alignment (Chapter 10) turned *off*. Skipped math class? Your best results will be by rescaling to exactly 50% for ImageWriters; multiples of 20% for Stylewriters; and 24%, 48%, 72%, or 96% for laser printers. Using these percentages, smaller images will have smoother, finer-grained shades of gray.

Scrolling through documents with pictures can be slow, because the Mac has to completely redraw the pictures with each movement. Most word processors provide a Hide Pictures command to replace the graphics with rectangular placeholders. After you get to where you're scrolling, you can turn the pictures on again.

Electronic Dictionaries

Every modern word processor includes powerful *spell checking* features, a godsend for those of us who never quite mastered the art of spelling in school. Fortunately, it's an easy function to use in most programs: simply set the insertion point at the beginning of the section you want checked and choose Spelling... under the Edit or Utilities menu.

> Our kids' high school teachers appreciate electronic spell checking, and claim it makes homework more readable.

The dialog box contains a button marked Start or Find. Click it, and the utility proceeds through your text, checking each word against an internal dictionary. When the spell checker encounters a word it doesn't know, it stops and highlights the offending word so you can change it. Your Mac displays a dialog box similar to the one in Figure 5.11. If it is a proper noun, technical term, or slang phrase the spell checker didn't recognize, you can add it to the dictionary at this time. A good spell checker will also give you a Suggest or Guess button to list the closest words it *does* know. Often, one of the suggestions will be what you really intended to type. Click the suggestion to insert it automatically in your text.

Spell Check Considerations

Not all electronic dictionaries are equal. There are noticeable variations in speed, dictionary size, and guessing techniques—any program can suggest "Chocolate" for "Choclate," but not many can cope with "Tofoo." (If *Tofoo* were Granpappy's trademark for an imitation bean curd, JJ would be able to click **Ignore** or add it to his dictionary.) Some programs flag the words you tell them to ignore, so they stay ignored the next time you open the document. Spell check utilities are also available as desk accessories, so you can add their power to other programs.

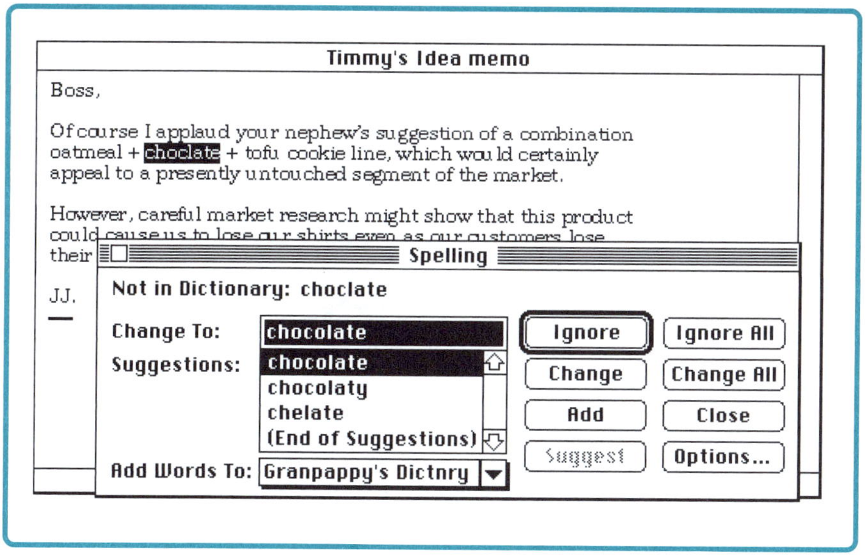

Figure 5.11

The Check Spelling utility in Word.

A Real Writer Would Never Use . . .

Another handy DA, often bundled with word processors but available separately, is a *thesaurus.* This tool is incredibly handy when you don't have the time to let inspiration provide "just the right word." To use a thesaurus, just highlight any word in your text, and the program suggests alternative words. You should also be able to select and check synonyms of the words the thesaurus suggests, to further refine your choice. A good thesaurus not only looks up synonyms, but also provides definitions and antonyms. Figure 5.12 shows the thesaurus we use.

The more words a utility knows, the more room it needs to store the words on disk. Dictionary and thesaurus files can be among the largest on your disk (on our machine, these references take more than 1½M).

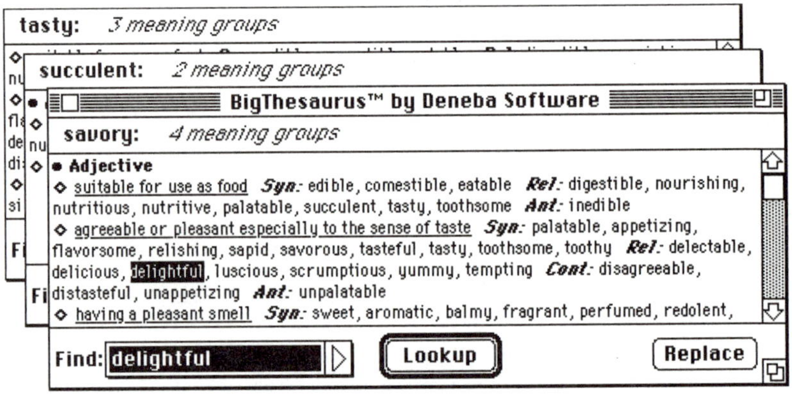

Figure 5.12

Just the right word . . .

> **TIP:** If you run your Mac from floppies, you can keep the dictionary files on a separate disk and not insert them until they're needed.

You May Have Already Won. . .

Large businesses frequently send out computerized form letters with "personalized" messages like the following one:

> Dear Mr. Jones,
>
> Imagine the surprise at 301 Elm Street, when your family gets its own...

Most good Macintosh word processors give you the capability to generate form letters (or personalize newsletters, or put individual names on multiple copies of memos). The command is usually called Merge... and appears under the File or Edit menu. To perform a merge, create a *data document* using your word processor. The first line should contain the categories of data you want to merge into the letter (such as *Name* or *Street*), separated by commas. Skip a line to make the document easier to read, then type the specific data, separating each category of information with a comma. Start a new paragraph for each recipient, until you have a document like the one in Figure 5.13. Most database programs will let you generate a text file to these specifications, which you can then open in your word processor (see Chapter 7).

Figure 5.13

Data document.

Now create your generic letter. In *Word*, start the first line with a « symbol, followed by the word **data**, the name of your data document, and a ». (The « and » characters are sometimes called European quote marks. Hold the Option key and press the backslash (\\) for «, and hold Shift–Option–\\ for ».) Then type the letter, and wherever you want the word processor to insert data from one of the categories, type the category name enclosed by the symbols (as in **«First Name»**). You can use a category more than once, or skip categories. Your letter should look like Figure 5.14. Category names are like Macintosh file names, in that capitalization is strictly for the convenience of the user. "First Name" and "first name" are considered the same in a mail merge operation.

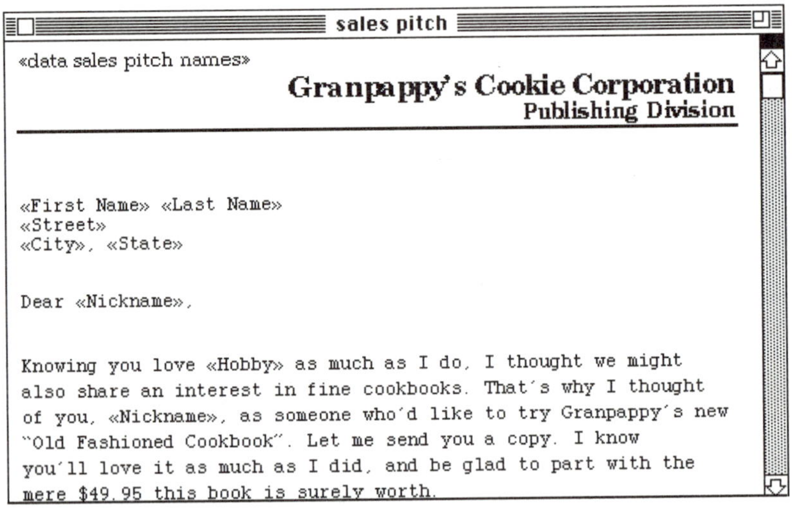
sales pitch

«data sales pitch names»

Granpappy's Cookie Corporation
Publishing Division

«First Name» «Last Name»
«Street»
«City», «State»

Dear «Nickname»,

Knowing you love «Hobby» as much as I do, I thought we might also share an interest in fine cookbooks. That's why I thought of you, «Nickname», as someone who'd like to try Granpappy's new "Old Fashioned Cookbook". Let me send you a copy. I know you'll love it as much as I did, and be glad to part with the mere $49.95 this book is surely worth.

Figure 5.14

Generic document for merging.

Save both files and make the generic letter's window active on your screen. Choose the Merge or Print Merge command (from the File menu), and you too can create effective or offensive form letters, just like the big companies (as in Figure 5.15).

Printing Your Document

There are three kinds of printers commonly available for the Macintosh: the ImageWriter (either the original or ImageWriter II), the StyleWriter, and the LaserWriter and its various laser clones. With very few exceptions, ImageWriters and StyleWriters are connected to a single Mac discussed later in this section. Laser printers are frequently connected through AppleTalk networks in an office (see Chapter 10).

ppy's Cookie Corporation
Publishing Division

ch as I do, I thought we might
cookbooks. That's why I thought

much as I do, I thought we might also

uch as I do, I thought we might
ine cookbooks. That's why I thought
ho'd like to try Granpappy's new
et me send you a copy. I know
did, and be glad to part with the
rely worth.

Figure 5.15 *One possible application of Mail Merge . . . .*

LaserWriter is Apple's trademark for its laser-equipped printers. But "laser" has become generic for all printers based on xerographic technology, even if they don't use lasers to generate light. (Our GCC laser printer has LEDs instead.) You can probably guess from the name that all these printers use the same basic mechanism as a Xerox copier. But imagine the legal and marketing headaches if Apple had decided to call it a XeroWriter instead.

Printing with the ImageWriter

There are two commands from the File menu that control printing. Use the Page Setup... command to set the options shown in the dialog box in Figure 5.16. If you want to print with the same specifications as the last document you printed, ignore this command. To change the specifications, choose this command anytime before you print.

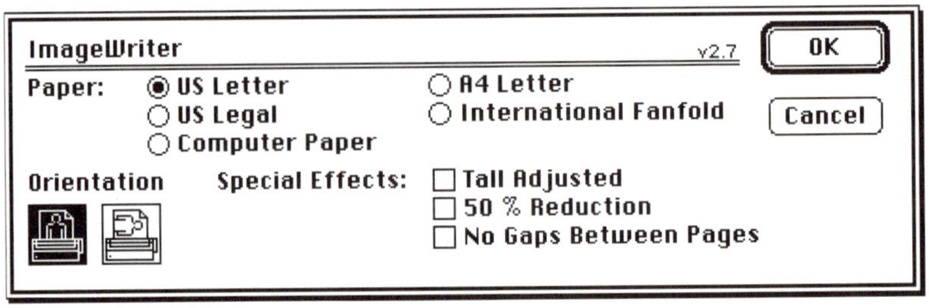

Figure 5.16
Page Setup dialog box.

Click Tall Adjusted if you've pasted critical pictures into the document. The normal setting is optimized for text but tends to squash graphics slightly. This is because the ImageWriter spaces dots slightly closer together vertically rather than horizontally. If you don't want your circles to look like ovals, Tall Adjusted will stretch the page a little. The other buttons on the Page Setup dialog box are self-explanatory. The Mac stores these instructions with the document, so you only have to set them once.

The Print... command (⌘–P) brings up a dialog box like the one in Figure 5.17. The Quality options can be a little confusing. Faster is not really fast, but it gives good output fairly quickly. One page of this manuscript took a minute and five seconds to print at that setting. Best squeezes the dots 1/144-inch apart for much higher qual-ity (like comparing the coarse dots of an old-fashioned newspaper photo to the much higher quality of a fine magazine). The price is speed; printing a manuscript page at the Best quality took four minutes and 20 seconds.

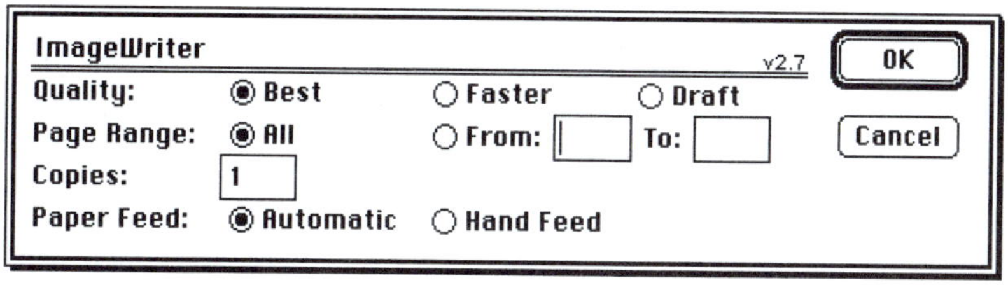

Figure 5.17

Print dialog box.

Best isn't always the best choice. To compensate for the shrunken dots, System 6 Macs use double-sized type and reduce it to fit. This means you need more type sizes in your system file. If you're printing 24-point Geneva type at the Best quality setting, you'll also need 48-point Geneva to get the best results.

TIP: You can eliminate the need for double-sized type in System 6 with Adobe Type Manager (see Chapter 10), or a separate TrueType INIT (see Chapter 13).

Draft prints quickly. The page of manuscript printed in 24 seconds. It printed so quickly because Draft used a plain typeface and skipped the graphics entirely. The result is more like a conventional computer printout than a Macintosh page, but it can be handy for proofreading or for long documents such as phone directories. Figures 5.18 shows a simulation of ImageWriter's three modes, to give you an idea of the quality difference. The erratic spacing in the Draft line isn't a publishing error. The ImageWriter used irregular spacing to match the line length of the higher quality output.

Figure 5.18

A simulation of Best, Faster, and Draft quality printout.

TIP: Type can look scrambled in Draft mode, as the ImageWriter tries to find its closest match to the sizes on your screen. To avoid this effect, set your entire document in 10- or 12-point Monaco type.

The rest of the options in the Print dialog box are self-explanatory. When you're ready to print, click the OK button. If you're printing many high-quality pages, find something else to do for a while. Unless you use a *print spooler* (see Chapter 12), printing ties up the entire computer.

ImageWriter Care and Feeding

There's very little that can go wrong with your Macintosh during normal use, because it has very few moving parts. The ImageWriter, on the other hand, is full of moving parts, so be prepared to take care of it:

- ▲ Pull off the cover every week or so to remove any accumulated dust or scraps of paper. Clean the printhead with a special cleaning ribbon available at most computer dealers.
- ▲ Keep plenty of ribbons around, so you don't have to use a faded one (which can also shed ribbon dust into the printhead). You can get solid-color ribbons for either ImageWriter model, and four-color ribbons for the ImageWriter II. (The solid ribbons work with any program. The four-color ones require color software.)

TIP: Best printing packs the dots so closely together that a brand-new ribbon will put too much ink on the paper! Save your new ribbons for Faster or Draft mode. After using a ribbon to print a few dozen pages, you can promote it to Best printing.

You can even get ribbons for ImageWriter that make iron-on transfers for T-shirts! RibbonLand, in Exton, PA, will send you a catalog of specialty ribbons if you call them at 1-800-221-4892.

Printing with the StyleWriter

The StyleWriter Page Setup... dialog box looks like Figure 5.19. Click your choices for size or orientation, and use the little arrows to reduce or enlarge the image.

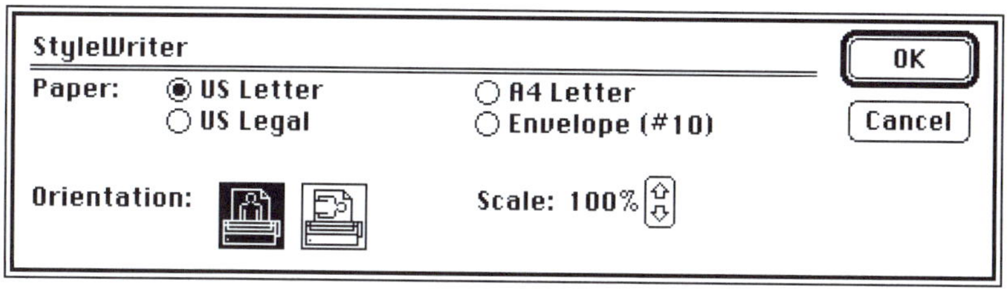

Figure 5.19
StyleWriter Page Setup dialog.

When you choose Print..., you'll see a dialog box like Figure 5.20. The Copies and Pages selections work exactly as you'd expect. The Manual button lets you feed single sheets for labels or transparencies. The Quality options represent a real tradeoff.

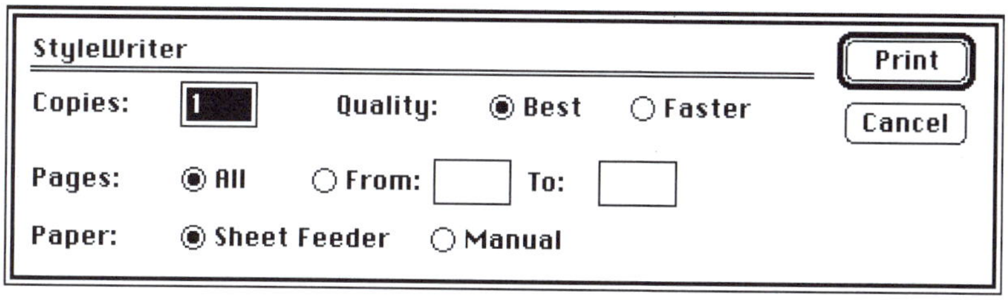

Figure 5.20
Printing choices with the StyleWriter.

Apple claims the StyleWriter "accepts medium-weight photocopier transparencies." We think they're being deliberately *unclear*: while it accepts transparency film, it won't *print* on most brands. To print transparencies, see the tip in the next section.

Best-quality StyleWriter printing can be excellent. The results are virtually indistinguishable from laser printing, if you use the right kind of paper and are lucky with your choice of graphics. You'll also need a lot of time: our test manuscript page took just under two minutes to print (current laser printers run about eight times faster).

Even the Faster option takes a while: about a minute and a quarter per page. Since the StyleWriter skips every other dot in this mode, the image is more gray than black. It looks like a high-quality fax.

The StyleWriter does a great job when you consider its size and price. For occasional short reports and business letters, it's an excellent value. But it will never replace the laser printer, which is why Apple (and many of other companies) still sells them.

Speed

Ordinary PostScript laser printers have their own intelligence. The computer tells it what to print, and the printer figures out how. The StyleWriter isn't as smart, and ties up your Mac while it locates every tiny dot on the page. With about 11,000,000 possible dot locations, this can take a while.

Apple's ratings for StyleWriter speed aren't even as good as our test results. They specify three minutes per page in normal mode, and a minute and a half in Faster. It has a lot to do with the number of words per page, and how fast your individual Mac thinks.

The StyleWriter must be used either with System 7, or with a special imaging utility. Apple includes a TrueType utility with the printer that functions under System 6. Unfortunately, it slows things down even more. We recommend buying Adobe Type Manager instead. Since the StyleWriter doesn't recognize PostScript commands, some graphics programs may give you unpredictable results.

Paper

Apple recommends 20-pound cotton letterhead bond for the StyleWriter. Ordinary low-cost photocopy papers, which work fine in laser printers, don't absorb ink well enough. Specially coated "Laser Output" paper, frequently used for printers' paste-ups, performs unevenly in a StyleWriter. Many of the colorfully printed desktop publishing papers, designed to spice up laser-printed newsletters and brochures, don't accept StyleWriter ink at all. If this is an important consideration, try some samples before you commit to a paper. Or use 20-pound cotton bond, and then photocopy to the specialty paper.

Overhead transparencies are a problem with the StyleWriter. Its ink won't stick to the transparency films available at most office-supply stores. Our local supplier suggested artists' "wet-media" acetate—the same stuff used by Hollywood animators—but it smudges horribly when touched. Unless you can get transparency film guaranteed to work with ink-jet computer printers, don't try to create overheads in a StyleWriter. Print on plain paper, and use the photocopier trick instead.

In This Chapter

MacPaint, the Model for All Paint Programs

•

Draw Programs

•

Draw/Paint Programs

MacPaint was included with new Macs until a few years ago. Because it was the first Macintosh paint program, it established the standards which all other programs follow. Once you learn how to use the basic painting tools described in this chapter, you'll be able to use them in any paint program. They all work essentially the same way, although they may appear on different parts of the screen in different programs. Operations you've learned in your word processing program, such as cutting, pasting, and saving, are exactly the same in the paint program, too.

6

Processing Pictures

When the Macintosh first appeared, one of the features which made it unique was that it was something more than the "educated typewriters" computer users used. The Mac let you use the mouse as a pencil or a paintbrush and draw pictures right on-screen. It was fun! For people who were scared of computing because they thought it meant entering arcane commands like "10 for x = 1 to 15: get a$: gosub 400: next x," it was a revelation! You could actually create something on-screen without ever touching the keyboard.

Of course, drawings created in MacPaint (see Figure 6.1) weren't great art, at least not at first. Even for people who already knew how to draw, making the switch from pencil to mouse took some effort. Most people's first efforts tended to look something like Figure 6.2. As they got used to using the tools and picked up a few tricks, the quality of the artwork improved, too.

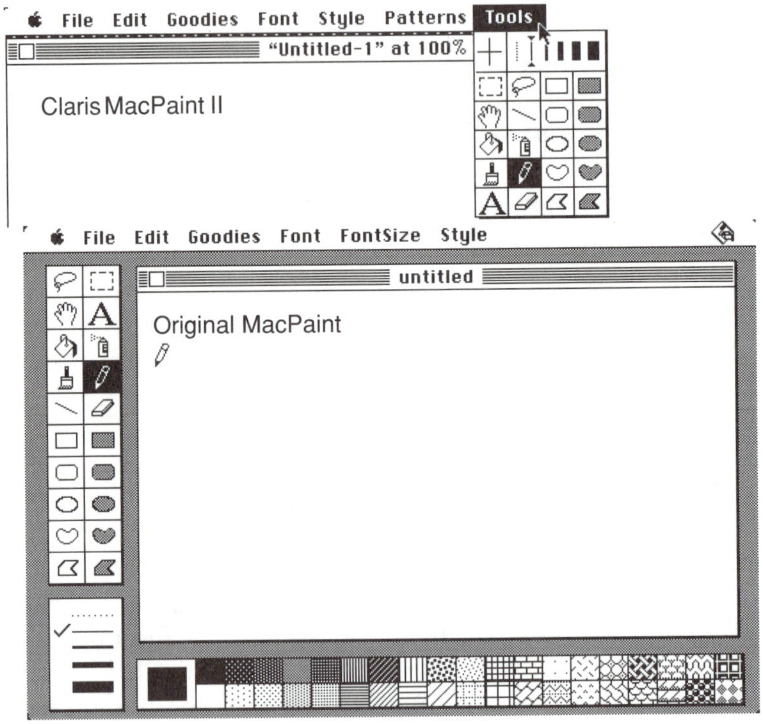

Figure 6.1

Differences between MacPaint and MacPaint II.

Figure 6.2

An early MacPaint picture.

The new version of MacPaint has changed the way the screen looks, but it's almost identical to the original in the way it's used. By the way, MacPaint II also has *tear-off* Pattern and Tool menus. After you pull them down from the menu bar, you keep holding the mouse button down as you drag the palettes wherever you want them. You can move them around by clicking on their tops and close them by clicking their close boxes, just like any other window.

Painting with a Mouse

You select your painting tools by clicking on them. (Just once! Double-clicking may take you into a tool shape menu, or do something else unexpected.) Here are some of the tools you'll use for painting, along with some techniques for using them.

The Pencil

The *pencil* is probably the most basic and most useful tool on your menu. It draws and erases one dot at a time. Position the pencil where you want it, and hold the mouse button down as you draw. Click on a black dot to turn the pencil into an eraser. Clicking on white toggles it back to a pencil. Figure 6.3 shows the pencil at work.

Figure 6.3

Using the pencil.

Hold down the ⌘ key while you select the pencil to get a magnified image of what you're drawing. The magnified view will be centered around the pencil point. Figure 6.4 shows the difference between regular and zoomed views. The original MacPaint menu called this *Fat Bits*, but now most painting programs simply refer to *zooming* in and out. You can also zoom in or out by selecting a zoom command on an options or "goodies" menu, or by using command-key combinations. Another shortcut for going into Fat Bits is to double-click the pencil on the tools palette. Double-clicking again takes you back to your previous view.

Figure 6.4

The "regular" view and the zoomed-in or "Fat Bits" view.

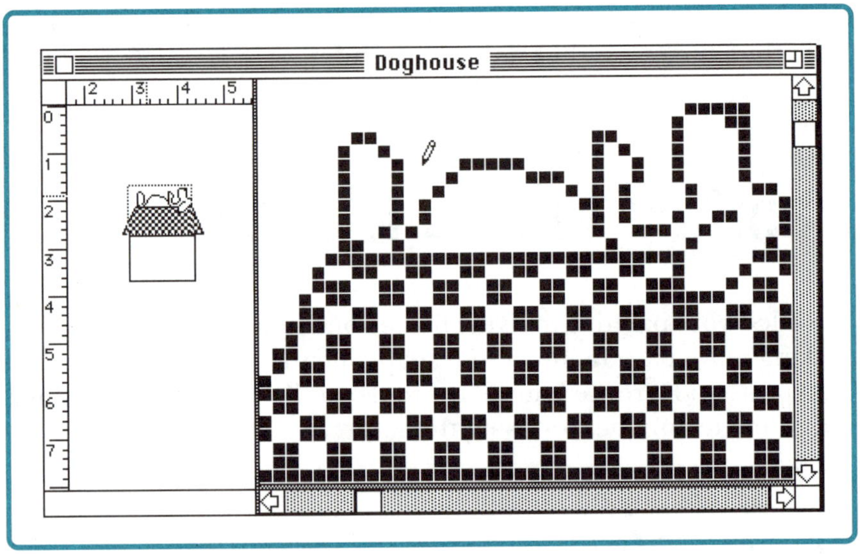

Most tools have *hot spots*, the business end of the tool. A hot spot is the single *pixel*, or dot, where the tool has its effect. Logically, the point is the pencil's hot spot. Other hot spots include the tip of the paintbrush, the drip on the paint can, and the end of the lasso rope. If you hold Shift down while you draw a line, it will automatically constrain the pencil to drawing a horizontal or vertical line. You can also use Shift to erase in a straight line, as you might in cleaning up the edge of a drawing.

The Paintbrush

You have a whole paintbox full of different brushes, and some programs even let you customize them to suit your needs. To choose a particular paintbrush, double-click the paintbrush symbol. You'll get a box which looks something like the one shown in Figure 6.5. Click a brush shape to choose it. A few of the brushes and the lines they make are shown at the left side of Figure 6.5. The dotted brushes give a stippled effect (a pattern of individual dots) if you click the mouse instead of dragging. When you drag the mouse while holding the button down, the brush draws lines.

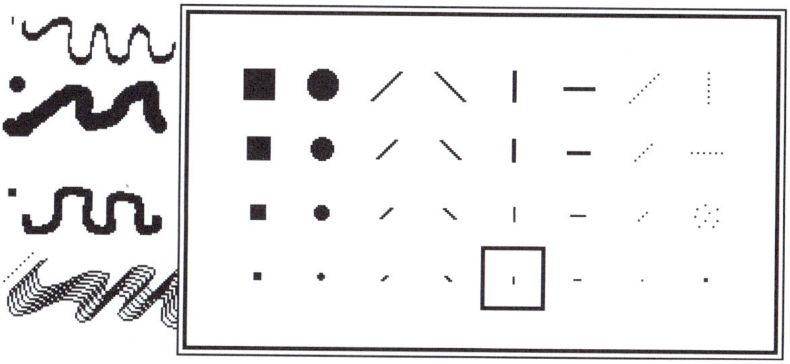

Figure 6.5
Choosing a paintbrush.

When you paint on the Mac, your brush fills with a pattern you choose from a *pattern palette.* Note that the palette, like the one shown in Figure 6.6, includes both all-black and all-white patterns. (Some programs also let you choose "none" as a pattern. This option is helpful if you're using a shape tool. A white-filled shape will hide whatever's under it. An unfilled shape won't.)

Figure 6.6
The pattern palette.

You choose a pattern by clicking on it. The large block displays the selected pattern. At the left of Figure 6.6 is a dialog box which allows you to edit the pattern. You get to this box by double-clicking the pattern you'd like to change. To edit the pattern, click individual dots in the enlarged pattern sample, just as you did to change the pattern on your desktop. Click OK when you're satisfied, and the pattern will appear on your palette. As long as you save the document you're working on, the new pattern will be part of its palette.

The Spray Can

The *spray can* applies patterns just as a real one applies paint. Just click the mouse to get a splatter of dots. Dragging the mouse gives a sprayed paint effect, as shown in Figure 6.7.

Figure 6.7

Spray cans are great for graffiti.

As with a real spray can, there's not much control. For denser paint effects, hold the can in one spot longer. Some programs also give you an airbrush tool, which is similar to an adjustable spray can. It's capable of very delicate work and can be adjusted to produce paint spots as small as a single pixel. Other programs let you adjust the spray can's flow by double-clicking on the icon.

The Eraser

Not surprisingly, the *eraser tool* works just like a real one. You select it, hold the mouse button down, and run it over whatever you need to erase. In SuperPaint, holding down Option as you erase gives you a quarter-size eraser, very convenient for erasing in tight spots without the need to zoom in for a larger view. Figure 6.8 shows the eraser at work.

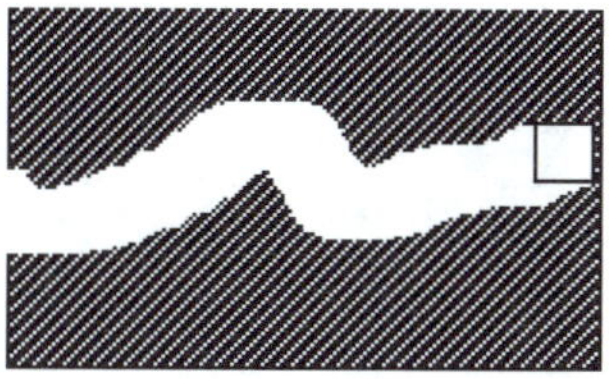

Figure 6.8
Using the eraser.

Double-clicking the eraser when you select it from the tool palette erases everything in the window! In some programs, but not all, holding Shift while you double-click erases the entire document. You can constrain the eraser to straight horizontal or vertical paths, as you did the pencil, by holding down Shift as you erase.

Drawing Lines

Never let it be said that you can't draw a straight line. The Mac makes it easy. Select the *line tool* and choose a line thickness. Hold the mouse button down at the start of the line, drag, and release the button at the end. For a perfectly vertical or horizontal line, or one at a 45° angle, hold down Shift as you drag the line.

The Paint Bucket

The *paint bucket* icon also has the expected result. It pours a pattern into a shape you create, as shown in Figure 6.9. First, select the pattern. Then select the paint bucket and position it inside the area you want to fill. Click once. Using the paint can is like using real paint because you have to be careful it doesn't spill. Really! If you pour paint into a shape that has a hole in it (isn't completely enclosed), the paint will flood the entire screen, as shown in Figure 6.10. If this happens, just undo. Then check your drawing for gaps.

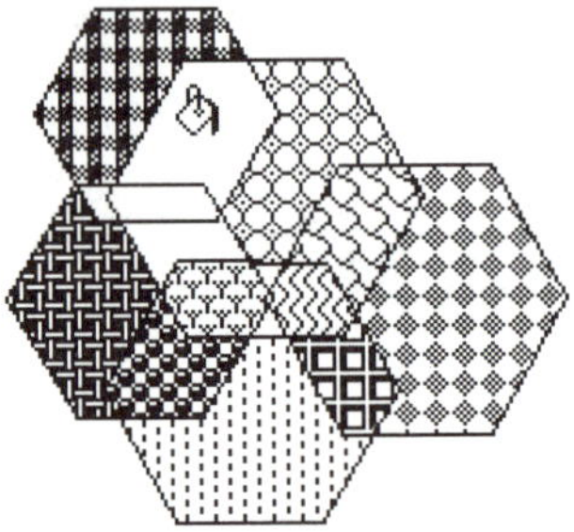

Figure 6.9

Pouring paint is fun!

Figure 6.10

Why paint spills (Fat Bits view).

Figure 6.10 shows a Fat Bits view of a square. Just one missing pixel can turn your whole screen to plaid. Sometimes, you might want this effect. Since the paint won't normally spill beyond the window, hold Shift while you pour to fill the entire document.

> **TIP:** Save your drawing before you do anything which could have damaging consequences, like pouring paint. That way, if you mess up your work and can't undo the damage, you can choose Revert to Saved in most programs. At worst, you can close the window (don't save the changes) and re-open the saved drawing.

The Shape Tools

If you want to work with filled shapes, there's a less risky way. Looking at the tool palette on MacPaint, you'll see two sets of *shape tools*: one with outlines, and one with gray centers. These tools will draw the shapes indicated in any size you wish (see Figure 6.11). Selecting a filled-shape tool automatically inserts the selected pattern into the completed shape, with no chance of a spill. (In SuperPaint, just select a pattern to fill the shape.)

Figure 6.11
Filled and unfilled shapes.

You can vary the thickness of the line around the shape by using the line-width indicator. The dotted line (or 0 line in some programs) is invisible, so you can lay down blocks of pattern with no visible boundary.

Unless you tell it otherwise, your Mac draws shapes from the outside edge. You select a starting point and drag the mouse until the shape is the right size. The starting corner remains where you placed it. You can also choose Draw from Center on the Goodies (MacPaint) or Options (SuperPaint) menu. This lets you position the center of your shape and drag outward until it's big enough. The edges expand as you draw. Drawing from the center is useful if you must position one shape inside another, as in drawing concentric circles (see Figure 6.12).

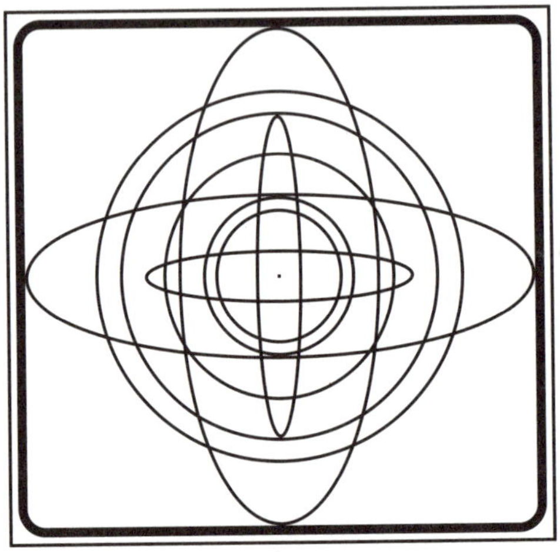

Figure 6.12

You could design stained glass windows, or diagram the atom.

To create Figure 6.12, we started by placing a dot in the center, to help keep the circles and boxes concentric. For each shape, we placed the cross hairs of the cursor exactly on the dot. Of course, you can go back in and erase the dot once you draw your circles. We left it, just to show you the trick. By the way, whenever Draw From Center is in effect, there are small crosshairs inside the shapes in the tools palette.

> **TIP:** There's a shortcut for shifting back and forth between Draw from Center and Draw from Edge. Just double-click on the square or circle tool on the palette. (This works in all the paint programs we've tried, except HyperCard's paint function. There, you can select it from the Options menu.)

The two irregular shapes are *freehand tools*. The curved one lets you draw and fill irregular or curving shapes. The polygon tool lets you draw angular shapes composed of angles and straight lines. To use it, click at each corner of the intended shape as you reach it. This will, in effect, nail down the line at that point. *Don't hold the mouse button down while you drag the line.* When you're done, cut off the line by double-clicking at the ending point of the polygon. To constrain lines to vertical, horizontal, and 45° angles, hold down Shift while using the polygon tool.

The Selection Box and Lasso

Yee-haaaa! Round 'em up and drag 'em around, with the *lasso tool.* Or, select a square or rectangular area with the *selection box* (the tool showing a rectangular, dotted outline). Either way, you can use these tools to move objects on the page, or to cut or copy a selected object. (Figure 6.13 shows the selection box, lasso, and other selection tools from two different programs.) The main difference is that the lasso selects only the object encircled, whereas, the selection box picks up everything inside it.

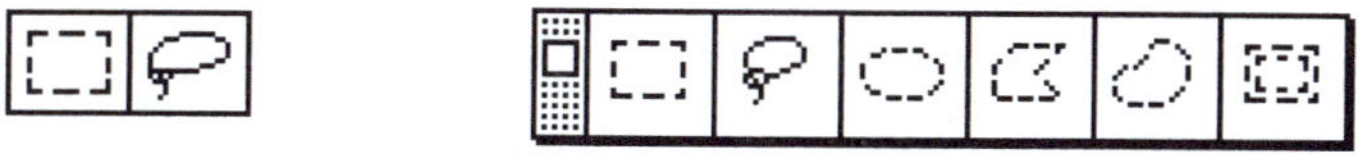

Figure 6.13

Some paint programs give you two ways to select (left). Others give you many more selections (right).

Double-clicking the selection box, in most programs, selects everything in the open window. Double-clicking an object with the lasso selects it, with no white space around it. Holding down the ⌘ key while you lasso selects a hollow object without the white space inside it.

Once you select an object, move the object by positioning the cursor on it. (You'll know the object is selected if the selection box flashes like a movie marquee, or if the lassoed object develops blinking diagonal lines.) Simply hold the mouse button down and drag it to its new location. (Figure 6.14 shows selected objects.) When you release the button, the object continues to flash, allowing you to change your mind and shift it a little more, if need be. When you're ready to stick it in place, click the mouse button, and it will stop flashing.

If you want to duplicate a selected object, hold down the Option key while dragging it. This is much quicker than copying and pasting single objects from the keyboard. Figure 6.15 shows one use for this trick.

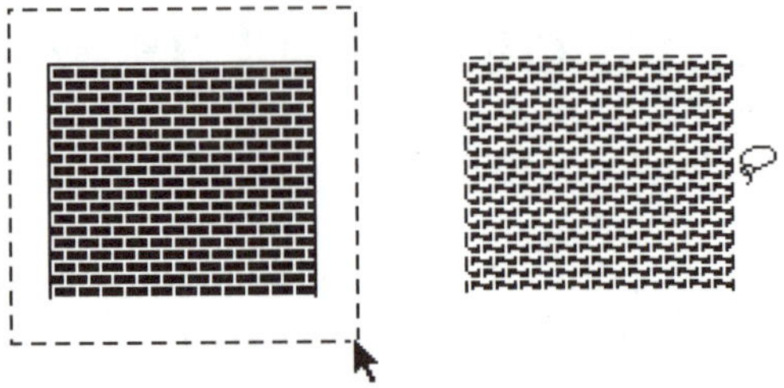

Figure 6.14

Now, imagine these in motion.

Figure 6.15

Hold down Option *and drag to turn one elephant into a herd.*

To make continuous multiple copies of an object, hold down both Option and ⌘ while dragging the object. The faster you move your hand, the more space there will be between copies. Slow movement gives you layers that are almost on top of each other. (See Figure 6.16.)

Adjust precise spacing between copies by selecting a line width to define the minimum spacing, and by dragging slowly. To keep objects in line, do the "three-finger drag": hold down the ⌘, Option, and ⇧Shift keys while you move the selected object. (See Figure 6.17.)

You can also use this trick to create a continuous pattern. In the example in Figure 6.18, we're extending the musical staff by selecting it and doing the three-finger drag.

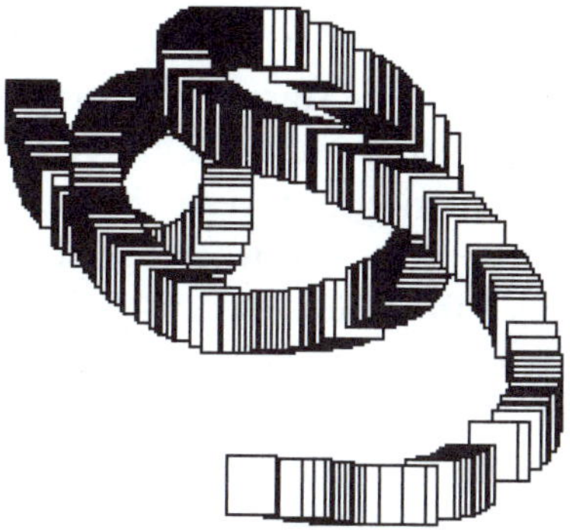

Figure 6.16

This trick works best with simple shapes.

Figure 6.17

Drag slowly to keep the spacing even.

Figure 6.18

When the melody lingers on . . . .

The Grabber

We tend to think of it as the "hand tool," but Apple calls it the *grabber.* It moves the open window around on the page. (Or, the window stays fixed while the hand moves the picture around behind it.) Double-clicking it lets you toggle back and forth between the whole page and the window. You can temporarily turn other tools into the grabber by holding down the Space bar.

The Text Tool

Use the text tool whenever you need lettering on the drawing you're creating. Once you've positioned the cursor, choose your font, type size, and style from the menus as you would in a word processor. If you make a mistake, use Delete to correct it. Each time you position the cursor or press Return, the Mac starts a new string of text. As long as you haven't moved the cursor, you can change the font or size of the words you've typed by selecting different choices on the menu. If you want to start over, either undo your work or use the eraser (except in the draw layer of SuperPaint). Some paint programs let you alter the text sizes and fonts by using special key combinations; others don't. Consult your manual.

TIP: If you're not sure what typeface would look best with your art, decide on an approximate point size and type the words. Then, select different fonts until you find one you like.

Goodies, Options, and Shortcuts

The File and Edit menus for paint programs are about the same as in any other Macintosh operation. Open, close, and save your documents just as you would in word processors. You have an option called Revert to Saved in most paint programs. It undoes everything (good as well as bad) that you've done since you last saved the document.

TIP: You know that ⌘-Z is the Undo shortcut. Here's an even shorter shortcut, for paint programs only. On newer Mac keyboards, press End (in the upper left corner of the keyboard). On older Macs, the key in the same location does the job, but it's the ' and ~ key. Pressing either key again is Redo.

In addition to Undo, you'll find Cut, Copy, and Paste on the Edit menu, just as in other applications. Some paint programs also include other interesting and helpful additions to the Edit menu. (SuperPaint puts them on the Paint menu.) Invert changes black pixels into white pixels, and vice-versa. (It doesn't turn things upside down. Flip Vertical does that.) Fill lets you select an area with the selection box and fill it with a pattern, making a borderless patterned area. (As we mentioned in the section on shapes, you can also do this by selecting an invisible line and a filled shape.)

Trace Edges creates interesting effects. Select the object you want to trace with the selection rectangle, and then select Trace Edges, or use its command-key shortcut. Figure 6.19 shows the results of one and two traces. Note that the open center of an object is also traced.

Figure 6.19

Tracing once gives an inverted effect.

You can trace an object repeatedly, but eventually it will become distorted. The rectangle in Figure 6.20 kept its shape, but the circle began to turn into a square.

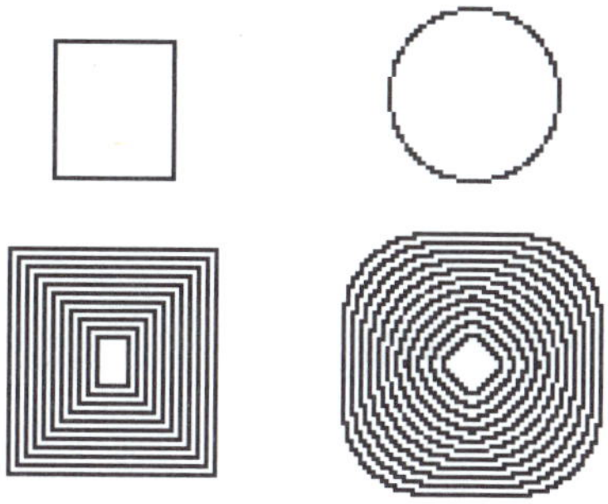

Figure 6.20

These objects were traced 10 times.

The Flip Horizontal and Flip Vertical commands are very useful, especially if you're attempting to draw a symmetrical object and can only get half of it correct. Simply select the half that's correct, copy it, and flip the copy. When you join them together you'll have a perfect mirror image, as shown in Figure 6.21. (Perfect as far as we're concerned. As we've said, we like cats.)

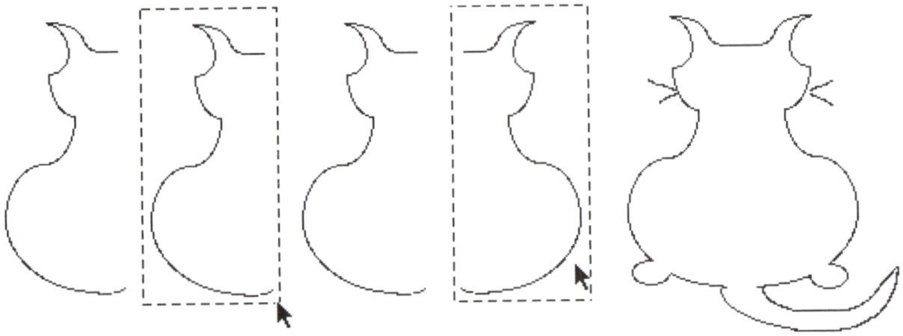

Figure 6.21

Draw, select, copy, flip, join, and add finishing touches.

Depending on which paint program you're using, you may have one option for Rotate, or you may have many. We produced Figure 6.22 in SuperPaint, using Flip Vertical, Free Rotate, Slant, Stretch, and Rotate Left. Keep in mind that the effects may not be what you expect with bit-mapped text. Jaggies and distortion may appear when you stretch and rotate text.

Figure 6.22

Wow 'em with fancy typography!

The Goodies Menu

Your paint program may call the Goodies menu something else. (SuperPaint calls it Options.) By whatever name, Goodies are useful and make creating Macintosh art easy.

Grids

You can think of a grid as a piece of "automatic" graph paper. When the grid is on, you can consistently line up all the lines and shapes you create. Each program sets the spacing for the grid a little differently. In MacPaint II, you set the spacing in the Preferences dialog box. In SuperPaint, selecting Grid and Rulers brings you a special dialog box. If you're using a different paint program, check the manual or poke around on your own. Snap to Grid makes everything on the page align to the grid.

The Preferences dialog box gives you many other options, as shown in Figure 6.23. In MacPaint II, you can select pattern effects; text effects; measurements in inches, centimeters, or pixels; and you can tell the Mac to keep your tear-off menus in the spots where you've placed them.

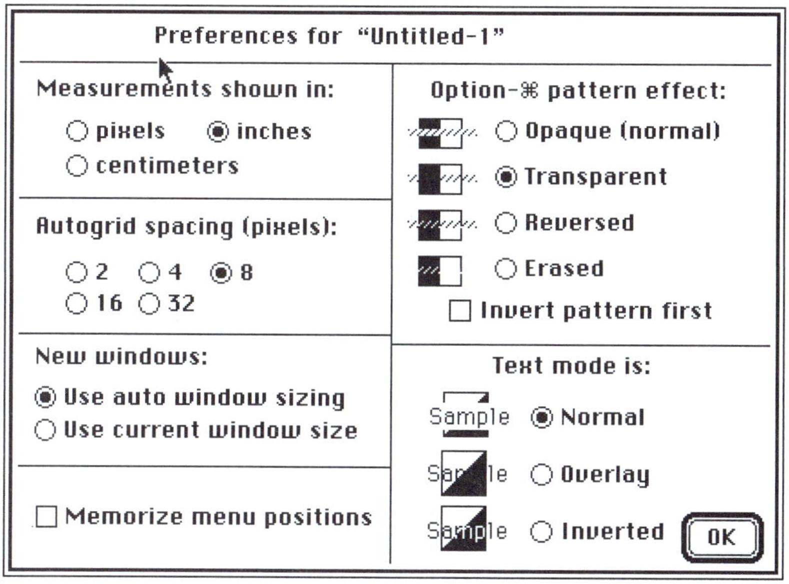

Figure 6.23

Grid spacing and much more.

Pattern Effects

You can create new patterns by superimposing one layer of paint over another. The Preferences box helps you do this. Figure 6.24 shows the effects of the various pattern options.

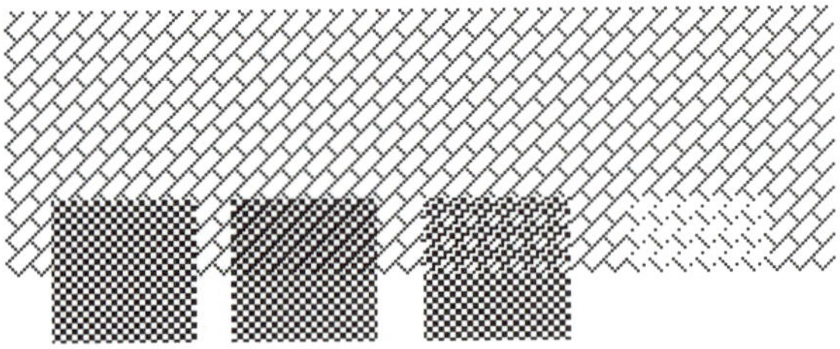

Figure 6.24
Opaque, Transparent, Reversed, and Erased patterns (called Paint-on-Black in SuperPaint).

Again, depending on which paint program you're using, you may find other goodies on your menu. You may even discover some tricks we haven't told you about. That's great! Half the fun of using your Mac is finding the secrets in the program.

TIP: The About... screen is just one place to look for "Easter Eggs"—unexpected, pleasant graphic or animated surprises. Some programs, including WriteNow, SuperPaint, and Disinfectant, put on a nice halftime show. You'll also find eggs in the Color control panel and About This Mac in System 7. (Try pressing the option and/or command keys as you click in the boxes.) To find secret characters on your keyboard, start by looking at Shift-Option-~ in different sizes of Geneva.

FYI Idea

Painting isn't just for artists. Anyone can use the text and simple line or shape tools to create posters, calendars, letterheads, memo pads, greeting cards, charts, doodles, ads, logo designs, maps, cartoons, menus, t-shirt designs . . . . We could go on and on, but you get the idea.

Even if you can't draw a straight line with a ruler and mouse, you can still get professional-looking art with a paint program. Clip art libraries are available at software dealers and downloadable from computer bulletin boards (Chapter 12). They're professional artists, as well as a blessing for the rest of us. They contain all kinds of images, drawn by expert Mac artists or scanned (see Chapter 10) from other sources. You can copy these pictures, manipulate them any way you wish, and incorporate them into your own creations.

We had fun designing coats of arms (see Figure 6.25) with bits and pieces from Dubl-Click's *WetPaint* series. There's a whole page of shields and emblems of all kinds, and you can flip them, scale them, and combine them in almost infinite ways. When you're working with clip art, lock the disks or use copies of the files.

Figure 6.25

A few odds and ends make instant history.

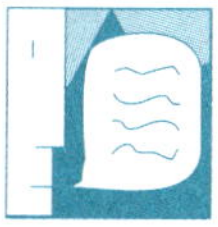

Design your own T-shirts with a Mac, an ImageWriter, and special iron-on ribbons (see Chapter 5). Create your design. Select it, and flip it. Print it on paper. Then, iron it onto your shirt. Iron-on toner cartridges are also available for the LaserWriter, but they're very expensive.

Other Paint Programs

We've talked about MacPaint and our personal favorite, SuperPaint (and we're about to talk a whole lot more about SuperPaint in another context). But you may have encountered, or even purchased, one of the many other paint programs on the market. At the low end (price-wise), there's *Easy Color Paint*, with 20 tools and 12 (!) 256-color palettes, and *Kid Pix*, which adds sound and rubber stamps. *UltraPaint* and SuperPaint are both slightly more expensive, and we'll explain in the next section which one we'd choose. *DeskPaint* and its partner, *DeskDraw*, give you virtually full painting and drawing capabilities in desk accessory form. They support color and full grayscale editing, and can print to both PostScript and QuickDraw printers (Chapter 10 explains the differences between these printers). *PixelPaint, Adobe Illustrator, Canvas,* and *Aldus FreeHand* are all high-end (very expensive) programs that do more or less the same things as the others, with a few professional ruffles and flourishes.

> **TIP:** There's one true bargain paint program, which you probably got free with your Mac! It's HyperCard. Although you might think of it as a filing system, it also has just about all the painting capability of MacPaint and works the same way. For more information about HyperCard and starting a stack of paintings, see Chapter 7.

Draw Programs

What's the difference between drawing and painting, you might wonder. There are several differences. *Drawing* á la Macintosh is closer to what you might think of as drafting. You can manipulate drawn objects, but you can't go in and clean up a single stray dot with your eraser, the way you could in a paint document. Here's why:

Paint programs, such as MacPaint, create what are called *bit-mapped images,* pictures made up of individual dots. Each dot is a separate object and can be moved or removed by itself or grouped with others. All you do is select the dots that make up an object, and drag them or delete them. Bit-mapped images are almost always at a *resolution* of 72 dots per inch. (If you started drawing a line of dots, and stopped when it was an inch long, you'd have placed 72 dots side by side.) The Macintosh screen and the ImageWriters both use this 72 dpi (dots per inch) format. The Mac saves and transfers bit-mapped images in paint format.

Draw programs, like MacDraw, treat the things you draw as separate whole objects, rather than as collections of dots. You select them by clicking, and drag them by their *handles,* dots that appear on the corners when you select an object (see Figure 6.26).

Figure 6.26

This cat's tail is not his only handle.

Draw programs are *object-oriented.* The program saves and manipulates files in the PICT format. Because draw objects are just shapes, a laser printer or typesetting machine will print them to the maximum resolution. Unlike the same shapes drawn in dots in a paint program or on the paint layer of SuperPaint, draw objects don't get jaggies when you print them on a 300 dpi laser, even if they look jaggy on your 72 dpi screen! It's a lot like the difference between on-screen text and laser type.

Now, as promised, here's why we like SuperPaint: it gives you both paint and draw functions in one program—even in one document! Think of SuperPaint as a drawing board with two layers of transparent paper. You can create an image on the paint layer, then copy it into the draw layer when it's perfect (although you don't have to—you can print from the paint layer). You can add type to the drawing, in the draw layer. (Type is handled much more easily in draw programs.) You can then print it on a laser printer without the jaggies you often see on ImageWriter drawings. (However, if an image in the paint layer has type with jaggies, copying the image to the draw layer will not make the jaggies disappear.) Figure 6.27 shows an example screen from a draw program.

Figure 6.27

Draw programs are great for creating this type of picture.

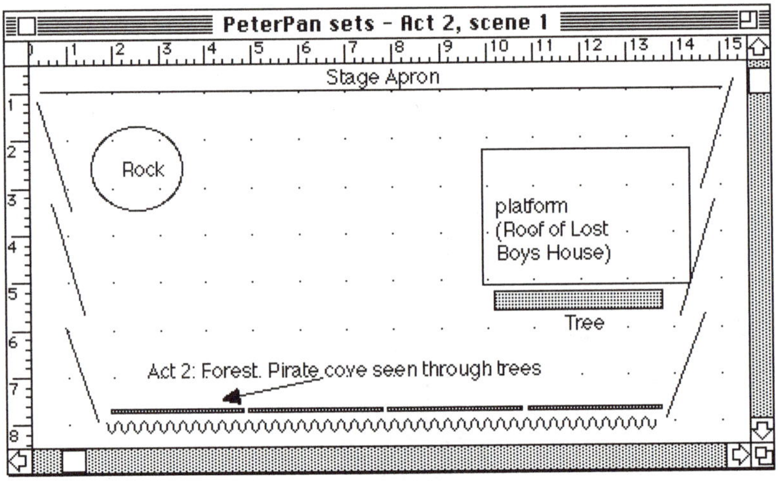

The most sophisticated draw programs are called CAD, for *computer-aided design*. Some of these are specifically for use by architects and engineers and may be economically beyond the reach of the average user.

Drawing Tools

Draw programs let you position objects precisely. This makes them ideal for drawing plans and schematics. A draw tool palette, shown in Figure 6.28, is less comprehensive than a paint tool palette, but the tools are similar.

You have lines of various thicknesses, shapes (which you can fill or leave empty), a text tool, and selection tools. The arrow, selected in Figure 6.28, is your primary selection tool. Lines, shapes, blocks of text, and pictures you copy into the draw layer from elsewhere all become objects. You select any of these by clicking on them while the arrow tool is selected.

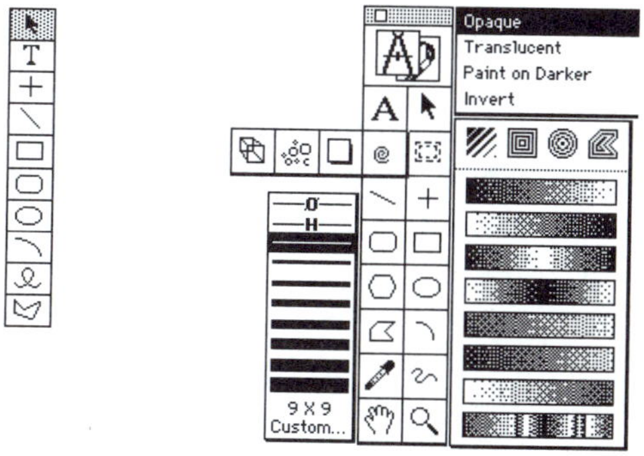

Figure 6.28

Early MacDraw (left) and current SuperPaint (right) draw palettes.

Ordinarily, you would select the objects in Figure 6.29 one at a time to move or change them. You can select all of them either by drawing a large selection box around them after selecting the arrow tool, holding the mouse button down and dragging a corner of the box, or by pressing ⌘-A. As you can see in Figure 6.29, selected objects have handles.

Figure 6.29

Several selected objects.

Once you've selected more than one object, you can *group* them, by choosing Group from the Draw menu or pressing ⌘-G, to turn them all into one large shape. (Separate them by pressing ⌘-U or choosing Ungroup.) You can distort them, flip them, change them in any way at all. If the object you drew was too small, or too big, you can stretch it or shrink it by pulling on one of its handles. (If you imported the object, it will distort when you stretch it. If you created it in the draw layer, it won't.)

Stacking Order

As you draw objects, each new one is stacked "on top of" the other ones that already exist in the document. You can bring some objects forward and send others to the back. This is helpful if you want to superimpose one piece over another, as shown in Figure 6.30. Choose Bring to Forward or Send to Back from the Draw menu. These commands will move the chosen object to the top or bottom of *all* other objects in the stack. If you have selected several objects, they'll keep their relative order when they move.

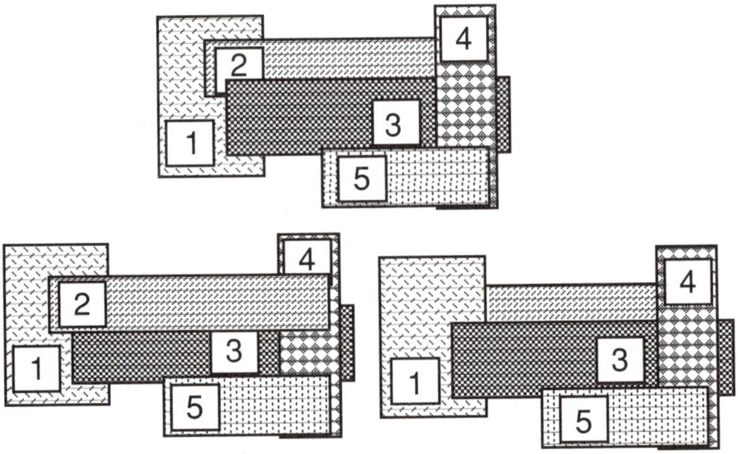

Figure 6.30

Shape #2 brought forward and sent back.

Duplicate and Replicate

You learned how to copy painted shapes by selecting and holding the Option key as you moved them or by pressing ⌘-C, ⌘-V to copy and paste. Duplicate and Replicate are more powerful ways to copy draw objects. (Replicate is not available in the paint layer of SuperPaint.) You'll find them in the Edit menu. Duplicate draws a copy of a selected object.

Replicate lets you rotate, scale, multiply, and move the copies, all at the same time. You get a dialog box which lets you choose your options. Figure 6.31 shows the dialog box, set to make multiple copies of a shape, and to move and rotate them. Figure 6.32 shows the result of applying the settings to a single triangle.

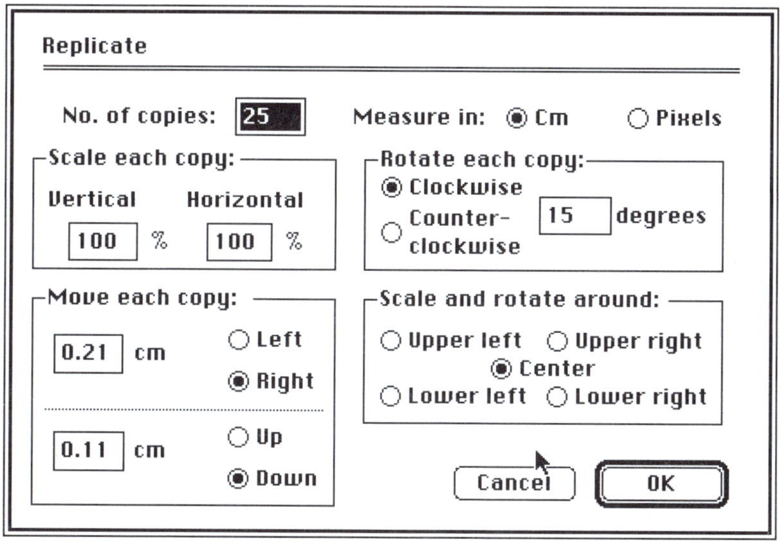

Figure 6.31

The Replicate dialog box.

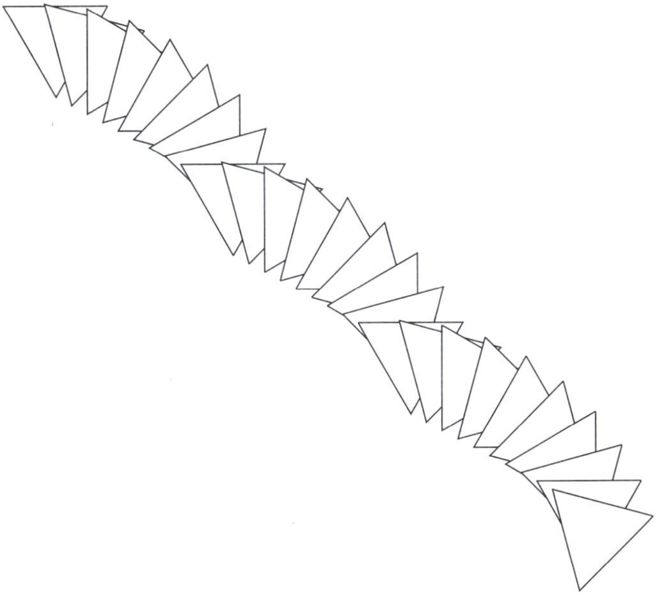

Figure 6.32

Use Replicate to make designs, patterns, and borders.

Use Replicate to create large patterns, to make grids, and to make precisely defined concentric shapes. It lets you create complex designs much faster and with greater precision than using separate tools or commands to scale, rotate, and duplicate a single shape.

Text Tricks

It's easier to work with text in draw programs or in the draw layer of SuperPaint than in a normal paint program. Using the text tool for entering and editing words is just like using a word processor. You can select a word, delete it, add letters or words in the middle of a line, change size and font, copy, and paste with the usual key combinations.

TIP: If you're copying a block of text into a page layout or word processing program, selecting it with the pointer will turn it into a PICT image, with precise type styling and dimensions. Copying it with the text tool (I-beam) will keep it as editable text.

Bezier Curves

That's Bezier, not bizarre. (Actually, it's pronounced bez-yay, as in Pierre Bezier, the French mathematician who defined them.) Use the freehand Bezier tool in a draw program to create editable curves. What that means is that you can draw a curve, and then tweak it until it's perfect. The lines produced by Bezier curves have control points along their paths. Reshape the line by selecting one or more of the control points. When you click on a control point, it will sprout handles, which you can then drag to change the shape of the curve. Figure 6.33 shows the Bezier tool in SuperPaint.

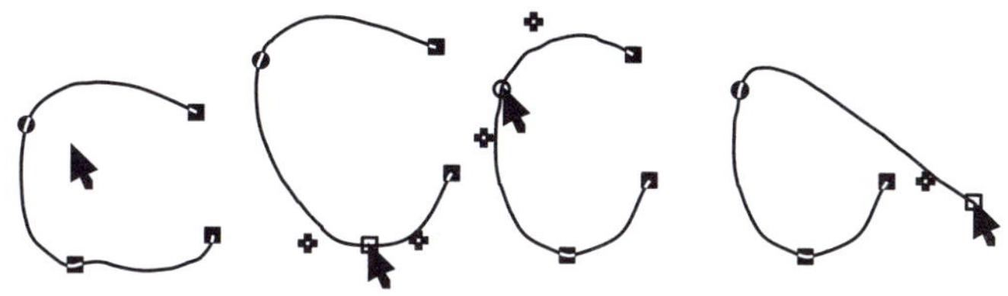

Figure 6.33

Drawing and changing a Bezier curve.

Each draw program handles Bezier curves differently. MacDraw creates a box with multiple handles around the drawn curve, and you change it by dragging the handles, as shown in the sequence in Figure 6.34.

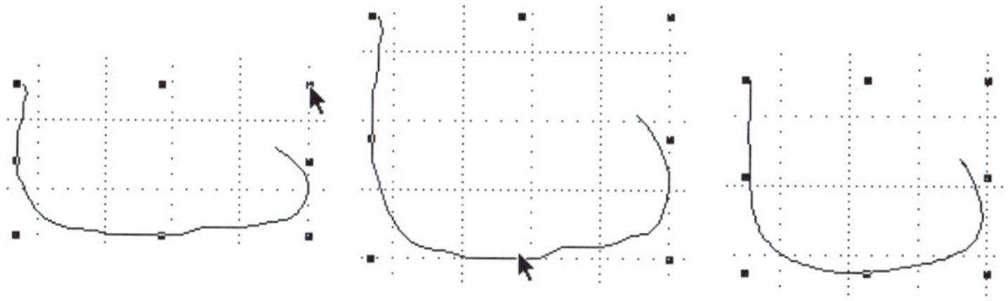

Figure 6.34

MacDraw's flexible curves.

You need to take one more step to finish the job. Select Smooth from the Edit menu, and it will even out all the lumps and bumps. There are, of course, many more things these programs can do. And they're lots of fun to play with.

Printing

At some point, you'll want to transfer your creations from the screen to paper. The previous chapter described the process of printing and using the ImageWriter and StyleWriter. If you have a laser printer, jump ahead to Chapter 10. If you're fortunate enough to have a color printer, check the manual.

Other Graphics Programs

What else could there be? A look through a technically oriented design magazine suggests there could be a lot more. There's *MacPerspective*, which lets you easily draw houses or boxes or anything else in accurate perspective. There are all kinds of drafting programs for engineers, and even a few for the homeowner. You can get an architecture, interior design, or landscape program that lets you lay out a top view of your backyard, new playroom, or dream house, and then view it from any side.

There are special programs for charting and graphing. *MapMaker* enables you to integrate all kinds of data with maps of the United States and abroad. There are darkroom programs, which we describe in Chapter 10. You can use special drawing programs to design your own typefaces and keyboard characters. There are animation programs to turn your Mac into a movie screen, or to let you walk through the house you've just designed. There's almost no limit to what you can do, once you start.

In This Chapter

How Databases Work

•

Working with Flat-File and Relational Databases

•

Apple's HyperCard, a Free-Form Database

•

Customizing Your Own HyperCard Stacks

Databases are like ordinary 3-by-5-inch file cards, if you can imagine a deck of cards that writes on itself, pretends to be a calculator when necessary, and sorts itself on request. Despite their power, they're easy to use, as you'll see in this chapter.

You'll also learn about HyperCard, supplied free with every Mac, which combines the features of a database with a painting program, animation, and a sophisticated programming language.

7

Databases and HyperCard

Back in the days of mainframes and punched cards, computer consultants would explain their systems to corporate executives with a simple analogy:

> *Imagine a room full of file clerks, with a room full of file cards. Your computer can do anything those clerks can—one step at a time.*

The executives, of course, would sputter something like, "File cards! We spent three million dollars for file cards?" and turn bright red. Then the consultants would add,

> *Of course, the computer does it zillions of times faster.*

Computers have gotten simpler (and consultants less sadistic), but it's still a good description. Even the most sophisticated Mac graphics program just makes a note of the color of each pixel, and sorts and flips it according to preset rules. Nowhere is the file card analogy more fitting than with *databases.*

Databases

A database is a file of *records*, each made of individual *fields*. The *database manager* sorts and manipulates the records. These terms are easiest to define if we use a common, noncomputerized database: Granpappy's recipe cards (see Figure 7.1). Each different area on a card (such as "title" or "list of ingredients") is a *field*. Each card in the bundle is a *record*, and the whole bundle is a *database file*. When Granpappy flips through cards looking for Christmas cookies, he's the database manager (just ask Grandma).

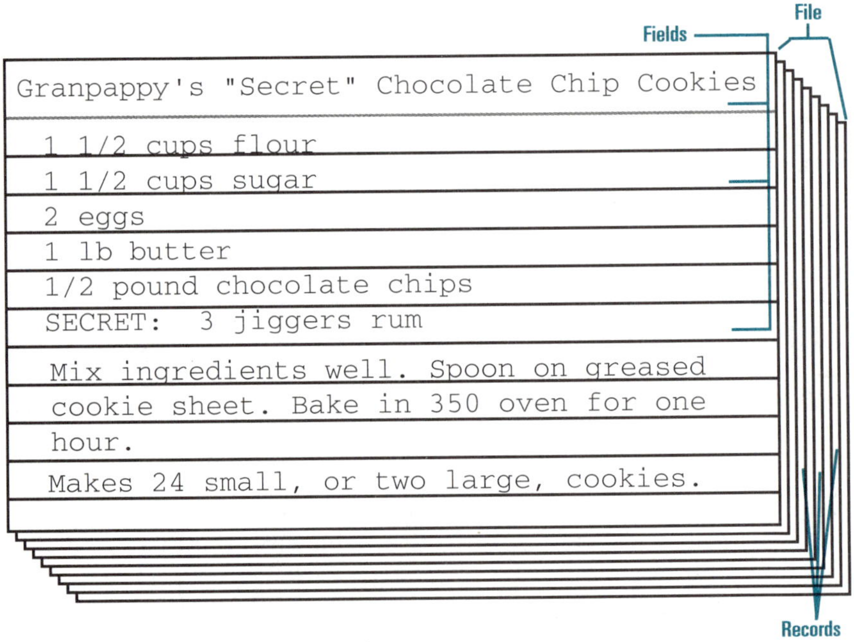

Figure 7.1
A cardboard database.

Computer databases don't have to be much more complicated than Granpappy's card file. A database-manager program works with different database files, just as a word processing application works with different documents. The terms *database* and *database manager* are often blurred. Even though the first properly refers to a file an the second refers to a program that reads it, people—and this text—will say "database" for both.

Mac Databases

A good Macintosh database will use all the tricks of other good Mac programs—graphics, typography, on-screen buttons, and sometimes even sound or motion. Figure 7.2 shows an on-screen display from Claris' *FileMaker Pro*. This record uses some text, numerical, and picture fields, but users can rearrange these and other fields into a different *layout* to meet other needs.

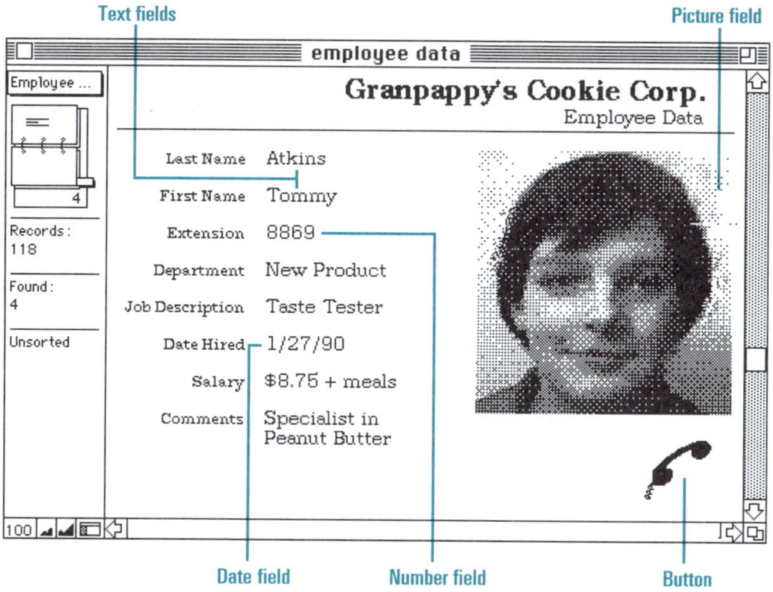

Figure 7.2

Database layout. Many fields from one record.

The Telephone button brings up a different layout (shown in Figure 7.3) with fields from multiple records. A file can have any number of different layouts for the same data. The steps for creating a new layout vary from program to program, but usually are a matter of point-and-click simplicity.

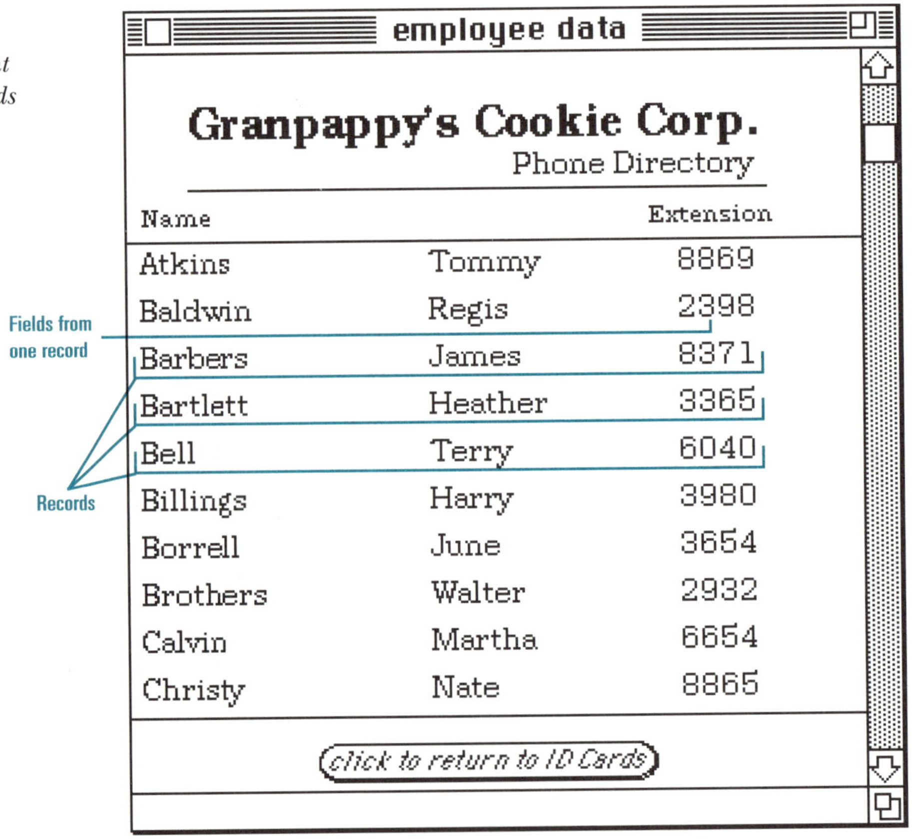

Figure 7.3
Same file, different layout—three fields each from many different records.

Entering Data

Macintosh databases use the same entry and editing conventions as other Mac programs. Press ⌘-N to open a new record, put the insertion point in a field, and type away. You can cut and paste text, and you can paste in graphics from paint or digitizing programs. But database entry frequently involves repetitive typing, so programs will also give you the following shortcuts:

- You can use *tabbing* to move the insertion point. As you finish in one field, hit the Tab key, and you're ready for the next.
- You can limit fields to accept only numbers (or only those within a given range), dates, or alphabetical information. They'll beep if you try to give them the wrong kind of data.
- You can set fields to beep if you make a mistake. Spell checking is common, and so is checking to make sure a name hasn't already been entered.
- You can even make a database do some of the typing for you. The database manager can automatically insert serial numbers, dates, or pop-up menus.

Fields can also automatically enter information derived from other fields (for example, to compute an invoice amount). Most database programs let you define a *calculated* field with no programming, through simple menus. Figure 7.4 shows the *formula* for the "Total Paycheck" field. It multiplies the "per hour" field by the "hours worked" field, and adds the "expenses" field. Other calculation options include a variety of statistical, financial, and scientific functions.

A field can be a *summary* of fields in other records, if you so specify when you create it. Summaries are usually running totals, maximums or minimums, or standard deviations. With some programs, you can create other kinds of summaries. A calculated field can even calculate text, comparing letters and letter positions within a different field. A formula could easily look at the second letter in the field "Name" and respond to "Ms. Johnson" differently than it would to "Mr. Johnson" (vive la différence). Or, it could ignore the first three letters and treat both Johnsons equally.

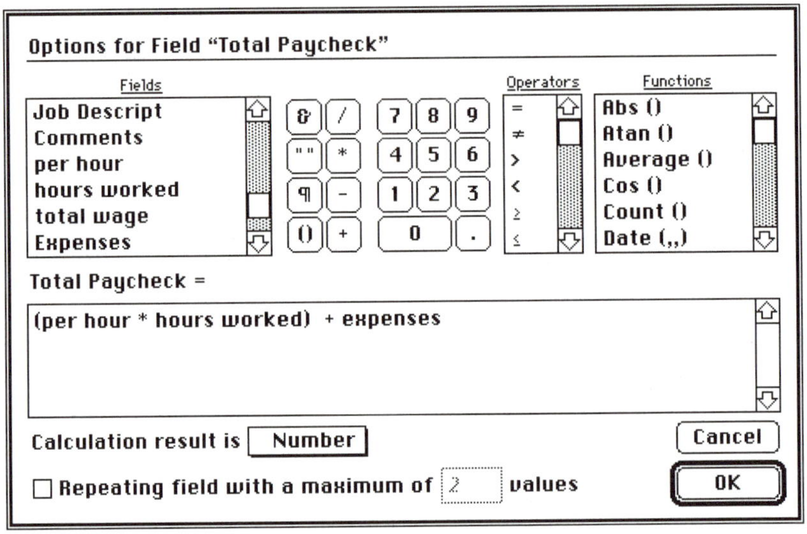

Figure 7.4

The FileMaker Pro Calculation box.

Saving Your Entries

Unlike most Mac programs, many databases don't have a Save command in the File menu. This doesn't mean all your data will be trashed. Instead, the programs automatically save information as you type it. Other programs ask if you want to save whenever you leave a record.

Database Reports

Reports are printed versions of on-screen layouts. But because they're designed to handle a printed page, a database's *report generator* often gives page-formatting options not found in screen layouts. (Some programs treat reports and layouts the same, and let you fully format and then print the on-screen version.) Reports don't have to look like directory pages or computer screens, however. You can arrange a file's fields as mailing labels, index cards, form letters, or even identification badges (Figure 7.5 shows some examples). As with layouts, there's no limit to the number of reports you can attach to a file.

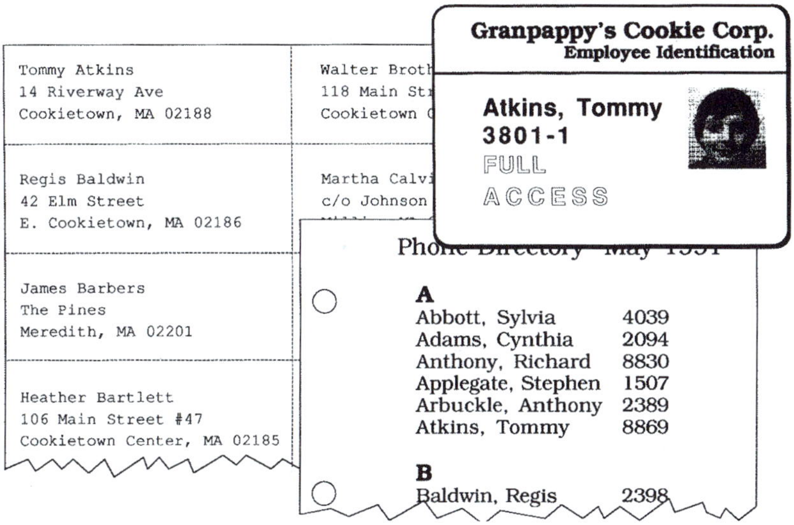

Figure 7.5

Just a few possible database reports.

Sorting

Database programs are capable of fast *sorting*. You specify a field (or number of fields), and the database manager arranges the records in that order. For example, you can print an accounts receivable report alphabetically by client, or rearrange it chronologically by invoice date. You can also specify *multiple sort keys*. The clients would first be arranged alphabetically, and then each client's invoices would be ordered by date for convenient dunning.

> Databases are smart enough to sort fields according to type. Alphabetically, "August 31" comes before "July 1" (making for an interesting summer), but if the field had been defined as a date, it will sort properly. Similarly, "133" comes before "23" when sorted alphabetically, even though a numeric sort function would know that 23 is smaller.

Sorting in most databases is simply a question of moving field names onto a list. Figure 7.6 shows the Sort dialog box in FileMaker Pro. The Globe icon lets you match your sort to the language and conventions of 15 different countries. Most databases will also let you program a button to perform a predetermined sort.

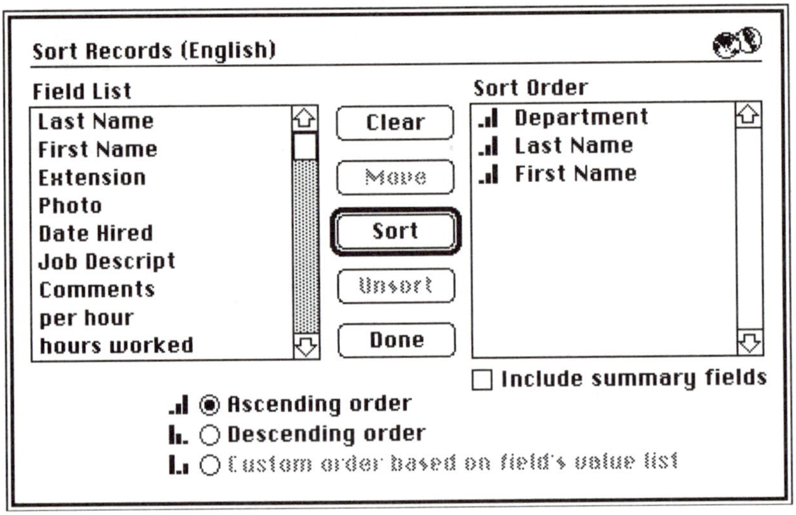

Figure 7.6

The Sort dialog box.

Database Access

Most sophisticated database programs can carry information across a network with no additional software. (You'll need legal copies of the program for each user, of course.) In a networked database, access can be set so distant users can read your files, add to them, or even change them. No separate file distribution is needed. Every user on the network sees the changes at the same time. (Well, almost at the same time. You set *network priorities* to keep the program from going schizoid if two people try to change the same field simultaneously.)

You can limit how people use a database, so general users can retrieve information but not change it, typists can enter fields, and the designer (you) can create new fields or layouts. Most databases let you attach passwords to different access levels.

Rich Relations

So far, the topics described pertain to all forms of Macintosh databases. The examples, however, were for databases that access just one file at a time. These are called *flat-file* databases, because they're like Granpappy's two-dimensional recipe cards. However, more advanced databases are *relational:* they can relate one file to the information in another, making it possible to chain and manipulate very sophisticated sets of data.

Imagine a cookie company with separate database files for recipes, vendor payables, and inventory. This information would be too cumbersome to combine into one flat file, and most of the time there'd be no need for the accounting people to look at a recipe anyway. But a relational database could relate a separate address file to all the others; and, if management wanted to get ready for a national oatmeal craze, they could access all four files at once.

A *structure* links relational databases. Figure 7.7 shows five files structured together as *Contacts* in Acius *FileForce.* In this example, sales reps could use the *People* file to keep track of three or four people with different phone numbers and buying histories working for the same company. Instead of having to repeat addresses in each record, the *People* file would look to the *Companies* file to retrieve the addresses. The bookkeepers would send out invoices based on the *Companies* file information, but could pass credit information directly to the parent *Conglomerate.* (This example also shows two smaller *subfiles* for information that loads into memory.)

Relational databases are powerful enough to handle all of the data in a large company. This power, unfortunately, usually makes them more expensive and harder to program than flat databases. If you're considering a relational database, be prepared to spend a long time learning how to set it up (or hire a consultant to do the job for you).

Figure 7.7

Structure of a relational database.

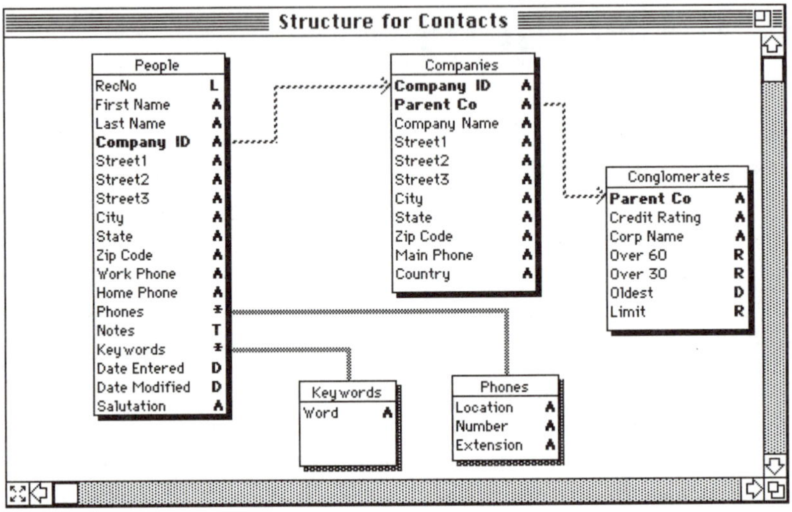

Apple's All-Purpose, Make-Your-Own Database: HyperCard

One particular database manager is extremely easy to program, can be used in a variety of applications, and for many users is absolutely free! In 1987, Apple started distributing HyperCard, a database-of-a-sort that was (and still is) as revolutionary as the original MacWrite and MacPaint.

HyperCard resembles a flat database with user-programmable relational capabilities. It's also a graphics program with almost the full capabilities of MacPaint, and an easy-to-understand programming language. It can create *hypertext* with almost no programming at all. Its creator, Bill Atkinson (creator of MacPaint), called it "a software erector set."

What is hypertext? Imagine a book where you point to a word on a page, and the book immediately flips to one or all other pages with the word. Then it tells you, in sound and pictures, what the word means. Finally, it prints out a dictionary of just the words you asked about. The touch-screen, like "information kiosks" you sometimes find at airports, is a simple example of hypertext.

In a way, HyperCard is the ultimate database for the Mac: *HyperCard is to ordinary databases what the Macintosh is to ordinary personal computers.* As of this writing, HyperCard is still included free with each new Macintosh. For its fullest use, you should also get a documentation and support package from Claris for about $50 (but that's still much cheaper than anything else on the market). Version 2.1 of HyperCard was released in late 1991. If you're using a 1.x version, buy the low-cost upgrade. It runs much faster, and gives you much more flexibility. (If you're using version 2.0, don't bother upgrading unless you're having problems making the program run on your system.)

Stack 'Em Up

At one extremely simplistic level, HyperCard is similar to a flat database like Granpappy's bundle of recipes. Individual records are, appropriately enough, *cards.* A file of cards is a *stack.* But individual or groups of cards can have much more sophisticated buttons than those in a traditional database. Buttons can look like the rounded rectangles you see in dialog boxes, they can look like desktop icons, they can be hidden in text or graphics, or they can be just hidden (invisible). You can also give fields button-like capabilities. Figure 7.8 shows some possibilities.

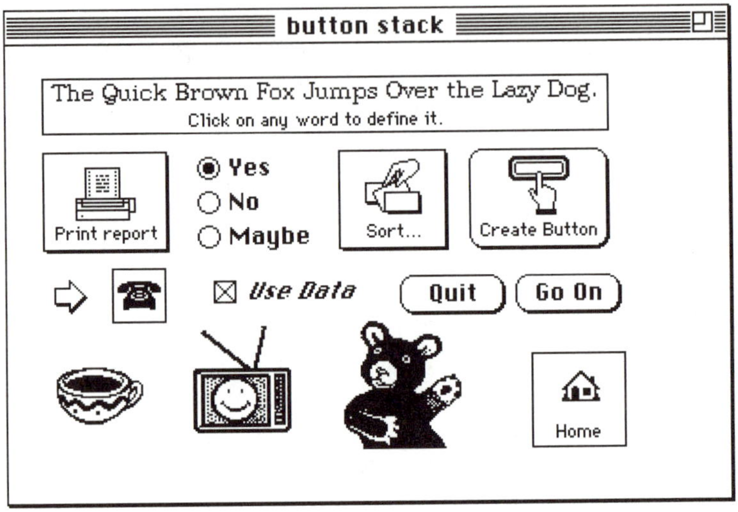

Figure 7.8
Buttons, buttons.

Click on any of the buttons, and the stack will do something appropriate. (In case you can't guess, the first three buttons on the bottom row are "Take a Break," "Show Video," and "Sing Teddybears' Picnic." You can make a HyperCard button do almost *anything*.)

Buttons are simply predefined screen areas. When the mouse enters or clicks in one of these areas, a program—or *script*, in HyperCard lingo—starts a series of programmed steps. Buttons are almost always rectangular but can have odd-shaped images superimposed on them. To see where the buttons really are in any stack, hold Option and ⌘ simultaneously. The button areas become gray rectangles, as in Figure 7.9.

About Stacks

The last button in Figure 7.9 takes you to the "Home" stack. Every HyperCard installation should have a stack with precisely that name; the program looks for it when you start up. (If HyperCard doesn't find a Home stack, it will beep angrily at you.) The Home stack normally stores information about the user, and special scripts that are common to all your stacks.

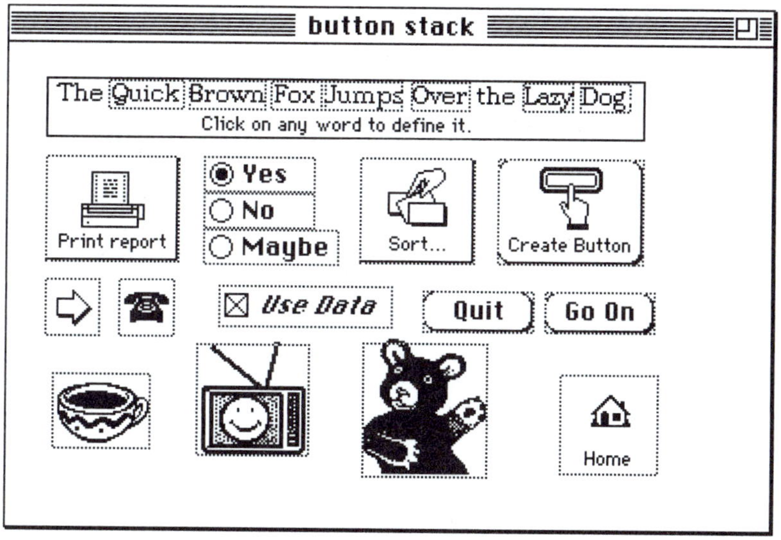

Figure 7.9

We've got the buttons!

To make a new Home, or any other stack, choose the New Stack... command in the File menu. But read the rest of this chapter first to see some of the things you'll be able to make that stack do.

Apple's Pre-Built Stacks

Apple includes some other stacks with HyperCard, ready for your own information. Even these basic stacks go far beyond the capabilities of ordinary databases. Figure 7.10 shows a card from Apple's *Address* stack. If you click the Show Notes button, the card changes to look like Figure 7.11 and reveals a Notes field. The button also changes. Buttons can also take you from one stack to another. If you click the Appointments icon, you'll open a totally different stack.

Apple's *Appointments* stack (Figure 7.12) has a different look. Its graphics, fields, and buttons make it work like a calendar. There's a different card for each day of the year. There's also a button to take you back to the Address stack.

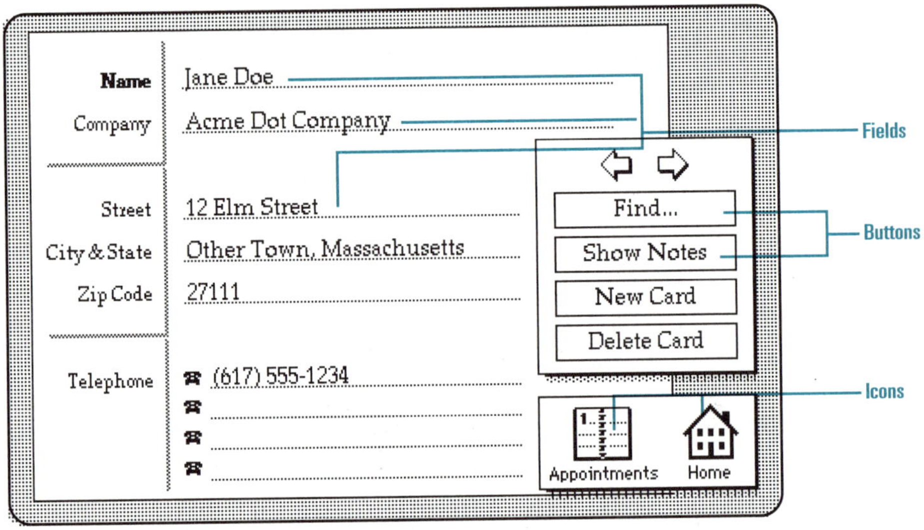

Figure 7.10
A card from Apple's Address stack.

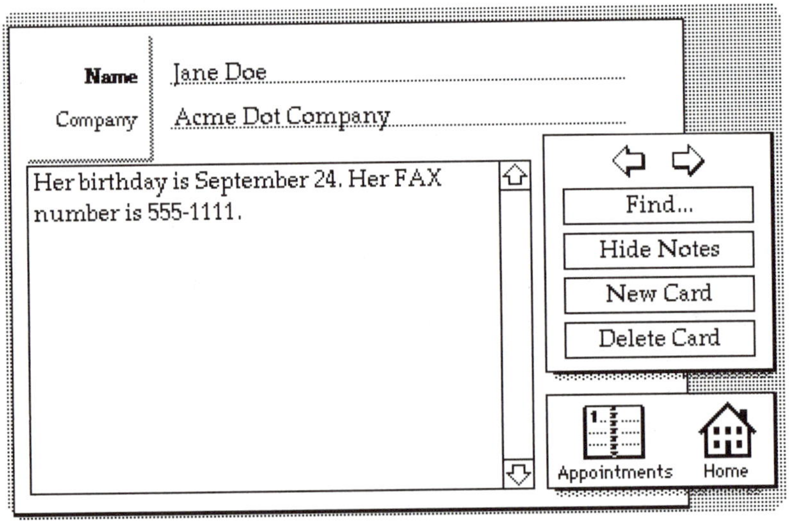

Figure 7.11
After selecting Show Notes, a previously-hidden field appears!

HyperCard Versatility

Stacks can do more than just store information. They can manipulate numbers and graphics. One early HyperCard stack consisted of just one card. As you typed in information about your car, the same card would compute your current miles-per-gallon and estimate yearly gas consumption.

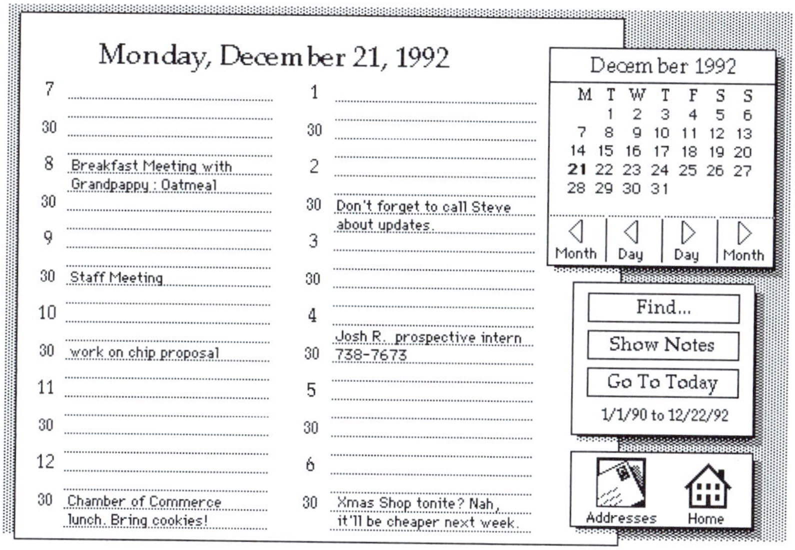

Figure 7.12

Apple's Appointments stack.

A stack Apple currently includes as a demo doesn't have any fields. It uses buttons and graphics to play choo-choo! You draw a track using the Build button, and watch the little train move around the card. It even makes appropriate noises. The *Train* stack (Figure 7.13) won't put Lionel out of business, but it does demonstrate some of the things you can make HyperCard do. Other stacks let you record or edit sound, draw graphs, or play games.

Moving through Fields, Dealing the Cards

HyperCard gives you a variety of ways to go from field to field, from card to card, and from stack to stack.

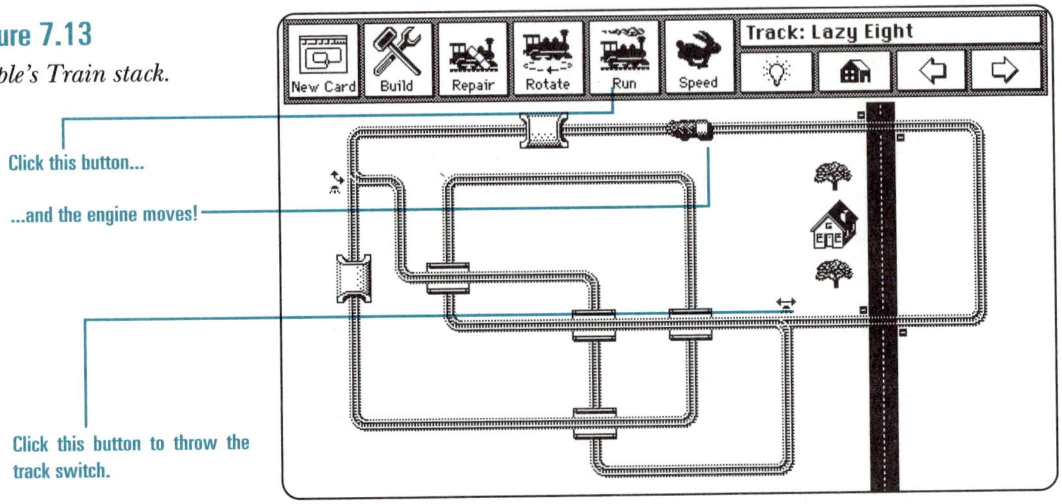

Figure 7.13
Apple's Train stack.

If you click in a Card field, the insertion point will jump there. If you're typing in one field and press the Tab key, you'll jump to the next field the author created. If you're typing and press Return, you'll either get a new line *or* jump to the next field. These tips don't always apply, depending on how the author has structured the stack. See "Level Playing Fields (and Buttons)," later in this chapter.

Navigating Within a Stack

You can move from one card to another using the Go menu, shown in Figure 7.14. If you don't see this menu, the author of the stack has hidden it. Look, instead, for similar buttons on the card itself. If you can't see any menus at all, try pressing ⌘-Space bar. This should make the menus reappear.

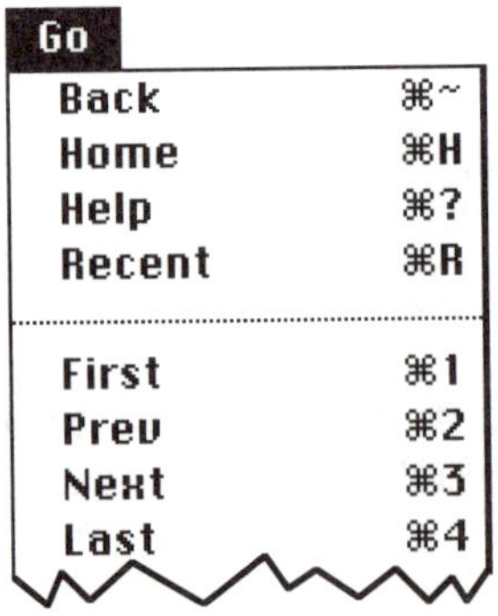

Figure 7.14
Part of the Go menu.

TIP: The command-key equivalents shown in Figure 7.14 work with most stacks, even if you can't see the Go menu on-screen.

The Back command takes you one at a time, in backwards order, through the last hundred cards you opened. The Help command takes you directly to the HyperCard Help stack (if it's on your disk). The First, Previous, Next, and Last commands take you to the appropriate cards in the current stack, and you've already learned what the Home command does. Recent shows you little (almost illegible) snapshots of the last 42 cards you've opened. Click on a snapshot, and you're there. (Figure 7.15 shows how the screen looks when you select Recent.) You can also move to another stack with the Open... command in the File menu, which brings up the standard Macintosh Open dialog box.

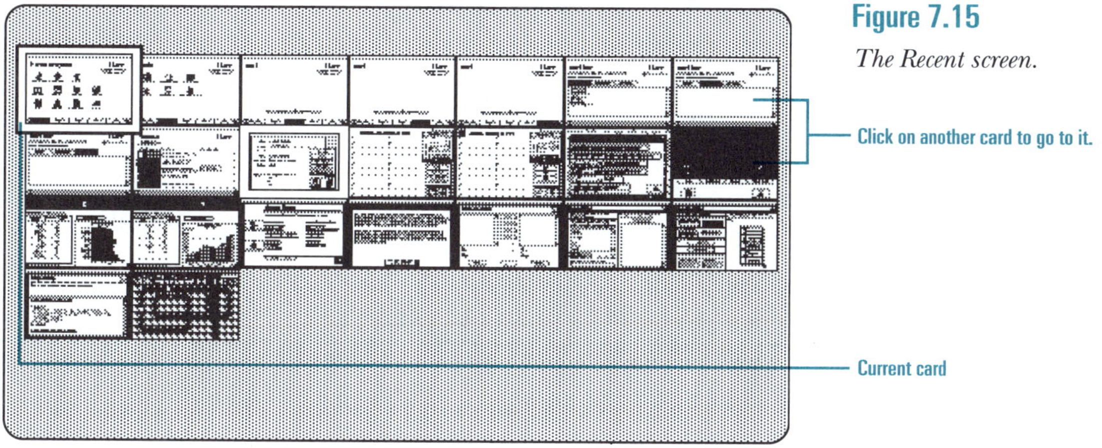

Figure 7.15

The Recent screen.

Level Playing Fields (and Buttons)

The problem with a "software erector set" is that everybody is tempted to try putting it together in different ways. HyperCard lets you protect your important stacks from unauthorized screwups through various methods, but the most common is by setting the *userLevel.* If you plan a stack for use as an information resource only, set a low userLevel to prevent people from changing the information. If you want to let others enter data but not mess with the scripts, choose an intermediate level.

> HyperCard capitalizes words weirdly. A capital letter in the middle of a word, like userLevel, means it's really two words jammed together for the requirements of the system.

You can give yourself a high userLevel while you're working on a stack, and then lower the level for other users. There are five distinct userLevels, as listed in Table 7.1.

Table 7.1 *HyperCard userLevels.*

userLevel	User Access
1. Browsing	Can read, but not change, data.
2. Typing	Can enter data in fields.
3. Painting	Can use the MacPaint-like tools.
4. Authoring	Can add or delete fields, add simple buttons, or delete *any* button.
5. Scripting	Can do anything you like with HyperCard, including defining new menu commands.

Set the userLevel by going to the last card of Apple's standard Home stack. (As a shortcut, press ⌘-H, followed by ⌘-4.) A card like the one in Figure 7.16 appears on-screen. You can make changes on this card to save as part of the Home stack. The next time you start HyperCard, it remembers the changes you made.

If you can't find the userLevel card (or want to make a temporary change), press ⌘-M to get the Message box. In the box that appears, type `Set userLevel to 5` or whatever level you want. Press Return to set the level, and ⌘-M again to hide the box.

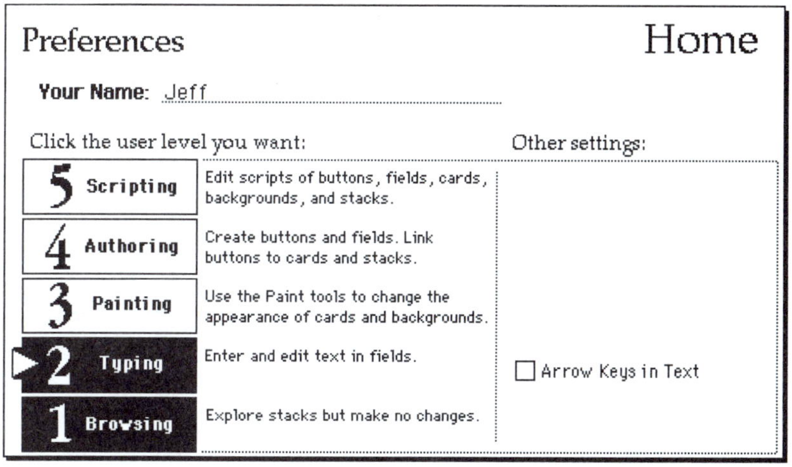

Figure 7.16

The userLevel Card, the last card of the Home stack.

> **TIP:** Fresh-out-of-the-box copies of HyperCard may have some "magic" in them. If you can't set a userLevel higher than two, click outside of a text field on the userLevel card, type **MAGIC**, and press Return. You won't see the word as you type it, but the higher levels should, uh, magically appear.

Entering Data in HyperCard

HyperCard fields follow the same conventions as most Macintosh word processing applications. If your userLevel is two or higher, you can change the data in a field. As you move the mouse over the field, you'll see the pointer change to an I-beam, as shown in Figure 7.17. Then you can type, drag, cut, or paste using the techniques you learned in Chapter 3. (Tab and Return might act funny. See the previous section, "Moving Through Fields, Dealing the Cards.")

A stack's author can lock a field when it's created, so only HyperCard can change the field contents. (For more information, see "Field Characteristics," later in this chapter.) If you move the mouse over a locked field, you won't see an insertion point.

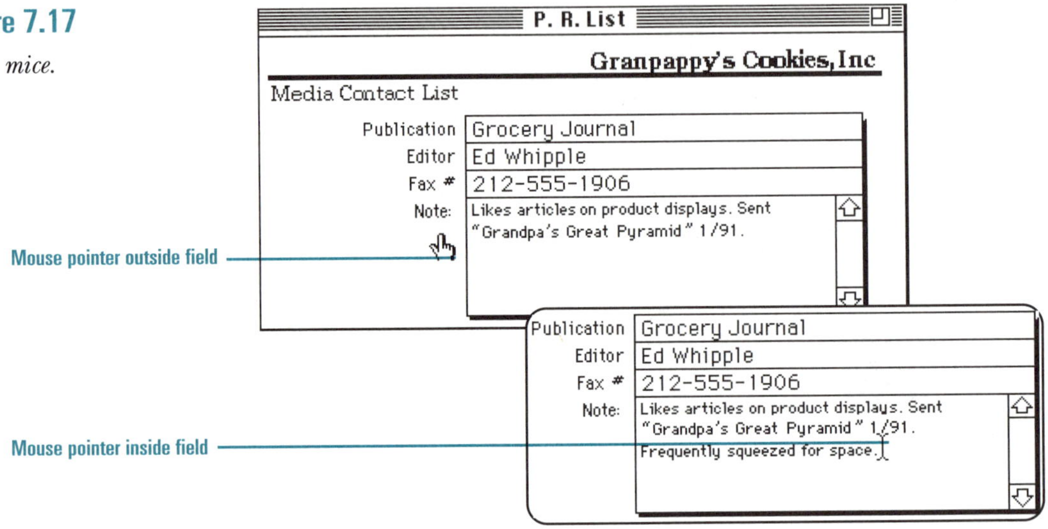

Figure 7.17

Field mice.

A field can hold up to 30,000 characters, depending on available memory. In a regular field, there's no way to see all of these characters (unless your Mac has an extremely large screen), but they're there, and a script can access them. In a *scrolling* field, you can move through data the same way you would when scrolling a document window. The Note field in Figure 7.17 is a scrolling field; if we entered more information about Grocery Journal, the scroll bar would become active.

The Missing "Save" Command

HyperCard's designers left the commands Save and Save As... off the File menu. This may disturb experienced Mac users. Relax. Saving is automatic in HyperCard. Whenever HyperCard is *idling*—that is, not performing any other activity—it checks for and saves any changes you have made to any aspect of the stack.

The down side of automatic saving is that you can't try something without destroying the previous version. If you're going to enter a lot of changes you're not sure of, use the Save a Copy... command first to duplicate the entire stack. If your changes don't pan out, you'll be able to trash the new version and go back to the copy.

Creating Your Own Stacks

With some database programs, you have to carefully plan how fields will appear in a layout. The fields you create have to be appropriate for every record in the file. With HyperCard, you can add or delete fields or buttons at will, even to individual cards. You can also create a new stack with no fields or buttons, and customize it from scratch. Use the New Stack... command in the File menu, and type a name in the dialog box that appears.

Cards and Backgrounds

HyperCard stacks are made up of *cards* and their *background*. Cards hold data, but are effectively transparent. The fields, buttons, and labels are usually on a background layer and show through. The concept is similar to database layouts and records, except each card can belong to only one background. It's as if Granpappy wrote his recipes on clear cellophane and kept the ruled index card lines on a master piece of cardboard beneath them (see Figure 7.18).

HyperCard works the same way. Fields, buttons, and graphics repeated in each card are put on the background layer. A background field can have different data on each card, just as a database field has different data in each record.

Figure 7.18
Granpappy's cellophane recipe cards.

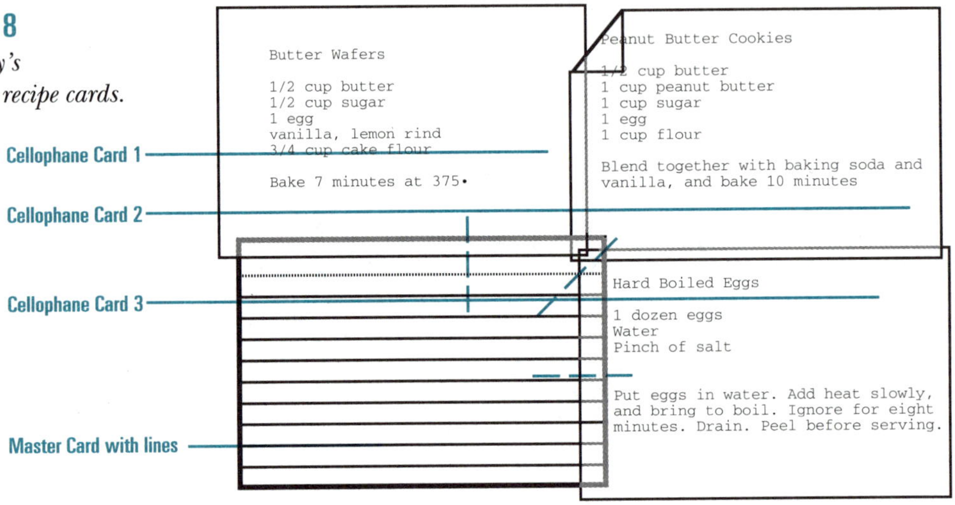

You can also put fields, buttons, and graphics on individual cards; all the other cards ignore these additions. Figure 7.19 shows how it all fits together in a card stack with two different backgrounds.

Figure 7.19
HyperCard stack with backgrounds and cards.

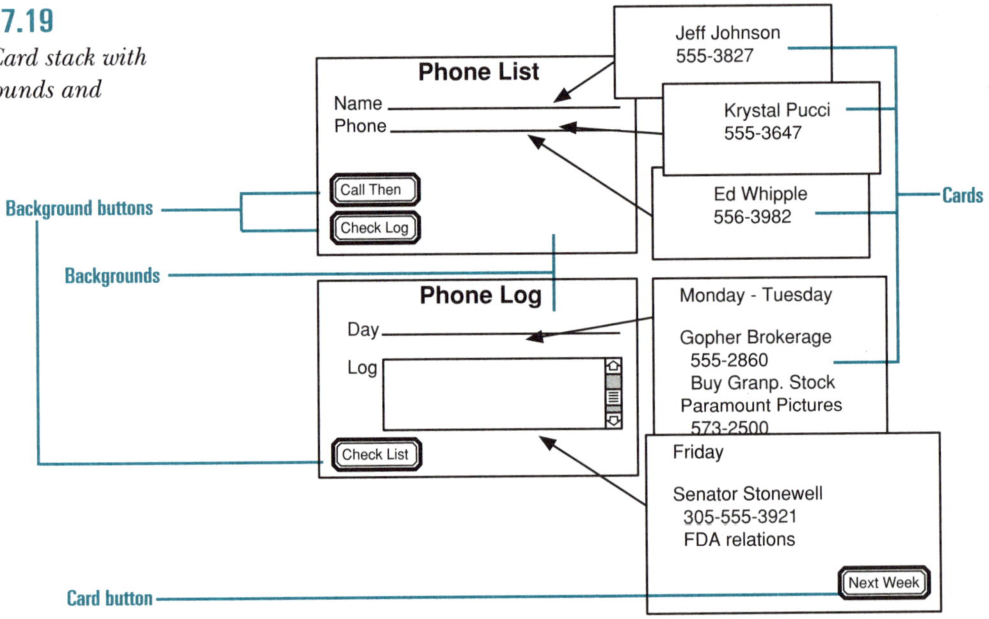

Modifying a Stack

Remember the PR List stack in Figure 7.17? Let's add an additional field to keep track of each editor's preference for gift cookies. Because this field will appear on every card, you should put it in the background. Choose Background from the Edit menu, and note the tiger stripes that appear on the menu bar (see Figure 7.20). The stripes appear whenever HyperCard is in the background layer. They let you know changes made here will affect every card with this background. If you don't see the stripes, your changes will affect only one card.

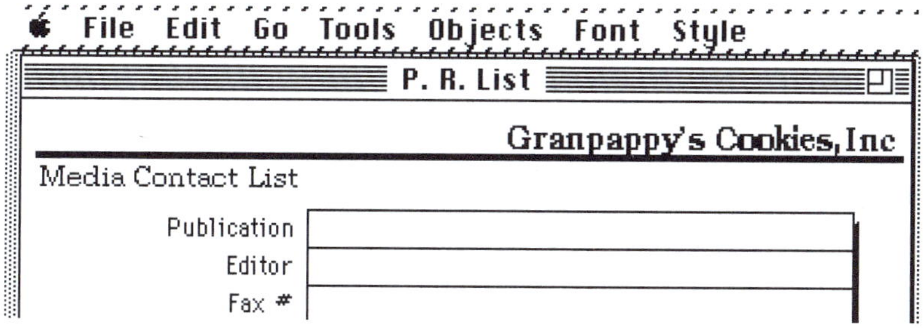

Figure 7.20
The background layer. Note the stripes on menu bar.

If you drag down from Tools on the menu bar, you'll see a tear-off palette instead of a list of commands (see Figure 7.21). This is the *Tool palette.* You can move it anywhere on-screen and use it to select HyperCard authoring and graphic tools. The graphic tools work just like their counterparts in MacPaint and can draw on either the card or the background layer. The three tools at the top are the *Browsing tool,* or *pointer* (for pressing buttons), and the *Button* and *Field tools* (for manipulating objects).

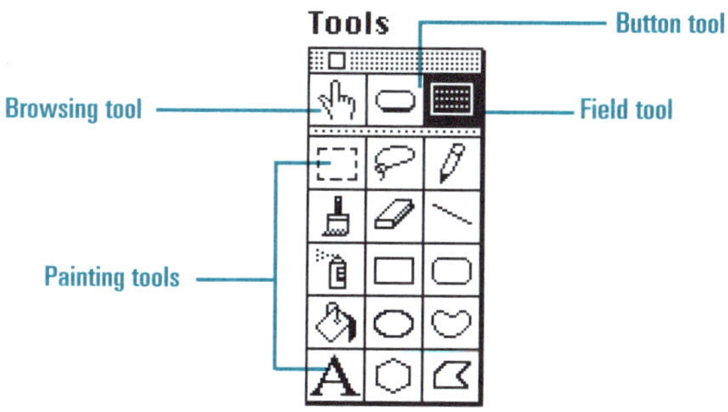

Figure 7.21
The HyperCard Tools palette.

Choose New Field from the Objects menu. This automatically selects the Field tool and plops a new field down in the middle of the card, as shown in Figure 7.22. The field border flashes to show it's active (in the figure, the field appears gray instead). Grab an edge of the field with the mouse, and drag it to a convenient place on the card. Then drag one of the corners to adjust its size. This way, you can position the new field precisely where you want it, as shown in Figure 7.23.

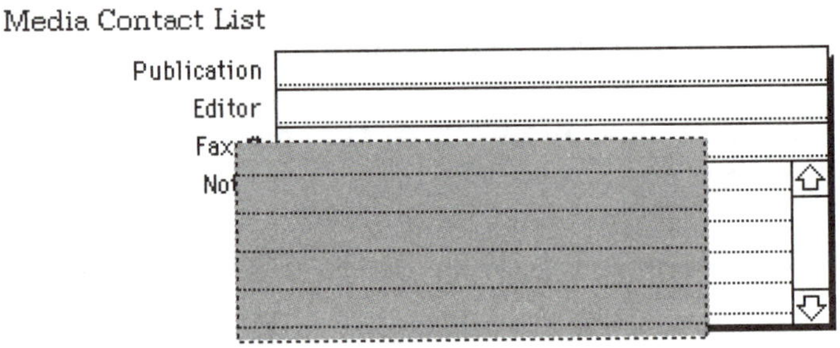

Figure 7.22

A new field.

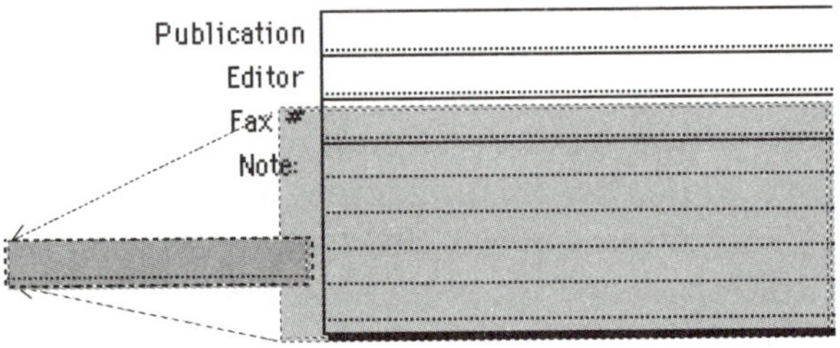

Figure 7.23

The new field moved to where it belongs.

Field Characteristics

Double-click on a new field to open the dialog box like the one shown in Figure 7.24, where you can name the field and select attributes. HyperCard doesn't require you to name each field, but typing a name now will make it easier to sort and retrieve information later. There isn't enough room to discuss all of HyperCard's field attributes in these pages, but they're thoroughly—if confusingly—documented in the Claris support package mentioned earlier in this chapter. Better yet, experiment!

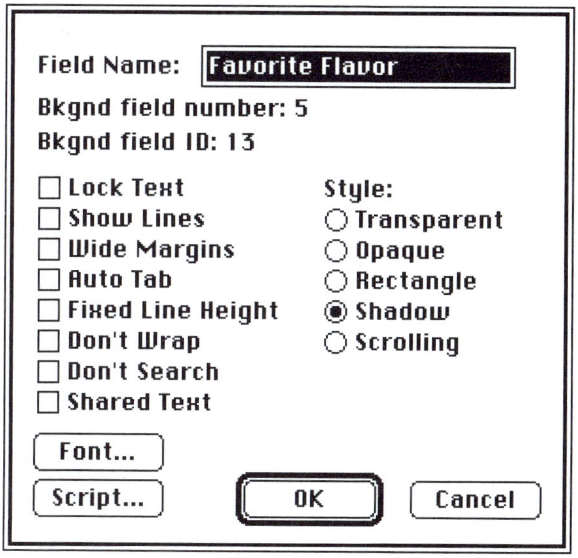

Figure 7.24
The Field Information dialog box.

It's a good idea to identify each new field for other stack users, to show what kind of information should go in it. You can add a little drawing (using the painting tools) or type a label on the background next to the field. The tools work just like those in MacPaint (see Chapter 6). For our example, we'll use the text-painting (A) tool to type the label **Favorite Flavor Cookie**. With the label in place, click Background again to leave that layer, and then choose the Browsing tool. The modified stack is now ready to use (see Figure 7.25).

Buttoning It Up

You can create a button to go to another card or stack just as easily. The procedure is almost the same as creating fields. (You can also create a button to do just about anything else, but that's not quite so easy. You'd have to learn the Hyper*Talk* programming language.)

To create a new button, go to the background and select New Button from the Objects menu. A new button appears. Move it where you want and double-click when it's in place. The dialog box shown in Figure 7.26 appears.

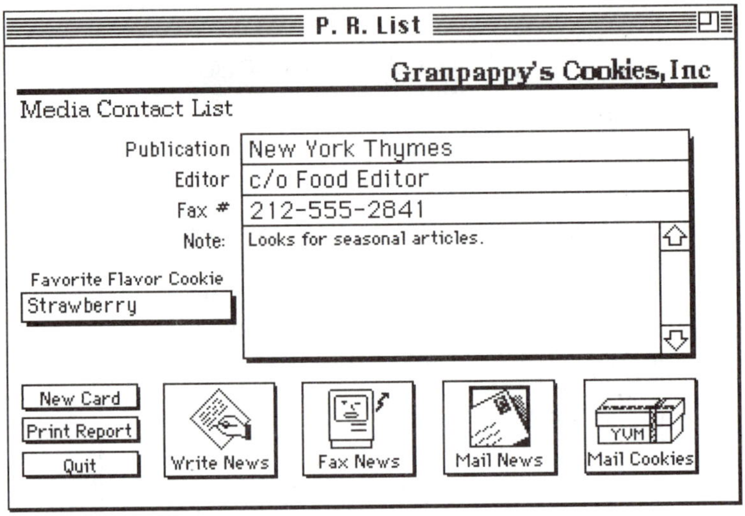

Figure 7.25

The modified stack, with the new Favorite Flavor Cookie field.

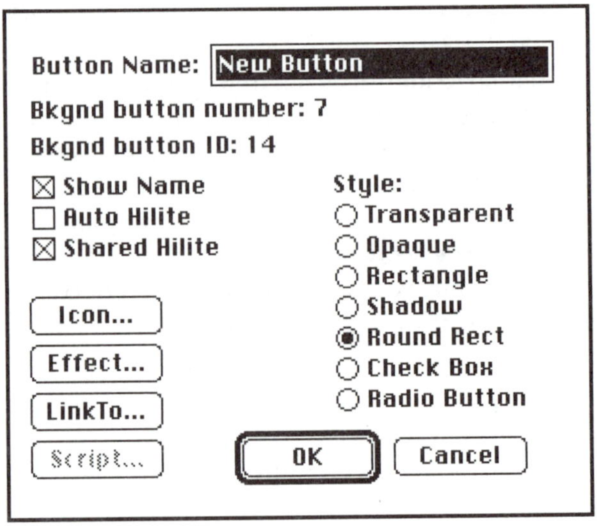

Figure 7.26

The New Button Information dialog box.

Naming the button is optional if you're going to use an icon, but if you don't name it, turn off Show Name. You don't have to be an artist to add graphics to your button. Just click Icon... and select one of the icons from the menu that appears (see Figure 7.27).

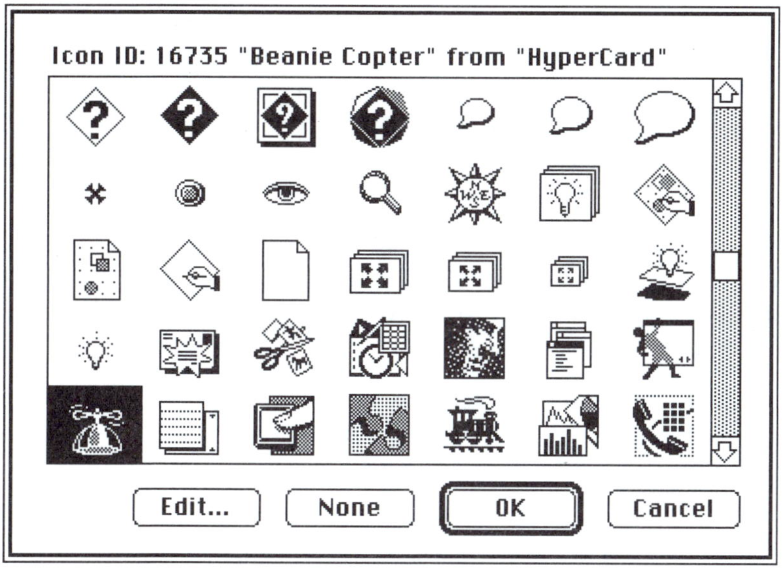

Figure 7.27

Icon selections.

If you are an artist, or don't like any of the choices presented, pick any icon and choose Edit.... The screen presents a Fat Bits version of the icon and some editing tools (see Chapter 6). Modify the existing icon, or pick New Icon from the File menu and start fresh.

Icons are attached to the button. Copy, cut, or move the icon with the button. Icon size also is limited. If you want a larger image as part of your button, choose Transparent in the info box and use HyperCard's drawing tools to add graphics underneath it. (That's how the Coffee Cup and Bear buttons were created as shown in Figures 7.8 and 7.9). But remember, the graphic you drew is just a picture, not a true icon. If you cut or move the button, the picture remains.

Choosing an icon takes you back to the background layer, so double-click the new button to see the info box again. Click Link To... to see the Link dialog box, shown in Figure 7.28. While that box is on-screen, go to any other card using the Go menu or the Open Stack command.

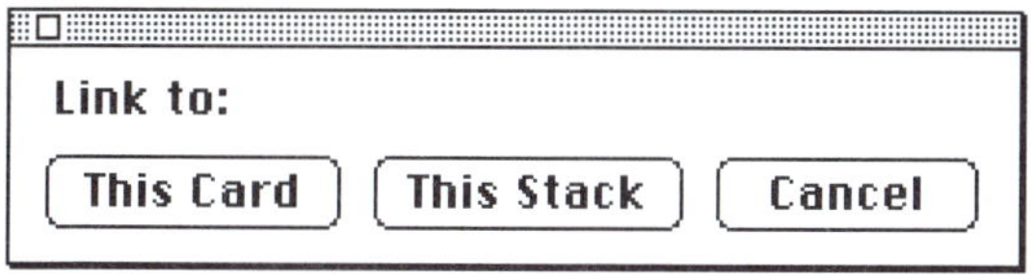

Figure 7.28

The Link dialog box.

The Link dialog box stays in place while you search for the desired card. When you get to the card you want, click a choice. This Card sets a link between your new button and the card you see. This Stack sets the link to the *first* card of the stack you're in. Either of these choices creates a script that will open the card you linked to whenever you press the button.

You can do one more thing to your new button: double-click it once more to get the info dialog box, and click Effect... to add a little Hollywood pizazz. We won't tell you all the effects you can get, but you'll have a lot of fun trying them.

Once your button is the way you want it, press ⌘-B to leave the background layer and reselect the Browsing tool. You can always go back to the Button tool later to change your new button.

Printing from HyperCard

HyperCard also can generate reports like any other database manager. In most cases, however, it's much easier than other database managers. You can also print individual cards, individual fields, or a whole stack as easily as a database manager-style report.

To print the card displayed on-screen, choose Print Card from the File menu. You can also use the shortcut ⌘-P. (Told you it would be easy.)

Printing a field is also easy. Just choose Print Field... from the File menu. A list of all the fields on the current card appears on-screen. Just select the one you want to print. This is useful when you want to print the contents of a long scrolling field or don't want to waste time printing graphics. Otherwise, Print Card is handier.

To print the whole stack, choose Print Stack... from the File menu. This gets only slightly more complicated. A dialog box appears (Figure 7.29), giving you the option to do the following:

- Print the cards full-sized or shrink them to fit more on a page (half-size is quite readable with most printers).
- Change the margins and spacing.
- Add a custom header to each page.

When you choose a different option, its effect appears in a preview window. When you're satisfied with the layout, click Print.

It's also easy to print only a few selected cards from a stack. That's what the Marked Cards button is for (not for gambling). Before you choose a Print command, go to each card you'll want to print. Choose Card Info... from the Objects menu, and click the Marked Cards button. You can also create a HyperTalk script that marks specific cards for you.

HyperCard also can print reports in a number of different formats (phone lists, mail labels, inventory sheets, and so on) and can send data to other programs using scripts. The range of options with these functions is almost dizzying and is certainly beyond the limits of this book. Once again, your best bet is to pick up a HyperCard text and experiment.

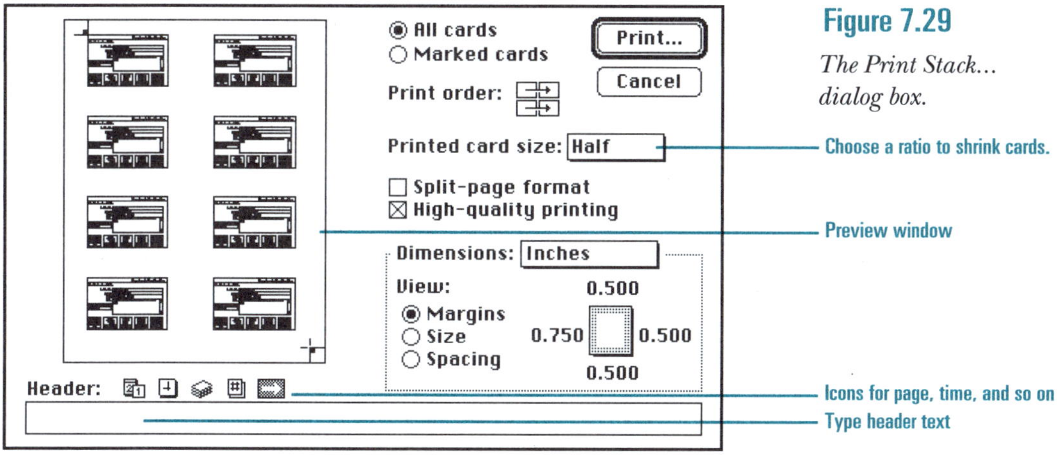

Figure 7.29

The Print Stack... dialog box.

Stacks and Stacks of Stacks

HyperCard and HyperTalk are so ubiquitous and easily-programmed that even inexperienced users design their own stacks for specific applications. Most dealers don't have HyperCard stacks for sale. There just isn't a demand for many commercial ones.

The good news is there are hundreds of clever and useful stacks. Most HyperCard authors are proud of their work and are willing to share it through computer bulletin boards or user groups (we have written six stacks in the public domain). At the worst, authors want a few dollars' shareware fees. You can have these stacks on your computer in minutes, if you have a modem. Or, you can buy disks of collected stacks from the user groups. (See Chapter 12 for more information.)

To illustrate the range of stacks available, we just called the Boston Computer Society's Macintosh bulletin board and downloaded the following few titles:

ADDRESS LIB	Correspondence management stack.
AMER GOTHIC	The classic painting animated.
ANIMAL YEAR	Converts your age to other animals' ages.
AUTOCAT	Catalog your floppies. Fast, reliable.
AUTOMATIK ART	Random art based on specific shapes.
CALCPAD	A small calculator written in HyperTalk.
CALENDAR	Very good calendar stack.
CHESS STACK	Working chess board.

CIRCUITS	Diagrams teaching electrical principles.
CONCENTRAT'N	From Apple Computer, the classic game.
CONSTITUTION	Full text of U.S. Constitution, by article.
CONVERSION	Converts between metric and English units.
CPR STACK	Animated CPR lesson.
DIPLOMA MILL	Create your own certificates.
DOT TO DOT	Kids' game of connect-the-dots.
FINANCE MATH	Computes interest rates & discounts.
FOLKTUNES	Traditional Irish folk tunes.
FRACTAL	Fractal tutorials with examples, bibliography.
GENEALOGY	Plot and save your family tree.
GRADEMASTER	Computes grades, compiles class lists.
GUITARIST	Guess the guitarist from the riff.

These stack titles came over our phone line in less than a minute and represent just a fraction of the hundreds of stacks available through the BCS. If we'd wanted, we could have downloaded any of the listed stacks to our Mac for the price of a phone call. After you've worked with HyperCard for a while, you'll probably have stacks of your own to share. Make a copy for a friend. Or two. Or three.

In This Chapter

Basic Spreadsheet Organization and Terminology

•

Using Spreadsheet Formulas, Databases, and Graphing

•

Checkbook and Financial Planning Programs for the Home

•

Complete Financial Analysis Programs for Business

In a roundabout way, spreadsheets are responsible for the existence of the Macintosh itself. Before Dan Bricklin invented VisiCalc, the first spreadsheet program, most people considered Apple's products either as teaching computers or expensive toys. VisiCalc changed that impression. The program was so useful that business executives had to deal with the Apple II it ran on. VisiCalc's look and feel—Bricklin's basic ideas of how computer and user should interact when processing numerical data—became the standard for every spreadsheet program that followed. This chapter describes Mac spreadsheets and other applications that can help you manage your home and business finances.

8

Spreadsheets

When you combine today's spreadsheets *with* the graphic power of a Macintosh, you get very powerful (and persuasive) programs indeed. And because the Mac is so easy to use, there are also powerful non-spreadsheet financial programs designed for us non-accountant types. Later in this chapter, we discuss home and small business accounting programs.

Spreadsheet Concepts

Accountants take columns of numbers, add them, multiply them by various factors, poke them into other columns, and eventually reduce them to a single bottom-line figure. This is where the concept of *number crunching* comes from. But an electronic spreadsheet does more than just automate the process. Because spreadsheets do in seconds what would take an accountant days, they make much more precise and complicated calculations practical. Electronic spreadsheets can also be much larger than their paper counterparts. Microsoft Excel can hold the electronic equivalent of a 250-square-foot accountant's reconciliation page!

When we say "a 250-square-foot reconciliation page," we're talking about an accountant with fairly small handwriting. A single Excel spreadsheet can handle up to 99,614,720 separate entries, depending on available memory. Of course, larger spreadsheets take much longer to recalculate.

Because it's so easy to recalculate an entire sheet after making small changes, spreadsheets encourage *What if . . .* exploration. Change one price or market share in a complicated formula, and you'll see the bottom-line results almost instantly. Predictions of future performance are easy. All you have to do is set up the right formula (and make the right assumptions about your company's future trends).

Columns, Rows, and Formulas

Because all spreadsheet programs share VisiCalc as a common heritage, they all work pretty much alike. Figure 8.1 shows a basic spreadsheet (from Microsoft Excel). The numbers down the side designate *rows*; the letters across the top are *columns*. The boxes formed by the intersections of rows and columns are *cells*, and can hold numbers, formulas, or text. We widened the first column, A, and typed some text into a few cells to show what our spreadsheet will do. Each cell is named, or *referenced*, by its column and row. Thus, the cell containing the number of widgets sold in January is called B2. Cell B3 contains the price for each. Because the Gross Sale would be the product of those two cells (Widgets Sold times Price Per Widget), we can put a *formula* into cell B4 that says, "Multiply Price times Units," or as far as the computer is concerned, "Multiply B2 * B3." A spreadsheet full of formulas and awaiting data is a *template*.

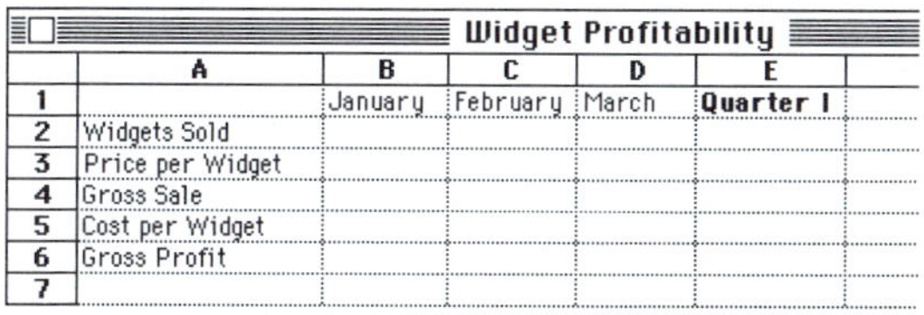

	A	B	C	D	E
			Widget Profitability		
1		January	February	March	**Quarter I**
2	Widgets Sold				
3	Price per Widget				
4	Gross Sale				
5	Cost per Widget				
6	Gross Profit				
7					

Figure 8.1

A basic, empty spreadsheet.

Entering a Formula

Depending on the program, double-click the cell where you want the formula, or click it and then the *formula bar* at the top of the screen (see Figure 8.2). A large X shows the bar is active. Now, either type or select from a menu what you want to do—anything from simple addition to complicated statistical analysis. Click or type the names of the cells that hold the data you want to use. Formulas in Excel should start with an equal sign. Other programs may use a plus sign or other mathematical symbols to indicate a formula. Once you've entered the formula, press Return to put it in the cell. The program will check your typing and point out any mistakes or mathematical impossibilities. Because we want to multiply two cells for our example, we'll click each and then type a star between them on the formula bar (Figure 8.2). For illustration purposes, we've told Excel to show the formulas in their cells in this figure. Normally, the results of the formulas would appear in their cells.

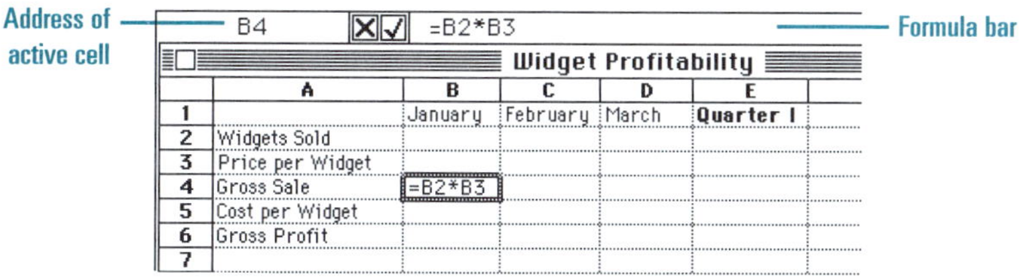

	A	B	C	D	E
1		January	February	March	**Quarter I**
2	Widgets Sold				
3	Price per Widget				
4	Gross Sale	=B2*B3			
5	Cost per Widget				
6	Gross Profit				
7					

Figure 8.2

A formula.

> Computer programs use stars or asterisks to indicate multiplication, to avoid confusion with the letter X. Mathematicians use a • for the same reason. So (3 x 4) =(3 • 4) = (3 * 4), depending on your occupation.

Formula Functions

Spreadsheets can do more than add or multiply. Most give you wide choices of mathematical, logical, text, and database functions you can select from menus. Figure 8.3 shows a few of the formula choices in Microsoft Excel (on the left) and Ashton-Tate's Full Impact (on the right).

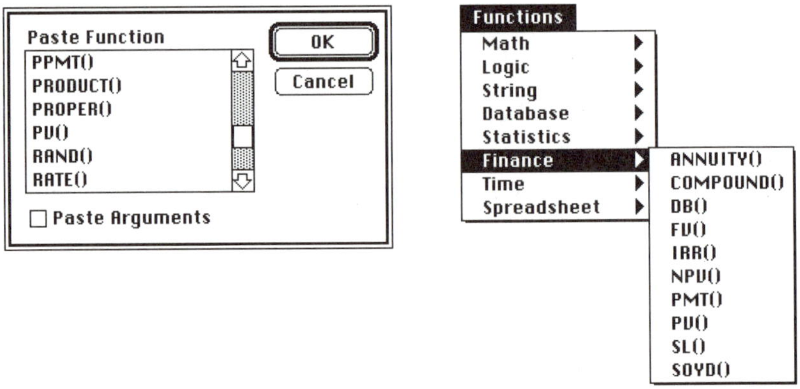

Figure 8.3

Function selection in two popular spreadsheets.

Formulas also can contain other formulas. When it's time to figure Gross Profit, we can think of the formula in cell B4 (Gross Sale) as if it were a number in another formula. Gross Profit equals Gross Sale less the cost of what was sold, which we've already defined as the product of the units sold (cell B2) times the cost of each (cell B5). So, we'll click and type that formula into cell B6, as shown in Figure 8.4. The entire formula is too long to show in its cell, but the program knows it's there.

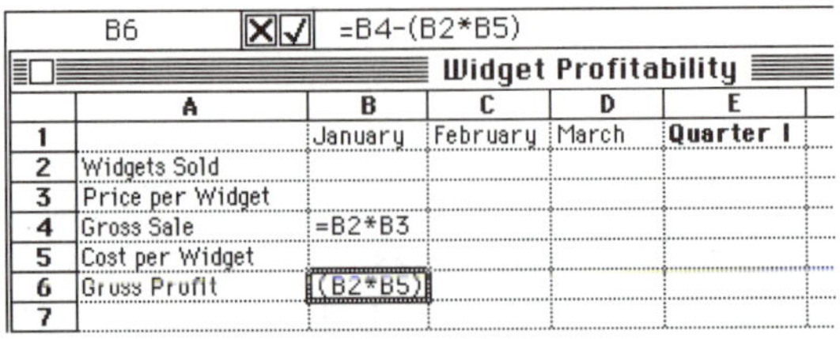

Figure 8.4

Formula referencing another formula.

Entering Data and Calculating

Now the fun starts. Click a cell that should get data (depending on the program, the insertion point will appear in the cell or in the formula bar). Type the number, and press Return. That's all you have to do. As soon as the program has enough data, it will figure out the formulas and put the answers where the formulas used to be (see Figure 8.5). Don't be concerned that the formula disappears from your screen. It's really still there, under the numbers, ready for your next set of data. Some programs use a menu command or shortcut (usually ⌘-= or ⌘-Space bar) to start calculation.

Navigating in a Spreadsheet

In most spreadsheets, pressing Return not only puts a number in a cell, but it also moves the insertion point to the next cell down. Pressing Tab does almost the same thing, storing the number and moving to the next cell horizontally. You can also use the arrow keys to move from one cell to the next.

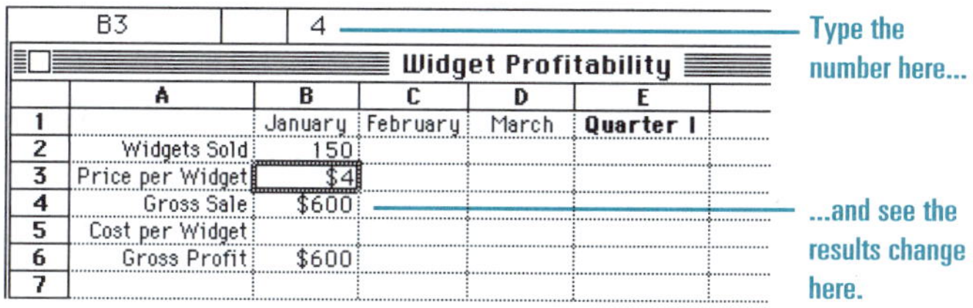

Figure 8.5

Enter a number. See the result.

Pasting Formulas and Relative Referencing

Putting the same formula into other columns shows off one of the neater things spreadsheets can do. February's Gross Profit should be based on February sales, not January ones. As we select and copy the formula from column B to column C, it will change its B-cell addresses to match! This *relative* addressing preserves the relationship between a formula and the cells that contribute to it. References will change their row, column, or both at the same time, depending on how you move the formula. Figure 8.6 shows how the formulas automatically use the proper month's data when we paste them into new columns.

Figure 8.6

Relative cell references.

Widget Profitability

	A	B	C	D
1		January	February	March
2	Widgets Sold			
3	Price per Widget			
4	Gross Sale	=B2*B3	=C2*C3	=D2*D3
5	Cost per Widget			
6	Gross Profit	=B4-(B2*B5)	=C4-(C2*C5)	=D4-(D2*D5)

Column letters change as you paste the formula.

You can specify *absolute* addresses by using dollar signs when you enter a formula. The reference B5 becomes C5 if you paste a formula with relative addresses into the next column, but B5 doesn't. You can also make part of the reference absolute and part relative. For example, $B5 always refers to a cell in column B; B$5 always refers to row 5.

Creating Spreadsheet Databases

A spreadsheet database has very little to do with the databases discussed in the last chapter. It's merely an area of the spreadsheet devoted to storing interrelated data. Usually, you should place this area off the screen (remember, spreadsheets can be *large*). An income tax table, with maximum gross income in one column and tax rates in the other, would be one example of a database. Databases can be more than two columns wide. For example, an employee database in a payroll spreadsheet could contain not only names and salaries, but also social security numbers and year-to-date tables for tax reports. These two types of databases are examples of *lookup tables*, which contain information formulas in other cells you might need to perform a calculation. Database functions within a spreadsheet usually don't include much more than sorting, summing, and finding averages. Although, many recent spreadsheets support a wide variety of functions and enable you to construct many more using macros and button scripts.

Charting

Most spreadsheet programs let you generate quick charts or graphs with just a couple of keystrokes. Depending on the program, you select the data that will make up the chart, choose from among dozens of possible styles, and add whatever text or callouts will make it most readable. Figure 8.7B shows an example of a spreadsheet pie graph. We could have easily turned the same data into a three-dimensional bar graph, multiple line graph, or scattergram.

It took less than a minute to turn the data from the ticket sales into a comparative analysis by class (Figure 8.7A) using Microsoft Excel. We created a new document in a pie graph style, selected one wedge, moved it, and added boldface type. Full Impact lets you make a chart part of the spreadsheet itself, circle important cells, or add other graphic highlights.

FYI Idea

Once you've completed a spreadsheet, it becomes the ideal medium for What If . . . calculations. It's easy to see what effect a 3% sales increase or a twenty-cent-per-unit cost reduction will have on the bottom line. Just insert the new figure, and watch the whole program recalculate. The screen shots in figures 8.7A and 8.7B show this kind of financial projection in part of a spreadsheet budgeting a school play. It's obvious that motivating every two kids to sell just one more ticket will have a significant effect on the play's financial success. (Most spreadsheets let you hide the cell borders, as we did here, to make the chart more readable.) More complicated spreadsheets can help you evaluate retirement planning, lease-versus-buy decisions, or how many votes a candidate can get by flip-flopping on a position.

Figure 8.7A

Spreadsheets become the ideal medium for What If. . . calculations.

Peter pan wksht

	A	B	C	D	E	F
1	Ticket Sales by Class					
3		Ticket Price		Tickets per student		Total tix sale
4		$3.00		2		$1,002.00
5						
6						
7	Class	Class size	No. Tix	Ticket total	Grade	Grade Total
8	Ms. Oscar	11	22	$66.00	K	
9	Mr. Reser	11	22	$66.00	K	$132.00
10	Ms. Val					
11	Mr. Gar					
12	Mr. For					
13	Ms. Puc					
14	Mr. Gob					
15	Mr. Boc					
16	Mr. Spe					
17	Mr. Irv					
18	Ms. Jir					
19						

Peter pan wksht

	A	B	C	D	E	F
1	Ticket Sales by Class					
3		Ticket Price		Tickets per student		Total tix sale
4		$3.00		2.5		$1,252.50
5						
6						
7	Class	Class size	No. Tix	Ticket total	Grade	Grade Total
8	Ms. Oscar	11	27.5	$82.50	K	
9	Mr. Reser	11	27.5	$82.50	K	$165.00
10	Ms. Valentine	18	45	$135.00	1	
11	Mr. Garfield	19	47.5	$142.50	1	$277.50
12	Mr. Fortune	11	27.5	$82.50	2	$82.50
13	Ms. Pucci	16	40	$120.00	3	
14	Mr. Gobo	15	37.5	$112.50	3	$232.50
15	Mr. Bock	18	45	$135.00	4	
16	Mr. Sperling	18	45	$135.00	4	$270.00
17	Mr. Irving	14	35	$105.00	5	
18	Ms. Jird	16	40	$120.00	5	$225.00

Figure 8.7B

Instant graphing.

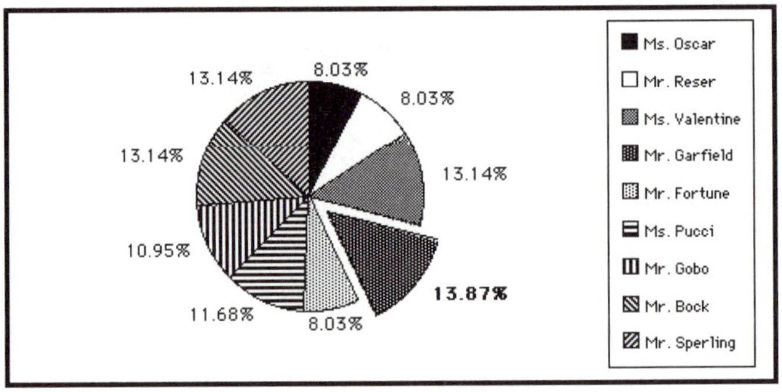

Spreadsheet Variations

Spreadsheet *logical functions* let you compare two numbers (or names, or dates) and complete a different operation depending on which is higher. This, in effect, is the basis of all computer programming.

Because of this branching capability, spreadsheets can do a lot of interesting things that aren't related to traditional bookkeeping. Figure 8.8 shows a few of the public domain templates written by users of Microsoft Excel, downloaded from America Online (see Chapter 12). There are also libraries of commercial Excel templates and timesavers for specific industries and applications.

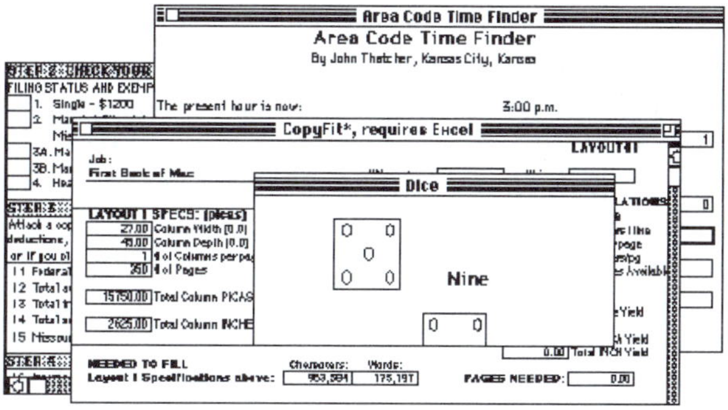

Figure 8.8

Some spreadsheets that are more than just piles of numbers.

Financial Management Programs

Spreadsheets are powerful ways to manage numerical data, if you know how the data should be organized in the first place (or can find a prewritten template that meets your needs). Unfortunately, "the rest of us" didn't go to accounting school, and the skills needed to successfully manage a business (or happily manage a large family) aren't the same as those needed to create a complicated template. That's why most people hire a bookkeeper for their business, go to a tax service every April 14th, and put off reconciling their checkbooks altogether. Or they purchase specialized accounting software.

Home Accounting Packages

Charles Dickens' formula for personal happiness ($Ci \quad Co$, where Ci is the amount of cash you make in a year and Co is the amount you spend, though Dickens expressed it more elegantly) has gotten a lot more complicated in an age of withholding taxes, credit cards, and IRAs. Home accounting programs go a long way to ease the burden, saving yards of adding machine tape. If your personal finances are complicated (with rental properties, freelance businesses, or investments), the time and bookkeeping fees you save can almost justify the cost of a Macintosh by themselves.

Most programs do at least three very important things:

- Create a budget (and see how well you're sticking to it).
- Track your income and expenses by categories that are acceptable to the IRS.
- Generate quick reports, in either graphic or tabular form, to help you plan your financial future.

The programs themselves need not be expensive. Software Toolworks' Dollars & Sense keeps track of multiple checkbooks and expense categories, and generates very useful reports and graphs. It's usually discounted to around $50. Meca's Managing Your Money keeps track of checks, generates reports (but no graphs), and gives friendly financial advice on everything from home refinancing to your life expectancy, for under $150. Reality Technologies' WealthBuilder by *Money Magazine* helps you pick investments to meet your goals, comes with a database of one thousand stocks and mutual funds, and costs about $100.

Checkbook Interface

Dollars & Sense organizes your transactions around electronic checkbooks (Figure 8.9). Checkbooks can represent actual checking accounts, other bank accounts, mattresses, or any other repository for your cash. To pay a bill, you type in the name of the payee, the amount, what the check is for, and a general category for the check. You can use categories provided by the program or add your own. There are prompts, shortcuts, and suggestions; the program will make intelligent guesses if it doesn't understand your input. You can print checks from the program or enter checks you've handwritten.

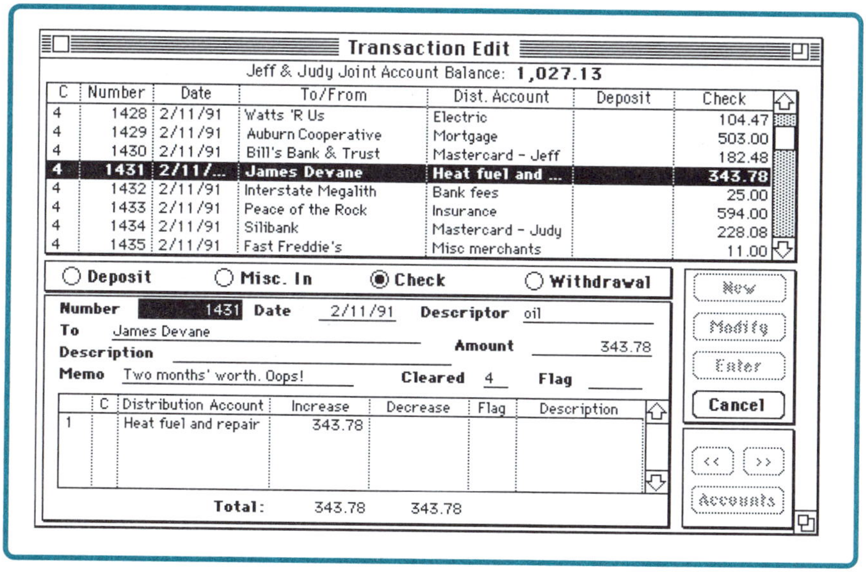

Figure 8.9

An electronic checkbook.

Reconciling a monthly statement is simply a matter of clicking check numbers and entering bank fees and interest. You can enter ATM and other checkless transactions as they occur or while you're reconciling.

Once checks are in the system, you can call for reports based on payee, nature of transaction, date, or other criteria. They can take the form of listings, balance sheets, statements, or graphs. Figure 8.10 shows some of the kinds of reports available with this low-cost program.

Quicken 3.0, from Intuit Software, is similar to Dollars & Sense and sells for about the same price. It doesn't provide quite the same flexibility with reports and won't create graphs, but it does add a few other useful features. Quicken can prepare files for tax preparation programs and manage common business payments, including payroll taxes. This electronic checkbook can even make paper checks obsolete: if you have a modem, Quicken can call the CheckFree electronic bill-paying service and have them make payments from your account.

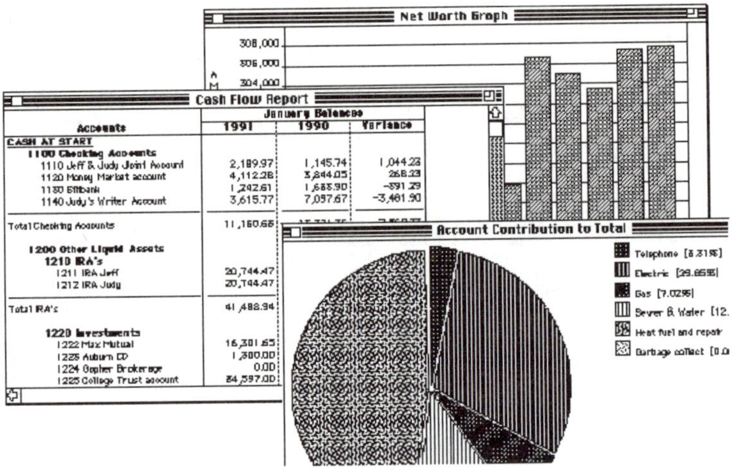

Figure 8.10

Reports in Dollars & Sense.

Floppy Advice

Not only does Meca's Andrew Tobia$ Managing Your Money ($150) automate your checkbook, but it also manages stock portfolios and retirement accounts, helps you plan for college, and advises you on insurance. (It doesn't generate graphs or charts.) Actually, the program doesn't really do *any* of those things. It just crunches the numbers you provide and adds generalized, rule-of-thumb guidelines. It's still up to you to find the investments, make sure the guidelines apply to you, and check the whole thing with a professional who understands tax law.

This is not to say that Managing Your Money doesn't take some strong stands on how you should spend or save. It adopts the insurance industry's position that cost of premiums is irrelevant and insurance itself is a Universal Good Thing. The program's smugness is offset by a well-written and comprehensive manual. If you're looking for financial advice (as opposed to Dollars & Sense's straightforward reporting), consider this program. Figure 8.11 shows some of its screens.

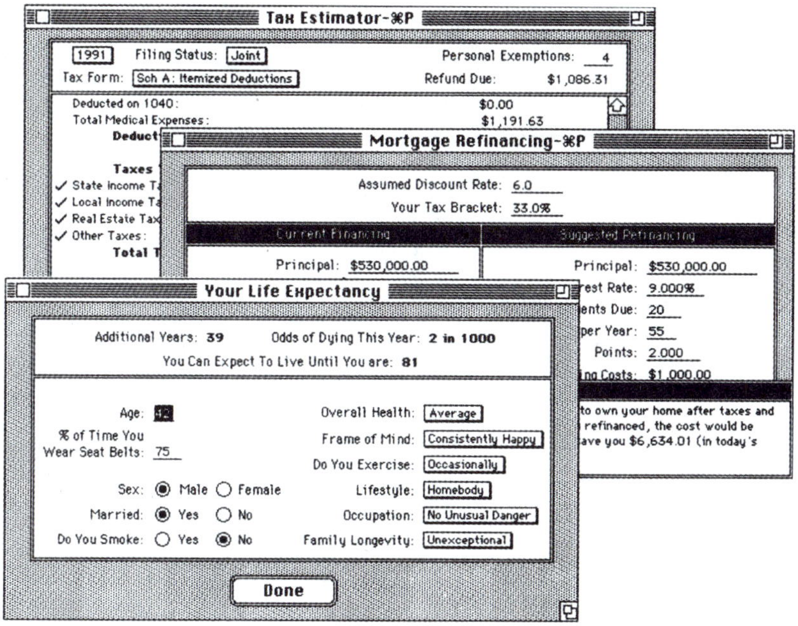

Figure 8.11

Financial advice, courtesy of Managing Your Money.

Tickertape Parade

If you've decided to pursue a slice of the American Dream, WealthBuilder by Money Magazine can help you avoid a pie in the face. The program, designed to work in tandem with a checkbook program, lets you establish goals in terms of a time line (as shown in Figure 8.12): how much you'll need for specifics like a house or retirement. It figures how much money should be set aside now to reach these goals. Then, it charts the historic performance of appropriate investments. While WealthBuilder won't recommend specific stocks, bonds, or mutual funds, it can let you compare investments based on performance and stability. Figure 8.13 shows the depth of detail in this $100 program.

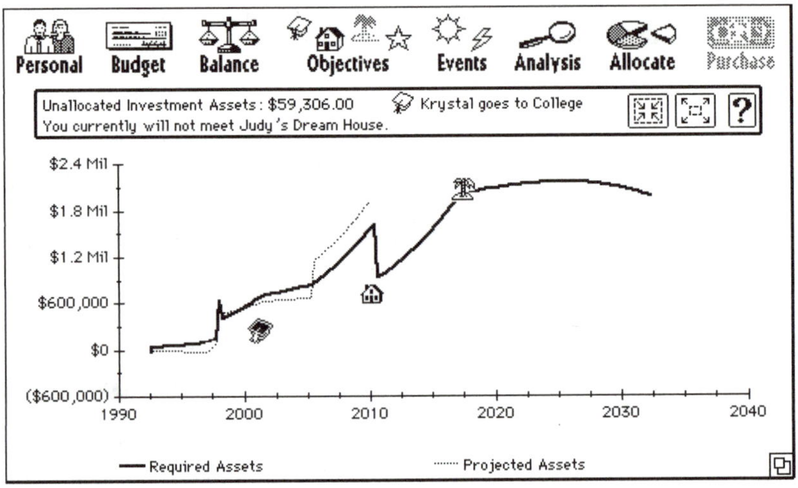

Figure 8.12

Charting your course in WealthBuilder. The icons stand for specific goals.

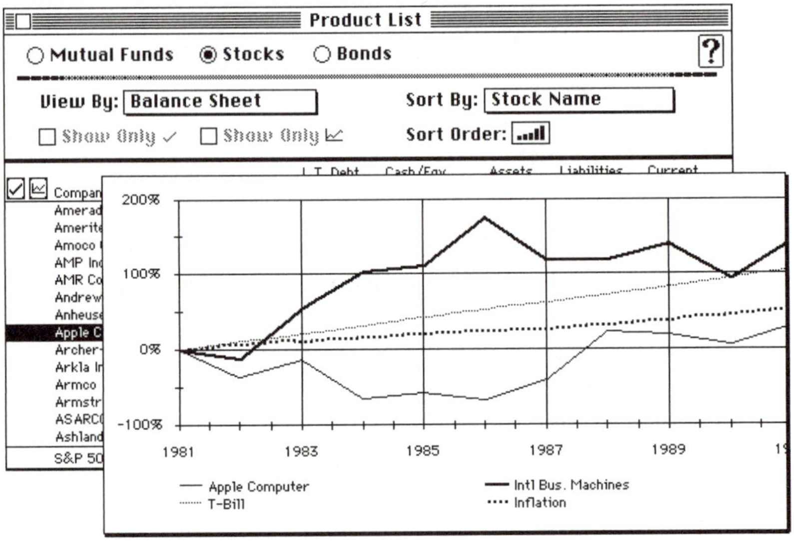

Figure 8.13

Tracking Stocks.

Since financial markets are volatile—just ask Donald Trump—the program's database must be updated quarterly on a subscription basis. This costs between $120–$200 a year, depending on depth. The program's own license agreement includes two very strong paragraphs disclaiming any liability for its recommendations. Still, if you're serious about investing, WealthBuilder can help you work your way through the maze of information in the financial pages—and serve as an independent authority to confirm the advice you get from brokers.

If the heart of a home accounting package is the checkbook, the heart of a business package should be the invoice. After all, buying and selling is what business is about. Business accounting packages are usually based around an electronic invoice, but they're more than programs for creating and printing forms. The invoice is actually part of a complex database. Figure 8.14 shows an invoice from Teleware's Mind Your Own Business and how some of the data on it is linked to other areas of the program.

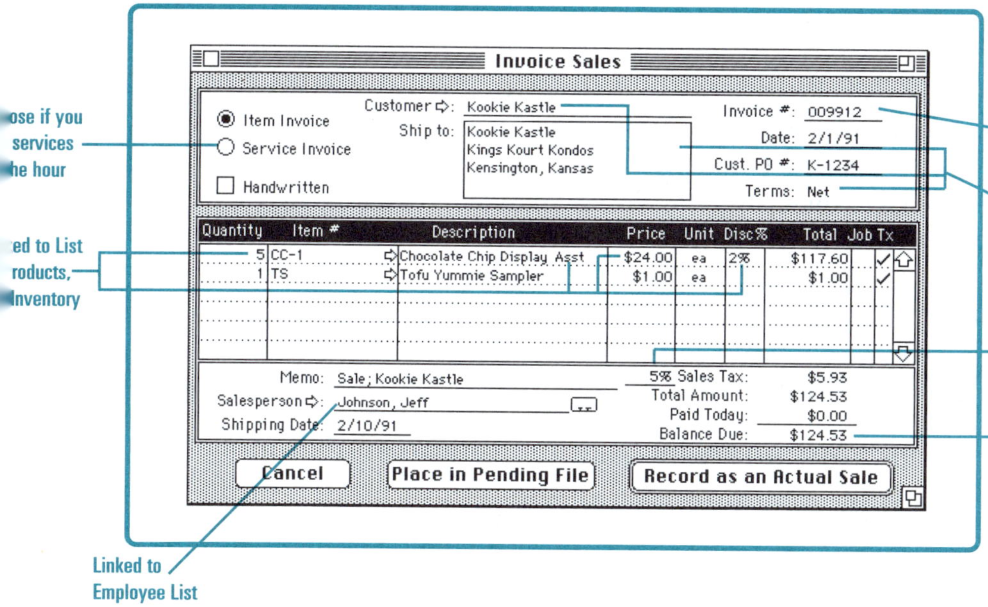

Figure 8.14

An electronic invoice.

These programs assume that your business sells a strictly defined list of products—with predetermined prices—to a strictly defined base of customers. This situation describes most businesses, but not all of them: chocolate chip cookies, or hours of psychiatric evaluation could be considered "products," but soprano recitals and book manuscripts probably couldn't (because the price is negotiable, and not related to the cost of its creation). If you're involved in that kind of business, you'd do better with one of the sophisticated home accounting programs described earlier. Similarly, if your business deals mostly with cash sales and a small list of suppliers—like a corner grocery store—you'd be better off with a dedicated *point of sale* system.

Bookkeeping for People Who Don't Have a Bookkeeper

Teleware's *Mind Your Own Business* seems to be designed for the entrepreneur with no background in accounting and no more than a couple of minutes a day to keep the books current. It lacks some of the features found in full financial programs (for example, you'll have to look up payroll deductions yourself), but makes up for it with a simple point-and-click interface and some handy non-financial features like automated to-do lists. It generates all the reports your accountant will need at tax time and most of the information a bank or creditor would want to approve financing. With a system requirement of only 512K RAM (very small, by today's program standards) it can be left happily in MultiFinder all day long, and referred to whenever the owner needs financial or inventory information. Figure 8.15 shows some of the possible screens in Mind Your Own Business.

BIG Business

Softsync's Accountant, Inc. is geared towards larger companies with many employees and possibly a full- or half-time bookkeeper. It's menu-driven and assumes you know what you're looking for. This program not only prints payroll checks, but also looks up appropriate deductions according to what state you're in, creates state and federal tax reports, and even prints W-2 forms for the employees. (You have to buy new modules for the program every time the tax laws change.) Figure 8.16 shows some of Accountant's reports.

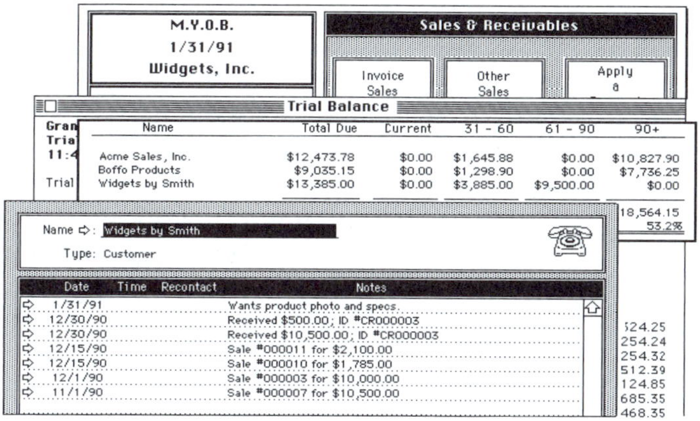

Figure 8.15

Mind Your Own Business.

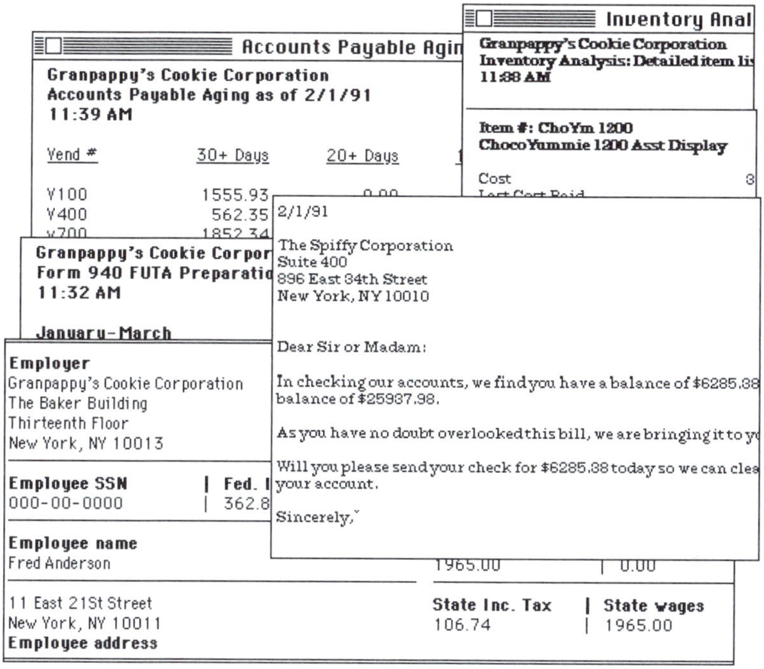

Figure 8.16

Reports in Accountant, Inc.

In This Chapter

Programs that Process Words, Numbers, and Pictures at the Same Time

•

Programs to Organize Ideas and Presentations

•

Tools for Communicating with People and Non-Mac Computers

•

Giving Your Mac a Voice

•

The MacDisney Version

It stands to reason that something as useful as a Mac would inspire many applications that the original designers never imagined. The fact is, there are hundreds of excellent programs that have nothing to do with picture and word processing (as well as some that process both at once). This chapter covers some of the more useful Mac programs that go far beyond MacPaint and MacWrite.

9

Other Programs

To keep things from getting too long, we've imposed a few limitations in this chapter:

- We don't include applications that are primarily collections of data. Business and Bible organizers, and programs that can create your résumé or your Last Will, are certainly useful. But their computing doesn't go much beyond word processing and database concepts.
- We had to leave out the vast library of public domain software. This is a heartbreaker because there are free or low-cost solutions to address just about every possible computer problem.
- We also left out a lot of sophisticated—and expensive—programs for media professionals. For example, there are at least three Macintosh-based sound editing systems available from audio dealers for between $15,000 and $40,000. Chances are your favorite CD was edited on one of them, but these are clearly not software for *the rest of us.*

All-in-One Programs

The Macintosh is loved for its ability to run word processors, paint programs, and spreadsheets or databases simultaneously, merging the results through the clipboard or Publish and Subscribe. Some companies have taken this a step further, selling *integrated programs* that combine multiple functions. Integrated programs usually include "Works" in their name, as in Microsoft Works, ClarisWorks, and (we're not kidding) BeagleWorks. They're usually discounted to around $200. Some packages also offer telecommunications, drafting, and outlining functions.

Working with the Works

All these packages boast of *seamless integration*, where the user has to deal with only one set of commands and can distribute data easily. This is a big deal for MS-DOS users but nothing special on the Mac. (Macintosh programs are already integrated by the clipboard and consistent user interface.) The real advantages of Mac Works programs are their low cost, ease of use, and small memory requirements. Instead of running three or more programs at once, you open just one program with switchable tools. Figure 9.1 shows how it all works together.

Most integrated programs are *frame-based*. You start a basic document in one function and draw little boxes on it to open other functions. For example, the memo in Figure 9.1 started as a word processor document. Where the writer needed a self-calculating chart, he added a spreadsheet frame. (The graphics object was drawn right on the page.) A few integrated programs don't use frames; instead, they have separate windows for each function. To integrate data, you cut and paste—just as you would with separate applications.

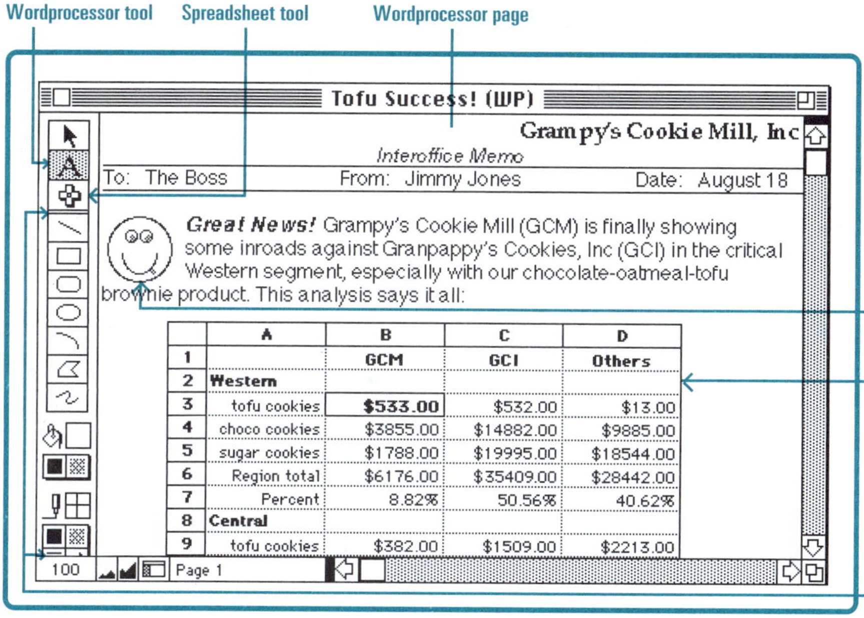

Figure 9.1

How ClarisWorks Works.

If It Works, You Still Might Want to Fix It

Works programs are definitely *not* for power-users. Almost as a rule, their separate functions are less sophisticated than the stand-alone programs they replace. For example, features that are standard in word processors—such as stylesheets or word counting—don't appear in integrated packages costing twice as much. Even packages that share a common heritage with the bigger stand-alones can be disappointing. Microsoft Word is much more versatile than the text tools in Microsoft Works. And Claris MacDraw Pro puts the graphics in ClarisWorks to shame. If you're serious about writing, designing, or number and data crunching, you'll probably throw the Works out.

On the other hand, these programs are ideal for simple or memory-restricted applications. Most fit comfortably into a 2M PowerBook or Classic, even with System 7. They give you most of the tools to prepare basic business documents. If you want to dress things up, you can export the text and graphics to more powerful programs.

Check carefully before you buy a Works program. Even some of the newest ones don't *actively link* data—if you change numbers in a spreadsheet, you have to manually update any graphs that reflect these numbers. You'll get better integration from stand-alone programs using System 7's Publish and Subscribe. Also, some Works limit your import or export options. If you're planning to start a document in WaterWorks and then move it to WordMasher, make sure the Works will do an appropriate translation.

CAUTION: Don't confuse integrated programs with *bundled* ones, like Microsoft Office or T/Maker Power Bundle. Publishers sometimes package stand-alone word processors, graphics programs, and spreadsheets in the same shrink-wrap box for a single discounted price. This can be a cost-effective way to get software, if you already like the programs on their own merits.

Idea Processors

You may call them outliners, chart makers, or desktop presentation packages, but what these programs really do is help you organize and present ideas. You can create anything from a quickie one-page action list to a full-blown color presentation complete with slides or overhead transparencies, speaker's notes, and audience handouts. You can even put your Mac into *slide show mode* and let it cycle through a presentation complete with Hollywood-style special effects.

The three idea processors you're most likely to encounter are Aldus Persuasion, Microsoft PowerPoint, and Symantec's MORE. All have essentially the same capabilities. (Taking full advantage of any of these programs requires a color monitor, but you can certainly perform the basic outlining and charting in black and white.) We created the next four illustrations using the program MORE.

Outlining

The basic tool of an idea processor is an outline similar to the ones you did in grade school before starting a research paper. In an outlining program, you can add ideas, or insert new topics, right in the middle of the path you've already begun. If a sub-topic (or a sub-sub-sub-topic) seems to be more important than you originally thought, it's easy to shift it to the correct place in the hierarchy. Everything else will fall in line behind it. Figure 9.2 shows the nitty-gritty part of the process of putting ideas into words.

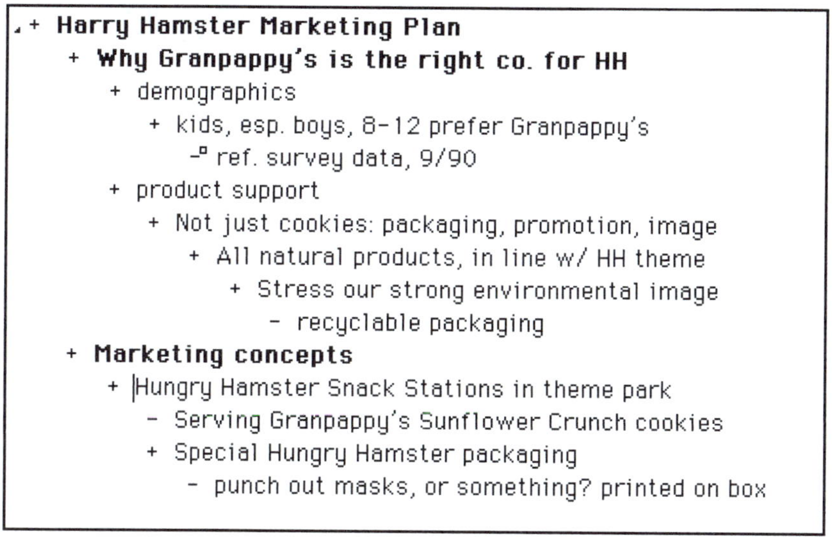

Figure 9.2

Organizing ideas in MORE.

Once you complete the outline, you can convert it into bullet charts or other graphic forms and turn them into overhead transparencies, pages for a presentation booklet, or even 35mm color slides. Or you can import your outline into a word processor as a basis for more complete prose. Figure 9.3 shows a piece of an outline transferred into a bullet chart and embellished with custom art. You can experiment with different layouts, clip art, and prebuilt templates.

FYI Idea

You can create slides or color overheads by sending the artwork to a service center for processing. Most accept Macintosh files directly on disk or via modem and will return your finished presentation overnight. For even faster service, get a GCC Technologies ColorFast printer for about $6,000. It makes color slides on special instant-processing Polaroid film.

Figure 9.3

A bullet chart doesn't have to have bullets.

Many of these programs have graph-making capabilities. You can enter or import data into a *worksheet*, a simple spreadsheet format. Then you can experiment with various graph formats and graphic styles. The result can be printed, output as a slide or transparency, or imported into a graphics program for even more fine-tuning. Figure 9.4 shows a sample chart created with MORE. Or you can link charts to wipe across the Mac screen automatically, drop into place, or do any of a few dozen different tricks as a *slideshow*. Figure 9.5 shows some ways to program the changes. You can build layers of frames, so you get the effect of single lines of text, art images, or pieces of chart suddenly animating themselves onto the screen.

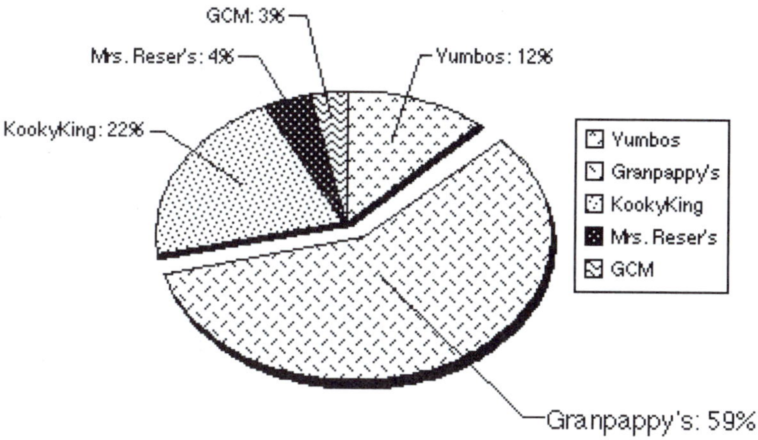

Figure 9.4
Data becomes an easy-to-read pie chart.

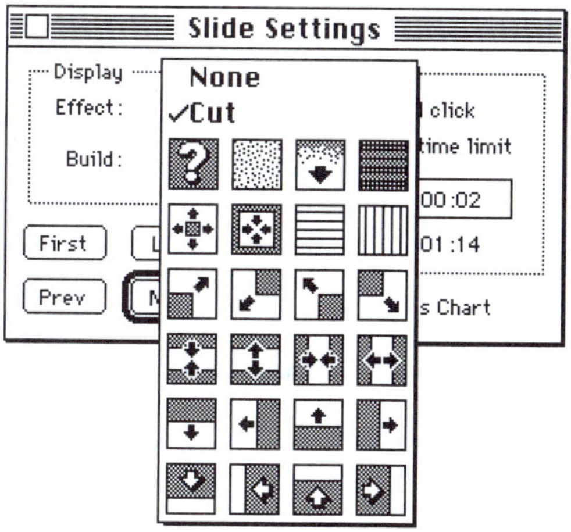

Figure 9.5
Cecil B. DeMille, move over!

You can also use the basic outlining program to create easy-to-read organizational charts. Just because it's an outliner, there's no reason to limit yourself to outlining. You can create virtually any kind of chart or graph you are likely to need. Use these programs to create and maintain time lines, phone lists, calendars, price lists, and dozens of things we haven't imagined.

Computer Helpers

Just as there are applications that help you organize your thoughts and communicate with others, there are programs that enable your Mac to do much of the same thing. Some of these "helpers" let you keep track of files or take an instant picture of whatever's on your screen. Others let your Mac send data to another Mac's screen, so you and the other user can work on the same file at the same time. You can even transfer a file to a non-Macintosh computer.

No Hands Hardware Sharing

Chapter 13 describes some of your options when connecting multiple Macs together to share files and software. One low-cost program also lets multiple Macs share keyboard, mouse, and screens: Farallon's Timbuktu/Remote. This is a handy way to show data to another user in your office or borrow somebody else's expert technique with some particularly obscure form of data-crunching. Instead of having them reach over your desk, you can call and have them manipulate your computer by remote control. You still have control but so does the distant user. A more expensive version, Timbuktu/Remote Access Pack, includes a modem and wake-up cable. You can call a distant Mac, work its keyboard and mouse from your local computer, and then turn it off again. Just the thing if you're constantly forgetting to bring files home to work on at night.

Take a Shot

Apple's ⇧Shift-⌘-3 utility for capturing screens doesn't work under all applications and wastes time and disk space if you're interested in only a portion of the screen. Two low-cost INITs do a better job: Wildflower's SnapJot and Preferred's Screenshot. These programs let you save a full screen, or just a portion of it, to either a file readable by a paint program or the clipboard. You can even capture color Mac displays for black-and-white Macs. We made all of the screen illustrations for this book with SnapJot.

Solutions' SuperGlue is a Chooser resource that lets you save files as graphic images. It retains formatting and special effects that would be otherwise lost in text files. You can then open the files in other programs and keep the effects intact. For example, headlines can be shaded and kerned in PageMaker and then imported in all their graphic glory to simpler word processors like WriteNow.

Barnyard Disk: Needle Folder: Haystack File

If you use—and lose—a lot of files, you'll probably get frustrated with Apple's standard Open... routine and Find File DA. Numerous utilities have evolved to supplant and replace them, including Now Software's Super Boomerang and NowMenus, On Technology's OnLocation, and Symantec's Fast Find. Most of these utilities add Finder-like capabilities to the standard Open... and Save... dialog boxes, showing creation date, size, and a file's Get Info... box. Some keep track of recently opened files, replace Find File with a much faster-finding DA, and let you open or read files from within the DA.

> **TIP:** Microsoft Word includes an elegant "find" function that can search all the files on a disk for specific text. The utility will even open non-text files (including some graphics and spreadsheets), and import them to text pages.

Mac to DOS and Back

It's a fact of the world that some users run IBM PCs or their clones, and occasionally you have to share files with them. Newer Macs can format high-density disks like those on newer PCs, but the files aren't compatible. DataViz's MacLink Plus bridges the gap with cables and software to move files happily from Mac to PC and back. The software/hardware package also includes translators to preserve the formatting of files from over 150 different Mac and PC programs. These translators are also available without the hardware for network use. Newer Macs with high density drives can (with software like Apple File Exchange) directly mount 3 ½-inch DOS disks.

Sound Processors

It may be hard to believe if you keep your eyes glued to a Macintosh, but most people also use their *ears*. Fortunately, the Macintosh is also a capable sound computer. Every Mac can play digital audio through a built-in speaker, and some newer Macs can play back in stereo and record as well.

Apple's Built-In Sound Support

Beep, boing, or clink. That's the total of Apple's built-in sound support. You can choose different alert sounds from the control panel. Newer Macs let you record your own voice to replace an alert sound. Some programs add to the standard boings with digitized telephone dialing tones, or music and sound effects. A system utility, MacinTalk, contains digital samples of English-language *phonemes* (the basic building blocks of speech) and some speech synthesis rules. Many games, HyperCard stacks, and utilities for the vision-impaired use MacinTalk for their voice.

A Sample Solution

MacroMind's $250 MacRecorder has become the standard for adding sound to the Mac. MacRecorder itself is a cigarette-pack-sized gadget that plugs into the modem port and *samples* sound, converting it from analog format into a digital format the Mac can use. It has a built-in microphone and a jack for an external signal, and its software does a better job than the current II and LC digitizing routines.

The bundled software, SoundEdit Pro, has become the standard for manipulating sound files. SoundEdit lets you do most of the tricks available in professional recording studios, and some are available on only the newest digital audio workstations. You can select and play sections of sound as small as a few thousandths of a second, copy and paste them with standard Mac techniques, and modify the sounds with surprisingly sophisticated control. You can also analyze sounds and export spectral data to other programs for scientific studies. Figure 9.6 shows SoundEdit's Effects menu and part of a three-track sound file. SoundEdit Pro software is available separately, without the MacRecorder hardware, for about fifty dollars less.

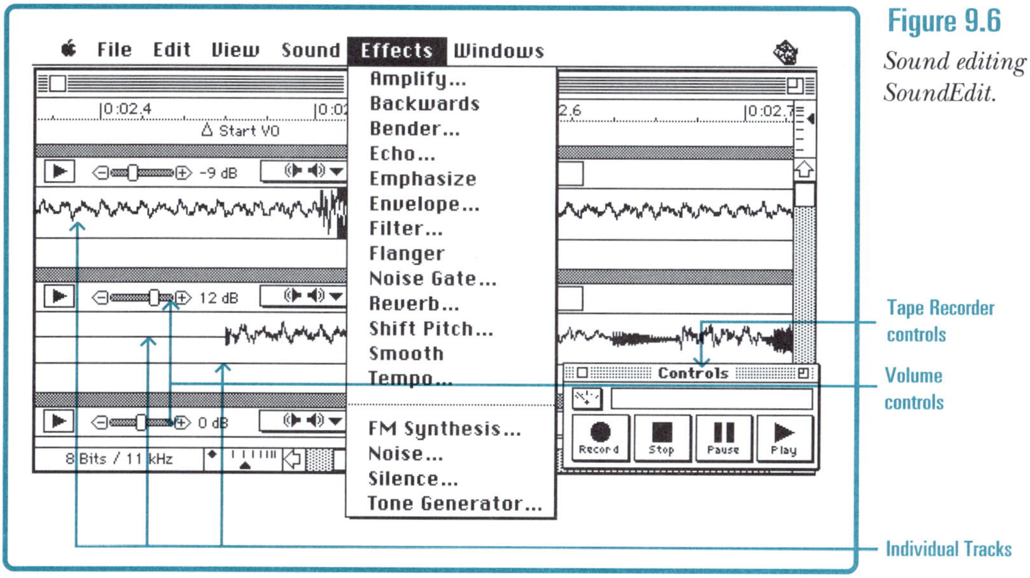

Figure 9.6
Sound editing in SoundEdit.

The only difference between MacRecorder and systems costing thousands more is speed and quality. But it's a significant difference: without expensive accessories, the Macintosh can't sound much better than an AM radio. Processing more than a few seconds of sound is time consuming (the high-priced systems speed things up with *Digital Signal Processing* cards). It's also disk-consuming. Even MacRecorder's limited format requires as much as 1.3M of disk space for each minute of sound.

> Even with the Mac's technical limitations, MacRecorder and SoundEdit are powerful. One of us has edited sound effects for a nationally known hamburger chain (whose name is curiously similar to our computer's) with this package.

The Mac Knows How to Score

Mac's sound quality limitations usually don't matter when making music, because musical synthesizers create the sound (the Mac just provides the control). The Mac's intuitive interface and ease of use have made it the machine of choice among professional composers. *Sequencers* work like word processors for notes. They let you enter an original music track (via mouse or synth keyboard) and then edit every musical aspect of each note. Mac sequencers are available at music stores with software starting around $100. Some of the effects in a professional sequencing program are shown in Figure 9.7.

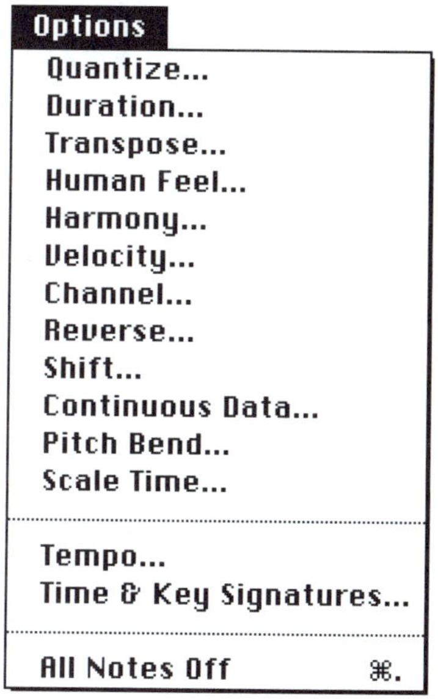

Figure 9.7

Musical options in Dr. T's Beyond software.

Musical Instrument Digital Interface (MIDI)

The key to making all this possible is a Local Area Network standard called MIDI: the Musical Instrument Digital Interface. MIDI is similar to AppleTalk, it sends data serially and you can configure devices in a daisy chain. Messages on the network tell various instruments when to play specific notes, how loudly, and whether to add special effects. MIDI does *not* carry the sound itself (except under unusual, non-real-time conditions).

Every current synthesizer and most studio sound effects have MIDI jacks. The Mac does not, but because MIDI is so similar to AppleTalk, low-cost adapters can convert the printer or modem port. The MIDI information is controlled by *MIDI Manager*, an Apple utility that lives in your System folder. A desk accessory, PatchBay, routes signals between sequencing, music-improvisation, and sound control programs running at the same time.

Mac Goes to the Movies

Well, maybe we're exaggerating a little bit here. You're not going to be able to create *Rocky XXIII* with a basic Mac program, or even *Rocky and Bullwinkle.* What you can do, with the help of the animation and multimedia presentation programs, is sequence and control objects on the screen so they appear to move. Mac animations are excellent presentation tools for engineering and finance, to explain prototypes of new products, to walk through proposed buildings, and for fun, of course.

Classical animation the Disney way required a massive stationary camera and thousands of individual pictures called *cels* (because they were painted on cellulose acetate). Animators stacked cels over a background, exposed a single frame of film, and moved or changed individual cels for the next frame: at best, a tedious and expensive process.

What's New, Doc?

Although some animation is still done this way, the winds of change are blowing. Macintosh animation is coming of age. A recent cereal commercial featured a three-dimensional cartoon character racing across the TV screen with a mob of live kids in hot pursuit. The character, one of Nintendo's Mario Brothers, was created on a Mac. The program added shading and simulated light sources, and created *in-betweening* frames for tiny increments of movement. It would have been a weeks' work for an animator, but it took the Mac less than a minute. Figure 9.8 shows pieces that can be animated to form a dancing doodad.

MacroMind Director can create slide shows for desktop presentation, as well as animated sequences for television. You can even make user-interactive animation sequences that respond to mouse-clicks or on-screen buttons. For example, you might create a forest scene with two paths and an animated bunny who doesn't know which path to take until the viewer clicks the "go left" or "go right" button. (The trees and flowers can respond, too. Director can handle up to 24 independently animated elements on the screen at any one time.)

Figure 9.8

The whole is the sum of its parts.

Hollywood Dreams on Brooklyn Budgets

Professional art and animation programs can set you back more than a thousand dollars. But simple moving objects can be animated in the free HyperCard program (you'll need some HyperTalk expertise, however). For more sophisticated cel-like effects, consider Motion Works' ADDmotion II, which adds animation and sound to HyperCard for about $100, and its big brother PROmotion, which can create stand-alone animation files and export to other animation programs. PROmotion, bundled with a CD ROM of over 100 animated characters and sounds, costs $250. Both programs use a similar interface.

Characters for these programs are created in a MacPaint-like environment, as groups of cycling cels. An automatic tracing paper option lets you see incremental changes from one cel to the next. Limited in-betweening is provided. Once a character has been saved, you can place it on a background and move it along a *path*, have it interact with background *props*, and give it sound. Figure 9.9 shows a sample animation being programmed. The pooch will move along the dotted path, while its legs cycle through six positions to simulate walking. The two palettes control points along the path, and tell the character to get smaller as it walks away from us. Once the animation is polished, the dotted line disappears and the whole thing can be laid over a drawing of a backyard.

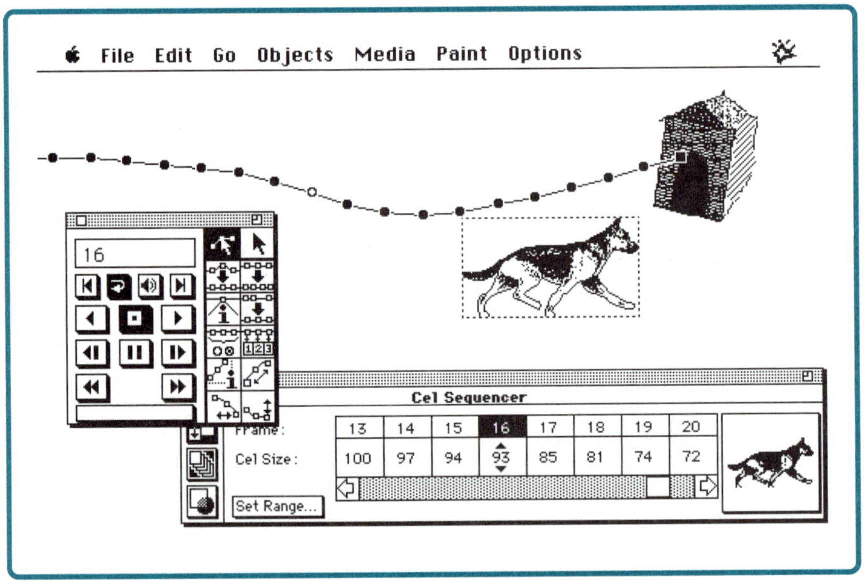

Figure 9.9

Animation being programmed.

PROmotion and ADDmotion files are exportable to QuickTime, a Mac system utility that coordinates animation, real-time video, and image compression to save memory. QuickTime Movies—short, slightly jerky video-and-sound sequences—can even be attached to properly equipped word processors or databases. QuickTime has been called as important a breakthrough for the Mac as the original Scrapbook, which let users save and import still images and text. Unfortunately, very few non-animation programs support QuickTime at this writing.

In This Chapter

Publishing Your Information

•

Making the Best Impression

•

High Quality Printing

In those not-so-good-old days before the Mac, creating a good-looking printed page required long strips of type set on paper, T squares, a sharp knife, and a pot of glue. It took hours to get everything stuck down neatly, and changes took even more hours.

This process is called *paste-up* and now you can do it painlessly with your mouse. This chapter will show you how to create beautiful flyers, newsletters, and ads with Macintosh paste-up programs.

10

Publishing with the Mac

Why do you need a special program to make beautiful pages? You may argue that you can do the same things with your regular word processor. It's true that programs such as Word, WriteNow, and MacWrite do enable you to insert graphics, change typefaces and point sizes in midstream, and even type in a multi-column format. You can create a good-looking presentation with a word processor (if you're willing to spend a lot of time on it, and settle for the standard stuff).

However, with Desktop Publishing, or DTP programs, you can create pages that really attract attention. Run type around a picture? Sure. Set a headline sideways? Why not? Add a photograph? Certainly. With a DTP program such as PageMaker, QuarkXPress, or Publish-It Easy there's literally no limit to the effects you can create except the bounds of your own imagination.

With DTP, you're not limited to creating newsletters and reports, either. You can create all kinds of interesting and useful items in a DTP format (see Figure 10.1). Custom forms are a breeze to lay out. Some programs include predrawn forms which you can customize to suit your needs.

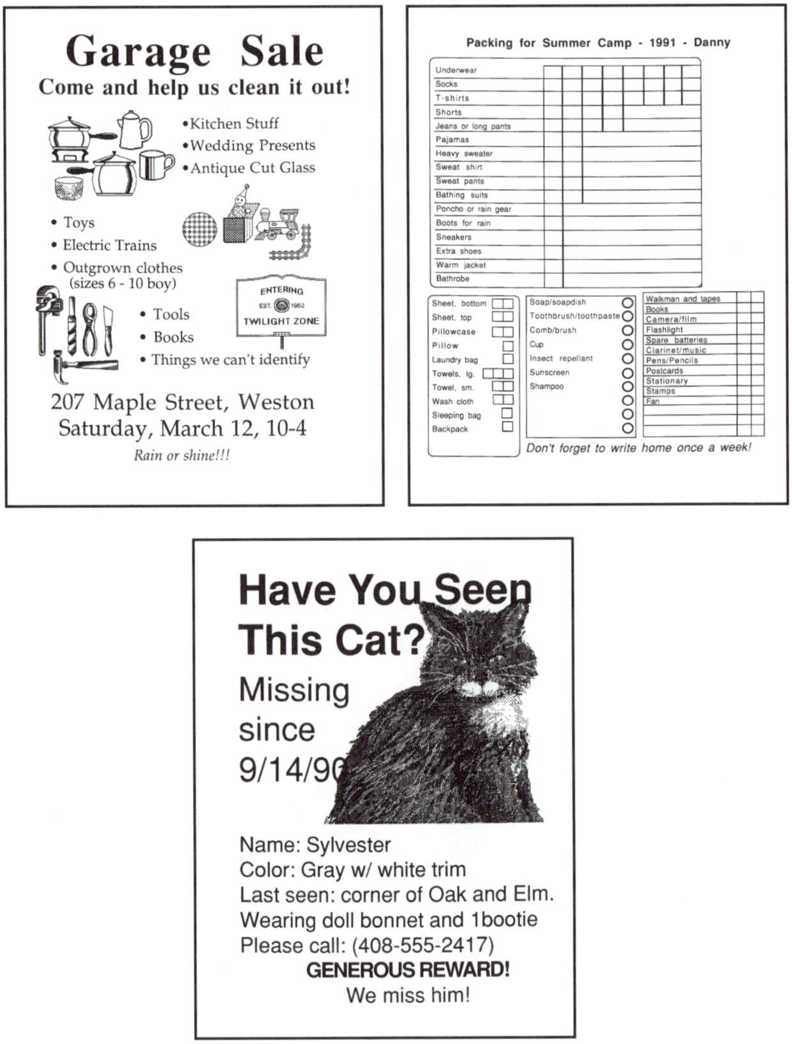

Figure 10.1

Other kinds of publications created with DTP.

What makes desktop publishing different from ordinary word processing? DTP programs integrate text and graphics in a different way than word processors do. *Graphics* can be loosely defined as nontext elements and may include drawings, scanned photos, logos, charts, and captured screens. Ordinary word processing programs treat imported graphics as ordinary characters. (Even if you're reading this book in the USA, it doesn't have domestic graphics. They were all *imported* into the text from separate graphics files.) Desktop publishing programs reverse the process and treat text as a graphic element to give you more design flexibility.

Drawing Board on Your Desktop

In many ways, using DTP is like pasting-up the old-fashioned way. You start by defining the borders for the piece. Instead of drawing the borders on the paper with a light blue (cannot be reproduced) pencil, in DTP you drag rulers down to mark the margins. (On a color Mac, margin rules even appear in light blue!) An old-fashioned paste-up artist would have had all the necessary type set in galleys, long strips of paper with text set in columns of type. Of course, he or she would have chosen type styles and sizes ahead of time, as well as *column width, leading, justification,* and *tracking.* The DTP artist simply copies the words from a word processing file (as shown in Figure 10.2), or types them directly into the DTP document. Either way, each block of text is a separate item, which can be resized and reshaped as needed to make the best use of the space.

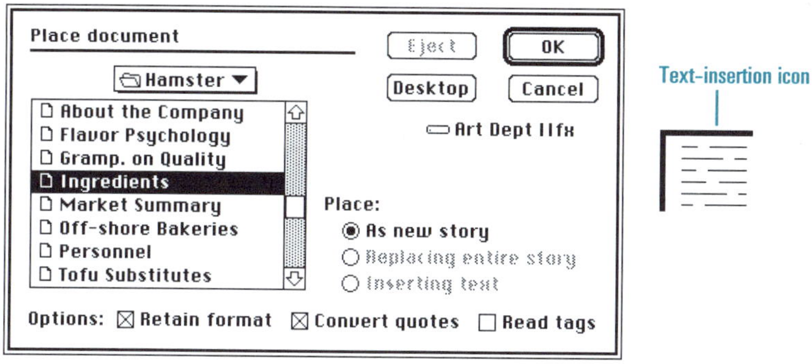

Figure 10.2

In PageMaker, selecting Place document gives you an icon which represents the upper left corner of your text block.

When we talk about a *block of text,* we mean a single "chunk" of words. It may be one line, one paragraph, one column, or an entire newsletter article. You work with text character by character, but you handle text blocks like graphics, as movable objects on the page. Edit text blocks with the I-beam pointer (text tool), but move them with the arrow pointer.

Art for Paste-Up's Sake

Putting a picture, even a photograph, into a DTP page is easy. You create one in a paint or draw program, find appropriate clip art, or scan a logo, photograph, or drawing from some other medium onto a disk. Then you find it with the Place...or Import Graphic...command in the DTP program's file menu. The picture—or a small icon representing it—appears next to your page. Then, you move it onto the page, and crop as desired. Simple. If you want to resize the graphic, you drag a corner of the picture box until it looks right. You don't need to call the photostat place to change your order. Figure 10.3 shows a picture appearing, and then moved into place and resized, in Publish-It Easy.

Figure 10.3

Placing or importing a picture.

Scanners

Scanners sound like something out of science fiction, but they're really quite simple. Not. A *scanner* is a hardware device which converts an image into a series of digital signals, which the computer reads as *pixels*. Pixels, by the way, is short for *picture elements*, those little dots that make up the image. Scanning, or *digitizing*, converts an image into ones and zeros, representing the color or grayness of individual pixels, and translating this representation to an image on the computer screen. Once the picture has been scanned, you can manipulate it, stretch it, shrink it, clean up the rough edges, and paste it into your DTP document.

There are various kinds of scanners, and the quality varies according to the price. If you have occasional need of a high-quality scanned image, it may be most cost-effective to find a local *service bureau* (we discuss them completely at the end of this chapter), with a *flatbed scanner*. Flatbed scanners look like copying machines and work in a somewhat similar manner. You place the image on a sheet of glass, and the scanner moves a bright light across the document as photosensors capture the changes in dark and light from one bit to the next. The more bits per pixel, the more accurately the scanner can reproduce grays. A very high-quality scanner, like the Microtek MSF-300ZS, can recognize up to 256 shades of gray, while a less expensive model may see only 16 shades (or none at all, if it's a monochrome scanner). Figure 10.4 shows an enlarged example of a scanned photograph with 16 shades of gray.

Another type of scanner, Thunderscan, uses the ImageWriter or ImageWriter II as a document carrier and replaces the printhead, temporarily, with the scanning device. Your original art or photo rolls through the printer while the scanning head "reads" it and sends the image to the Mac. The maker claims that the current model can scan up to 64 levels of gray, bringing reasonable quality at relatively little cost to all users with ImageWriter printers. However, you only can use a picture that will roll through the scanner. Unmounted photographs work well. A painting on canvas won't.

Figure 10.4

A photo of the authors' son converted to 16 shades of gray; enlarged to show detail.

If you need to scan only small images, or have the patience to reconstruct larger pictures from several passes, a hand-held scanner may be just right. Hand-held scanners look something like an oversized electric razor. You roll the scanner over the material you want to copy, and it sends the data to the Mac. With 400 dpi capacity, the LightningScan looks like a good investment for occasional scanning.

> **TIP:** For a better quality image with Thunderscan, you can scan the image at 400% its size. Because Thunderscan normally scans at 72 *dpi* (dots per inch), scanning at 400% gives you an image that's four times better (288 dpi), which you then reduce back to normal by printing it at 25% on your ImageWriter. Scanning a full page at 400% takes as much as an hour, though, so be prepared to wait.

Color scanners translate a color photo into an image you can view on a Mac II, but color scanners are extremely expensive and require a great deal of memory (at least 4 to 5 megabytes of RAM to handle a single large picture). Some color scanner systems convert 35 mm slides into screen images, or make four-color separations for printing.

At approximately $8,000–$10,000, color scanners are out of the range of the average Mac owner. Some magazine publishers use color scanners, and a service bureau in your area may have one.

Another type of scanner uses a video camera as an input device. You simply focus your home camcorder on whatever you want to scan: art, photos, or a three-dimensional object. (You could, theoretically, scan a person, but most people can't hold still for the 30 seconds it takes.) Then take a snapshot of the image, using a hardware connector such as MacVision or Computer Eyes, or a videoboard in a Mac II. You can open the file and retouch the image, change the contrast, crop, and so on, before pasting the image into your DTP document.

> **TIP:** You can create a sense of depth when digitizing an object by placing it at a slight angle to the camera. Using an angled spotlight will also help give better shading.

There's also a snapshot approach to getting images. For about $650, Logitech's FotoMan system includes a fixed-focus, point-and-click electronic camera with a built-in flash and enough memory for 32 pictures, and the necessary cables and software to transfer its pictures into your Mac. It's more expensive than an old-fashioned Kodak and a hand scanner, but it's a lot faster and doesn't use any chemicals. Cannon and Sony also make electronic still cameras, available from large photo dealers, that connect to video input boards.

Image Libraries

Suppose you need something to brighten up your document, but you can't draw, and don't have a camera. Now, suppose you could go to a file with hundreds of pictures of all kinds of things and simply cut or copy the images you need.

You can do this on the Mac. There are thousands of images available from various publishers, including several series on CD-ROM, as well as disks. Figure 10.5 shows some examples of clip art taken from Dubl-Click's Wetpaint series. Unlike paper clip art, you can modify these computerized pictures in any way you like using a paint or darkroom program. In fact, modifying them is highly recommended, especially if you want to borrow a piece of artwork to use as your logo. You wouldn't want to see your favorite piece of clip art on your competitor's letterhead.

Figure 10.5
Three clipped elements, combined in SuperPaint.

TIP: Be sure to read the licensing agreement that comes with any clip art package you buy. Know what you can and can't do before you do it.

Nobody's Perfect . . .

Old-fashioned, non-electronic photographers often retouch their pictures. With a few puffs of an airbrush, they can remove tiny flaws like double chins in a portrait or telephone wires in a landscape.

Programs such as Aldus' Digital Darkroom and Adobe Photoshop let you do the same tricks on your Mac. You can combine images, sharpen or blur selected parts, or even draw in new details. These programs work with *bit-mapped gray scales,* setting each pixel to one of 4, 16, or 256 different shades (depending how you've set the Control Panel).

With the control provided by darkroom tools (see Figure 10.6), you can lighten parts of an image and darken other parts much more precisely than by photo *dodging* and *burning.* If there's something distracting in the background, you can remove it. Was Cousin Leroy making faces at the camera? Mask him out. (Just copy gray tones from elsewhere in the picture and fill in the holes.) You can rotate, distort, flip, stretch, or scale any image. If your picture of the Washington Monument makes it lean like the Tower of Pisa, give it a nudge so it's straight again. You can selectively sharpen or blur an area or a whole image. You can invert blacks and whites to turn a positive image into a negative image. You can make photos into line drawings by tracing edges.

Figure 10.6
Darkroom programs can improve your 'photography'.

Your darkroom tool kit includes a brush and an airbrush tool for touch-ups, as well as cutting and pasting tools. Using these is like using them in an ordinary paint program, except that they're handling screened images and can pick up tones. Of course, on a Mac II, you can do these tricks in color. You can also do tricks *with* color. Adobe claims Photoshop lets you "make any of more than 16 million colors pop." (And presumably snap and crackle, too.) Of course, even the best color monitor can't show you all 16 million colors, and your printer can't reproduce more than a couple of hundred, but you *can* do all sorts of wizardry with the colors you have.

Darkroom programs are somewhat tricky to master, but if you have the patience to work through their tutorials, you'll learn how to do some very neat things with your images. They're also slow on any but the fastest Mac IIs or Quadras because of the quantity of data they have to handle. It helps, of course, if you have some experience with "real" photography, so you'll know which tools to use to get the effects you want. It also helps to use a large monitor so you can see what you're doing.

Designing to Get Attention

We could probably devote a whole book to explaining the fundamentals of design, with lots of explanations why some things work and others don't. Because there isn't room for all that here, we'll try to give you a minicourse in the basics of the basics.

Balancing the Page

First, there is *balance*—the notion of keeping the different areas or elements of the page in a harmonious relation with each other. This is not to say that things must be symmetrical, as shown in the examples in Figure 10.7. *Symmetry*, when every element has a sort of mirror image of itself, is boring.

Figure 10.7
Which is more interesting?

You can break up a heavy, gray block of type with illustrations or *pull quotes* (see Granpappy's comment in Figure 10.8 for an example). You also can change the space between lines to make the block of text easier to read. You can achieve balance, as Figure 10.9 shows, by setting a graphic element down at the lower right to offset a bold logo at the upper left.

Figure 10.8
Keep a sense of balance and proportion. Notice the pull-quote in the right column.

Figure 10.9
White space makes the page more appealing.

Proportion

The second design element to consider is proportion. Proportion helps you show the reader the relationships between various pieces of your design. You need to accompany a huge, screaming headline with bold subheads and reasonably large text. Otherwise, the page looks unbalanced.

To keep a sense of proportion and give the reader something to focus on, organize your page around one dominant element, whether it's a headline or a piece of art. A single, large headline will help focus the reader's attention. Several subheads, with nothing dominant, tend to look confusing.

Leading the Eye

You can use subheads to break up long stretches of plain text, but there should be something to lead you from one subhead to the next. Lead the reader's eye through the page by creating a sense of direction. We read English from top to bottom and left to right. Therefore, you want to move the reader's eye in those directions. Give the reader a reason to start at the top left and work down. Headlines at the top of the page draw the eye to the text's logical starting place. Starting from there makes reading the rest of the information easier.

White Space

White space is more than just blank paper. It's an important design element which adds emphasis and contrast. White space can balance out a page with lots of text. Visually, it contrasts with the overall gray tone of closely set type and helps eye leading. White space around a graphic makes it stand out and seem more important.

Sometimes, you may need to shorten the text to improve the design of the page. Don't be afraid to trim your own copy. Remember that the ultimate goal of your published piece is communication, and anything which doesn't get read doesn't communicate.

TIP: Design facing pages together. Most DTP programs give you this option. What works on a single page might not work if the adjoining page fights it. Don't forget to leave *gutters,* the white space in the middle of a two-page spread for the binding.

Typographic Tactics

One of the things which immediately separates the amateurs from the pros in DTP is the way type is used. (Remember Figure 5.6, which looked like a ransom note?) Because there are so many *fonts*—or type styles—available (see Figure 10.10), it's very tempting to take advantage of the variety. Mixing more than two or three type styles on a page is seldom, if ever, effective. If you use a specialized typeface, use it only for special effects.

Figure 10.10

The typeface you choose should depend on what you're selling.

Some of the typefaces in Figure 10.10 have *serifs*. Others don't. (Serifs are those little lines that stick out at the end of a letter, originally designed to even out the stonecutter's art when typesetting was done with a hammer and chisel.) Some designers believe that serifs make a page of text easier to read, because they guide the eye along each line. Others prefer *san serif* or *gothic* typefaces—ones without the little marks—for a more casual feeling. You can mix both styles in a document, but it's a good idea to set them in different sizes or in different areas on the page.

> **TIP:** Avoid using Macintosh shadow or outline versions of any typeface. Even though they're on the Style menu of every application, they aren't attractive or even readable for most purposes. As a rule, forget these options exist!

Size and Style

Make sure the type options you choose are readable in your text, not just in the program's dialog boxes. Some don't look good in smaller sizes, and a few don't enlarge well. One of the many advantages of DTP is that you have the freedom to experiment. If something doesn't look right, you can always change it or undo it. In general, your most important words need to be in the biggest type. Your headlines might be 24-point Helvetica, with the subhead 18-point Helvetica Condensed, and the text in 12-point Palatino (as shown in Figure 10.11).

This is 24-pt. Helvetica Bold

The subhead is set in18-pt. Helvetica Condensed

And here's a column of text in Palatino. Even though Palatino is a serif font, it relates nicely to a Gothic (sans serif) font such as Helvetica.

Figure 10.11
Some of the many possibilities in type.

Some DTP programs let you extend or condense type by putting more or less space between letters. There are also extended and condensed versions of many typefaces. You can find *bold* and *demi-bold* (medium weight) versions of some fonts, and the Mac also lets you select bold or italic type as an option in your DTP, graphics, or word processing program.

TIP: Remember that type sizes are measured in points, with 72 points to the inch. Type widths are measured in *ems.* An em is the same width as the type's point size. For example, a 12-point em is 12 points wide. *Em* comes from the width of the letter *M,* the widest character in a font.

Kerning

If every letter in the alphabet were a perfect rectangle, we wouldn't need to do this. But because letters are odd shapes, some combinations need to be moved closer together than others to look good. *Kerning* is the process of adjusting space between letters, so they fit better. DTP and a few word processing programs can automatically kern combinations like *Ta, To, Tr, WA, Ya, yo,* and others. Automatically kerned combinations may still not look right in certain point sizes. Most DTP programs also let you add precise amounts of kerning, for special effects or to balance the masses of different letters. Figure 10.12 shows differing kerning on the letters W, A, and Y.

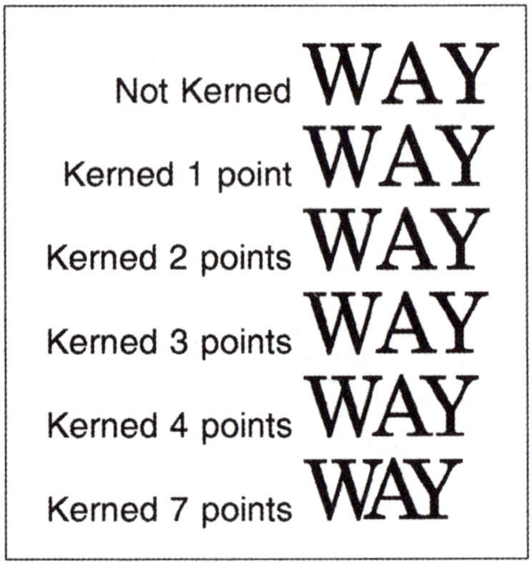

Figure 10.12

WAY, cool. Different amounts of negative kerning.

The various DTP programs have different ways of adjusting kerning. In Publish-It Easy, you set a number of points to kern between letters. Each negative point brings the letters tighter together, as shown in the figure; positive points spread the letters out. In PageMaker, you place the I-beam between the two letters and press ⌘-Delete to tighten or ⌘-⇧Shift-Delete to loosen. *Track kerning* or *tracking* means adjusting the kerning uniformly through a block of text.

Leading

Leading (rhymes with "bedding," not "bleeding") is the amount of space between lines of text. On an old-fashioned typewriter, you had two choices, single-spaced or double-spaced lines. The Mac offers almost infinite options for leading. You can adjust leading by as little as a tenth of a point. The goal is to make the text easier to read, by giving it enough space between lines not to appear crowded, but not so much space that the eye doesn't link the end of one line to the beginning of the next. Leading also affects the "grayness" of the page. A smaller font, leaded generously, might be easier to read than a larger font with the lines squashed together.

Normally, you should specify leading at least 20% of the font size. Depending on the program, this means selecting either 12-point spacing or 2-point leading for 10-point type, and so on.

> Most DTP programs let you specify *negative leading* to bring the lines closer together than normal. Negative leading means spacing lines less than a full character height apart, such as 10-point spacing for 12-point type. Parts of the letters may be clipped off on the screen. But they'll print properly on a PostScript printer.

Justification

You can set type with several kinds of justification. What the term *justified* generally means is that the type touches the margins on both sides of the column. *Flush left* indicates that the type is flush with the left-hand margin. *Flush right* aligns type to the right margin. *Centered* type floats evenly between the margins.

Hyphenation

Some DTP programs will place hyphens for you, according to electronic dictionaries. For example, PageMaker gives you a choice of automatic or manual hyphenation. You can insert a hyphenation break where you want one or choose among options. If your program hyphenates automatically and you want to add another hyphen, press the Option and hyphen (-) together to avoid confusing the computer.

More Professional Publications

The more you do, the better you'll get. You can also train your sense of design by looking at what others have done. Study ads to see how the designer uses type. Look at other people's newsletters, to see how text passages are broken up. If you see things you like, figure out why they work, so you can apply the knowledge to your own projects. The following tricks can help you add professionalism to the documents you publish:

- Use quote marks instead of prime marks (straight quotes). Select the SmartQuotes option (if your word processor has one) when you first type the document, or use the correct keystrokes, as follows:
  - Press Option-] for ‘
  - Press Option-Shift-] for ’
  - Press Option-[for “
  - Press Option-Shift-[for ”

- Press the Space bar only once after a period, not twice. (If it's an unbreakable habit, just do it and then select Change.... Type two spaces in the Find box, and one space in the Change To box. Then, select Change All.)
- When you're dashing off a quick phrase—use the right dash! The hyphen is not a dash. You can get an em-width dash (—), the one you mean when you type —, by pressing Shift–Option–- (—). An en-width dash (–) is available when you type Option–-. Use an en-dash between numbers (as in 10–20).
- Don't underline words for emphasis, use italics. Or use bold type, larger type, or a different typeface.
- If you're not sure whether to justify text, don't. Text set flush left, ragged right, is just as easy to read and often looks better because the spacing between words remains consistent.
- Watch out for widows and orphans. *Widows* are one or two ending lines of a paragraph or page carried forward to the next column or page. *Orphans* are beginning lines of a paragraph separated from the rest of the paragraph in the next column or page. Some DTP programs, such as PageMaker, automatically adjust for these. Otherwise, adjust leading or column size to avoid them.

Templates

PageMaker also includes premade *templates* for many of the common forms and layouts you might need. All you need to do is open the template file and insert your own information, logo, or other element. Then, save the file and print it as your own document. Figure 10.13 shows some PageMaker templates.

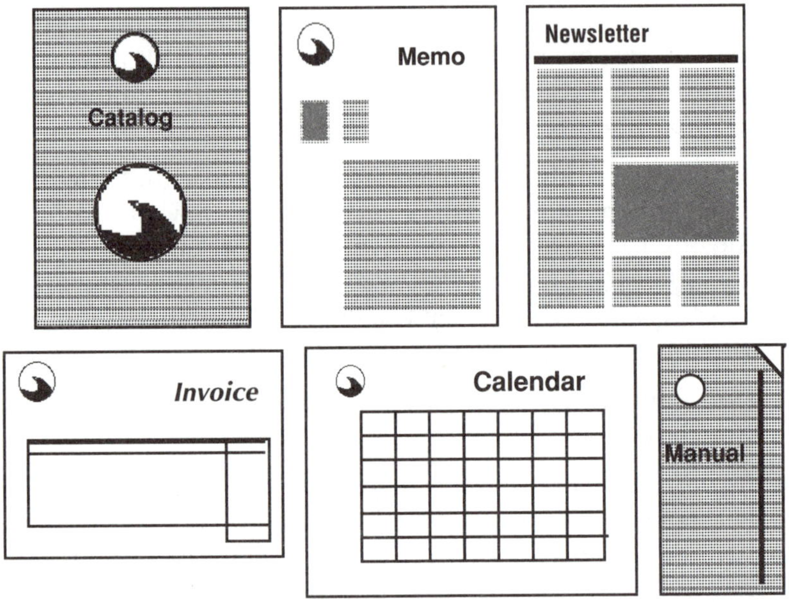

Figure 10.13
Instant design with templates.

PageMaker automatically opens a copy of a template, rather than the original. If you're using a different DTP program, remember that you should always work from a copy of the template file. That way, the original file remains unchanged and you can use it again. You can keep a modified version of a template for future use by clicking Save as Template when you select Save As... from PageMaker's File menu. In other programs, lock the template file from the finder, so you can't accidentally modify or erase the template file.

High-Quality Printing

Now that you've got your DTP document looking good on the screen, how can you transfer it to paper? Back in Chapter 5, we talked about printing on the ImageWriter and StyleWriter. While a StyleWriter is theoretically capable of better images than a laser printer, its limited paper choices, low speed, and tendency to blur make it a poor choice for professional applications.

By the way, the word *laser* isn't just a marketing gimmick. There really is a laser beam inside most printers (a few use LEDs for the same effect). Laser printers work much like copying machines, except they copy rapidly flickering beams of light rather than pages. When you select Print from any application, your Mac sends the printer a detailed description of the page using the Adobe *PostScript* language. A computer inside the printer converts the description to individual flash-on or flash-off commands—90,000 of them per square inch. (Some printers don't have their own PostScript computers, but use the Mac's brains instead. See Chapter 17.) An electrostatically charged drum rolls past the laser. Individual flashes of light change charges on tiny areas of the drum. The drum then passes through a tray of *toner*—little black ink particles which cling to the charged areas. The drum then presses against a charged sheet of paper, transferring the particles. Heat and pressure melt the particles in place.

Print Languages and Printers

There are two different kinds of laser printers: those that use PostScript and those that don't. Back in the early days of laser printing, when Adobe first developed the PostScript interpreter, it charged kilo-bucks for use of the system. The price has since come down, but non-PostScript printers are still less expensive. They hook up to the computer's SCSI port, just as the hard disk and scanner do, and use the Mac's built-in QuickDraw language instead. (You can have both a hard disk and a laser printer plugged in, as long as they have different SCSI addresses.)

> *SCSI* (pronounced "skuzzy," not "sexy," alas) stands for Small Computer System Interface and refers to the place on the back of the Mac where you plug in a hard disk or other device. SCSI is an industry standard that allows for very fast information transfer.

PostScript printers offer the advantage of using the AppleTalk network, so several computers can share one printer. There's a wider range of type fonts available in PostScript. When printing, PostScript printers don't tie up the computer as long, because much of the necessary processing happens within the printer.

Type Managers

There's a way to get good looking type on your screen (and on your ImageWriter, which also "sees" 72 dots per inch), with fewer of those annoying jaggies that make your headlines look like they're built from kindergarten blocks.

SYSTEM

The technology is built into System 7's *TrueType* and is available separately in Adobe Type Manager. In Figure 10.14, both A's are set in 120-point Palatino type. The one on the right was produced on a system using Adobe Type Manager—ATM, for short. The one on the left was typed on a System 6 machine without ATM installed. The differences are just on the screen. Unless you're setting type in a paint-only program (see Chapter 6), you'll get perfectly shaped letters from your laser printer in either case.

Figure 10.14

What you see on the screen, before, and after ATM.

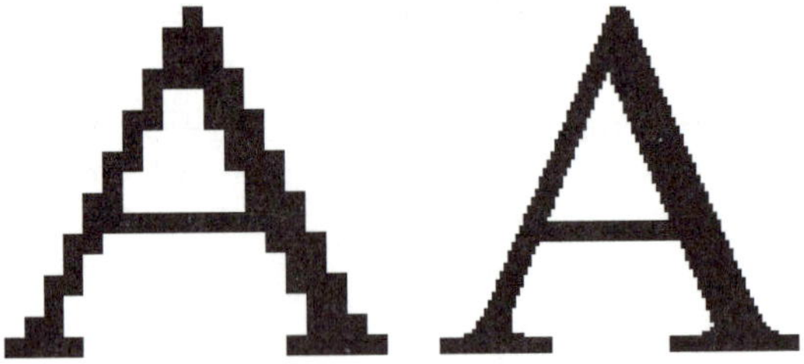

ATM and TrueType smooth the letters to their maximum possible resolution. This slows things down a lot, especially on older Macs. But the advantages outweigh the disadvantages. If you're serious about DTP (even if you have a PostScript printer), ATM and TrueType let you design based on actual letterforms, rather than jaggy approximations. They do this by generating a *bit-mapped* image of each letter.

Bit-mapped fonts are patterns of individual dots, which is why they look like the left side of Figure 10.14. Bit-mapped fonts are intended only for use on the screen and low-resolution printers like the ImageWriter. Laser printers use *outline* fonts: instructions about the lines and curves that make up each letter.

> **TIP:** StyleWriters come with a separate TrueType utility that System 6 users can drop in their System folders. You don't need to use it. StyleWriters work just as well with ATM, which runs faster and can access the larger library of PostScript fonts.

Using Laser Printers

To send a page to a laser printer, open Chooser from the Apple menu and click the icon representing the LaserWriter (even if it isn't an Apple brand printer). Or select the icon for the special print driver supplied with your QuickDraw printer.

If you created your document with a different printer selected, the Mac will ask you to choose Page Setup to verify that the settings are correct. The Page Setup box may vary slightly from the one shown in Figure 10.15, depending on the application and some special printer drivers. A few obsolete applications, such as early versions of HyperCard and MacPaint, print without Page Setup.

US Letter (8 ½ x 11 inches) is the default paper size. US Legal is 8 ½ x 14 inches. A4 letter is the European standard (8 ¼ x 11 ⅔ inches), and A5 is the standard Japanese paper size, (7 ¼ x 10 ¼). If you change the paper size, be sure you physically change the paper in the tray, and the settings on the printer itself, for the printer to work properly.

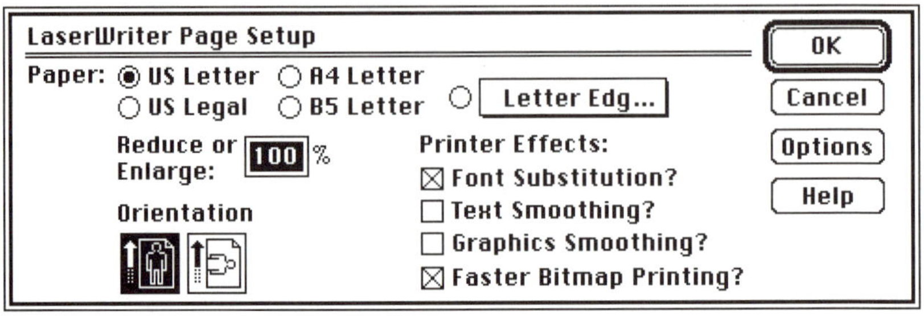

Figure 10.15
The LaserWriter Page Setup box.

The pop-up menu *Letter Edge to Edge* lets you select other page sizes, if your printer can handle them. In some versions of Page Setup, this is replaced with Tabloid (11 x 17 inches).

You can *Reduce* or *Enlarge* the print on the page from 25 to 400% of the actual size. *Font Substitution* automatically substitutes high-quality fonts for Geneva, New York, and Monaco.

Text Smoothing does a better job with the remaining screen fonts. It takes longer to print but can reduce some of the "jaggie" problem. If you're using PostScript fonts or TrueType, this option has no effect. *Graphics Smoothing* smoothes the printed image of some paint-layer graphics.

Faster Bit-mapped Printing does what it says—speeds up bit-mapped printing by preprocessing the information before sending it to the LaserWriter. Apple warns that `...some documents may not print with this option turned on`, but we haven't had this happen in several years of daily use.

The Options button calls up the dialog box in Figure 10.16. The little critter at the left side of the box flips as you click the check boxes, to demonstrate the effect of the selected option.

Invert Image gives you a negative image, or white type on a black background. It takes buckets of toner and can gum up the printer in the process. The blacks are nowhere near as good as those produced by a photostat. Our advice—unless you have a good reason to invert the image, don't.

Precision Bit-mapped Alignment reduces the page 4% to compensate for a slight error when the laser prints pictures from a paint program, so that images exactly an inch wide on the screen stay exactly an inch wide on the page. If you leave this option on, however, it can throw off precise calibrations in some drawing and page layout programs.

Larger Print Area lets you leave smaller margins, if the application allows it. *Unlimited Downloadable Fonts* gives the printer permission to *forget* a downloaded font after it has used it, and to use the printer's RAM for the next one. This tends to slow down documents with many typefaces or on multiple copies of the same document.

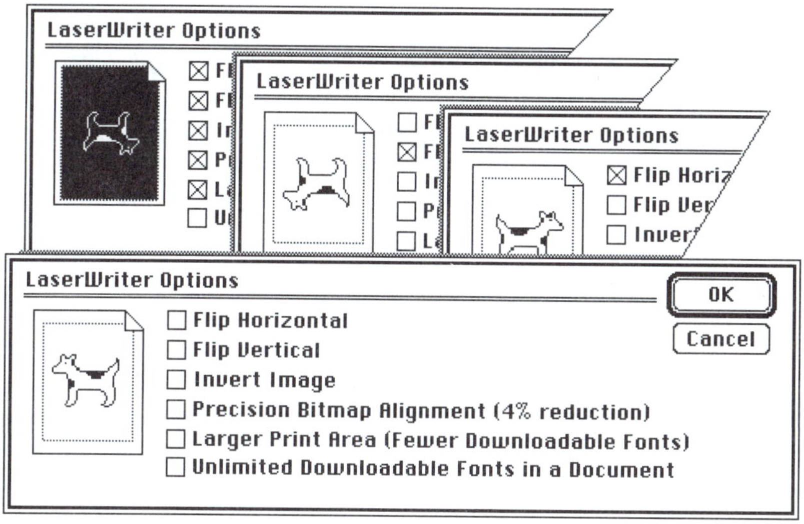

Figure 10.16

Some Page Setup options. Watch the critter do her tricks.

Putting It on Paper

Now, you're finally ready to print. How your finished job looks depends, in part, on what kind of paper you're printing it on. LaserWriters can handle many different kinds of paper, as well as adhesive labels and transparency film. For everyday use, you'll get the best results from the least expensive paper stock you can find. Cheap paper has a low fiber content, so it is quite smooth. The smoother the surface, the sharper the image. Also, more expensive papers have a fine dusting of powder between the sheets to keep them from sticking together. This powder tends to get fused in with the toner, making the image less dense. Be sure to keep your paper in a dry place. Humidity swells the fibers and causes problems.

If you're printing the masters of your newsletter or brochure as *camera ready* art (to be sent to the offset house or photocopier), it's worth paying a few dollars extra for a ream of special reproduction-quality paper. Hammermill's Laser Plus is one of several available. It has a very smooth, slightly waxy surface, and the package states, "for pre-press proofing and camera ready masters."

CAUTION: Do not use letterhead or envelopes that have been preprinted with a raised, textured ink. This *thermographic printing* will melt when the laser printer's heat hits it, gum up your printer and make a mess of the letterhead, too.

If you're not sure what kind of paper to use for a special job, or if you want to check out a variety of fancy papers, the best (if not least expensive) choices we've seen come from PaperDirect, Inc. and Queblo. They have sample kits with more than a hundred different styles, colors, weights, and finishes—all appropriate for laser printers. The kits aren't free, but being able to see and feel the difference between stocks is well worth the cost. Queblo's samples are punched for a notebook; PaperDirect's are loose pages you can use for finished projects. Call PaperDirect at 800-A-PAPERS or Queblo at 800-523-9080.

Color Laser Output

Process color uses varying mixtures of three or four basic inks to print full-spectrum images from photographs or Macintosh art. High-end graphics and darkroom programs produce the necessary *color separations,* and many color printing companies can work directly from Mac disks. Personal color laser printers, however, are still too expensive to be practical. Even color *thermal transfer* printers—producing accurate but slightly textured images used to proof magazine pages—start at about $4500. They may be rentable at your local service bureau (see next section).

But you can also get beautiful color printing from an ordinary desktop laser, for about $100, with a cute gadget available at art supply stores. Letraset's *ColorTag* consists of a heated roller and colorful foil sheets. You place the colored foil over the laser image or type you want to color, and run the roller over it. Whatever was black will magically change color! The foil sheets come in about two dozen very saturated colors, including metallics. They can really spiff up a report cover package dummy.

You can also use ColorTag with photocopies of StyleWriter or ImageWriter pages, or just about anything else. The process works with any dry xerographic toner, so it's equally at home with office copiers.

Service Bureaus

Sure, you can do wonderful things with a LaserWriter. But they cost a lot of money. Is there an alternative? Yes—it's called a service bureau. These are places where you can rent computer time, get your output laser printed, have something scanned into a disk file, get photo-quality type at 1,200 or 2,400 dpi, and usually get good quality copying done at the same time.

You can find service bureaus in the Yellow Pages under *Computer Rentals*, *Copying*, or *Typesetting*. Some service bureaus will take your disk and print from it, or let you send files by modem. Others will rent you time on a Mac, and charge you an hourly rate plus a fee per page printed. (Most charge only for the pages you actually keep, but policies vary.) Service bureau personnel can be quite knowledgeable about the Mac and DTP in general. Don't hesitate to ask questions.

If you're planning to give the service bureau a disk to print from, check first to see how you need to format the material. You can preview the print job on your ImageWriter. It's a good idea to send a preview copy along with the disk, in case there are questions. Make sure you have the right screen fonts for the type you want to use, and they have the proper application to read your files. Be sure to shop around. Service bureau prices, quality, and capabilities differ greatly. Some have *ordinary* laser printers. Others may have, or have access to, the very high-quality output devices such as the Linotronics.

TIP: Before you go to a service bureau, back up any disk you take with you. Work from copies. Rental Macs can be viral. If you bring home a disk you've used on a rented Mac, scan it for viruses before you use it on your own system. (See Chapter 14 for information about virus protection.)

In This Chapter

A Brief History of Computer Games

•

Games Today

•

Learning Games

•

Other Fun Features

•

Startup Screens, and Screen Savers

If using the Macintosh makes working fun, think what it can do for all those non-working hours! There are Mac games and programs to enchant virtually every member of the family, even family pets. (Cats have a particular affinity for computers, we've found. Perhaps it's the mouse?) This chapter will show you some of the legal ways to have fun with your Mac.

11

Impractical Applications

The earliest computer games were developed long before the Macintosh era and tended to be either "chase the blob of light around the screen with another blob of light" games or scripted adventures.

One of the very first games was Spacewar, developed at MIT, which allowed the player to fire what were variously described as bullets, missiles, or torpedoes at a dot of light representing an alien space ship. Games, like Spacewar, are sometimes called twitch games, because you play the game using delicate motions with some form of controller—either a knob, a joystick, or a mouse—or by toggling some combination of keys on the keyboard.

Out in California, where life tended to be mellower, a different kind of play evolved. Adventure games were based on scenarios such as

> *You are standing at the end of a road before a small brick building. Around you is a forest. A small stream flows out of the building and down a gully.*

The game was programmed to recognize typed commands, and the player navigated through the Tolkienesque setting, gathering treasures and fighting off monsters by typing such two-word instructions as "go east," or "get sword." Adventure and the many text games which followed it obviously owed a lot to the Dungeons and Dragons role-playing games.

One of the earliest adventure games for the Macintosh was Infocom's Hitchhiker's Guide to the Galaxy, loosely based on the book by Douglas Adams. Figure 11.1 shows the opening screen for this game. As Arthur Dent, you blundered through the galaxy in search of a good cup of tea and a way to save Earth from being bulldozed to build an interstellar bypass.

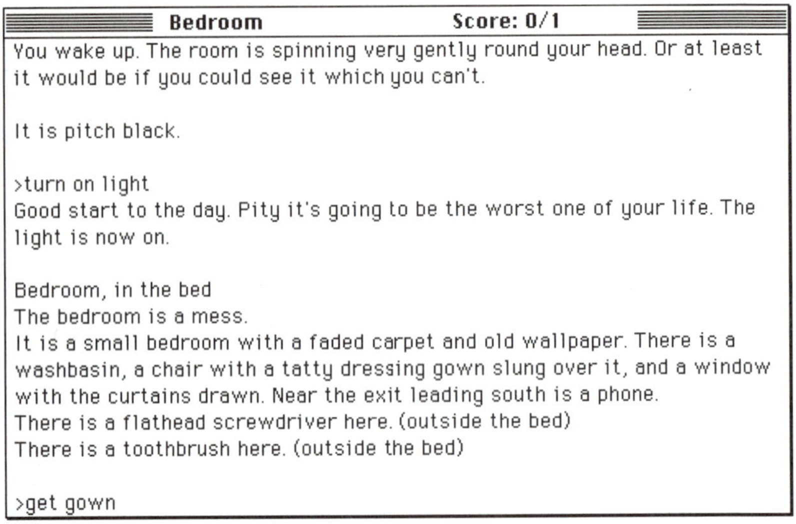

Figure 11.1
Opening screen of Hitchhiker's Guide to the Galaxy.

Game play required typing very short sentences, as Figure 11.1 also shows. You had to type just one direction at a time. You could print out your game as you went along, but you couldn't scroll backward to see where you'd been.

TIP: In Hitchhiker's, the "thing your aunt gave you that you don't know what it is" turns out to be a carrying bag, of huge capacity. Put the stuff you collect along the way into the bag. You can't lose the "thing," no matter what you do.

Hitchhiker's Guide, despite its drawbacks, became an instant hit. Other companies developed games which combined text with graphics, making the adventures more interesting. Current adventure games add animation, sound effects, and elaborate graphics, in full color on color Macs. Among the more popular games are the Space Quest, Kings Quest, Police Quest, and Leisure Suit Larry series from Sierra On-Line, and their newest adventure, EcoQuest, in which players battle pollution and oil spills in an underwater world. Figure 11.2 shows a scene from Space Quest III, typical of Sierra's adventure games.

Figure 11.2

Will space explorer Roger Wilco find a way out of the space station? Maybe . . .

Text/graphic games also owe a lot to a very early computer game, Hunt the Wumpus, first played on a teletype-style printer! Wumpus hunters had to work through a maze, avoiding the dreaded Wumpus, and picking up gold coins. Brøderbund's popular Prince of Persia is a modern maze game in which players must work their way through the dungeons fighting off the guards to rescue the princess. A scene from Prince of Persia is shown in Figure 11.3.

Figure 11.3

That guard won't bother you again . . . but there are more.

No discussion of Macintosh games is complete without mentioning the very first Mac games: the desk accessory Number Puzzle and Amazing! Figure 11.4 shows a screen of Amazing!, which came on Apple's Guided Tour for the original Mac. It was designed to teach new owners how to use a mouse. (You might say it was also the Mac's first educational software.) With four levels of difficulty and dozens of different mazes, this maze was—and still is—a nifty little game. Unfortunately, it won't work with some current Mac models. The Puzzle DA is still supplied with new machines and runs in color under System 7.

You can change the picture on the Puzzle in System 7 by copying any PICT image and using the paste menu command while the puzzle's open. If your new picture is larger than the puzzle, it'll be scaled (and possibly distorted) to fit.

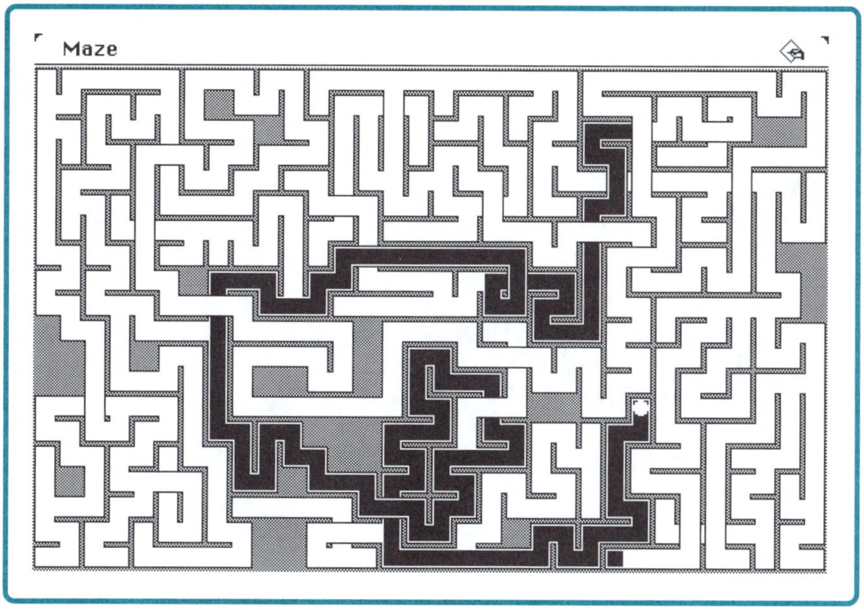

Figure 11.4
Mac's Amazing Mouse Maze.

Simulations

Today's generation of Macintosh games includes something for everyone. If you're not in the mood to zap aliens or meander through Middle Earth, you can pilot a space shuttle or fly a Cessna 182 without ever leaving your desk. You can sit behind the wheel of a Formula One race car. You can even practice your surgical techniques.

Life or Death from Software Toolworks, shown in Figure 11.5, lets you diagnose a variety of abdominal problems, perform an appendectomy, and finally repair an aortic aneurysm. The treatment is medically correct, and the graphics are startlingly accurate (be glad the illustrations aren't in color). This kind of realism is heady stuff, indeed, for the armchair medic! But be careful: a missed diagnosis or a slip of the scalpel sends you back to medical school.

You can coach a pro football team, ski down a mountain, play eighteen holes of golf at some of the world's most challenging courses, or drive a race car. You can pilot any number of different aircraft, including the P-51 Mustang, Fokker Triplane, Cessna, and

Learjet 25G, with any of several different Flight Simulators. XOR's MacSki, shown in Figure 11.6, lets you practice your slalom technique on a dozen different ski slopes and design your own mountains, too.

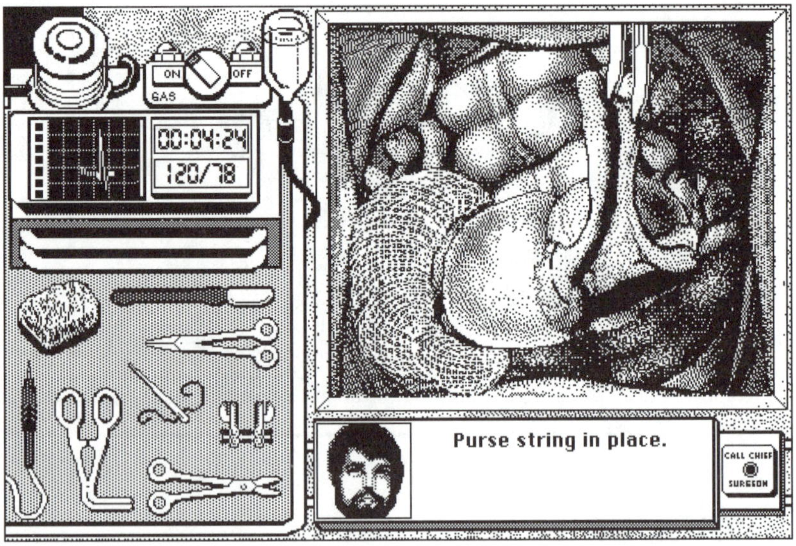

Figure 11.5

Now, place the upper and lower clamps, and sever the appendix.

Figure 11.6

It's all downhill from here.

TIP: A day's worth of skiing can be fun if you're using real snow, but take frequent breaks when playing any game on your computer. To avoid eye strain, blink, focus on a distant object, and then look at the screen. To prevent wrist and forearm soreness, position the mouse or keyboard so you can rest your elbow and forearm on the desk, requiring only small movements of the wrist or fingers during game play.

If you crave something more sedentary, there are shareware Mac versions of the classic games chess, go, whist, and cribbage. Feeling lucky? Be a high roller at baccarat or craps. Play blackjack, poker, or roulette without losing your shirt. Or you can buy puzzles of all kinds, including the very popular Tesserae and Darwin's Dilemma from Inline Design and Activision's Shanghai II (shown in Figure 11.7).

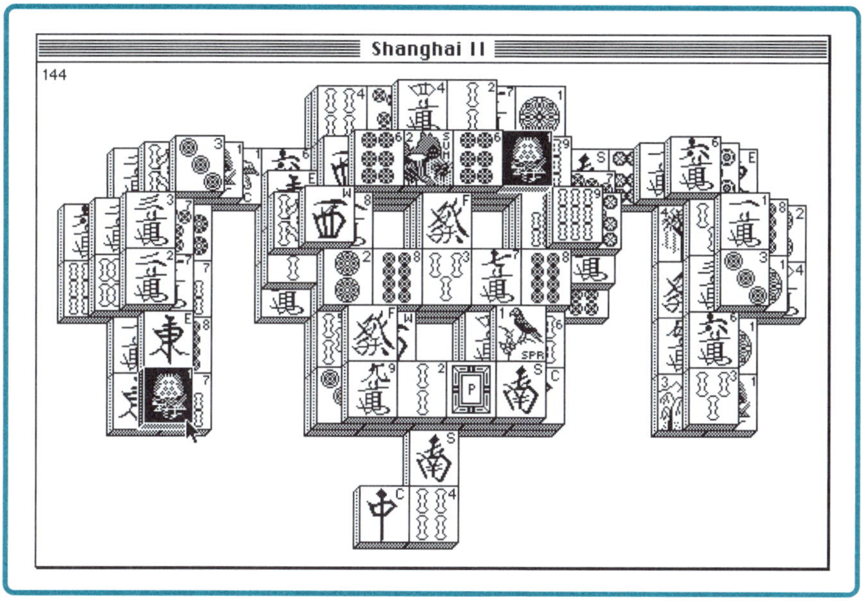

Figure 11.7

The trick is to remove pairs of tiles until all are gone.

Within the past few years, a new kind of simulation has gotten popular. You're the Mayor of Maxis' Sim City. You can either develop a city from scratch or select one of many prebuilt ones. You have to keep the citizens happy as you build roads, construct factories or power plants, dedicate parks and stadiums, and—if possible—avoid raising taxes. Sim City won't get you elected to your local city council, but it does provide a fairly good representation of the interrelationships of politics and economics. Sim Earth does the same thing on a global scale. You have to manage a planet from creation through development of intelligent life. The newest Sim-ulation is Sim Ant, where you and your fellow bugs attempt to conquer a suburban backyard. Not for the squeamish, Sim Ant features blood-sucking spiders, treacherous ant lions, and the deadly foot-with-shoe!

> **TIP:** If your Sim City is facing bankruptcy, raise money in a hurry by typing **FUND**. (In capital letters. Capital, get it?) Each time you do, the cash on hand goes up by $10,000. We wish this worked in our checkbook program, too.

Join the Clutter Club

Whenever you purchase a new game, be sure to save the instruction manuals and other strange-looking items that come with it. You may need them. Wise users don't buy copy-protected disks, since there's usually no way to back them up or mount them on hard disks. So game makers have resorted to other tactics to protect their software from "user distribution." (That's a euphemism for piracy, theft, and general sleaziness by people who think it's okay to rip off software writers by passing a program around the whole neighborhood.)

One way to protect a program is to make the player enter secret information before or during the game (as shown in Figure 11.8). If you don't have the necessary book, card, or decoder handy, you're out of luck. The program will usually shut down after a few wrong guesses. At the moment, the author's desk is littered with a doctor's beeper from Life and Death, manuals from at least two dozen other games, and the six-inch-round decoder wheel from Pipe Dream.

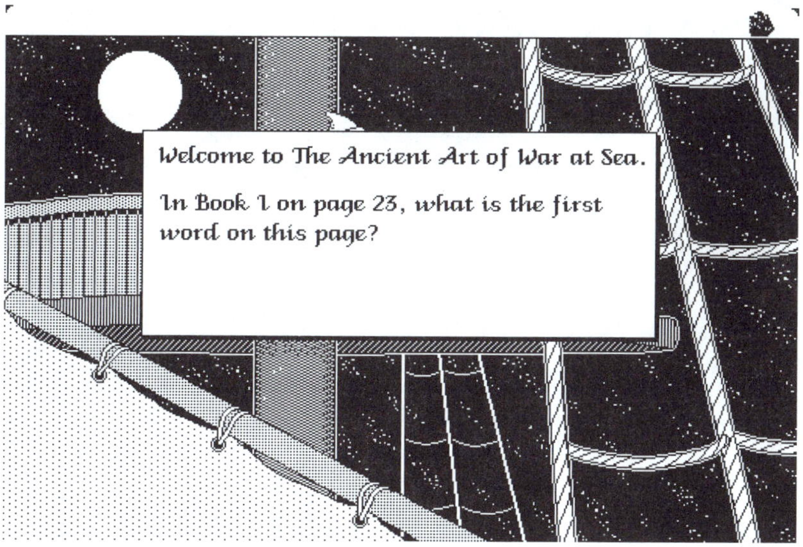

Figure 11.8

Instead of copy protection, we have entry protection.

Kid Stuff

Games aren't just for grown-ups, though. The Macintosh is as child-safe as a computer can be. Even pre-alphabet two- and three-year-olds can use the mouse—and they do, happily, for relatively long periods of time. In the process, they develop hand/eye coordination and gain prereading skills. Games such as Brøderbund's Playroom and Spelunx let kids explore the possibilities of the Mac as they explore the well-equipped playroom or the network of underground caves. In Figure 11.9 we're not just exploring caves, we're learning physics. We drop-ped a rock into the pit. The gauges tell us how fast it's traveling each second it falls. Then, we'll see how long it takes to hear the splash.

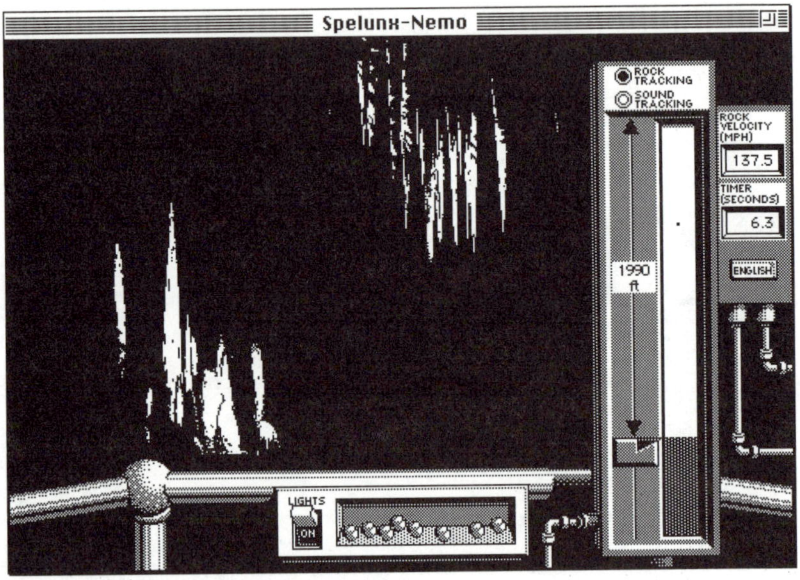

Figure 11.9

It's dark in these caves! One of over fifty different Spelunx activities.

Sleuthing

Older kids and teens can brush up on history and geography while they play detective, tracking down arch-criminal Carmen Sandiego. Brøderbund's Where in . . . . is Carmen Sandiego? series has sold well over two million copies! Various versions of the game have you trace Carmen or one of her co-thugs through Europe, around the world, across the USA, or even through time. (That's what the four dots in the title stand for. Not what you were thinking.)

Super Sleuthing

If Carmen is for kids, Moriarty's Revenge is the grown-up version. Mysterium Tremendum's detective game, while superficially similar to the Carmen series, is far more challenging. There are close to 1,000 different city/country clues, and several thousand appearance clues.

The game comes with an atlas and a sleuth handbook that warns, "Not everything is described here. As in any endeavor, you must find some things out for yourself." Figure 11.10 shows screens from Moriarty's Revenge.

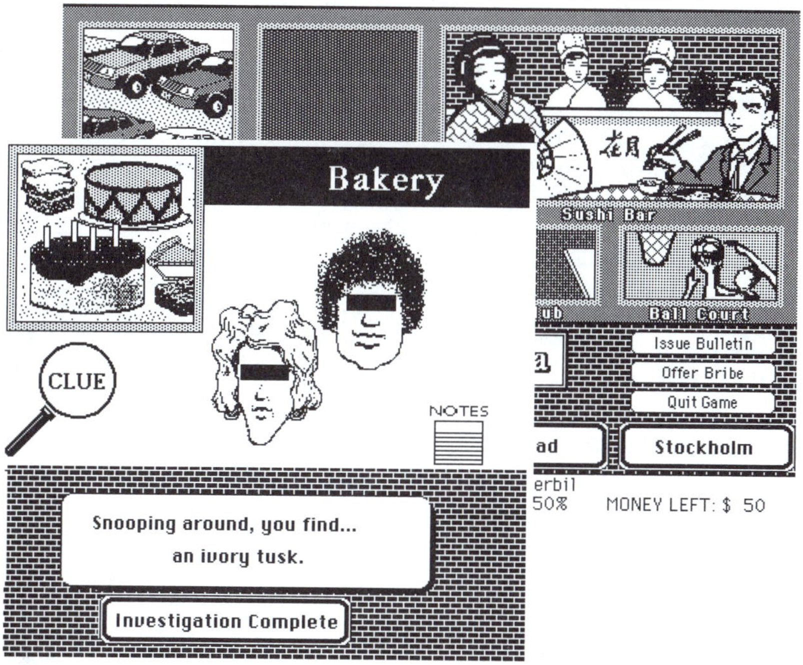

Figure 11.10

Clues tell you where the crook went. Bystanders give physical descriptions.

Players not only find the criminal, but interview bystanders to work up an accurate description—and they don't always tell the truth. At the same time, you have to keep track of time and money (both of which often run out before you catch the crook).

Arcade-Style Games

It's true that games on the Mac, especially non-color models, may not be as exciting as those on the latest 32-bit games-only timewasters for which the kids beg. On the other hand, Mac gaming can be a lot more interactive than TV screen adventures where players have only a joystick and a jump or shoot button.

Many of the hot games for Nintendo and other game machines are also available for the Mac. Tetris, shown in its DA version in Figure 11.11, was developed by two Russian computer enthusiasts. The game is simple, but fiendishly difficult to play. Pieces fall from the top of the screen, and the player must rotate them and shift them from side to side to pack as many rows as possible into the playing field. Spectrum Holobyte also publishes Faces, Welltris, and Super Tetris. Their newest Tris game, Word Tris, requires you to make words from falling letter tiles. Difficult, but fun.

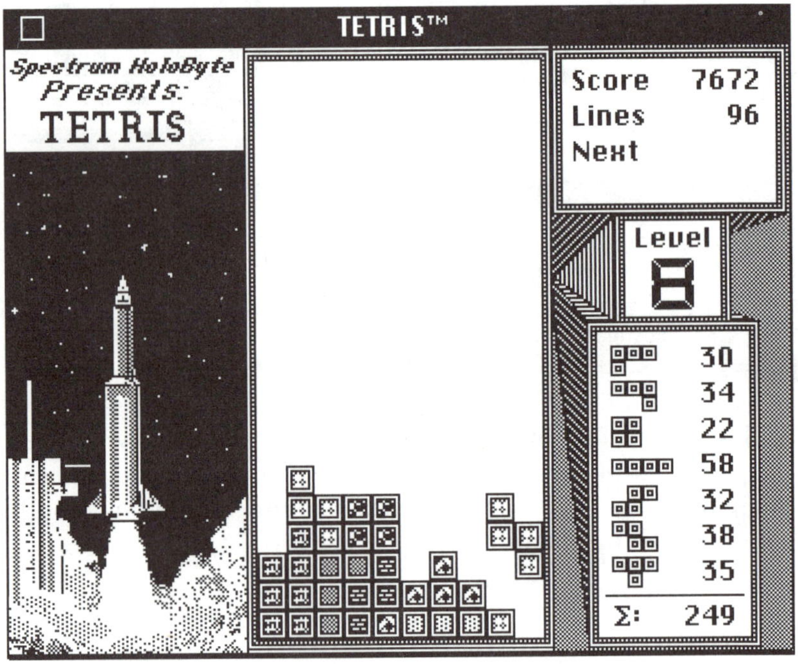

Figure 11.11

Tetris, one of the all-time best-selling games.

Get an Education

Games such as Tetris are educational, teaching human-computer interaction and hand/eye coordination. But if the goal is more concrete learning, there's another category of software. Educational materials range from pre-kindergarten to college levels, and teach everything from the alphabet and telling time to foreign languages and physics experiments. Even younger users can find educational games, such as Reader Rabbit and Number Munchers—popular teaching programs for the younger set.

Learning Materials for Older Kids

Several software publishers offer study guides for the SATs, as well as the GMAT and LSAT exams. Review questions, tutorials, and practice tests provide a good warm-up for the real thing and are probably as effective as exam prep classes costing 10 times as much.

Language tutoring programs on the Mac are usually HyperCard stacks of electronic flash cards, including native voices with correct pronunciations. Penton Overseas' VocabuLearn series includes cassettes as well, and comes in French, Italian, Spanish, German, Russian, Hebrew, and Japanese. HyperGlot's Word Torture is blessedly silent, but its automated vocabulary drills take you through 1,400 words in Russian, French, Spanish, or German. *Kanji Master* teaches spoken and written Japanese with high quality digitized sounds.

Other Fun Features

Sure, the Macintosh is supposed to make you more productive, and save time on such things as writing, keeping track of finances, and sorting all kinds of data in usable formats. But now that you've saved all that time, what can you do with it? You can play games on your Mac, of course. But aside from games, there are a number of other ways you can play with a Mac. One of us considers HyperCard scripting as a sort of word game, and writes in this simple language for fun. Our teenaged son, an accomplished artist, calls the color drawing capabilities of the Mac II the best-ever video game!

Meet the Moose

Back in the mid-1980s, one of the best-known and most-beloved of shareware programs was a thing called Talking Moose. It used a phonetic speech translator (called Macintalk) to make the Macintosh talk! A little animated moose head appeared in the corner of the screen, spouting such gems as, "How come you never take me anywhere?" or "Turn on the modem. I want to make a long-distance moose call." You could also add your own phrases. The Moose would appear at random times, unless you turned him off from the control panel. Unhappily, Apple's System 5.0 was not moose-friendly and the wisecracking beast became extinct! Careful breeding by Moose author Steve Hall and Baseline Publishing have produced a new, hardier Moose, along with a bunch of animated friends. They all exist peacefully with System 7 and can interrupt your work in color or black and white.

TIP: You can record your own strange sounds, too, and use them as alerts, write them into HyperCard stacks, and do whatever you want with them. The Control Panel device called Sound on newer high-end Macs lets you use the accessory microphone to record customized "beeps" up to 10 seconds long, and Farallon's MacRecorder lets older Macs do much the same thing. For more information, see Chapter 9.

Fun with Screens

Most paint programs let you replace the usual Welcome to Macintosh that pops up when you turn on the computer. Figure 11.12 shows one of our favorite startup screens, which we created in SuperPaint. If you want to make your own, work in the upper left corner of the document. Use clip art, scanned images, screen shots from your favorite games, typed words, or anything else—it's your Mac. SuperPaint's Full Screen mode lets you see exactly what your finished screen will look like.

Figure 11.12

Our cat says welcome in his own way.

Once you've completed the picture, call it StartupScreen—the title should have no spaces—and select the StartupScreen format from the Other Formats men in your paint program's Save dialog box (Figure 11.13 shows the choices in SuperPaint). Put the document in your System Folder, restart your Mac, and admire your work. Feel free to give your StartupScreen to friends: the program you created it on doesn't have to be on their Macs for it to show up.

> **TIP:** A few paint programs, including SuperPaint, let you open and edit existing StartUp screens. If yours can't, be sure to save a copy in the program's normal format.

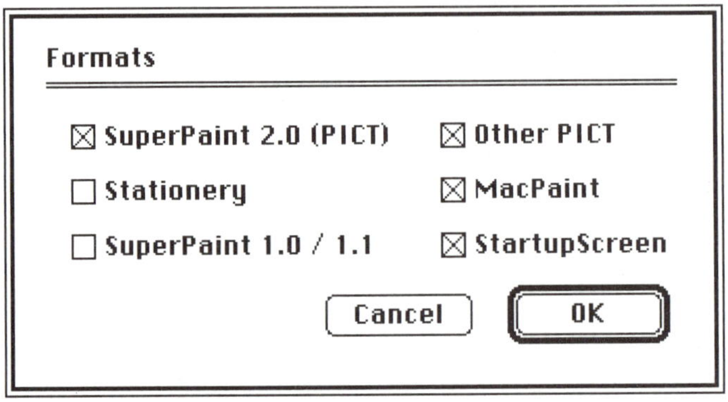

Figure 11.13

The StartupScreen format.

You can even make parody versions of other programs as a startup screen. First, take a screenshot by hitting ⌘-Shift-3. When you use this command, the Mac takes a picture of whatever is on the screen and saves it as a paint document openable by most graphics programs. You'll find the image on your desktop, labeled Screen 0. You can take up to nine screen shots, and the Mac names them Screen 1, Screen 2, and so on. (Once you get past 10, the numbering starts over, replacing the first screen shot with a new one. If you want to make more screen shots, move the first set of screen shots into a folder.)

Screen Savers

Screen savers probably should be called Ghostbusters, because what they really do is prevent ghost images from becoming a permanent part of your screen. A computer screen works just like a TV picture tube. A phosphor chemical is sprayed on the flat glass at the front end of the tube. A beam of electrons hits the phosphor, causing it to glow and form the image you see. Overuse can exhaust the phosphors, creating dark spots (called burn-ins or ghosts) on the screen where the light has shone longest. On the Macintosh, burn-ins tend to appear at the top of the screen, on the menu bar.

Screen savers, sometimes known as screen blankers, will black out the screen after a set period of time and give the phosphors a chance to recover. Obviously, a screen-saver program has to keep track of what you're doing so the screen doesn't go blank while you're working. The two best-known Mac screen savers are Pyro and After Dark. They're fun to watch, too, since they provide a sort of video wallpaper when your Mac dozes off. After Dark features fish, flying toasters and lots of other zany designs. The pattern remains on the screen while the mouse and keyboard are idle. As soon as the Mac gets a better offer, it redraws the proper screen and goes back to work. After Dark and its control panel are shown in Figure 11.14.

Figure 11.14

Our Mac has gone fishing.

Why not just turn the computer off? It's actually better for the electronics if you leave the computer on, instead of turning it on and off every time you stop for coffee. Most failures occur at start up because of power surging through components. It also wears down the switches and disk drives. If you don't have a screen saver, it's a good idea to dim the screen using the brightness control.

Screen savers are *not* a good idea with PowerBooks. It's far better to use Apple's built in Sleep mode to conserve battery life without losing your work.

These are just some of the ways to have fun with your Mac. Playing games is a good way to learn what the computer can do, and to begin to understand how it works and what you can do with it. Computer games are a tradition that goes back as far as computers themselves. It's OK to play!

In This Chapter

Getting Help

•

Finding Other Mac Enthusiasts

•

How Computers Talk to Each Other

•

Who Ya Gonna Call?

•

E-mail and More

•

Shareware

When you need technical help with a program, you can call its help line or get help from a user group. User groups often have magazines and bulletin board services to help you meet other Macintosh enthusiasts, and they are a source of shareware (low-cost software often written by nonprofessionals) and freeware. This chapter teaches you how to get in touch with other Mac users to share your knowledge and experience.

12

Modems and User Groups

Now that you've learned what your Mac can do, and a little bit about how to do it, you may be wondering how to find out more. Your dealer can answer many of your questions. When all else fails, you can read the manual.

While you're looking for the answer to your questions in a product manual, look also for the phone number of the company's *help line.* This is (usually) a toll-free number you can call when you need assistance making things run. It may also be called *user support, customer service,* or *technical support.* Like the manuals themselves, the cost and quality varies. Often, smaller publishers provide the best support. A few large companies have 900 numbers, answering your question promptly but adding a service fee to your phone bill. Some of the biggest names leave you on long-distance hold for what seems like hours, listening to elevator music until your brains turn to tapioca and you forget the question.

If you're calling for help, have the computer turned on and ready to go, and the following information in front of you:

- The name and version number of the program (You can find this with the About... command or by selecting Get Info from your desktop.) You'll also need the serial number of your registered copy of the program.

- What you did just before you encountered the problem.
- The exact wording and error code numbers (if any) of any dialog boxes that appeared.
- Which model Mac you're using and how much RAM it has.
- Versions numbers of the system and finder you're using, and names of any INITs or extensions you've installed.
- If you're using System 6, whether or not MultiFinder is active.

With this info in hand, and a pencil and paper for notes, call from a phone next to your computer. Often, the technician will talk you through the problem, telling you step-by-step what to do. But you'll have to be able to read the screen back to them for this to work effectively.

Of course, when you've got a problem the folks you need may be three time zones away, eating lunch, or even out of business. Where else can you turn for help (besides this excellent book)?

User Groups

Ever since the first personal computers appeared on the scene, there have been groups of computer enthusiasts who have shared information and helped each other with what was, at first, a brand new science. These *user groups* may be dedicated to computers in general, to a particular kind such as the Mac, to a kind of application, or even to a particular program. Often there are *special interest groups,* or SIGs, within the club. A listing of subgroups in one Macintosh users' group includes SIGs for education, business, HyperCard, legal, music, and 4th Dimension (a database program).

Help from Boston . . .

In addition to running classes and seminars, Mac user groups keep lists of volunteers to provide telephone support with certain programs or problems. The Boston Computer Society's Macintosh Group (BCS·Mac) lists well over two hundred volunteer experts, including two dozen who specifically focus on beginners. Best of all, it's free. Of course, you may have to pay for a long distance phone call, but the help list includes experts in all parts of the country.

BCS·Mac publishes a monthly magazine, *The Active Window.* In addition to Dial Help listings, it includes software reviews; news of new products; hints; lists of new disks in the shareware library; and a calendar of monthly events, SIG meetings, beginner's nights, and seminars. BCS membership costs $40 per year and includes privileges in all 44 user/interest groups (including BCS·Mac), low-cost access to humongous shareware libraries, discounts at computer and software stores, and subscriptions to the *BCS Update* and special-interest publications such as *Active Window.* Call them at (617) 864-1700.

. . . to Berkeley

The other really large user group is the BMUG. It was originally the Berkeley Macintosh Users group, but became BMUG (bee-mug), when the IRS decided that a Mac user's club was an Apple advertising gimmick and therefore taxable. In response, the group officially adopted its nickname, removing "Macintosh" from the corporate identity. This, bless them, made the IRS happy. BMUG publishes a newsletter—actually a large volume of news and tips—twice a year. It also maintains huge libraries of shareware, a bulletin board and help line, and a database of the best pizza and Chinese food in Berkeley. Call them at (510) 549-BMUG or (510) 849-HELP.

There are also hundreds of smaller, local Mac user groups. Your computer dealer should be able to refer you to some. If not, a local college or high school with computer classes can help, or call Apple's 24-hour toll-free user number (1-800-538-9696 Ext. 500) for information about groups in your area.

Should You Join a User Group?

Yes, for the following reasons:

- *User groups are your source for unbiased information.* Dealers are in business to sell you something. (That's no surprise.) Some try to sell you things you don't need, usually to solve problems you shouldn't be having. User groups are full of people who understand the problem and are happy to tell you how to solve it—for free.
- Special Interest Groups (SIGs) help you connect with others who share your interests and enthusiasm.
- User groups are a good source for usually virus-free, legitimate shareware.

No, if you already know all the in's and out's of your system, never want to upgrade it, and have determined that it'll never break down. Or if you use your Mac as a doorstop.

Shareware

Shareware is noncommercial software, developed by users and distributed via user groups and bulletin boards. Most shareware is entertaining or useful software that somebody wrote for fun—or to solve a unique problem—and thought others might enjoy. There are also demo versions of commercial programs and fully working versions of programs that might become commercial in the future.

Shareware developers need and deserve encouragement. Postcards are nice and cash helps. Authors request minimal payments—usually in the neighborhood of $10—for programs you keep using. Try the application a few times to see if you like it. If you don't, erase the disk or pass it on to a friend. But if you do keep it, you really should ante up. (It sure beats shelling out big bucks for commercial programs that don't meet your needs.) The system works only if users keep up their end. If we don't, then developers may stop turning out all these nifty and inexpensive new games and tools. Shareware fees often bring tangible rewards as well, in the form of expanded versions or keys to unlock functions. Figure 12.1 shows some typical shareware screens with requests for small fees.

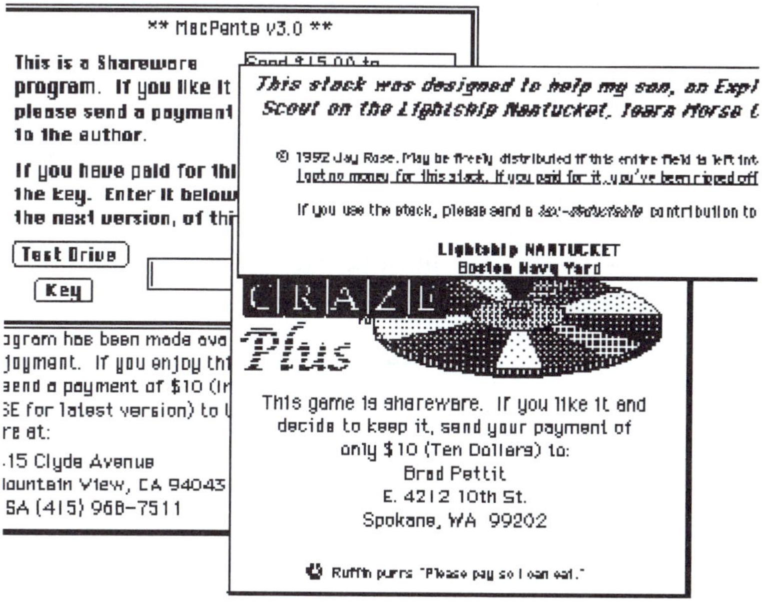

Figure 12.1

Shareware authors don't ask for much.

The point is, shareware is *not* automatically freeware. You may encounter some programs that are free—the About... screen will say so—but even then, thank-you notes to the creators are a nice idea. With that in mind, the authors publicly thank and praise John Norstad and Northwestern University: their freeware *Disinfectant* anti-virus program (discussed in Chapter 14 and available from most user groups and bulletin boards) has saved a lot of data from damage, worldwide.

> Can you copy shareware for friends? Yes. It's published for that purpose. But first, pay your shareware fees and encourage your friends to pay theirs. It's only fair.

Where to Find Shareware

You can get shareware disks and CD-ROMs from user groups. If you join an on-line service like Delphi, CompuServe, or America Online, you can download from vast libraries of shareware. BMUG, BCS·Mac, and many other groups also have on-line libraries for downloading.

Don't forget, you can also *upload* to an online service. If you write a really useful stack for HyperCard or a game your friends love, why not spread it around? You, too, can collect minuscule amounts of money from grateful users. If you come across a good piece of shareware that someone else has written, spread it around. Just don't try to upload copyrighted software (check About... if you're in doubt). Not only is it illegal; it's also ineffectual: most board operators delete any copyrighted files they get.

CAUTION: Be careful about the source of your shareware. Shareware disks from an unknown company or user group could be carrying a virus. Follow the procedures in Chapter 14 to keep your system healthy.

Magazines and Books

The two major Mac-oriented magazines are *MacUser* and *MacWorld.* They're both good. In fact, they're virtually interchangeable. Both have product reviews, features on Mac-relevant topics, and tips for users. Both are beautifully put together and easy to read. Both have lots of ads, which we read as avidly as the editorial material. *MacUser* appears to be aimed at more advanced users and costs a buck less at the newsstand (both offer substantial discounts on subscriptions). There's also *MacWeek,* with a lot of current industry and computer business news, but not much for the end user. Other magazines have specialized Mac info: *Portable Computing*, for example, gives excellent coverage to PowerBooks, laptop Mac clones, and appropriate software.

Computer stores and general-interest bookstore chains often have large selections of computer books. While these are weighted toward IBM PCs and their clones, you can usually find a few dozen different Mac titles in stock, ranging from general surveys to software-specific guidebooks. Computer publishing is a booming business (as the makers of this fine tome can attest), and new books come out four or five times a year. Because of this, it's impossible to recommend specific titles with any accuracy.

The Mac Reaches Out

For many computer users, the Mac isn't just a tool, it's a window on the world. With a Mac and a modem, you have access to encyclopedias and reference services of all kinds, stock quotes, travel information, up-to-the-minute news and weather reports, and forums on topics ranging from antiques to zoology. After a hard day's work, you can close up the database or word processor and settle back for a friendly game of poker with the regular gang, download a new desk accessory, or chat with friends in other parts of the country.

What makes this communication possible is a device called a modem. *Modem* stands for *mo*dulate, *dem*odulate. It's needed because your computer thinks in a digital format. So does the computer it's going to be talking to. But your local phone lines don't.

At least not yet, in most places. The telephone folks are slowly introducing *ISDN*, or Integrated Systems Digital Network. ISDN handles digital signals dozens of times faster than modems, on ordinary telephone wires. The system carries high-fidelity audio, video, and computer data at only slightly higher cost than today's voice-only calls.

So, to communicate with another computer via phone lines, you have to use analog signals the phone company can handle. (Figure 12.2 illustrates the difference between digital and analog signals.) That's what a modem does. It plugs into your computer on one side and the telephone line on the other. It *modulates* a voice-like frequency with digital data. At the other end, the signal gets *demodulated* back to digital signals by another modem. In between, the telephone company sees a signal that looks (electrically, at least) very much like human voices. Fax machines do the same thing, for the same reason.

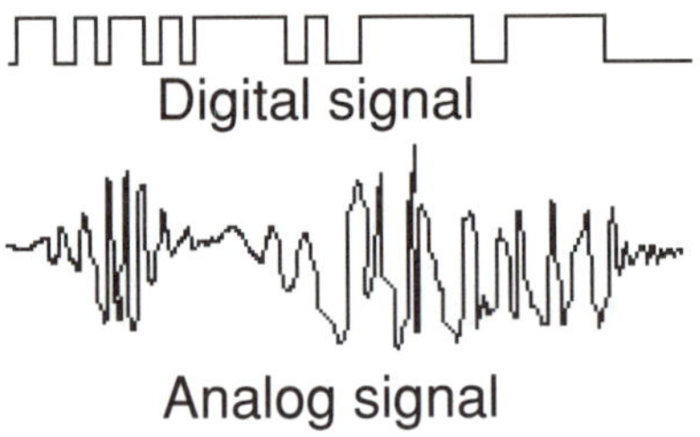

Figure 12.2

The data leaves the computer as a digital signal but travels down the phone line as an analog signal.

There's more to this package, though. You need software to make it work: a *communications program*, instructions that tell the computer how to put information into a format that can be recognized at the other end of the line.

A Question of Protocol

As far as the phone company is concerned, a modem call is just another phone call. (See Figure 12.3.) It's up to the computers involved to make sure data actually is sent. If both computers use the same protocol, they can talk. People work the same way: if you make a call and the voice on the other end says "Bonjour" and you remember your French, you simply shift language and proceed. But if the voice says "Ishpediska?" or "Qwerffle?" all you can do is mumble.

How do the computers know whether both can use the same protocol? The answering computer first sends a *carrier signal*, a two-toned whistle that says, "OK, I've answered the phone. Who are you?"

Immediately, both computers start a process called *handshaking*, verifying they speak the same language and use the same protocols. *Protocol*, by the way, has pretty much the same meaning here as it does at the State Department. It's the ground rules for how computers recognize each other.

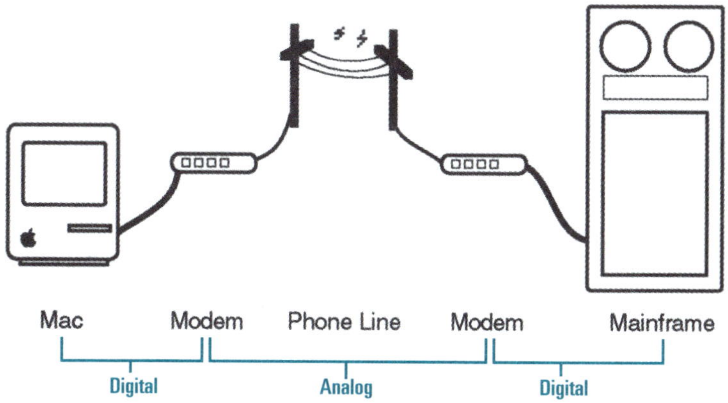

Figure 12.3

Any computer can talk to any other computer, so long as they agree on protocol.

How Fast?

There are three critical protocol issues on which the computers have to agree. The first is the *speed* of the communication. It could be anywhere from 300 to 9,600 bits per second, or even higher. Frequently, you'll see this referred to as *baud rate*, because at low speeds one baud equals one bit of information per second. (High-speed modems use data compression that makes this comparison meaningless. Baud persists because it's easier to pronounce than bps.) If you're connecting to a friend's computer, both modems must be manually set to the same rate. The number means the same thing, even if one program calls it bps and the other calls it baud.

Higher speeds are obviously more efficient. They're also more subject to error caused by static on the phone line. Commercial users have sophisticated modems which automatically *fall back* to slower speeds when they encounter noise. Most bulletin boards adjust themselves to the user's rate during handshaking. ISDN, by the way, is capable of at least two simultaneous, *64,000* bit-per-second conversations!

How Polite?

People don't communicate well when everyone talks at once (cocktail parties excluded). Computers are more flexible, so the second protocol issue is *duplex* mode. It decides how the two computers share the line. Can they both talk at once (on different frequencies), or do they take turns? In *half duplex,* one computer talks and stops, and then the other one begins. In *full duplex,* both can send and receive at the same time. Most of your communications will be in full duplex mode.

When you're on-line, what you see isn't really what you type. The words on screen are really an *echo* of your typing, transmitted through both modems to the host, and then back again to your screen. This way, you can check for garbled data. A third duplex mode, *local echo,* is for the few hosts that don't support this feature. It sends your typed characters to the screen and modem simultaneously. If you select local echo with most telecomm services, you'll see each character twice. LLiikkee tthhiiss..

How Now, Brown Cow?

The third element controls the elocution and grammar of your electronic conversation: *data format.* The characters on your screen are represented by *bytes,* made up of eight individual digital ones or zeroes. The modem can send only a single one or zero—a *bit*—at a time, so it organizes them into *words.* Different systems, starting with the earliest teletypes, have different standards for words. Your computer can adapt to most of them.

The data format includes word length, *start and stop bits* to help the computer separate words, and *parity bits* that guard against line noise. Once both users agree on the format, you can ignore it. You type, and the system makes sure the proper words arrive at the other end. Most bulletin boards and services use *N-8-1,* meaning *N*o parity, an *8*-bit word, and stop bit.

ASCII (pronounced AS-key) stands for American Standard Code for Information Interchange. ASCII Code is an internationally recognized standard, relating a specific 7-bit word to each letter, number, and symbol most computers can make. An eighth bit rounds things out, and is used by the Mac for special characters like ^, ▲, or ≡ . Most other computers can't recognize the first two symbols and refuse to acknowledge that last one. Special ASCII codes also do teletype-related things, like rolling the paper down or ringing a bell to wake the operator up.

Choosing a Modem

Consider how you're going to use the modem. For ordinary modem use—joining an on-line service or a local bulletin board—an ordinary modem is fine. But you can also get ones that also send and receive faxes: they're cheaper than separate fax machines, save paper, and produce a more professional-looking message on the other end. You'll need a modem that can handle at least 2,400 bps. Some desktop models transmit at 9,600 or even 14,400 bps, but this has limited use at present. CompuServe and some other commercial services support higher speeds, but charge a premium to use it. Many local boards can't handle more than 2,400 bps.

Modem Costs

The 2,400 bps modems cost under $200 and are usually available at discount for as little as $100. Many modems include bundled software. Sending faxes adds about fifty dollars, and receiving them costs another fifty or so (these features are available separately): figure about $250 for a full-service fax/modem. For another $100, DoveFax+ adds *voicemail* to your Mac. It can answer calls and record or play messages when the caller hits Touch-tone keys, sounding just like a large automated telephone system. Many modems offer *data compression,* helpful when sending to compatible equipment, but not supported by most dial-up services. If you want to buy a 9,600 or 14,400 bps modems, be prepared to spend anywhere between $500 and $1000.

You might still find 300 baud modems on sale for as little as $25. Avoid them. They're frustratingly slow, and what you save on hardware you'll waste on connect charges—if you can connect at all. Many on-line services and user groups have phased out their 300 baud operations, on the grounds that they tie up their lines too long.

CAUTION: Most, but not all, modems use *Hayes commands,* also called AT commands. (Hayes is the company that set the de facto standards for modem communications.) Make sure any modem you buy is "Hayes-compatible."

Installing a Modem

FCC rules require that direct connections to the telephone system be made through standard plugs and jacks. If you don't have a modular phone jack (type *RJ-11* or *RJ-14*) near the computer, you'll have to put one in. Most office supply and electronics stores sell easy-to-install jack kits, as well as extension cords and Y-connectors. RJ-11 jacks are used for single-line installations. RJ-14 ones have an extra pair of conductors, for two-line phones. You can use a standard modem with either jack: if it's an RJ-14, the modem will connect to "Line 1."

Many people use their regular telephone line for both voice and computer communications. Others have a second line installed just for the computer. You can plug a standard single-line phone into the back of any modem and use it for voice calls when you're not telecomputing. Figure 12.4 shows how it all goes together.

The actual hookup of the modem is simple. It has a power cord, a modular phone cord, and a cable to the computer. Be sure everything's turned off before you plug it in. Unplug your phone from the wall, and plug the modem's phone cord in. Figure 12.5 shows what the modem jacks on the back of your Mac may look like.

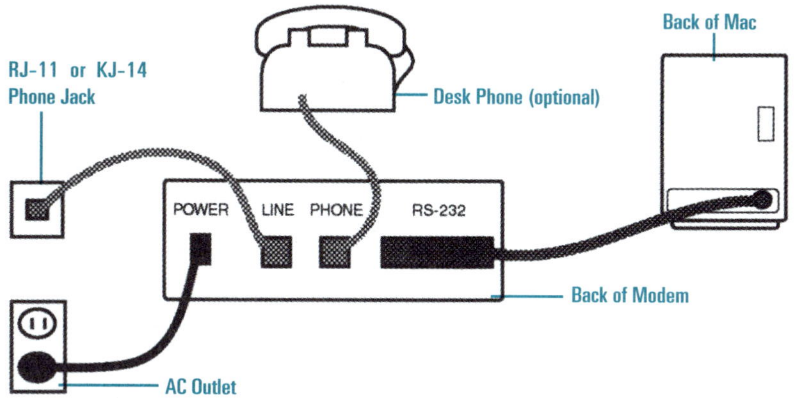

Figure 12.4
Back view of a modem setup (other Mac cables not shown).

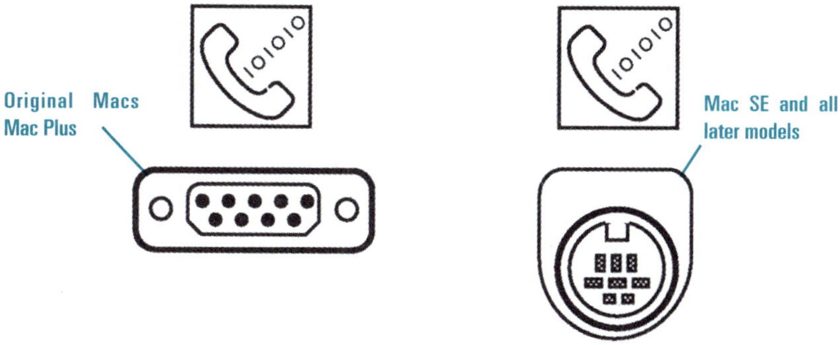

Figure 12.5
Possible modem jacks and the modem port icon.

The modem port on the back of the Mac is next to, and looks just like, the printer port. Both jacks work almost alike, but the computer gives the modem priority. This helps make sure communications aren't interrupted. Depending on the age of your Mac, the connector will be one of the two shown in Figure 12.5. No matter which kind of Mac you have, the phone icon identifies the modem port. (One popular modem, the Global Village TelePort, connects to an ADB keyboard or mouse jack. But don't worry about getting it confused. The plugs are different and the TelePort comes with complete instructions.)

Plug in the power cord, or power adapter. Most modems use low voltage and have wall transformers like the ones found with cassette recorders or video games. If you can't fit the transformer on your wall, it's okay to use an extension cord.

Telephone Traffic Cops

You can't use the phone and the modem at the same time. Picking up a local extension (or worse, dialing) causes noises that can disconnect most modems. But you don't have to post little yellow stickies on all the extensions, saying "Touch this and you DIE!" You can invest in privacy switches which disable the other phones when a single phone or modem is on the line.

> You can pick up privacy switches at electronics stores for less than $10 each. Ask for a Radio Shack Teleprotector or similar device. You'll need one for each phone, but it's still cheaper than a second line.

More elaborate *Automatic Line Switches* listen for specific handshaking tones and connect the line to your modem, fax machine, or telephone. These cost around $100, depending on features, at electronics and office supply stores. They may require some wiring. They work best when installed where the phone line first comes in from the street, so they can control all your phones at once. If you're going to install one this way, make sure it has *secondary ringing* and can ring extension phones when a voice call comes in.

If you have Call Waiting or a similar telephone company service, you'll need to disable it while you're on-line: the beep that indicates an incoming call can knock you off a bulletin board. Dial *70 before you place the call or insert *70, in the modem dialing instructions—the comma indicates a pause. If you have a rotary (pulse) phone, type `1170` before the number you're calling. When you disconnect, Call Waiting turns back on. (You can also do this from a telephone, if you don't want to be interrupted during an important voice call.)

Checking It Out

When the modem and computer are connected and turned on, you'll notice some lights on the front of the modem. They let you know what's going on inside the box, as follows:

MR	Modem Ready. Power is connected and circuits ready.
SD	Send Data. Flashes when data comes from your computer.
HS	High Speed. 2400 bps (as high as 14,400 bps on some modems).
OH	Off Hook. Modem has picked up the phone line.
TR	Terminal Ready. Mac is properly connected. If you see the TR light, you're almost ready to go on-line.
RD	Receive Data. Flashes when data comes down the phone line.
AA	Auto Answer. Modem is set to automatically take calls.
CD	Data Carrier Detect. Lights when properly handshaked.
FM	Fax Mode. Found only on fax modems.
VM	Voice Mode. Found only on modems with voice capability.

Telecommunications Software

You'll also need special software to activate your modem. Many on-line services provide their own *Graphical User Interface* or GUI (usually pronounced "gooey," believe it or not). These special programs let you call a particular service, such as Prodigy or America Online. They control your modem with Mac-like icons and menus but call only their own system. You can't use one service's GUI to call another service, even if the other is also graphically oriented. An example of one of these *dedicated* programs, for America Online, is shown in Figure 12.6. If you want to call a text service or local bulletin board, you'll also need a general purpose application—alternatively called *telecomm* or *terminal programs*—discussed below.

Figure 12.6

A friendly interface for America Online.

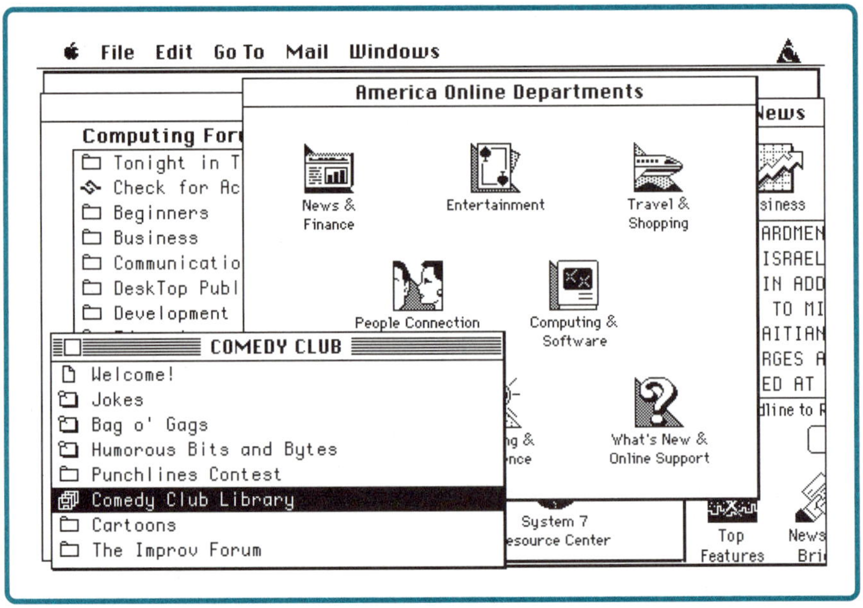

Some modems come with a telecomm program disk. This may not have all the features you want or need. Some of the things that make a useful telecomm program include: the ability to program custom functions (often called *macros*), multiple protocols to communicate with different types of modems, call-answering (making you the *host*), automatic redialing, and the ability to act like everything from old-fashioned teletypes to the latest Digital Equipment Corporation graphic terminal.

There's always going to be a trade-off between features, price, and ease of use. If all you want is user-friendliness and low cost, look for Dave Alverson's Z-Term: a shareware telecomm program available from user groups and commercial services. It supports most file transfer protocols, including the preferred ZMODEM format. You may also find a free telecommunications stack in HyperCard collections. It won't support graphics, macros, or anything else fancy, but it will get you on-line with a minimum of fuss. If you want something more powerful, you'll have to pay a few dollars.

White Knight

White Knight, a powerful and constantly evolving terminal program by Scott Watson, started life as one of first pieces of shareware. Updated versions of Watson's Red Ryder were distributed by user groups until a few years ago. Users kept calling for new features, so Watson formed the Freesoft Company to support new development and changed the name to avoid a lawsuit by the Red-Ryder-Cowboy people. This venerable program still remains the benchmark by which other telecomm software is judged.

The shareware versions of Red Ryder were reasonably uncomplicated. As the program matured, it also grew more powerful but harder to understand. It now comes with a 275-page manual. Some commands are definitely not intuitive. White Knight includes its own programming language and a built-in compiler. Users can write scripts that log onto a service, check for mail, and up- and download files on their own. Or the program can look over your shoulder and write a script that mimics your activities. It handles up to 30 user-defined buttons, 65,000 on-screen colors, an infinite number of linked scripts, and has the widest range of file transfer protocols of any telecomm program. (As a boon to the nearsighted, it also can display text in any font or size.) White Knight is usually discounted to around $90.

MicroPhone

The other major telecomm program, MicroPhone II, is definitely easier to grasp. It also costs about two-and-a-half times as much. At a street price around $225, it's one of the most expensive telecomm programs available. It's worth the price for people who want power without programming. Microphone II comes with four disks of prewritten scripts for just about every popular service, including Dow Jones, GEnie, and CompuServe. Once the program logs you in (and checks your mailbox if you want), it starts to work almost like a GUI. Figure 12.7 shows how you can push MicroPhone's buttons to make things happen.

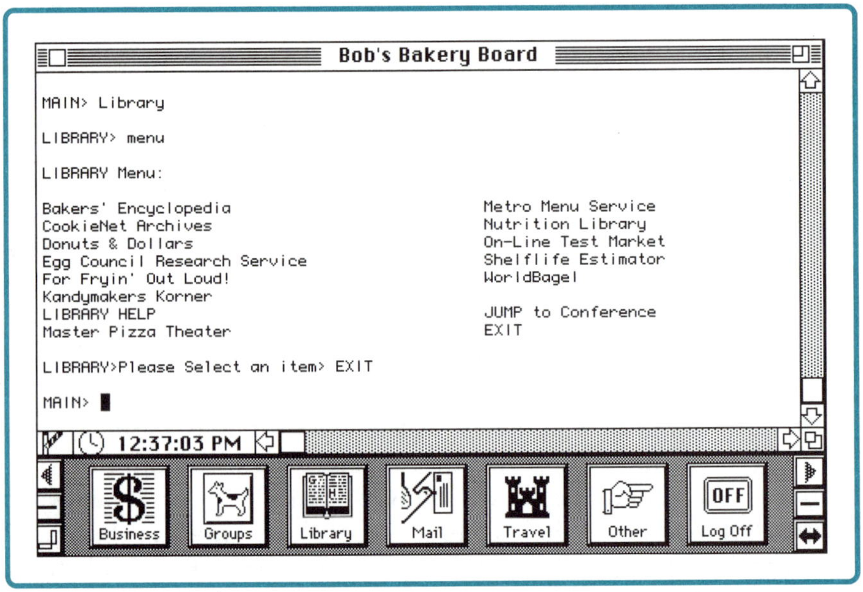

Figure 12.7

Click an icon to move around in MicroPhone.

MicroPhone comes with two manuals. But unlike White Knight's programming-and-philosophy texts, these books are for beginners. They walk you through procedures, show you how to use preprogrammed scripts, and then explain how to build your own. You can even create icons and subscripts for your favorite on-line activities.

Using a Modem and Telecomm Software

No matter what program you're using, there are four essential steps to communicating via modem.

1. Select the settings. Tell your computer how to send information and how to display what it receives. Chances are, you'll only need to do this once for each service you call.
2. Make the connection. Dial the number and give the service your identification and password.
3. Transfer data. This includes file transfers, real time chats and games, researching in a data library, or whatever else you want: it's all transferring data.
4. Disconnect. Tell the service you're leaving, and tell the modem to hang up the phone.

The rest of this section explains the details.

Step 1—Selecting the Settings

You need to establish communication protocols before you communicate. Look for a menu item called Modem Settings or Serial Port Settings. Figure 12.8 shows White Knight's. First, tell the program where you've plugged the modem: usually the modem port—with the telephone icon—but sometimes the printer port. (The next two items on the White Knight control panel affect how the computer speaks to the modem; you can leave the default values shown.)

Figure 12.8

White Knight's serial port dialog box.

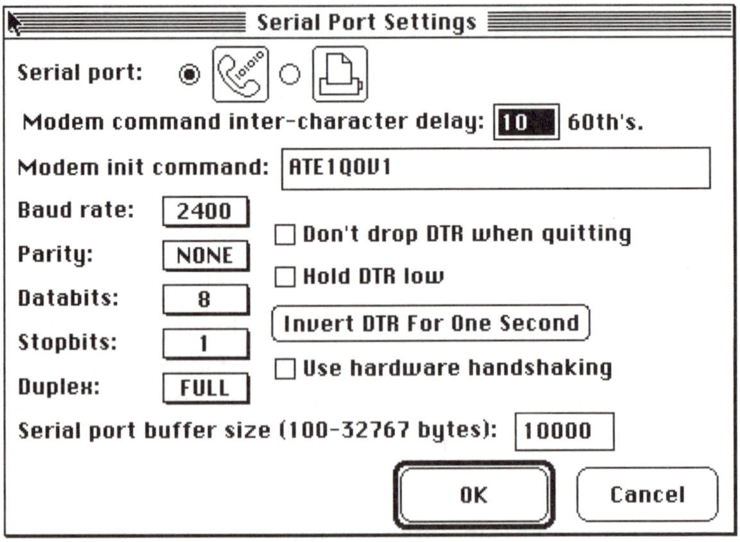

The next step is already done if you're using a GUI like the ones supplied with America Online or Prodigy. Otherwise, you'll have to set the protocols we discussed earlier. Figure 12.9 shows the pop-up menus in White Knight. If you're calling another individual, always use NO parity, 8 data bits, 1 stop bit, and HALF duplex. Set the baud rate according to the slower modem. If you are going to call most bulletin boards or on-line services, use NO parity, 8 data bits, 1 stop bit, and FULL duplex (Frequently expressed as N-8-1 FULL). Most services support the 2,400 baud setting.

Figure 12.9

Make setting selections on the pop-up menus.

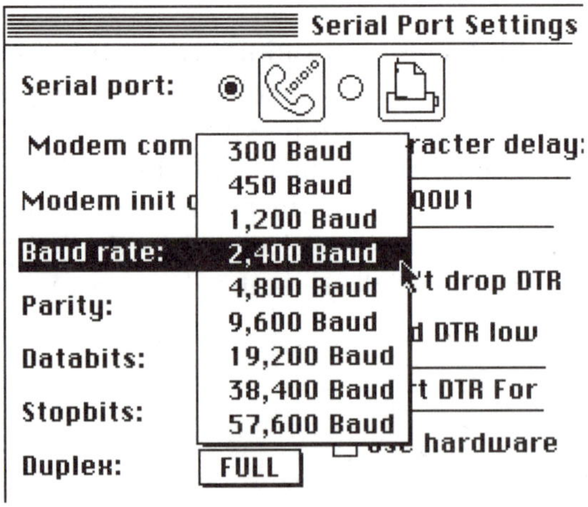

Now that the computer knows how to send information, you have to tell it how to receive. This is called *terminal emulation,* because it emulates a teletype terminal or video terminal. (Again, preprogrammed GUIs don't need this setting.) Figure 12.10 illustrates the choices in White Knight.

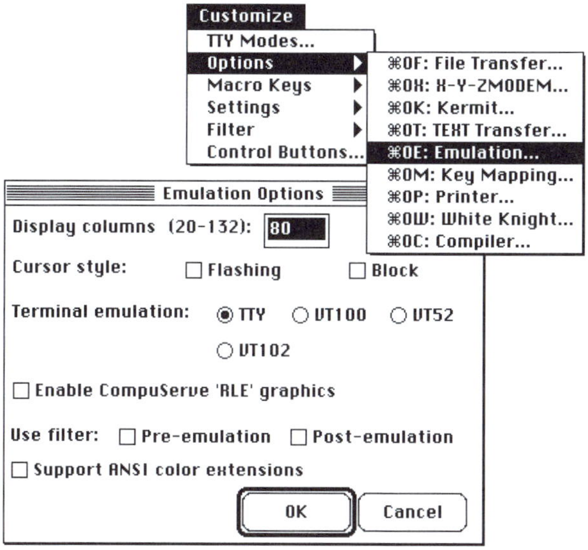

Figure 12.10

Emulation settings and the menus that get you there.

Most boards are set up for an 80-column display, which fits a compact Mac perfectly when using 9-point Monaco (the default typeface in most programs). The cursor can be an underline or a block to tell you where to type—a block cursor is illustrated at the bottom of Figure 12.7—and it can flash to call attention to itself on the screen (something we couldn't accomplish in this book).

TTY emulation (also called CRT on some systems) is sometimes called dumb terminal, because a teletype knows only a few commands. Use this if you're talking to an individual—even a smart one. The VT modes represent Digital Equipment Company devices, the standards for on-line compatibility (VT 100 and VT 102 are sometimes called ANSI-compatible terminals.) If you're calling an on-line service, start with TTY and work upward through the VTs. The higher ones make your keyboard's arrow keys more Maclike, and may enable line-graphics on some boards. CompuServe RLE graphics are highly detailed drawings, suitable for everything from clip art to weather maps. (Enabling this on other services can have unpredictable results.) Use filter options are for advanced users on non-standard boards.

Step 2—Connecting

Most modems initialize themselves when they're turned on. If yours doesn't, or it's working strangely, type **ATZ**. *AT* means *Attention,* telling your modem to do whatever command follows. *Z* stands for initialize. Once the modem has reset, it will respond OK on your screen. Before you call, see whether your phone uses tones or pulses. (Tone systems beep when you dial. Pulse systems click.) If you're calling from a tone phone, type **ATDT** and the phone number of the service. *ATDT* means *Attention, Dial (using) Tones.* If you have an ordinary rotary dial on your phones, use **ATDP** (*Attention, Dial Pulse*).

What happens after this depends on who you're calling. Here's a *log* of a call to the Boston Computer Society's Telecommunications Bulletin Board (the BCS has three other boards, including one that specializes in Macintosh). Our commands and text are in **bold, color, computer font**. The computer's responses are in computer font.

```
atz
OK

atdt 786-9788
CONNECT 2400

[here, we hit "return" a few times]

OPUS-CBCS v1.73a

Welcome to BCSNet Telecomm BBS - 101/122 in FidoNet.
This board is run on behalf of the Telecommunications
Group of the Boston Computer Society.
We request the use of proper names on this BBS system
and you should enter your FULL NAME when prompted.
```

```
What is your FULL NAME: Jay Rose
Password: ........


Welcome to BCSNet Telecomm BBS!
-------------------------------

Press ENTER to continue

[Return]

MAIN:  M)essage_Section      F)ile_Section     G)oodbye
B)ulletin  S)tatistics      Q)uestionnaire
P)age_SysOp C)hange_setup     H)istory    L)istUsers
V)ersion N)ews_update     *)Macro     @)MakeMacroMenu
?)HELP


Select: M
```

We initialized the modem, and got an OK. So we placed the call. Because most modems have built-in speakers, we heard the beeps as the modem dialed. When the host computer answered, we heard a whistle followed by a burst of handshaking noise. Once protocols were established, we saw we were connected at 2,400 bps. Then we hit the return key a few times, to let the board know that a human being was ready to communicate. The next step depends on the board.

Different systems use different forms of identification. This one asks for a real name. Others assign numbers to each user, or ask the users for a nickname or *handle*. Some ask for your city and state. No matter what the computer calls you, it then asks you to verify your identity with a *password*.

Password Precautions

The eight dots in the next line of our log represent the password we entered. Most services hide the password as you enter it to protect your Mac from prying eyes. (Bank ATM systems do the same thing.) Most non-commercial bulletin boards let you join by simply filling out an on-screen form and choosing a unique password—any combination of numbers and letters at least six characters long. When you join a commercial service, you'll probably receive a temporary password and user identification number. The first time you sign on, you'll be asked to supply your real name and a preferred password.

Be careful. Your password is your private key to a service. Don't give it to anyone—even a representative of the service. Unauthorized users can run up charges or have merchandise shipped in your name. They can also change your password, so you won't get in the next time.

Step 3—Exchanging Data

Now that you're on-line, what are you going to do? You have all kinds of options. You can receive news, weather, stock quotations, and sports scores; travel services including profiles of cities and countries you're considering visiting, as well as SABRE and PARS (which let you make airline and hotel reservations); reference libraries, including encyclopedias (available on most services); on-line games; electronic mail; forums and bulletin boards on all kinds of topics; live conferencing on most services; and shopping by modem.

Many services maintain large libraries of downloadable shareware. Figure 12.11 shows a small part of the games listing on CompuServe.

File Transfers

Telephone lines are noisy, and even a relatively minor pop or click can scramble a character, possibly turning your whole document into garbage. Special *error correcting* file transfer protocols make the task safer. As with handshaking, both sender and receiver have to agree on a file transfer protocol.

The granpappies are *XMODEM* and *Kermit.* XMODEM is the most common format, an option on all commercial services and on most BBSs. There are several variants, which some telecomm programs support. Unless both host and recipient can handle XMODEM-CRC or XMODEM-1K, stick with the plain vanilla version. Kermit is frequently used for mainframe transfers.

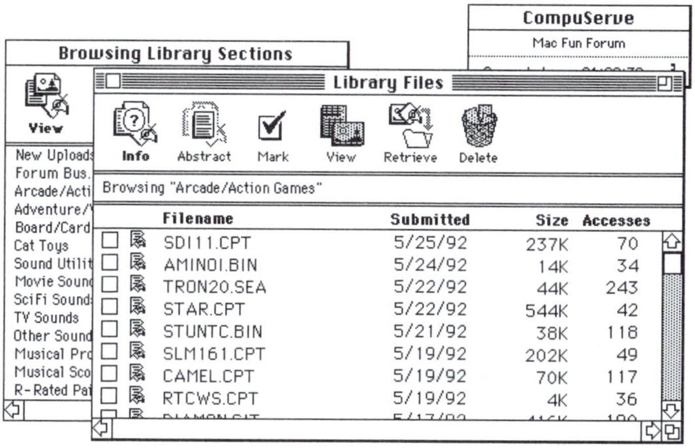

Figure 12.11

A few of the two hundred or more games available on CIS.

YMODEM can send batches of files, rather than single files as XMODEM does. It is considerably faster, but has no error checking mechanism and should be used only with very clean, reliable systems.

ZMODEM is the newest, and arguably the best, of the file transfer protocols. It combines the best of all the others. It's fast, handles batches of files, and checks for errors. It can even be interrupted in the middle of a transfer and pick up where it left off (saving frustration if line noise stops a download that's three-quarters finished). Many BBSs and on-line services now support ZMODEM, but some terminal programs can't use it.

When you're transferring a file you'll get a status box like the one in Figure 12.12. It tells you how long the operation will take and gives you something to look at while it happens. Your terminal window, the place where text generally appears, is inactive during the transfer. Most terminal programs let you use DAs or other applications under MultiFinder or System 7 while they're transferring, and beep to let you know they're finished. (The GUI supplied with America Online cheerfully announces "File's Done!" through the Mac speaker.)

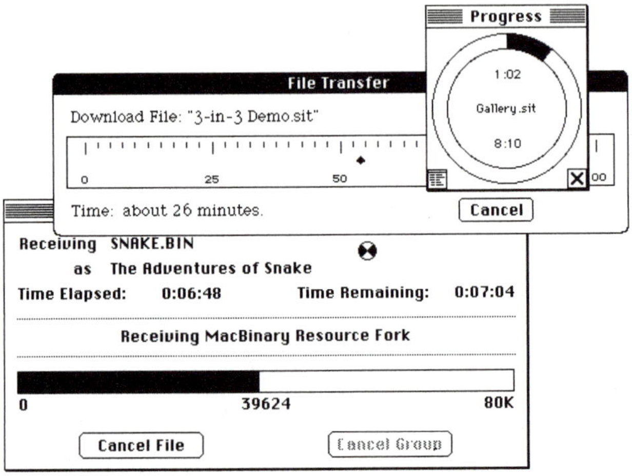

Figure 12.12

Three systems for keeping track of download progress.

> Applications that use a lot of processing—like twitch games—can significantly slow down file transfers. If you're in a hurry for a file transfer, don't try to run another program.

On-Line Activities

Aside from file transfers, you can read information and post your own messages on a bulletin board or forum. Figure 12.13 shows a screen shot of a typical message on America Online. You can exchange E-mail with other service members. Commercial services also let you shop and bank on-line, check today's news and tomorrow's weather, and get the latest sports scores. When you're all done, it's time to log off.

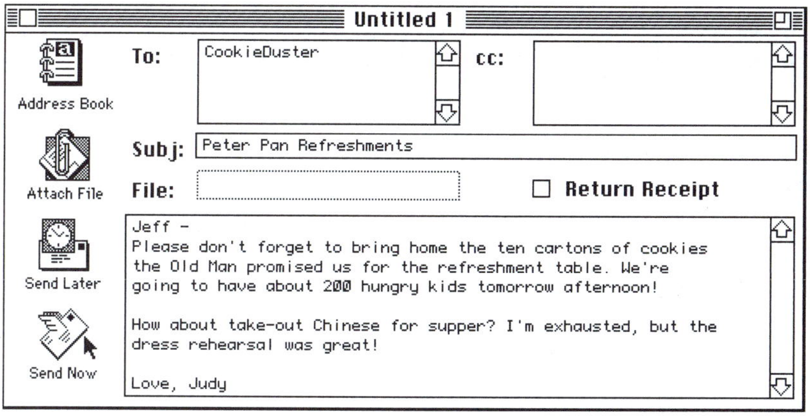

Figure 12.13
Sending E-mail via America Online.

Step 4—Disconnecting

Since most commercial services charge by the minute, you'll want to be sure you've actually signed off when you think you have. Disconnecting appears as a menu item in some GUI programs, or as a box to click in others. Text-based services like Delphi have you type **`exit`** or **`bye`** to leave (or, occasionally, **`/signoff`**). After you've finished the signoff procedure, the modem will report `NO CARRIER`. Tell it **`ATH`** to hang up the phone. Sometimes a system will appear to freeze while you're on-line. You may have gotten accidentally disconnected (*turfed*, as Delphi users call it), or the host may be having problems. In such a case, the best thing to do is to turn the modem off and on again. This will hang up and reinitialize, so you can start over.

> Don't sign off by turning off the modem if you're still connected to a small bulletin board. This can freeze the host system, anger the system operator, and get you permanently disconnected.

Choosing a Service

There's a service for you, no matter what your interests are. How to choose? Check for specials, free trials, and satisfaction guarantees. Most modems include bundled offers from Prodigy or CompuServe. GEnie promises to refund your first month's basic charge if you don't like what you find. Another way to decide is to talk to friends who belong or who may have used a service and dropped it. Each of the services has its strengths and weaknesses.

CompuServe

With more than a half million members, CompuServe is certainly the biggest commercial service (see Figure 12.14). It's also the most confusing. Furthermore, at $6.00 per hour for evening connections—and *much* more during the day—it can get expensive. You can waste hours in the never-never land of forums and libraries without ever posting a message or downloading a file. Its layers of menus are complicated, and its commands, even with the GUI and menus, are less than user-friendly.

> The CompuServe Information System (CIS) is often referred to by non-subscribers as CI$.

CompuServe's Navigator software can help. It lets you list what you want to do before you log in. Then it logs in, performs your commands, and gets out with computer efficiency. The whole idea is to save you from having to pay for being on-line while you're looking at menus or thinking what to do next. Figure 12.15 shows how it works. Navigator, unfortunately, costs extra and doesn't access all areas of CompuServe. Since CIS functions as a straight text service, you can use an ordinary terminal program. But if you're on CompuServe a lot, you might find their special programs a good investment.

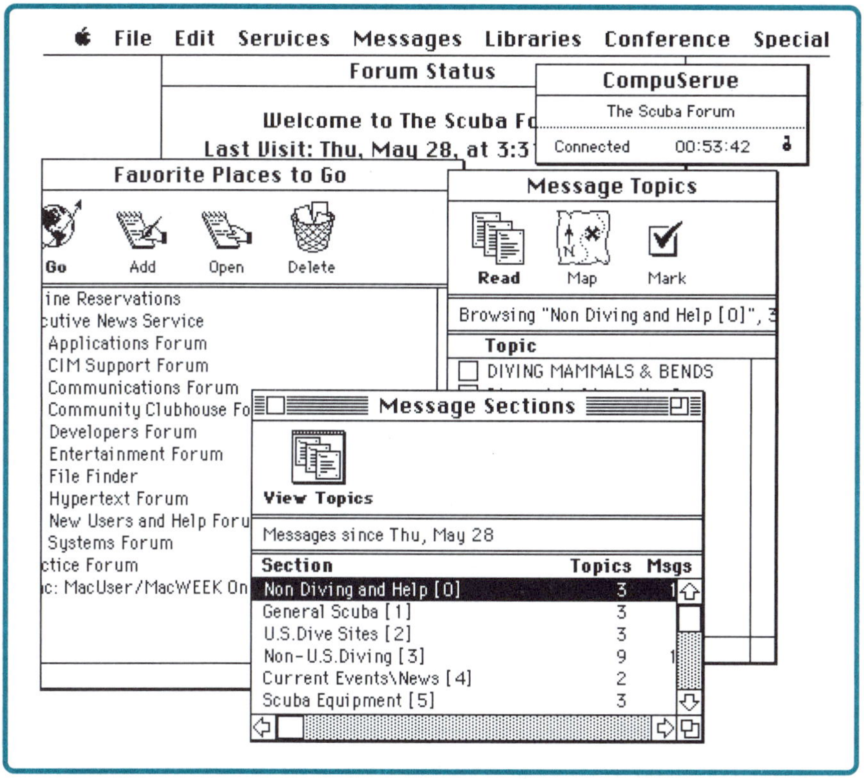

Figure 12.14
A typical CompuServe session using CIM.

Prodigy

Prodigy is a joint creation of IBM and Sears, so its orientation is not surprisingly IBM PC—and its basic premise is "shop 'til you drop." Its screen looks more like an ad than an information service (see Figure 12.16). Because downloading takes time away from advertising, the software doesn't provide a way to print most screens or save files. (A shareware INIT, P*-to-Disk, lets you save Prodigy text. It's downloadable from most commercial services—except you won't find it on Prodigy.)

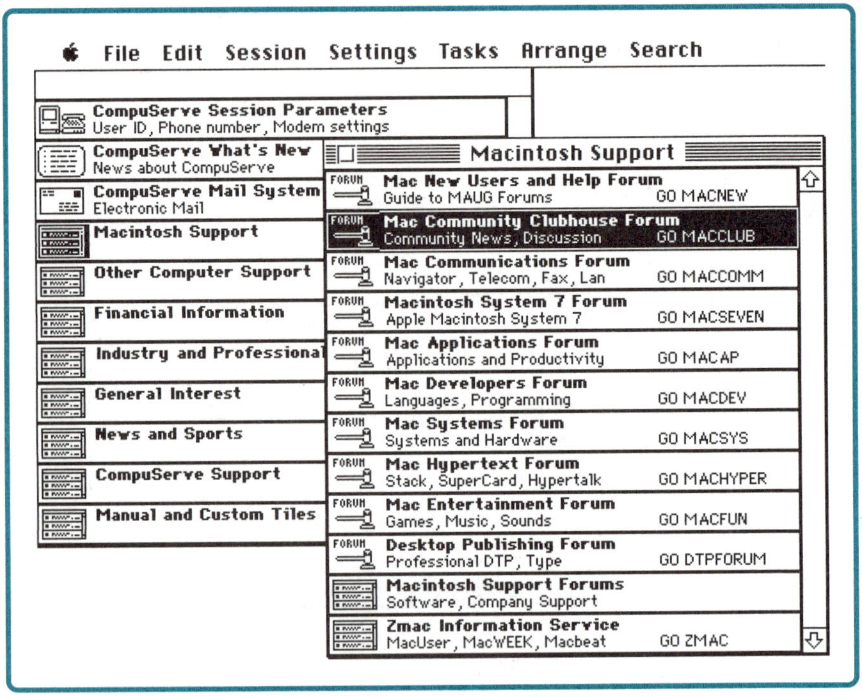

Figure 12.15

Smooth sailing with the Navigator.

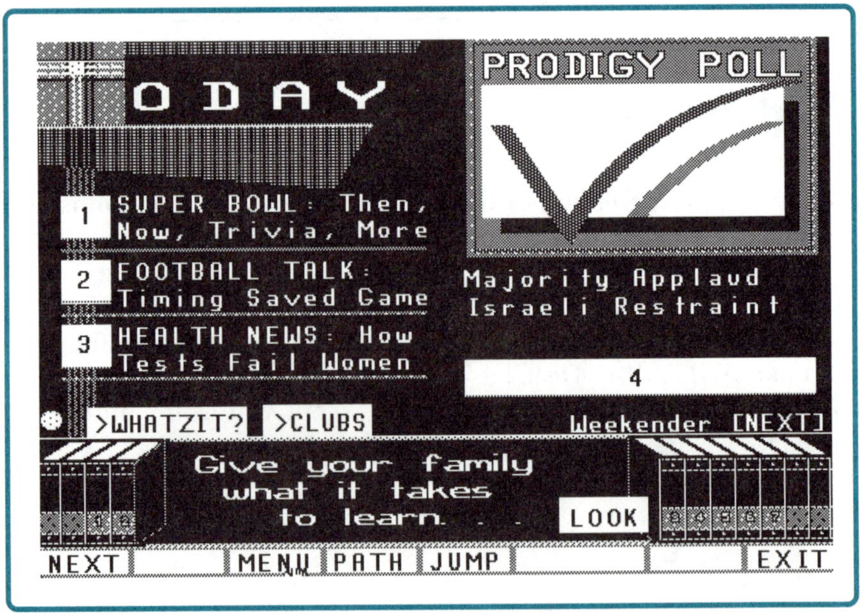

Figure 12.16

A Prodigy screen.

Prodigy was designed for the IBM, and the Mac version came much later. The built-in capabilities that make the Mac so friendly—including the Menu bar, MultiFinder, and DAs—are ignored by Prodigy. The built-in imaging hardware is also ignored, and screens have to be painted bit-by-bit. This process is s-l-o-w. It can take as much as a full minute to log in and 20 seconds to go from one screen to the next. Even fans call it PLOD-igy.

Mercifully, Prodigy doesn't charge by the minute. $12.95 per month covers unlimited day or evening access (there's a surcharge for over 30 E-mail messages a month). Most of the costs of the service are paid by on-screen advertisers. An interesting aspect of this advertising mentality is its notorious censorship. Messages are refused if they cover adult subjects, competing commercial products, or say anything negative about Prodigy. They're even refused if they're *depressing*—making Prodigy the only national service without a Forum for the disabled. Censorship is final, and the service "terminates" members who keep bringing the matter up.

America Online

When you sign on to America Online, your Mac's speaker says "Welcome." Right away, you know this service is going to be different. America Online was formerly part of Apple's official AppleLink service for developers, and it was taken over by Quantum Computer Services to let the rest of us in. As you might expect, it's the most Mac-like service. You click icons and use scrolling menus to get around. Since the functions use Mac's built-in text and graphics routines, they're fast and familiar. There's an immense amount of Mac information with forums supported by Apple, Claris, Microsoft, *MacWorld Magazine*, and just about every other major player. You'll also find the usual on-line goodies like news, weather, travel, and large downloadable software libraries.

Unlike the other services, America Online's GUI disk comes with very few instructions. It doesn't seem to need many. It's easy to figure out where you are in America Online and how to do what you want. Downloading is MultiFinder-friendly, so you can start a long download and still use your Mac for something else while the data comes in. America Online costs $5.95 per month, plus $4.00 per nighttime hour. Some typical screens were shown in Figure 12.6.

GEnie

Unlike the first three services we described, General Electric's on-line service is strictly text-based. You must use a terminal program to get in. It also uses an unusual protocol. Set your terminal software to HALF, instead of FULL, duplex. Once you've dialed and see `CONNECT`, *don't* just hit return. Instead, type **`HHH`** and then hit [Return]. This must be done within the first few seconds after connection. In a few moments, you'll see `U#`. Now enter your User ID number, followed by a comma and then your password. If you don't follow this exactly, the system won't work.

Many of GEnie's downloadable programs are in MS DOS format and useless on a Mac. But the reference materials and other services are text-based and can be read by any word processor. And the forum areas are incredibly diverse. GEnie's two-tiered pricing structure can be the absolute lowest in the industry. For $4.95 a month, you get unlimited evening access to basic services including selected forums, classic games, travel and entertainment services, unlimited E-mail, and news and weather. A time-based connect fee kicks in once you start to do other things, at about the same rate as CompuServe.

Delphi

Also a text-based service, Delphi is easy to use and often seems friendlier than CompuServe or GEnie. You can browse by typing simple commands. For example, **GR SF** takes you to the Science Fiction Forum, one of many Delphi Groups. **ENT TQ** enters the on-line Trivia Quest game in the Entertainment section. (During trice-weekly trivia tournaments, members compete for prizes and trade wisecracks.) Elsewhere in the game area, the Poker tables are always open, and many fantasy and board games await.

Delphi's conference area is by far the easiest of all the on-line services. Typing **/Help** at any menu gives you a list of options, as shown in Figure 12.17. Delphi also charges by the minute, but at rates substantially less than CompuServe's: twenty dollars, for the first twenty hours per month.

```
BOSTON>Which Service? /help
 - Immediate "/" Commands -
/EXIT - same as Control-Z
/BUSY - disables conference messages
/LENGTH 24 - sets page size to 24
/NOBUSY - re-enables conference messages
/PROMPT - sets prompt mode to MENU, VERBOSE, or BRIEF
/TIME - show time
/WIDTH 80 - sets terminal width to 80
/WHOIS username
- Use /HELP FULL to get a complete list.
```

Figure 12.17
Getting help from Delphi.

Making the Choice

The national on-line systems are different, not in their basic services (all have news, bulletin boards, shopping, and reference materials), but in their specialties. Some are better for research, others are better for gaming. Professional and special-interest forums vary widely. And of course, rates range widely also. But you'll also find that styles vary. What's taken as friendly chat on one board may be totally out-of-place on another. Try them all . . . you may even find that a free local board meets your needs completely.

While some national services will send you a bill every month, most prefer to charge their fees to your credit card or direct-debit your checking account. If this concerns you, as it does us and many members of the Boston Computer Society who have reported hard-to-correct errors and unauthorized credit card charges, you may be able to get direct billing by asking for a business account.

Local Access

Some services, such as Prodigy, pride themselves on having local access numbers all over the country. Others have limited local access and use a gateway system such as Tymnet, Telenet, or the Canadian Datapac system to provide a connection without long distance charges. The service you select will be happy to tell you how to gain access via one of these gateways.

> **CAUTION:** Even without long distance charges, on-line fun can cost money! It's not hard to spend a couple of hours in conference or playing games. Downloads take time, so even freeware can cost several dollars per program. Sophisticated terminal software keeps track, in dollars and cents, of how long you've been connected. If yours doesn't, keep a timer next to the Mac.

On-Line Etiquette

The best way to learn how to chat on-line is to plunge right in. CompuServe usually sets one or two channels of its CB simulator aside for newcomers. America Online's Lobby area and Pub also welcome first-time chatters, and the Delphi conference system is friendly to novices. There are just a few things to remember. Spelling mistakes are inevitable, and should be ignored. But it's considered bad form to leave CAPS LOCK ON (the equivalent of shouting through a bullhorn).

On-line chatters are a friendly bunch, and you can expect every entrance to be greeted with a round of `Hi`, `{{hugs}}`, and `smooch`. You might also encounter a few shorthand symbols, called *emoticons* (emotion icons). If you can't quite make them out, hold this book on its side.

:-) or :)	Smiles
`;-)`	Wink
`:-(`	Frown
`:-P`	Sticking out tongue
`:-o`	Surprise
`@—>-—`	A rose for milady
B-)	Wearing glasses

Other common shorthand expressions include:

BRB	Be Right Back (used when you're leaving the keyboard for a minute.) Similar to AFK (Away from Keys).
BTW	By the Way.
GA	Go Ahead (generally used after someone has sent several lines of a long thought, or in a more formal conference).
GMTA	Great Minds Think Alike (when two members have typed virtually the same comment).
IMHO	In My Humble Opinion . . . (Watch out for this one! Soapbox time . . .)
LOL	Laughing Out Loud.

OTOH	On the Other Hand.
ROFL	Rolling on Floor Laughing (also appears as ROTF-Rolling On the Floor).

Many on-line friends become off-line friends as well. But a word of warning is in order here, too. There are some very strange people in the world, and a few of them have modems. Some go looking for the computerized version of a one-night stand. Others simply pretend to be someone or something they're not. The classic story reported in *CompuServe Magazine* involved one of their on-line CB Hostesses, who supported "Pregnant & Pretty" through nine months of maternity advice only to learn that P&P, male, was neither. There is a fair amount of "hot chat" on some of the services. CompuServe and America Online put descriptive titles on the CB channels being used for "adult" conversation. It's not a good idea to let the kids go browsing on these services unattended. Telecommunications could be more educational than you realize. Prodigy's censors, of course, guarantee a G rating. You can give your children their own Prodigy numbers and not worry about what they'll see. Most of what they see will be commercials.

In This Chapter

Adding More Memory to Save Time

•

Bigger and Better Storage with a Hard Disk

•

Backup Storage Options

•

Tips for Choosing Software and Supplies

Most Macs are complete when you take them out of the box. But by adding a few extra gadgets, you can make any machine more efficient. This chapter covers some of the ways to make your Mac more capable, including tips for buying memory, storage options, and the best ways to acquire software and supplies.

13

Enhancing Your Mac

Our first personal computer, in 1979, boasted a whopping four thousand bytes (4K) of memory and saved its programs on an old cassette recorder. While we could use that computer for simple math and even wrote a graphic pinball game (which was so inept it should have been called Cheeseball), the system wasn't even powerful enough to balance a checkbook. The main function of this machine was suggesting what personal computers would do in the future.

Within three years, we had 60K more bytes of RAM and two 90K floppy disks. The system was still slow and limited—it had a fraction of the power of the earliest Macs—but we were able to use it for basic business functions like word processing and data handling. Of course, all those chips and cards were strung together with ribbon cable and the whole mess was pretty unreliable. We were looking at a state-of-the-art, all-in-one 64K machine, but couldn't afford it.

Two years later, we bought a Mac. It had twice as much memory and a 400K drive. Its programs were almost as large as our original disk drive. We were in heaven...until we realized our applications required even more memory and a second drive. Within a year, that Mac had grown to *a hundred times* more memory than that original machine.

And it still wasn't enough.

We're not saying a computer is a Bermuda Triangle for memory chips (and finances). But chips get cheaper, processors faster, and drives bigger. Programmers take advantage of this growth and write more powerful applications that need the bigger drives and multiple chips. Users upgrade their computers to run the new programs and expect a payoff in productivity, sales efforts, and the bottom line.

The most obvious example of this is Apple's new System 7: most users need at least *2M* just to turn it on!

The nice thing about this runaway computer expansion is you can do nifty things on a desktop that were virtually impossible on a mainframe several years ago, like quickly generating the chart in Figure 13.1 to illustrate our little story.

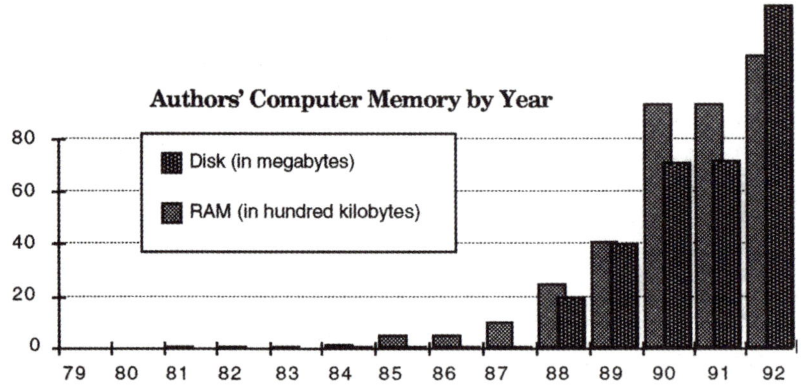

Figure 13.1

A quick illustration.

Should You Upgrade?

The rule of thumb for upgrading hardware is the same as the rule for upgrading software: *if it ain't broke, don't fix it.* If you're happy with your computer's capability and the software it can run at its present size and structure, there's no reason to change. Spend your money elsewhere. Or, better yet, save it for when you'll want one of Apple's latest Mac models. But if you're noticing bottlenecks—that is, if you're losing time, productivity, or patience—consider enhancing your hardware. You should think about upgrading if

- ▲ You frequently shut down one application to copy data to another. You need more memory.
- ▲ You want to take advantage of System 7 on an older machine. You need more memory, and possibly an accelerator.
- ▲ You already have four or five megabytes of memory, and you're still shutting down one application to copy data to another. You need System 7's Virtual Memory feature.
- ▲ You spend a lot of time swapping disks. You need another drive.
- ▲ Backing up is tedious. Get a bigger backup medium.
- ▲ You've got a hard disk, but it's getting slower and slower. Surprise! You probably just need some software to perk up that disk. See Chapter 14.
- ▲ You have crammed clip art collections and distended databases. It's time for a CD-ROM drive.
- ▲ You need absolutely permanent storage. A Write-Once, Read Many Optical Drive uses lasers to store your data as thousands of points of light.
- ▲ Complicated page layouts and spreadsheets are slowing you down. You need an accelerator to help the Mac get through graphics and calculations faster.

You also may need to enhance your Mac just to run new software. Some programs require hefty minimum memories. Others need a hard disk to run efficiently.

About Memory . . .

Computer memory comes in two types: *volatile* (the contents disappear when you turn off the power) and *nonvolatile* (the more permanent kind). In Macs and most other personal computers, the volatile memory is on chips (*RAM* chips, or *Random Access Memory*), and the nonvolatile is on floppy or hard disks.

RAM is very fast. Disks are slower. Operations that need frequent references to a file (program instructions, spreadsheet data) go much faster in RAM. RAM is also expensive. A floppy that costs two dollars or less holds more information than a hundred dollars' worth of chips (as of this writing—one of the most volatile aspects of RAM is price).

RAM is the stuff people usually refer to when they talk about the *size* of a computer and is the first number in size specifications. For example, a "Classic II 4/40" is a Classic II with 4M RAM and a 40M hard disk. In fact, RAM is what we usually mean by "memory." Floppies and hard disks are more often called "storage."

This leads us to an important definition. Remember that computers think in terms of *bits:* one or zero, on or off, black or white. This way of thinking is great for specifying a single dot on a screen, but kind of limiting if you want to pick, say, one letter out of 26. The smallest useful chunk of computer information for human beings requires about seven bits, to fully describe 128 possible choices.

Computers are most efficient processing things by powers of two (2, 4, 8, 16, 32, and so on), so designers simply rounded the seven bits to the next power, defining *a byte as eight bits (or a choice of one out of 256 possibilities).* With a little applied Latin, *kilobyte* (*K* or *KB*) becomes one thousand bytes, and *megabyte* (*M, MB*) is a million of them. Actually, because of that power-of-two rounding, one K is really 1,024 bytes.

MultiFinder and Layering

Macintosh has a marvelous tool, *MultiFinder,* which essentially lets your Mac have a split personality (see Figure 13.2). If you want to touch up a graphic and paste it into a memo (while your modem is sending something to the home office), you can keep all three programs running at once. You just keep each program's document on your screen, and click the one you want to work on. (The PC world has recently added similar capabilities in *Windows.*)

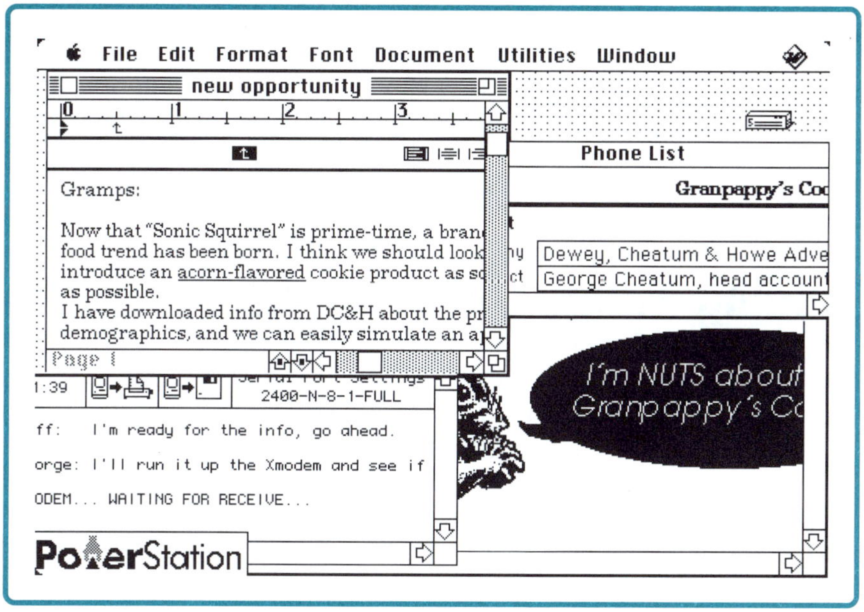

Figure 13.2

MultiFinder at work (System 7 has a similar feature). Each window activates a different program.

MultiFinder needs memory to support all those programs—as a general rule, slightly less than 1M of RAM for each (this varies with the programs. Some graphics and database programs are memory hogs), plus more for the MultiFinder itself.

MultiFinder runs best with System 6.0.5 or 6.0.7, and all you need is Apple's MultiFinder and DA Handler files, which you received free with the system disk. System 7 includes a built-in function that lets you keep opening programs until you run out of memory, so you won't need MultiFinder. The effect is about the same.

Once you've installed these files in your System Folder, you can activate MultiFinder by selecting it under Set Startup in the Finder and restarting. If an application is open, you can still get back to the Finder to open any other (up to limits imposed by memory). You can switch between open applications and the Finder by selecting them in the Apple menu, clicking the small icon in the upper right corner of the screen, or clicking any on-screen window from the application.

Even if you don't plan to use MultiFinder, extra memory can still save you time. Some applications use *layering* and load only part of a program when they start. As you request a function, the system gets it from disk and forgets others. This takes time. Applications that use layering let you turn it off, but only if you have enough memory. Many programs also give you multiple documents or let you enlarge a drawing or spreadsheet, depending on available memory.

Adding Memory to Your Mac

You can add RAM to any Macintosh, up to limits determined by the machine's internal construction. However, memory was soldered in place on very early Macs. Upgrading these machines now is probably impractical. (Back in 1985 and 1986, there was a thriving market in *board swaps*. You'd exchange your Mac 128's brains for a board upgraded on an assembly line. Your old board would go back to the line to be upgraded for someone else.)

Starting with the Plus, Apple organized Mac memory on *SIMMs*: single in-line memory modules. Many users think of SIMMs as "snap-in memory," because the modules are really plug-in cards. Unfortunately, plugging them in requires opening up your Mac (and in some cases, clipping or soldering resistors).

CAUTION: Opening a compact Mac is hazardous if you're not a trained technician. Both Apple and this book urge you not to try. If you feel you *have* to crack open a compact Mac, read the warnings in Chapter 14 and get the specialized tools. Then, don't do it.

Mail-order computer stores will send you a videotape showing their experts installing memory. The tape is a marketing ploy to sell more chips. If you have a Mac II (or a PowerBook and are willing to void the warranty) you may be successful. If you have a compact Mac, forget it. We're not assuming you're a klutz. The insides of any computer are delicate and generally unprotected. Anyone can make a fatal slip and render a $2,500 box inoperative. At least if a service shop makes the mistake, they have to fix it.

Prices for memory fluctuate, but for the few years prior to this writing, the price has been drifting downward from $60 to $35 per megabyte through mail order, and $10 or $15 more per megabyte professionally installed. High-speed Mac IIs need faster, slightly more expensive chips to perform properly. PowerBooks need medium power memory cards, currently running $80 to $150 per megabyte. Portable Macs use low power memory chips that cost about $350 per megabyte, if you can still find them.

Storage Devices

The more programs and documents you use, the more storage space you'll need to keep them in. It's easy to install additional storage, and you can choose from a range of storage options that goes far beyond the original floppy (and perhaps hard disk) supplied with your Mac. This section describes some of the storage devices available. Generally, the more a device costs to buy, the less it'll cost in the long run. But functions, features, and speed vary among manufacturers, so compare before you buy.

Floppy Disk Drives

You need one floppy disk drive in any system, to load software and make backups. Unless you do a lot of disk-to-disk copying, there are only a few reasons to buy an external floppy.

- You have to read disks written on a PC or current Mac and have an early SE or Plus with a noncompatible 800K drive.
- You've got a very old Mac 512 or 128 with just one drive and no provision for a hard disk.

- ▲ You can't afford a hard disk.
- ▲ Some copy-protected software relies on peculiarities of the 800K track format, and SuperDrives can't read them. If you have a newer Mac, you may need to find an external 800K floppy to use these disks. See Chapter 14, first, for a warning.

You can buy a 1.4M SuperDrive for about $230 by mail order. For little more than twice that amount, you can buy a hard disk that's thirty times larger. On a bits-per-buck basis, a floppy is not a good deal. It also runs much more slowly. On the other hand, it's easy to install: just plug it in to the back of your Mac. With a SuperDrive, you can use low-cost 800K disks or more powerful 1.4M HD ones; the differences are discussed in the next chapter. Here's a brief summary about floppy drives.

Pros	Interchangeable with any MacPortable and easily distributed
Cons	Slow Limited storage area
Price	Initial: About $230 Media: 75¢ - $2 per disk
Cost per megabyte	About $230 initially $1.25 per stored megabyte

Hard Disk Drives

This is the standard for any serious computing. Today's hard drives are inexpensive, fast, and reliable. You'll see an immediate improvement when you switch from floppy to hard drive. Your system and programs will start faster, and you won't be constantly swapping disks. (You may also *hear* a difference. A few brands of hard disk are relatively noisy.) Some older copy-protected software won't run from the hard disk, but most publishers have abandoned this form of protection.

The disadvantage of a hard disk is that all your computing eggs are in one basket. If a hard disk crashes, you can lose your system and all your files at once. (Floppy disks are more likely to crash, but they're smaller so you risk less.) Some ways to protect yourself are discussed in the next chapter.

Internal versus External Hard Drives

Most new Macs have hard drives built-in (the super-powerful Quadras don't), but many older units use floppy disks only. If you want to add hard-disk storage to a Quadra, or you're upgrading an old or used machine, you'll be faced with the choice between an *internal* or *external* drive—one that lives inside the Mac and draws power from it, or one that has a separate box and power supply. There's no functional difference between them. In fact, the magnetic mechanisms of both are identical, and they handle data with equal efficiency.

The eggs-in-basket consideration we discussed in the last section applies even more to internal hard drives. If an internal drive needs repair, you lose your entire computer while it's being fixed. If your computer's brains need repair but the disk is still functional, you can't easily move its data to another machine. Installing an internal drive on most Macs is a job for a technician.

External drives are safer and far easier to install, but they cost about a hundred dollars more than their internal brothers. The drive prices in the rest of this chapter refer to external units. You can add an external hard drive to any Mac—even if it's already got an internal one—with a simple SCSI connection. (See Chapter 16 for more information.) The Mac 512 and 128 don't have SCSI jacks, so their hard drives use the much slower modem connection.

Size versus Price

The most costly parts of a hard disk system are the power supply and mechanism, not the magnetic surface, so the cost-per-byte declines drastically as the disk gets bigger. A typical mail order 40M external hard drive will set you back about $500. For $100 more, you can get one twice as big. Or you can pay four times more—slightly less than

$2,000—and get a drive a dozen times bigger! These super-sized drives, running between 500M to 650M, are usually reserved for professional audio or graphics applications.

Don't waste your money on a 20M hard disk. A few powerful applications and an enhanced system will quickly eat up half its space, and a busy database can fill up the rest. Unless you're going to use the Mac in a very simple home office (or are particularly strapped for cash), go for a bigger unit. (We wish somebody had pointed this out to us a few years ago.) A Mac with 45M to 80M offers plenty of room for everything except massive graphics or database projects. If you do fill up your small hard disk, you can easily add others to your SCSI chain (Chapter 16).

We also recommend you don't buy a *used* hard disk. A hard disk is constantly spinning, whenever the computer is turned on. If anything's going to wear out with age, it will. (The other parts of a well-cared-for Mac will live forever. We've been as happy with second-hand Macs as with new ones.)

TIP: If you have a lot of files in a large drive, the Finder can slow down trying to draw them all on the desktop. You can *partition* a drive into smaller sections that are easier to handle, using software supplied with the unit. Each partition acts like a separate disk, even though they're physically connected.

Here's a summary of information about hard disk drives.

Pros	Fast Large storage area More reliable than floppies
Cons	Moderate initial cost Not portable
Price	Initial: $450–$700 Media: n/a
Cost per megabyte	About $7–$10 initially No on-going cost.

Removable Hard Disk Drives

Imagine a hard disk with the features of a floppy. You could move files from computer to computer and lock the files up in a safe at night. If the disk got full, you'd just stick in a new magnetic platter. *Removable hard disk drives* hold 45M to 88M—the equivalent of between fifty and a hundred standard floppies—on a single cartridge. The drives connect through the SCSI port, and, as far as the computer is concerned, are just another hard disk. The only drawback is the cost of the transport—about fifty percent more than similarly sized nonremovable hard disks. The cartridges cost about the same as an equivalent number of floppies—$75 to $100 dollars each—but give you a hard disk's speed, reliability, and compactness.

Pros	Fast Large storage area Secure and portable
Cons	Expensive initial cost
Price	Initial: $650 - $850 Media: $75 - $100 per disk (price depends on size)
Cost per megabyte	About $15 initially $1.20 per stored megabyte

Tape Backup Systems

While tape systems are available from Apple and third-party vendors, they're just now catching on, and most dealers still don't carry them. There are two principal formats. Large-tape drives are slower but cost about the same as removable hard disks; their cartridges cost $30 to $40 (about fifty cents per megabyte). Drives using 4mm DAT tapes may cost twice as much, but the cassettes cost as little as *fifteen cents* per megabyte! Because of their size and low media cost, these systems are excellent for backups and long-term storage. But the real price you pay is speed and convenience. Tapes have to be *formatted* to receive the data, a process that can take more than half an hour. And since the heads don't jump around like a hard disk, they're much too slow to use as a primary medium.

Optical Drives

Optical drives aren't subject to the magnetic interference or aging that plague other drives. A tightly focused laser reads and writes the data, so optical disks pack more bits in less space. (The principle is the same as CD audio, which stores a lot more music in a smaller package than traditional long-playing albums.) It's easy to connect optical drives through the SCSI port. Because they hold so much data, you might need special software to keep track of your files on an optical drive.

CD-ROM

CD-ROM storage devices use disks identical to music CDs, and some of the drives can also play music. Because CD-ROM is virtually crash proof, easy to store, and can hold hundreds of megabytes, it's ideal for distributing large files. Manufacturers now distribute packages of related programs, clip art and photo libraries, and reference materials on CD-ROM. Modern drives are fast and are an excellent complement to a hard disk. The drawback is that they're *ROM*: read-only memory. Home CD players can't record songs, and CD-ROMs can't save data. Data duplication houses prepare the disks on special equipment.

CD-ROM drives cost between $500 and $1,000. The time and space savings makes them a bargain for professional applications. Disk prices vary according to what's on them, but range from about $40 (for the equivalent of 700 floppies' worth of public domain software) to more than a thousand dollars for up-to-date compilations of technical journals. Typical home-office reference materials—including encyclopedias, atlases, and collections of clip art—cost around $250.

Pros	Very large storage area Relatively fast and portable Low per-byte cost

Cons	Can't save user data
Price	Initial: $500 - $1,000 Media: varies according to copy-righted data
Cost per megabyte	About $1 initially About 5¢ for public-domain software

Writable Optical Drives

Recently, prices have started to decline on *flopticals*, systems that combine the best features of optical drives and floppies. The drives cost about fifty percent more than an equivalent removable hard disk would, if one were available: $1,500 to $2,000, for systems holding between 128M and 600M. (High-speed gigabyte-sized systems cost more than $3,500.) The disks themselves are fast, small, robust, and relatively cheap at $50 to $200. Some optical systems give you *WORM* (Write Once, Read Many) ability. Once you save a file, it can't be altered by you or any other user: an important feature in accounting and financial tracking systems. WORM disks are even cheaper.

Pros	Crash-proof, long-life storage Big and fast Extremely low per-byte cost WORM feature provides audit trail
Cons	Highest initial cost
Price	Initial: $500 - $1,000 $3,500 for super-sized systems Media: $50 - $200
Cost per megabyte	$3 - $6 initially (depending on size) 30¢ - 40¢ per stored megabyte

System Accelerators

System accelerators are actually extra computers that fit inside your Mac and take over some of the processing load, often with a more powerful chip than Apple originally installed. They can provide significant speed advantages in programs that do a lot of calculating, like spreadsheets or image manipulation programs. The added speed won't help much in text-based or database applications, because these programs spend most of their time waiting for you to type, but you may notice that disk accesses are faster with certain accelerators.

If you think you need one, consult your local Mac guru. Accelerators have to be matched to your computer and application, and the price can range from $350 to almost $2,000. Have it installed professionally in a compact Mac, and ask the installer to clean the connector with "Cramolin" (available from Caig Laboratories, Escondido, CA) on any machine that's more than a few years old. Since every Mac activity will pass through the accelerator, dirt or oxidation can cause catastrophic crashes.

Buying Software

The best indication of Macintosh's success is how many companies have sprung up to support it. In 1984, you could buy only Apple-brand disks and software, only at authorized stores, and blank disks cost $5 each. Now you can choose among products offered by hundreds of software publishers, and disks are a buck each at the corner drugstore. This tremendous competition means prices vary widely. Very little is sold at list price, and discounts range as high as 40% for some mail-order software. It pays to shop around.

Buying New Programs

While Mac software is usually more flexible and easier to use than DOS versions are, very few programs are as flexible as the ads promise, or as easy as the demonstrators make them look. Unless you're absolutely sure an application is right for you, arrange to try it out before you buy it (or make sure you can return it if you're unhappy). Some software may have unique hardware requirements. Check, before you buy, to make sure a program will run properly on your equipment.

> One of the authors also demonstrates computer systems at trade shows and knows personally how deceiving a demo can be.

Computer Stores

This may not be the best place to choose software. If you're a novice user or use Macs in your small business, you may find it convenient to buy your hardware and software in the same place. But buying software from a computer store may limit your selection. Stores that concentrate on hardware might not be equipped to demonstrate different applications. They may have a few popular programs on the shelves, but probably won't have much information about alternatives. On the other hand, you might be able to negotiate a sizable discount on software and supplies if you buy them as part of a package with hardware.

Software Stores

Some stores sell nothing but software (and an occasional box of disks), particularly programs for the Macintosh and PC. You can expect to find a variety of programs for any purpose, and at least one salesperson who's actually used each program. These stores will let you browse and ask questions, and frequently walk you through any problems with new software. They generally offer discounts, in the vicinity of 10 or 20%, and do a good job of initiating new users to Mac computing.

Look for a software store that will either let you try out a program on their Macs or be willing to accept returns on a "no-questions-asked" basis. A home trial is always preferable to an in-store demo. Make sure you can return a program *after* you've tried it (that is, with the seal broken); otherwise, a home trial is useless.

Mail-Order Software

In the early days, mail order was the black hole of computer shopping. You'd place an order, wait a few weeks, and be stuck with whatever the company shipped. Outright fraud was not unheard of.

As the computer market moved from hackers and hobbyists to corporate and collegiate buyers, the mail order industry cleaned up its act. The big Macintosh specialty distributors now offer excellent telephone support, deep stocks, deep discounts—sometimes as much as 40%—and at least a 30-day trial period (if the manufacturer allows one). Most companies won't charge your credit card until they ship the software, and for a few dollars extra, they'll guarantee next-day delivery. Many of these companies even have automated fax reference libraries: if you call a special number and enter a code from a touch-tone phone, their computer will send back copies of the product's literature.

If you have a good idea what you want and can wait 24 hours to get it, you can save money with these companies. Check a user group for referrals, or look for the companies with five- or six-page color ads in Macintosh magazines.

Secondhand Woes

It's illegal and immoral to sell copies of commercial software, but there's nothing wrong with selling your original (as long as you don't keep a copy for yourself). Many users will legitimately advertise a secondhand program on bulletin boards or in classifieds, because they've outgrown (or grown bored with) it or need quick cash. While you can often get a good deal this way, you don't get any protection from a bad deal. Hence, the following caveats:

- Make sure you get the original program disks and manuals. This is essential if you have any hope of getting support and upgrades from the manufacturer. While you're at it, make sure the manufacturer's still in business.
- Make sure it's a current version of the program. If it's not, make sure it will run on your system and meets your needs. Avoid buying version 1.0 of anything (it may be buggy), unless you're absolutely sure you can upgrade for a rcasonably low cost.
- Check the program's operation. Make sure the disk has all the files the manual says should be there.
- Find out the current (discounted) price. Program prices frequently go down over time, and "it's yours for half of what I paid" might not be such a good deal.
- Scan for viruses. (Chapter 14 contains more information on viruses.)
- Write the manufacturer to change the registration name. (But be aware: some don't accept changes.)

You can check current versions through user groups, America OnLine, or *Macworld* magazine.

Buying Supplies

System and software prices are not truly competitive. If you want the features of a Mac IIsi or Microsoft Word, you have to look for the best deal within Apple's or Microsoft's pricing policies. This isn't the case when you buy computer supplies. There's not much difference between any one nationally advertised line of products and any other, so you can shop for the best price. Here are a few words to the wise buyer.

Floppy Disks

You'll need lots of these. Even if you have a hard disk, you should make floppy-disk backups of all software and every important document. And while disks are erasable, they're so cheap that most people don't bother: they keep them as backups, instead.

Brand Name versus Generic Disks

Some computer stores sell unbranded disks, for about three-quarters the price of the national brands. These are usually either bulk disks, originally intended for duplicators and quite usable, or manufacturers' fallouts that didn't meet specifications. Unfortunately, there's no way to tell which is the case by looking at the disk. We've had bad luck with unbranded disks, and have frequently seen 2 disks out of a box of 10 fail to initialize. So much for the savings.

You don't need to spend money on premium disks. Any of the standard national brands will do quite well. Just make sure the manufacturer's name is stamped on the metal shutter. You also don't need *preformatted* disks, which have simply been shoved into Macs at the factory and initialized. Unless your time is *very* valuable, you can spend the 60 seconds doing the job yourself. The prices in the next few paragraphs are for nationally branded disks, and represent the range between discount office supply houses (frequently the cheapest place to buy) and full-service computer stores.

Types of Disks

Newer Macs need *high-density* disks to take advantage of the SuperDrive format. These disks hold 1.44M of data, about twice that of the 800K "standard" disks that will run in almost any Mac. They also cost about twice as much as standard disks—$18 to $28 for a pack of 10. Look for "HD," "2HD," or "2SHD" on the box, and a second hole opposite the disk locking hole, as shown in Figure 13.3.

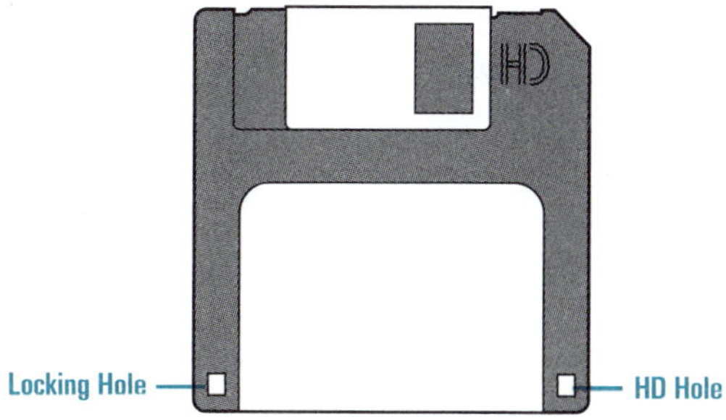

Figure 13.3
A high-density disk.

> If you cut a properly located second hole on a standard disk, SuperDrive will think it's high density. (You'll also run the risk of getting little plastic scraps all over the inside of your drive.) But it's not a good idea: the magnetic surface isn't designed for the higher density format, and you'll probably lose most of your data.

You can put a high-density disk into a standard Mac, but it will initialize as an 800K standard disk. It's much cheaper to use *double-sided, double-density* disks. These are designed for standard Macs, and sell for $10 to $15 per 10-pack. Look for "DS-DD" or "2S-2D" on the box. If you put one of these disks into a SuperDrive Mac, it'll work fine; it just won't save more than 800K.

The earliest Macs used *single-sided* disks holding 400K of data, which are virtually impossible to find these days. However, you can put a DSDD disk into an early Mac and format it as single-sided. (Don't try to reformat an old single-sided disk as a double-sided one. It may initialize, but you'll run the risk of losing data on the untested side.)

ImageWriter Supplies

ImageWriters need little except ribbons and paper. You can get both in a computer store or through mail order, but they're frequently cheaper at a discount office supply store.

Cheaper grades of paper are usually cut unevenly. They may jam in your printer, or leave little scraps of paper inside from their perforations. Look for paper with "laser cut" or "clean cut" edges. It runs better and will give your printouts a more professional look. Computer or electronic chain stores usually carry color and preprinted papers.

ImageWriter ribbons come in black (and, through the mail-order houses, in several colors). You can also get four-color ribbons for single-pass multicolor printing on ImageWriter II, but the color resolution isn't very good.

> **TIP:** Can't find ribbons marked "Apple ImageWriter"? Look for ones for the C.Itoh *Prowriter*, or the NEC *PC8000* series. They're exactly the same.

Laser Printer Supplies

Laser printers use the same supplies as modern office copiers: toner kits, imaging drums, and plain paper. There's a full discussion of appropriate papers for laser printers in Chapter 10. Toner and drums vary according to the printer (some models combine them); you can purchase them at your dealer or through the manufacturer. Apple LaserWriter toner kits are fairly easy to find.

Apple toner cartridges can be *recharged.* Even after you've used up the black inky stuff, the other imaging parts in them are still usable. Service companies will put more ink into your old cartridge for about half the cost of buying a new cartridge. You can find these companies advertised in the back of Mac magazines. (Other brands of printers frequently use toner cartridges that don't have imaging functions. These cost about a quarter of the Apple variety and aren't worth refilling.)

> **CAUTION:** The quality of recycled toner cartridges varies. Some can damage your printer by leaking toner, others have a low life span or poor quality toner. Still others work fine. Be careful.

StyleWriter Supplies

Ink—available from Apple dealers—and 20-pound cotton bond paper are recommended. For a discussion about printing on other materials, see Chapter 5.

Additional Hardware

The computer stores are full of them. Here's where a hobbyist can go crazy, with everything from furry mousecovers to fitted Mac-customized desks. (Don't ever say you can't think of what to get the authors for Christmas.) Not every accessory is frivolous, however. The Mac add-ons discussed in this section will enhance operating speed, convenience, or reliability.

Input Devices

Many people aren't comfortable with the Apple mouse or PowerBook mini-trackball, finding it either isn't precise enough for detailed graphics or takes up too much mouseroom on the desk. (Musicians who prop a Mac on top of a synthesizer don't have desks at all.) Fortunately, there are plenty of mouse alternatives.

Optical Mice

Optical mice look like the standard Apple variety but use a beam of light instead of a rolling ball (Figures 13.4 and 13.5 contrast the two mouse types.) The beam bounces off a specially prepared mirror. As the light beam crosses tiny lines engraved in the mirror, it registers movement. Because light is frictionless (and doesn't pick up dirt from a desk surface), the action feels smoother and more precise. Optical mice cost about $80, the same price as replacement rubber-ball mice.

Figure 13.4
Standard (rubber ball) mouse.

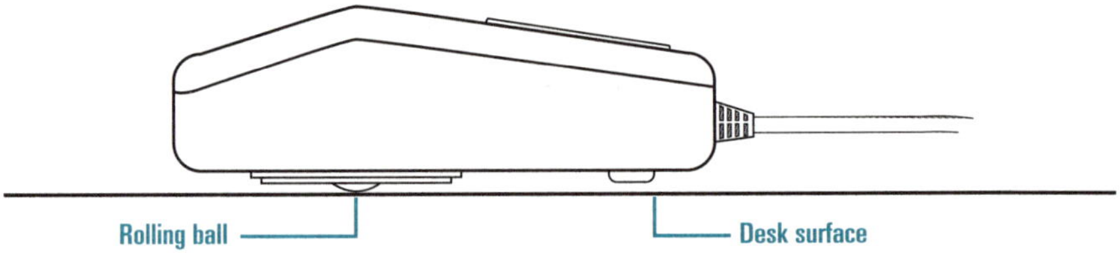

Figure 13.5
Optical mouse.

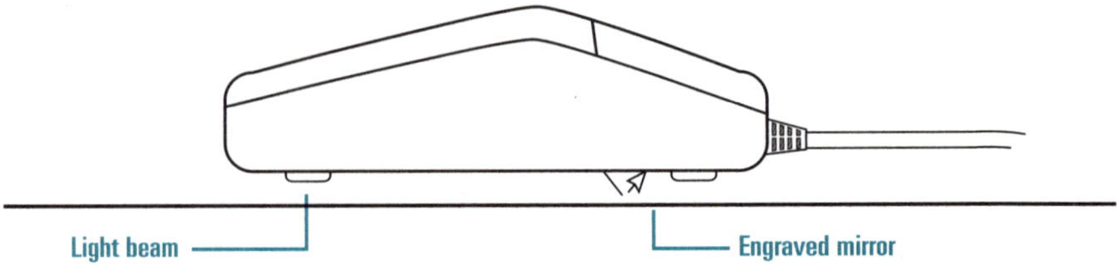

Graphics Tablets

Graphics tablets work according to the same principle as an optical mouse, only they bounce the light (or very low power radio waves) from a pen-shaped object instead of a palm-shaped one. Prices vary between $250 and $800, depending on the size and special features like pressure sensitivity (many graphics programs let you draw heavier lines by pressing harder on a properly equipped tablet). For professional artists, the extra control is worth the cost.

> **TIP:** Don't forget, with the Apple Desktop Bus (ADB), you can have more than one input device connected to the same computer. See Chapter 16.

Trackballs

Imagine a mouse on its back. Instead of pushing it around, you tickle its tummy. That's how a *trackball* works. Instead of a small rubber ball, the trackball has a two-inch diameter billiard-ball clone that you spin with your fingertips (see Figure 13.6). A quick flick can send the pointer shooting across the screen. Because the housing for the ball never moves, the trackball doesn't require much desk space. Trackballs are a favorite of musicians, video game addicts, and one of the co-authors. Cost: about $100.

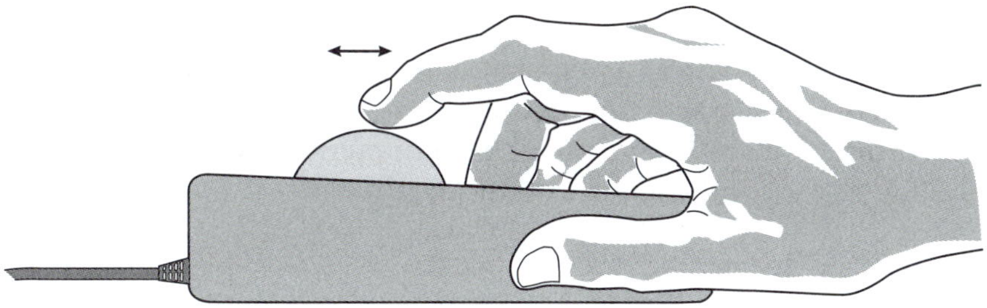

Figure 13.6

A trackball.

Touch Screens and Tablets

One could argue that the ultimate pointing device is a human finger. *Touch screens* and *tablets* let you use yours, and respond to fingertip pressure. Computer interfaces to read a pointing finger are expensive, however, and don't offer much advantage over a trackball or graphics tablet. A simple touch tablet that sits on your desk costs about $250. A more elaborate touch screen that fits over the screen on a compact Mac costs about $500.

Mouse (and Wrist) Helper

If you're using a traditional Apple mouse, consider getting a *mouse pad:* a small square of fabric- or plastic-covered rubber that serves as a resilient surface on your desk. They make the mouse easier to control, and keep its ball cleaner. Mouse pads cost between $5 and $15, depending on whether they're plain or preprinted (with colors, company logos, or bikini-clad Californians).

Wrist pads are thick pieces of rubber that fit along the front of your keyboard, providing wrist support for those of us who never learned touch typing or piano. For about $18, they're claimed to reduce carpal tunnel syndrome, a nerve injury sometimes caused by long typing sessions.

Conditioners, Controllers, and Filters

Until such time as we've got cold fusion generators in the basement, we're all at the mercy of the commercial power grid. Blackouts are relatively uncommon in a well-maintained system, but the opposite—very quick *spikes* or *surges* of high voltage—are the unfortunate result of lightning storms and switching equipment. Therefore, consider adding power conditioners to your Mac.

Filters

The Mac's power supply can cope with a lot of problems, but fast voltage jumps aren't on the list. Simple plug-in *filters*, available from electronics chain stores and computer dealers, are cheap insurance against the expensive repairs that can result from power spikes. For less than $20, you can get a simple gadget that plugs into any grounded outlet; your Mac plugs into it. For a few dollars more, you can get one combined with a multiple-outlet power strip that'll protect the printer and modem brains as well. Smaller filters are available with telephone plugs to stop phone-line spikes from hurting a modem, and some large units do everything at once.

Check the power filter warning light or window frequently. The circuit elements will sacrifice themselves to protect your Mac. If they absorb too big a surge, they'll burn out and stop offering protection. If your neighborhood has so-called "dirty lines," you may find the power filters burning out frequently. Keep using them—it's a lot cheaper to replace a filter than to repair a power supply. Or better still, invest in a device that will generate its own clean electricity (as discussed in the next two paragraphs).

Blackout-Proof Your Mac

If power goes out while you're computing, you'll lose anything you haven't saved to disk. If power goes out at the exact instant the system is creating a file, you can lose a whole disk (but you probably can recover it with techniques discussed in Chapter 14). Users in blackout-prone areas should consider an *Uninterruptible Power Supply* (UPS): these monitor the power line and switch to an internal battery if things go dark. The battery is usually powerful enough to maintain power for 15 or 20 minutes, long enough for you to save your work and shut down properly. When the power comes back on, the battery recharges.

The better UPS units convert incoming power to low-voltage direct current (matching the battery), filter everything, and then reconvert it to look like wall current. For this reason, they can give much more efficient surge suppression than ordinary filters. Uninterruptible Power Supplies are available from larger computer dealers and commercial electronics houses, for about $225 to $400 (depending on how long they'll keep your Mac humming).

Power Control Switches

One of the peculiarities of computer systems is that sometimes they won't work if you turn things on in the wrong order. Hard disks and other SCSI equipment should be powered either before, or simultaneously with, the main computer. If not, the Finder might not see them.

If you have a hard time remembering the proper turn-on sequence, or just don't want to be bothered reaching around behind the equipment, you can get a central switch box. These put all the power controls in front of you, and frequently provide a master switch, line filtering, and a swivel base as well. (They also contribute to the mess of wires behind your Mac, because each peripheral's power cable has to plug into it.) Depending on the manufacturer and features, count on spending around $100.

Sophisticated Circuits' PowerKey is a central switch you can keep out of the way, because you never have to touch it. It turns on your system with the "triangle" key found on the SE and later machines, and has a built-in timer for presetting turn-on time. PowerKey costs around $100 depending on discounts. Add another $40 for a feature that lets you turn on your machine by modem.

Screen Filters

This last kind of filter controls light, rather than electricity. If you use your Macintosh during the day in a room with a window, you've probably seen serious glare on the Mac's picture tube. Polaroid and a couple of other companies make custom-fitted glare filters that match compact Macs and cost about $50. Larger ones for graphics monitors cost as much as $250, depending on the size. These filters can't eliminate glare totally, but they do cut it down to reasonable limits in an average office. They'll probably do the job, unless you've got a corner office on the 70th floor (in that case, you can hire someone else to deal with the glare).

If you're worried about the electrical fields that emanate from computer screens, you can get a glare filter with built-in electronic shielding. These are only slightly more expensive (the small Polaroid one is under $60), and have the added benefit of dissipating static so dust won't cling to the screen.

In This Chapter

Deflecting Disk Damage and Disentangling Disappeared Data

•

What to Do When Your Computer Can't Read a File or Disk

•

How to Avoid Viruses and Have Safe Sectors

•

How to Fix Your Mac, Even if You Can't Work a VCR

•

Things You Shouldn't Try to Fix

As wonderful as the Mac is, it's not perfect. Your software and files are at risk from disk failures, system bugs, and viruses. Even the hardware can suddenly stop working. But you can help keep things running smoothly with a few simple steps. This chapter tells you how to avoid or fix routine Mac problems. You'll also learn to recognize those times when it's better—or safer—to let an expert take over.

14

Mac Care and Feeding

The *good* news: Only two things can go wrong with a computer. The *bad* news: These two things are the hardware and the software.

Computers are among the most reliable appliances you can buy (except for the earliest Macs, which had a tendency to blow out the power supply). But computers are complicated systems, and even a minor problem can give the best-thinking machine a headache. The simple rules in this chapter will help you keep your Macintosh in top condition.

I Had the File a Minute Ago . . .

The most devastating computer problems are ones that destroy data. You can fix hardware and buy substitute software, but nothing can replace a report that took you a week to write.

This is unfortunate, since the magnetic media where your data lives is the most delicate part of the system. Hard disks, though reliable, do occasionally fail. The 3-½" floppies in the Mac (while a tremendous improvement over the 5-¼" floppies still used by some PCs) are fragile and can wear out. Problems with other parts of the system, from software bugs to confused operators, can also scramble files. All this isn't cause for panic, but it is reason to be concerned and take precautions.

Sooner or later, no matter what kind of computer you use or how careful you are, something will fail. And when it does, you'll lose data. You just can't beat the odds.

Before You Go Forward, Backup!

The best way to stop a flat tire from ruining your trip is to keep a spare in the trunk. This works for files, too. A *backup* copy of software or data is a perfect clone of the original. If anything ruins the original, you can load the backup and get back to work. To backup a file, folder, or an entire disk, simply drag its icon to another disk. There are also backup and compression utilities, discussed later in this chapter, to simplify the task. Make backup copies of everything important. Following a few simple rules will protect you from losing vital data.

Backup Rule #1

Always copy new software and system disks as soon as you get them. Lock them so they can't be accidentally erased (or infected with viruses). Then put the originals in a safe place and use the copies.

This kind of copying isn't software piracy. You can make as many copies as you need for safety, so long as you don't let anyone use the copies on any other computers. In fact, most software publishers urge you to make backups.

Backup Rule #2

Backup any new document of value as soon as possible. Many users have regular backup sessions once a week. Cautious, paranoid, and power users backup daily.

How frequently you backup depends on how much risk you're willing to tolerate. We made two backups of every chapter of this book, one on floppy disk and the other on the hard disk of another computer. If your livelihood depends on files you frequently update, you'll learn to backup frequently as well.

Backup Rule #3

Make fresh backups of any files that change on a regular basis.

Don't neglect files that change every time you use them, like spreadsheets or databases. If you're not sure which files have changed since the last backup, go to the Finder and select View by Date. (Figure 14.1 shows a window with files and folders organized according to their creation dates.) You can also print this list, by pulling down Print Directory... from the Finder's File menu while the window is open.

Backup Rule #4

Keep your backup disks in a safe place. This is almost never anyplace near your computer.

Disks are sensitive to stray magnetism, extreme heat, and spilled coffee (see "Disk Disasters" later in this chapter). Anything that bothers one disk will probably also bother any other disks near it, so make sure you don't store backups in the same place as working copies. (Some users keep their household backups in the office, and their business backups at home.

Backup Utilities

Many hard disk drives come with free automatic *backup utility* software to organize the procedure. Backup programs are also available commercially and on public-domain bulletin boards. To use a backup utility, just follow the on-screen directions and keep feeding your Mac new floppies. Figure 14.2 shows an example of a dialog box from a backup utility. Many backup utilities convert your files to a special format, and you need to run the software to reconvert them before you can access the file.

Figure 14.1

View by Date.

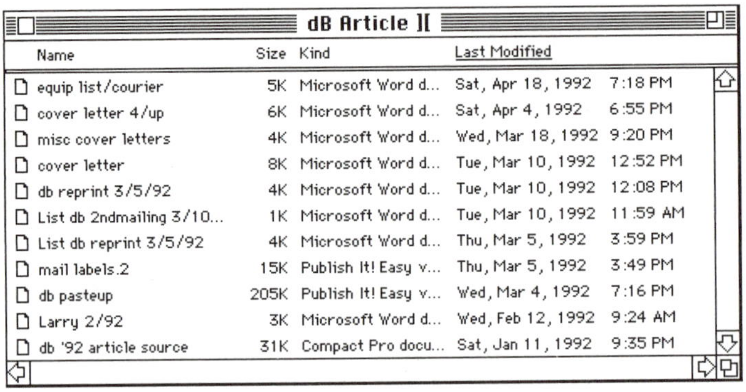

dB Article][

Name	Size	Kind	Last Modified	
equip list/courier	5K	Microsoft Word d...	Sat, Apr 18, 1992	7:18 PM
cover letter 4/up	6K	Microsoft Word d...	Sat, Apr 4, 1992	6:55 PM
misc cover letters	4K	Microsoft Word d...	Wed, Mar 18, 1992	9:20 PM
cover letter	8K	Microsoft Word d...	Tue, Mar 10, 1992	12:52 PM
db reprint 3/5/92	4K	Microsoft Word d...	Tue, Mar 10, 1992	12:08 PM
List db 2ndmailing 3/10...	1K	Microsoft Word d...	Tue, Mar 10, 1992	11:59 AM
List db reprint 3/5/92	4K	Microsoft Word d...	Thu, Mar 5, 1992	3:59 PM
mail labels.2	15K	Publish It! Easy v...	Thu, Mar 5, 1992	3:49 PM
db pasteup	205K	Publish It! Easy v...	Wed, Mar 4, 1992	7:16 PM
Larry 2/92	3K	Microsoft Word d...	Wed, Feb 12, 1992	9:24 AM
db '92 article source	31K	Compact Pro docu...	Sat, Jan 11, 1992	9:35 PM

Automatic file backup programs give you the option of *incremental* backups. These copy only those files that have changed since your last backup, or other date you specify. The program asks for specific disks from your last backup as it runs. (Incremental backups rely on the Macintosh internal clock to work properly. If you've changed the clock or have a weak battery, the program may not work correctly.)

All this backing up doesn't mean you have to cover your shelves with floppies. Once you've made a backup, it's okay to re-use the disks from the previous one. On the other hand, disks are relatively cheap. Many users save the last *two* backup copies, just in case the most recent one fails. Some people even keep all their backups, on the off chance that they'll need to document changes to a file.

File Compression

You can also save shelf space by making the files smaller and fitting more of them on a disk. *Archiving* utilities and some backup programs go through your data and create a shorthand for patterns that appear frequently. When it's time to read thc file, the program uses a key to replace the shorthand with the original patterns.

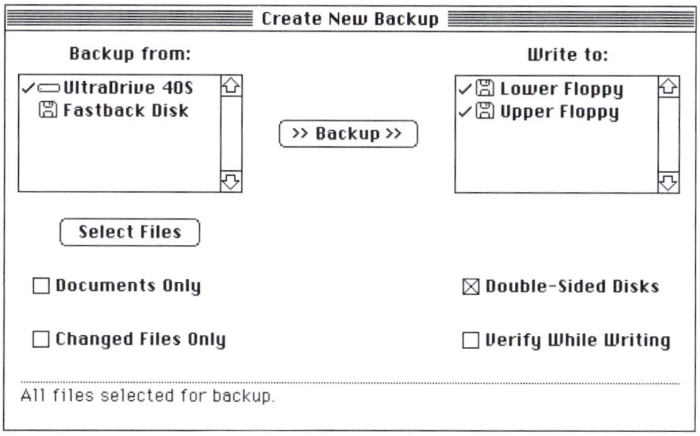

Figure 14.2

A dialog box from a backup program.

Figure 14.3 shows a simplified example of this kind of compression. The other strange characters stand for combinations of characters in the original text. Even though we created this example manually using a word processor, it makes the file ten percent smaller than the original.

Archiving utilities are, of course, much more thorough. They may also use multiple compression techniques for the best result. Such programs as Stuffit, Compact Pro, and Disk Doubler often shrink files between 30 percent and 60 percent. The only penalty (other than software or shareware cost) is time. It takes a while to find all the patterns in a long file.

Avoiding Ruptured Disks

Disks store data magnetically. Electric coils in the disk drive (the *heads*) magnetize tiny particles on the disk surface. The resulting pattern of North and South poles become the ones and zeros of your letter to

Aunt Isabel. The disk drive heads work like the school science experiment of magnetizing a nail with an electromagnet and then testing it with a compass, only a *lot* smaller. Here are some guidelines to keep your floppy disks healthy.

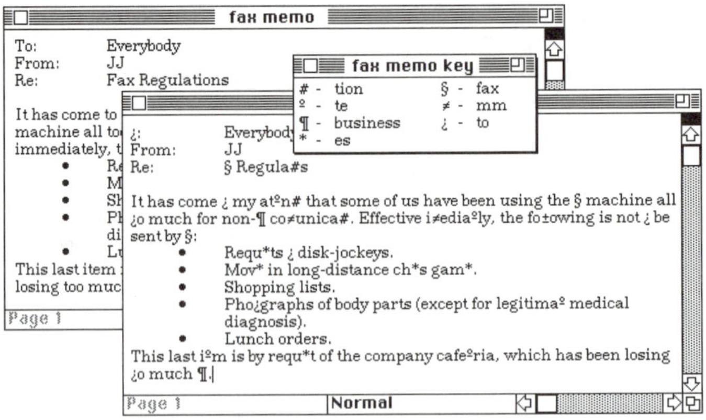

Figure 14.3

The authors do by hand what archiving utilities do better electronically.

Keep Clean The oil in a fingerprint is thick enough to interfere with the magnetic particles on a disk, and a human hair or particle of cigarette smoke is a relatively gigantic piece of debris. A single speck of dust can cause the read/write heads to *crash* into the data on disk.

Keep Closed Macintosh floppy disks are somewhat protected by the plastic jacket and metal shutter, but dust and smoke can work their way through—so keep your computing area clean and smoke-free. Even little pieces of pencil eraser can sneak in, so be very careful if you erase a disk label.

Keep Dry Disks aren't spill-proof. Liquids can flow right through the openings and distort the magnetic surface, or cover it with contaminants.

Keep Isolated The tiny magnets on a disk surface are easily scrambled by bigger magnets. Watch out for telephone handsets, stereo speakers, and electric motors. A steel desk drawer that once held a magnetic paper clip holder can become magnetized itself. Magnets also lurk in pocketbooks and briefcases, so be careful carrying disks.

Even the power supply in compact Macs radiates enough magnetism (along the left side of the case) to hurt a floppy. Always keep external drives underneath or on the right side of these models. Don't leave disks on an original ImageWriter either: there's a magnet under the cover.

Keep Cool Heat can destroy any magnet, especially the microscopic ones in a floppy disk. Don't leave disks in the sun, on top of a radiator, or (since heat rises) on top of the Mac itself. Make sure drives and the Mac are well ventilated.

Keep Still Hard disks are more robust than floppies because the heads and the magnetic platter are factory-sealed. But they're more sensitive to vibration, and moving a hard disk while it's spinning can cause the head to crash right onto the disk surface. (That's where the term *computer crash* originally came from.) Even when a hard disk is turned off, shocks and extreme vibration may cause problems. If you're shipping any kind of drive, pack it carefully. Put a blank or unimportant disk into floppy drives before you ship them, to keep the mechanisms from bouncing around.

Keep Calm Just remember—avoid heat, magnetism, dirt, and shocks. If you do this, your data should last a long time.

TIP: Airport X-rays themselves are safe, but the motors in x-ray machines frequently aren't. Walk-through metal detectors can also present a problem. Give your disks and PowerBook to the guard for hand inspection (and be prepared to turn on your PowerBook, to prove that it's real).

Hard Disk Fragmentation

Relax. *Hard disk fragmentation* doesn't mean your disk shatters into little pieces. It means the data on them has been shattered by your computer's natural file routines, and now it has to spend extra time gluing them together. It happens to disks all the time.

How a Disk Fragments

Let's say you started with a clean, virgin disk and saved a few files on it. For this book, we'll show each file as a separate sentence, as in Figure 14.4.

Figure 14.4
Three files.

1: The quick brown fox jumped.

2: Mary had a little lamb.

3: "Run, Spot, run!" said Jane.

The disk saves space by jamming all the files together and keeping a list of which *sectors*—the smallest division on a disk surface—contain which file. The list is called the *directory* (and *directory errors* are incredibly devastating to a disk). In our illustrations, we'll put the directory at the top, and jam all the text below it. Figure 14.5 shows the result.

Figure 14.5
Three files with a directory.

1:sect1-27••2:sect38-50••3:sect 51-77••

The quick brown fox jumped.Mary had a little lamb."Run, Spot, run!" said Jane.

So far, fine. When you want a file, the system reads the directory and then jumps to the appropriate sectors. When you delete a file, you tell the directory to ignore—and eventually write over—that file's sectors. (The data actually stays in place when you delete files, until some other data replaces it.) Figure 14.6 shows our example with one file deleted.

1:sect1-27••~~~~~~~~~~~~~~~••3:sect

51-77••

The quick brown fox

jumped.~~~~~~~~~~~~~~~

~~~~~~~~~~"Run, Spot, run!" said
Jane.

Figure 14.6

One file thrown out.

But when you try to save another file, things might stop being so efficient. The system starts writing the new file in the newly available sectors. Unfortunately, the file might be longer than the one that was deleted, so the system has to look elsewhere for space to put the rest of it. Figure 14.7 shows a possible result.

1:sect1-27••2:sect38-50,78-

124••3:sect 51-77••

The quick brown fox jumped.Now is

the time for all "Run, Spot, run!"

said Jane.good men to come to the

aid of their party.

Figure 14.7

Fragmentation.
~~~~~~~~~~

Hard to read? Imagine how hard it is for the computer. Each time you access that file, the system has to check the file's *extension* and jump the heads over to find them. All this checking and jumping takes time. After a few months of heavy use, hard disks can get so fragmented that starting up or reading long files can take noticeably longer.

Disk Defragmentation

There are two ways to *defragment* a disk (put all the pieces of each file back in adjoining segments). The cheaper way is tedious and time consuming. Copy all the files onto another hard disk (or a bunch of floppies), totally erase the main disk, and then copy them back. Totally erasing a disk removes everything from the directory (except for some vital housekeeping files), so the data gets written back without extensions.

The easier way is to use a disk defragmenter. One of the most popular—and our favorite—is The Norton Utilities for the Macintosh. The package includes programs that can (under the right circumstances) restore crashed hard disks, recover trashed files, and lock out damaged sectors. It's a handy disk to have around, though some of the other utilities include automatic backup software, and encryption routines.

Defragmenters copy information from one sector to another until each file is continuous. The better defragmenters, including the two mentioned above, also relocate files to reduce future fragmentation and keep head movements to a minimum.

If Your Mac Can't Read a File

A lot of things can make a file unreadable. Here are a few of the more common problems.

- Media errors, including dirt or damaged sectors.
- Temporary glitches or power losses during the file-handling routines.
- Software bugs that damage a file.
- User errors, like inadvertent trashing or giving two files the same name.
- Viruses.

Except in the last case, you can probably recover your file with the proper steps. Viruses are more damaging (but are rare). We'll discuss them later in this chapter. If your programs won't load or a precious data disk comes up Unreadable..., follow these rules:

1. **Don't do *anything*.** Scream, curse, pound your fist on the table (but not too close to the computer), or whatever you normally do when dismayed. But don't touch the computer. *Do* stop and think.
2. **Analyze the problem.** Is it a file that's unreadable or the whole disk? Is the system otherwise normal? The most common file-reading problem is actually quite benign. You double-click on a file icon, and see a message like `The file "Peter Pan" could not be opened/printed. (The application is busy or missing.)`

   When you double-click a document in the Finder, it looks for the exact program that created it. Occasionally, the creator information gets scrambled. Start the application first, and you'll probably be able to open the file with no trouble. If you don't have the exact program that created the file, try whichever word processor, spreadsheet, or graphics program you *do* have. Most of today's programs are quite forgiving about opening up competitor's files.
3. **Try again.** Many file or folder opening problems are temporary. If you can't open something by double-clicking, try the Open command. If you can't open something from within an application, Cancel and start over.

> Scrambled creator information can make an application fail to recognize its own children, and a desired file won't appear in the Open dialog box. Cancel, and hold Option when you retry the Open command (or press Option-⌘-O). This will make the program recognize *all* files.

If none of the files on a floppy disk are readable, try ejecting the disk and reinserting it. (If this happens often, you might need a hardware repair.) In extreme cases, Restart and try again. (If your system is on a floppy disk, try starting with a different system floppy.)

4. **Reach for the backup copy.** You do have a backup copy, don't you? You *don't?* Well, now you know why we stressed them at the start of this chapter. But all is not lost.
5. **Reach for a file-recovery utility.** The Norton package, described above, has an excellent file-recovery section. Other commercial utilities, including Microcom's 911, are also powerful. Apple's own Disk First Aid (supplied with the system disk) is the least effective. Don't give up if the Apple program doesn't fix your problem. Plug in the third-party disk and follow the instructions.

If a file is damaged and you don't have a recovery utility handy, *lock the disk immediately*. Don't try to write anything else on that disk until it's thoroughly fixed. Not only can writing something to disk cause you to lose more data, but it'll probably also make the damaged file totally unrecoverable.

If Your Mac Can't Read a Whole Disk

This section assumes your Mac is otherwise up and running. If not, skip ahead to the next section. If your Mac displays a box saying something like `This disk is unreadable`, or `This is not a Macintosh disk`, try these similar steps:

1. **Don't panic.**
2. **Think about the problem.**
3. **Try again.** This rule is only common sense and applies to most noncomputer situations as well.
4. **Just say "No."** You may see a message like this when you insert a damaged floppy: `This disk is unreadable. Do you want to initialize it?`

   You don't. Initializing will absolutely destroy any chance of ever recovering the data on that disk. Click Eject, then lock the disk so nobody else can accidentally initialize it.
5. **Try a different drive.** Sometimes a drive gets out of adjustment. Try opening the disk on another computer. If you can, copy it: the copy might work perfectly on your original machine.
6. **Reach for a backup or recovery program.** They work on full disks as well as on individual files.

If Your Mac Won't Start at All

Yikes! Your computer is totally dead, and a report's due in an hour. Again, panic isn't indicated. While you might have hardware problems that require repair, it's more likely that you've got software or media troubles you can fix quickly yourself. Try the following suggestions:

1. **Check the hardware.** With the power off, make sure all the cables are securely plugged into the Mac. (While you're at it, make sure there's power. A tripped circuit breaker in your basement can make even the best computer look broken.)

If you turn on a properly powered system and nothing happens, or you get a strange tweed or herringbone pattern on the screen, you do have a hardware problem. Seek professional aid for your computer and a colleague for that report.

2. **Try another startup disk.** Turn off the computer and insert a floppy that has System and Finder files on it. (The backup you made of your original Mac *System Disk* is fine.) Then turn the system back on. If you've got an external hard disk, give it 15 seconds to warm up before turning on the main computer. The Mac might take a few more seconds to start itself with the unfamiliar disk, but pretty soon you'll see the desktop. If the desktop shows your hard disk icon, you're in good shape. Try steps 3 or 4. If you have a hard disk but don't see it on the desktop, skip to step 5. If you can't read the System Disk at all, you've got a hardware problem: go back to step 1.

3. **Reset your PRAM.** Information about startup disks, the internal clock, and other user preferences are stored in a section of Mac memory called the *Parameter RAM*, or *PRAM*. This memory is always on, powered by an internal battery. But if PRAM gets corrupted, your Mac can forget you've got a hard disk.

   To reset the PRAM for a Mac 128K, 512K, 512e, or Plus, just turn it off, and remove the battery from the back. Leave it off at least 15 minutes, making the PRAM forget the wrong information it's learned. When you put the battery back and start up again, the Mac should recognize the hard disk. Its clock will also need resetting.

   To reset the PRAM on an SE or newer machine running System 6, press and hold down ⌘-Shift-Option, and then open the Control Panel while you hold these keys. The system will ask if you want to zap the PRAM. Let go of the keys and click Yes. Start up again, and things should be fine.

   To reset the PRAM under System 7, restart the system and hold down ⌘-Option-p-r while the system is resetting. When you hear the startup chime the second time, release the keys. The system will automatically start again, and you're ready to go.

After you reset the PRAM, you may also have to reset user preferences like the desktop pattern or alert sound. Use the Control Panel DA for these settings. While you're at it, check the printer and user name in Chooser: these may have gotten zapped also.

4. **Replace the system.** No, don't throw away the darned computer. Just copy the *System* and *Finder* files from the successful startup disk. It seems as though system files get corrupted more than other programs (probably because they get more use than other files). If you're not running System 7 you'll lose any special DAs or fonts you've installed, but they're easy to put back. If a system disk won't work as the startup disk even after these steps, you probably have INIT conflicts. See the next section.

5. **Reinstall the disk driver.** This is a file on every hard disk that tells the Mac how that particular disk was built. If it gets messed up, the Mac can't read the disk. The *Installation* or *Management* floppy that came with your hard disk can reinstall the driver. Check the manual to see how to use the disk. If you have an internal Apple hard disk, look for the file *Apple HD SC Setup* on the system or utility floppy.

6. **Grab that recovery program.** Bugs, power glitches, or user interruptions can absolutely scramble a disk, if they happen precisely when the system is writing to the directory. Recovery programs can usually rebuild the directory with minimal data loss. In the case of a hard disk, they can make the difference between saving or losing hundreds of files.

If you get the idea we like file-utility programs, you're right. These $100 programs are cheap insurance if you use your Mac for anything important. Get any one of the utilities that offers file and disk recovery. In the unlikely case the package you buy can't fix your problem, give the crashed disk to friends who have a different one and ask them to try.

Those Insidious INITs

INITs are little subprograms that wedge themselves into the Mac's operating system during startup—hence the name INITialization—to add useful functions that Apple forgot. You can add screen saving, print spooling, faxing, type management, virus inhibition, or a lot more. (Most INITs show little icons across the bottom of the screen when the Mac first turns on, as in Figure 14.8.) INITs work like benign viruses, finding their way into loopholes in the System program and temporarily taking control.

Unfortunately, two or more of them might try to get into the same loophole at the same time, or use one that Apple closed in a subsequent System version. If this happens, your computer won't start properly: it'll freeze, show you a Sad Mac, or endlessly try to keep restarting. The solution is simple:

1. Start your Mac from a different system disk.
2. Open the System folder on the disk that's having trouble, and move all the INITs into a different folder on your desktop. (You may want to make a new folder for this purpose.)

Figure 14.8.

A screen full of INITs at startup.

If you're running System 6, view the System folder by Kind, and move any files called *Startup documents.* If you're running System 7, move anything in the System folder's *Startup Items* folder, and any *system extensions* in the *Extensions* folder.

3. Now for the fun. Put the INITs back where you originally found them, one at a time, starting with the ones you find most useful. Each time you move another INIT, Restart the Mac. By a lengthy process of elimination, you'll find the combination that's giving you trouble.

Or get an INIT management program, like INITPicker or the one in the Now Utilities.

Your Mac Starts but Your Programs Fail

Occasionally, users with a lot of INITs or other extended functions might find otherwise healthy programs unexpectedly quitting, dropping them back to the Finder. The Mac will courteously post a message like `The application FormFudger has unexpectedly quit (108)`, but that's little consolation if you neglected to *save* the form you were fudging.

If you get a lot of these failures with different programs, chances are your system needs more *heap space*—a section of computer memory reserved for temporary data storage by active programs. (INITs eat into this memory, shortchanging the programs.) The easiest cure is a free public-domain utility, Bootman™ by Bill Steinberg, available from most user groups. Follow the instructions in its window, and Bootman will analyze your system requirements and do a heap good fix.

Viruses and the Macintosh

Despite a general panic by the media, Macintoshes have not been very badly hit by *virus infections.* Viruses are real and do real damage, but those discovered on the Mac are fewer in number and much less damaging than those found on IBM PCs and their clones. Some of the reasons we've heard are that the PC is more favored by the hackers who write viruses, that DOS is easier to infect, and that Mac people are kind and gentle and would never hurt their fellows. Some of these reasons might be true.

Viruses are like the germs they're named after. They spread from host to host through a medium of infection, they reproduce, and they interfere with the hosts' normal functions. Unlike germs, however, computer viruses won't kill you. They're ill-considered pranks, not a possibly deadly product of nature. And they don't even really infect their hosts. No known Mac virus stays with the computer circuits. If you start from scratch with healthy files, no trace of the infection should remain. This includes all system and application files, as well as the data files from a few programs.

Non-Viruses

Don't confuse viruses with the other forms of malignant software, *worms* and *Trojan horses.* A worm is a program which spreads over a network, copies itself into every computer it finds, and then devotes the computers' time and energy to making additional copies. It can fill a mainframe's disks with meaningless copies of itself, dragging the system to a halt. (The famous Internet worm tied up several thousand government and university machines in 1988.) As of this writing, there are no known worms on Macintosh AppleTalk networks or graphic-interface bulletin boards. A worm can't spread over ordinary text-based bulletin boards. But you could be tricked into downloading a Trojan Horse with worm-like proclivities.

A Trojan horse is a program that appears to do something interesting or useful, while it's really attacking your system. A HyperCard stack called *Sexy Ladies*, passed around a few years ago, was really a Trojan horse. While users would ogle the uninhibited graphics, a software routine would quietly start erasing all the files on the hard disk. Other Trojan horses occasionally surface, but they're quickly spotted and reported in magazines, at user groups, and on bulletin boards.

Safe Sectors

It's possible to have a normal Macintosh social life and stay free from infection. You can use public domain software, try out a demo program, and download files from bulletin boards . . . as long as you follow the simple rules we list here.

1. **Know you're at risk.** The point of this rule is you should read and follow the other rules. If kids use your Mac (they love to copy software), or if you move your disks from machine to machine, you have a chance of picking up a virus. Service bureau and university lab machines are notorious. Even sealed commercial software disks have been found infected, to the dismay of their publishers.

2. **Get a good *virus protection program* from a reputable source.** Some of the best anti-virus programs are virtually free. Every Mac owner should have them. They're distributed through user groups and on the national bulletin boards. The Boston Computer Society's Macintosh group will send you a disk with the best and latest programs for a minimal fee. Call (617) 864-1700 and ask for their *Virus Protection Disk.* They can also give you advice about other virus protection programs. (Reputable user groups *hate* viruses, which tend to break down user-to-user communication.)

   Be wary of getting copies from a friend or downloading from a marginal board. You might be getting a virus at the same time.

There are some commercial virus protection programs available, but for most users these won't offer any additional protection over the nearly free programs.

3. **As soon as you get the virus-protection disks,** LOCK THEM! Do this before you ever put them in your computer. (There is no known virus that can infect a locked disk.)

4. **Use the virus protection programs now, and keep on using them.** Scan every system and applications disk you own for viruses. As soon as you've determined your master of a program is virus-free, *lock it* and put it in a safe place. You'll need these if you're ever hit by a virus.

   Then scan all your working program, system, and data disks (including your hard disk). Do them all at once—don't scan a few, run a game or spreadsheet, and then scan some more—or else a virus might spread back to what you thought was a clean disk. If you're reluctant, re-read the first rule listed in this section. No one is immune.

There are two ways to protect against viruses: detection and denial. You should use both. How much of them you use depends on how much at risk you are.

Virus Detection

Every virus has a characteristic signature. A *virus scanning program* looks through the files on a disk and compares it with known signatures. It can also try to remove the viral parts and keep the rest of the data, but we don't recommend this if you've got clean backup copies.

Figure 14.9 shows the main screen of the best public-domain detection program, Disinfectant (by John Norstad of Northwestern University). It's remarkably easy to use. Select a disk and click Scan. Disinfectant will give you a list of any infected files it finds. If you choose Disinfectant Help in the Apple menu, the program displays electronically indexed instructions and an excellent discussion of viruses and their symptoms. You can send the documentation to your printer (it makes a 59-page book) or word processor by using the File menu.

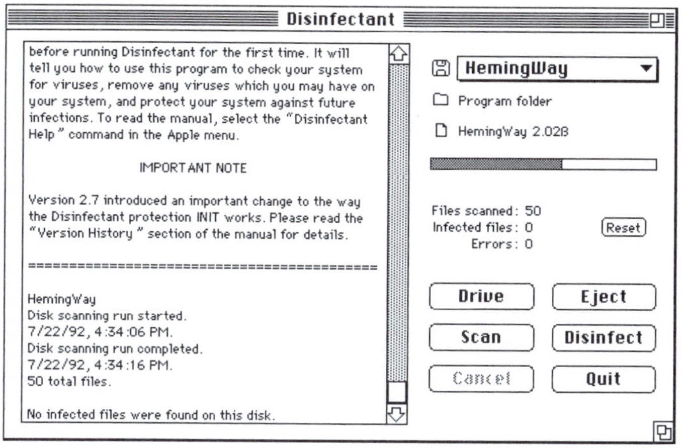

Figure 14.9

The Disinfectant screen.

Even the best detection program can only detect a virus for which it has a signature. These programs have to be modified to recognize new viruses isolated by experts. Always use the latest version of the scanning program. Disinfectant can also put an INIT on your system that checks for signatures as you insert disks, but a more powerful combination of INITs appear in denial programs.

Denial Programs

Imagine a magic pill that makes you immune to all future attacks of the common cold. The medicine would wait while the cold virus was dormant, but as soon as the virus became active it would put a barrier around your sinuses. (At the same time, it would page your family doctor's beeper to announce the attack.) That's exactly what denial programs do. Consider that computer viruses don't damage your system until they start modifying or erasing other files. If something inhibits these modifications, the virus won't hurt your system at all. (But it can still spread to other computers, which is why you need a detection program.)

Gatekeeper, by Chris Johnson, is a public domain INIT that looks for file changes. Of course, some change is desirable (Font/DA Mover, for example, changes your system file), so Gatekeeper keeps a list of programs that have file-changing privileges. If an unlisted one tries, Gatekeeper stops the process, flashes a dialog box to warn you, and asks if you want to go ahead.

Gatekeeper appears as a Control Panel device, as shown in Figure 14.10. It's not difficult to work, but it does require a little thought in determining which programs to add to the list. If an otherwise legal program isn't listed, Gatekeeper will bother you for permission every time you use it. You can always change the list. This program also has an excellent on-line Help facility, available from the top menu.

Startup utilities load in alphabetical order. Gatekeeper is actually a file called " Gatekeeper" (notice the little space between the quote mark and the G), so it can load first and watch over the rest of the startup. It may conflict with other INITs or CDEVs. If this happens, rename the offending utilities so they load before Gatekeeper, using the following steps:

1. View your system folder By Name. The offender will be listed somewhere below Gatekeeper.
2. Change the INIT or CDEV's file name by adding *two* spaces in front of it. The Finder won't let you start a filename with a space, so you have to fool it: type an **x** and two spaces, renaming the file to something like "x MyInit". Click elsewhere to deselect the file, then click on it again and delete just the x.
3. Close the folder and restart your Mac.

Virus Recuperation

If one of these programs reveals that you have a virus, don't panic. Recovery—once you're aware of the infection—is painless. Use the following steps to get rid of a virus:

1. Turn off your computer, and start up again from a locked, uninfected system disk.

2. Remove the *System, Finder,* and any infected files from your working disk. Trash them and empty the trash.
3. Reinstall the files from your locked master disks.
4. Scan your hard disk and *all* your floppies for viruses.
5. Tell your friends, co-workers, and anyone else who might be sharing disks that you've had an infection. There's no shame in it, and you might be able to stop the virus from spreading.

Figure 14.10
Gatekeeper in the Control Panel.

Hypochondria

It's tempting (especially given an occasional panic in the media) to scream "Infection!" whenever anything goes wrong with your computer, but lots of things can happen that don't have anything to do with a virus. This chapter discusses some of them. If your system still misbehaves and none of the suggestions in this book or the software manuals seem to help, ask a local Mac expert or user group.

Having Healthy Hardware

The current generation of Macintosh computers is more reliable than most electronic equipment you might have in a home or office, but how long it lasts depends on the care you give it. This section gives guidelines for keeping your hardware healthy.

Heat Kills Computers

Too much heat will make any electronic component grow old before its time. The converse is also true. If you keep an electronic gadget cool, it will last longer. The Mac is actually more tolerant of the external environment than most human operators. Apple suggests an operating range between 50° and 95° Fahrenheit (10°–35° C). But the temperature *inside* the machine will exceed those limits quickly if anything blocks the vents on the back or sides (or the top of older Macs).

Dust also causes heat damage. Too much of it will form a nice, warm blanket on the printed circuit cards and chips. Unfortunately, the ventilating fans in most Macs also suck dust into the machine! This doesn't mean you should disconnect the fan. The only solution is to keep your operating environment relatively dust-free. If dirt is a problem, get a fitted dust cover at a computer dealer. Cigarette smoke residue can also trap heat and cause the disk problems noted earlier. We've seen too many circuit cards covered with a thin layer of cigarette tar.

To summarize:

- Keep your Mac cool.
- Keep it dust-free.
- Keep it smoke-free.

Connections

Never plug or unplug anything into your Mac while the system is on. Surprise! This is the number two cause of early Mac failure.

Connectors work fine while they stay in one place, but when you move them, some of their little pins make contact before some of the others. If the power is on, this can unbalance the chips that service those connectors. The chips for the SCSI port are particularly vulnerable.

Regulate!

Erratic wall currents, including brownouts and quick high-voltage *transients* or *spikes*, can damage your computer. Transients can also ride the telephone line and damage your modem. Protection is relatively cheap (see Chapter 13).

Don't Be Stupid

Ordinary common sense rules also apply to the Mac (use a properly grounded outlet, don't operate it in the rain, never hit the keys with a defensive linebacker, and so on). We'll assume you don't need to be reminded of these.

Things You Can Fix Yourself

Don't be afraid to attempt some hardware repairs. The Mac was designed to make these easy, even for nontechnical people. This section discusses things you can fix yourself, and how to do it.

Clean Your Mouse

If the pointer doesn't track smoothly on the screen when you move the mouse, chances are the mouseball or rollers are dirty. They're easy to clean. Just follow these steps.

1. Turn off the Mac.
2. Open the plastic ring on the bottom of the mouse. There are two different kinds of mouse rings (see Figure 14.11). Turn yours as indicated in the figure.

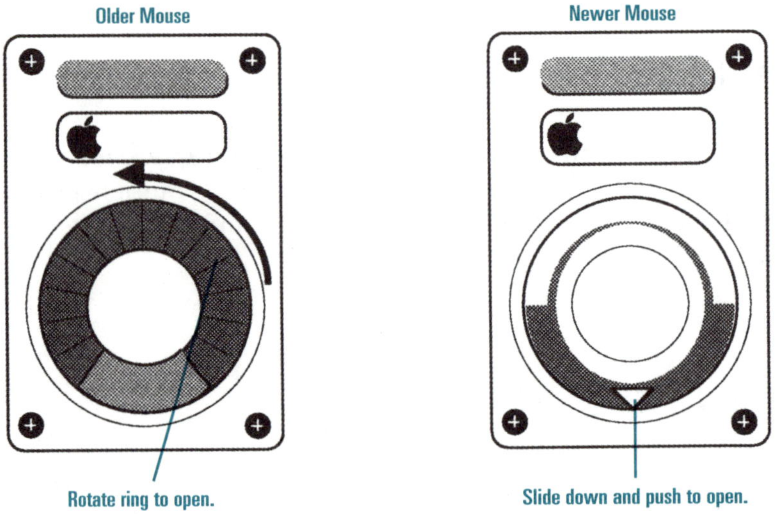

Figure 14.11
Opening a mouse.

3. Shake the ball out.
4. Locate the three rollers that support the ball (shown in Figure 14.12). Chances are, these rollers have picked up a trail of gummy dirt from your desk. Clean them with a cotton swab and alcohol.
5. Wipe off the mouse ball with a soft, dry cloth.
6. Gently blow into the mouse to chase out any dust or dirt.
7. Reassemble the mouse. It should now work smoothly. If it doesn't, there may be something wrong with the optical sensors, and it will need professional repair or replacement.

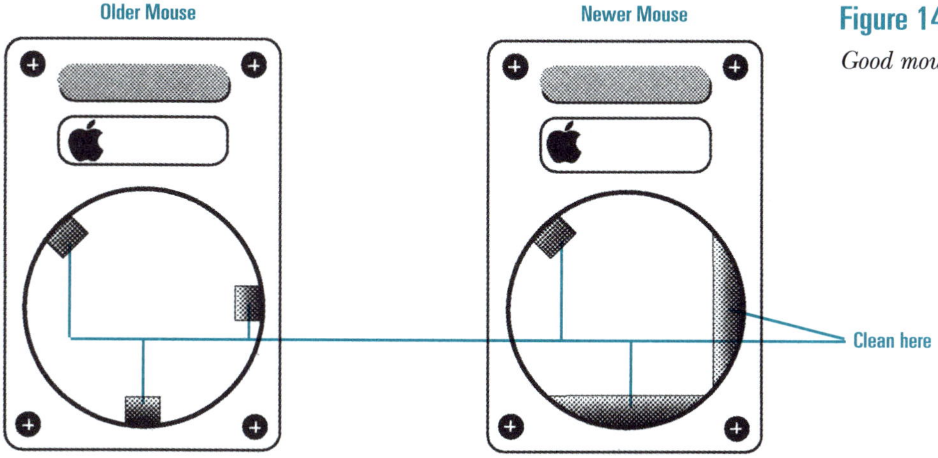

Figure 14.12

Good mousekeeping.

> Third-party mice are available for around $75. Some of them work much better than the Apple version.

Clean Your Disk Drive?

A couple of companies sell disk-drive cleaning kits, usually packaged with screen and keyboard cleaning supplies. These look like regular disks, except there's a piece of cloth in place of the magnetic surface. You wet the cloth with a special cleaning solution and stick it in the drive. As the drive-cleaning disk spins, it allegedly wipes accumulated grime off the heads.

Apple has never suggested using these kits, in close to ten years of operating manuals. This is probably because the kits, if used incorrectly, do more harm than good. Too little or too much cleaning solution can damage the heads. A worn out or dirty cloth disk can deposit more dirt than it removes. A bad housing can knock delicate parts completely out of adjustment.

On the other hand, if a drive is *consistently* having trouble with disks that work fine on at least two other drives, it's *possible* things could be helped with one pass of a cleaning kit. At least, you probably won't make it worse.

Clean Your Printer

A dirty printer puts ink every place but where it should go. A clean printer (with proper supplies) gives remarkably good reproduction. ImageWriters can get fouled with tiny scraps of paper and with fibers from the ribbon. Simple cleaning instructions appear in Chapter 5.

StyleWriter ink cartridges can get temporarily gummed up, especially if the cartridge hasn't been used for a while (or is fresh out of the box). Fortunately, Apple provides a quick and clean way to clear ink jams:

1. Turn the StyleWriter off.
2. Press and hold down the Ready button.
3. While the Ready button is down, press the Power button. Then release both buttons.

The printer will enter a self-cleaning sequence, which takes about twenty seconds. (By the way, you can use a similar procedure to print a test page—just substitute the Form Feed button for the Ready button in the above instructions—so you can check the printer without using your Mac.) The only other common StyleWriter problems we've encountered are dirty rollers—open the front panel and wipe the two black rollers with a dry cloth—or misfeeding caused by a temporary separating of the paper feeder from the printer itself. Make sure the front and back of the printer assembly are snugly together and that the two latching buttons on the sides of the feeder are firmly forward.

Laser printers are stuffed with boxes of black powder, charged wires that try to keep the powder in the right place, and heated rollers that gum themselves up with assorted melted crud. Routine toner replacement is simple, but each brand (and just about each model) of printer is slightly different, so check the owners' manual. Anything more complicated may need special parts and techniques. If the manual doesn't make it look easy, send the whole dreary mess to a service shop.

Change the Battery

Every Macintosh has a small battery to keep the clock going and the PRAM alive. The first symptom of a weak battery is usually an inaccurate clock.

The battery in the original Mac and Mac Plus lasts about a year. To change it, open the little door near the power switch and pop in a new Eveready 523 (or equivalent) 4.5-volt battery. They may be hard to find, but a computer dealer or photo supply store can get them.

The battery in newer compact models is soldered in place. The one in Mac II machines sits in an unsupported plastic holder on a delicate circuit card. Fortunately, these batteries are rated seven years. Replacement in both cases is best left to the technically adept. The multiple batteries in PowerBooks have their own complex rules: see the booklet that came with the computer.

Check the Cables

If you move your keyboard around a lot, the cable will start to show wear. If it wears down too much, the keyboard will become erratic. Get a replacement ADB cable at your dealer. Replacement keyboard cables for the Plus and earlier machines are a lot less rugged, but are harder to find when they break. Even though they look like ordinary telephone cords, they're not. Apple perversely wired the Mac keyboard cable backwards (compared to the millions of telephone cables), even though it's otherwise identical. You might still be able to order a replacement cord from an authorized service shop.

> *Authorized* service shops can be hard to find. Apple's authorization process is notoriously rigorous.

There's a strong likelihood you won't be able to find a replacement keyboard cable for an original Mac, and you'll have to make your own from an ordinary telephone handset cable. This requires a little soldering (or a friend with a soldering iron). Figure 14.13 shows the two types of cable you're likely to encounter. Either match the four colors as in the top drawing; or, if the cable has only two colors of wire, lay it on a flat surface and flip it as in the bottom drawing. Test your work with an ohmmeter before you use it: shorted splices can damage your computer. But if you do a good job, it'll be electrically identical to the Apple original. Make sure you use a handset cable—the cord that goes to the wall has different connectors.

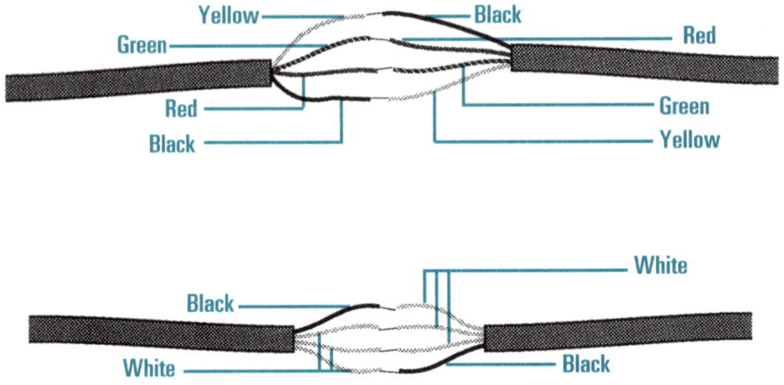

Figure 14.13.
Modifying a telephone cord for early Mac keyboards.

Things You Shouldn't Try to Fix

If your Mac is displaying the following symptoms, send it to a repair shop at once:

- Absolutely dark screen.
- Shrinking screen.
- Persistent "Sad Mac" icons (that's the one with little x eyes).
- Burnt or smoky smell.
- Abnormally loud noises (early Macs have been known to radiate a soft, high-pitched whistle with no ill effect, except on the user's nerves).

The best source for reliable repair shop recommendations is a user group in your area. Otherwise, you're at the mercy of the phone book and your dealer. In addition to the repairs you *can't* do, there's one thing you *shouldn't* do unless you know exactly what you're doing. It's risky, both to the computer and to your personal safety.

Don't open your Mac! Hazardous voltages remain in compact models, even after you disconnect the power. There's a good chance you'll hurt yourself. Even if you avoid the high voltage, there are still lots of tiny contacts and components to misalign, and you can snap the picture tube in half by leaning on the wrong circuit card. The Mac II series is a little bit safer (because there's no picture tube), but it's just as delicate.

This includes installing memory. Mail order firms sell do-it-yourself memory kits and will even give you videotapes of their experts popping chips around. (We've also seen videotapes showing a 97-pound weakling become a Schwarzenegger overnight.) Remember, these are primarily *sales* films. You can save $20 or $30 by installing your own memory. . . and you can also cause a few hundred dollars' worth of damage.

In This Chapter

How to Choose the Best Mac for You . . .

•

. . . and How to Shop for It Intelligently.

•

Used Machines: Bargains or Bummers?

•

Complete List of All New and Used Macintosh Models

•

Where to Look

The Macintosh isn't a one-size-fits-all computer. Twenty-two different models are now available. Some are brand new machines, some are older or used (but still good investments), and a few are unfortunate mistakes that Apple should never have released. You can choose from all-in-one units, battery-operated portables, or modular machines with separate monitors.

This chapter will help you select the right kind of Mac for your application. It suggests a few handy rules about buying computers and ends with a model-by-model description of the entire line.

15

A Mac of Your Own

Every Mac shares the features that make Macintosh computing so friendly: a mouse (or equivalent pointer), a high-resolution screen, and the Macintosh operating system. Except for the very earliest Mac, all run most of today's software (though some run it very slowly). All have connections for a modem, printer, external speaker, mouse, and keyboard (even the PowerBooks, with their built-in trackball and keyboard). Perhaps the best way to differentiate Macs is in terms of *footprint*—how much space they take up on or under your desk. Smaller ones tend to be easier to set up, but have fewer options. Bigger ones tend to have more powerful brains.

Compact Macs

These are the standard Macs seen on executive desks and parodied in comic strips, and the simplest for day-to-day use. The line ranges from the earliest 128k through the current Classic II and includes such other classics as the powerful SE/30 and the low-cost Mac Plus. All compact Macs have a 9" black and white screen. Cards can be added for grayscale or color, but this should be done only by technicians. Many models have internal hard disks, and all—except the very earliest—can use an external hard disk efficiently.

Modular Macs

These keep their brains in one box, and their picture tube in another. The result is flexibility. Grayscale or color monitors of various shapes and sizes can be added, and additional cards can be plugged in for video capture, sound processing, or other tasks not yet invented. The line ranges from the original (and underpowered) Mac II to the monster Mac Quadras and includes the LC series—low-cost machines that can be adapted to run Apple IIe software found in many elementary schools. Modular Macs are generally more powerful and faster than compact ones, but there are notable exceptions—as you'll see from their individual descriptions.

Folding Macs

We wanted to call this category laptops, but Apple insists their PowerBooks aren't laptops but *notebooks.* In addition to the three PowerBooks, the line also includes the Mac Portable introduced a few years ago. All of them fold in the middle, with the keyboard on one half and the screen on the other (just like virtually every other laptop on the market). All use batteries for power, have LCD screens that lack the brightness or contrast of plug-in Macs, and require special low-power chips for expansion. And all of them—including the overweight and unwieldy Portable—are great for people who use their computer on the road.

About Speed

If all you do is enter text, the Mac will usually wait for you. Even the fastest touch-typist can't keep up with a computer and modern software. But if you want to crunch numbers, move or edit graphics, or even do such word-processing tasks as change headline sizes or check spelling, speed becomes important. Computer speed is determined by three factors: how many tasks the basic chip *(Central Processing Unit, or CPU)* can do with one instruction, how fast the system cycles these instructions, and—to a lesser extent—how much memory is installed.

All Macs use processors in the Motorola 68xxx family, ranging from the 68000 through the 68040. The higher the number, the smarter the chip. Some machines also add a *Coprocessor* or *Floating Point Unit [FPU]* to speed things up. These separate chips specialize in number processing, letting the CPU worry about other tasks. This isn't just for spreadsheets, since an FPU can speed up many graphic or multimedia applications.

Mac processors run at 8 to 40 megahertz—millions of cycles per second—depending on the model. This doesn't mean they carry out your instructions that quickly, since each human instruction can represent thousands or even millions of individual computer operations. But a faster processor means a faster Mac, and the differences are more than a few millionths of a second. An operation that takes five seconds on a Quadra can take a full minute on a Classic, and even longer on a Plus.

The amount of memory a computer has influences its speed, depending on the program. If there's enough room to fit a document in RAM, most programs can manipulate it more quickly. Memory organization and how data is routed between RAM and disk can also influence speed. That's one reason why a Quadra 950 at 33 MHz can do things faster than a 40 MHz IIfx.

Secondhand Mac

Macs have few moving parts (only the disk drive, keyboard, and mouse) so "used" doesn't have to mean "used up." If you're willing to shop around, you'll find bargains galore, especially with the competitive pressure from newer models. You should be able to get an excellent deal on a Mac that someone else has outgrown.

Earlier we said that buying a Mac was like buying a car. Buying a used Mac is like buying a used car. There are things to watch out for, and uninformed salespeople (we won't say "unscrupulous") will try to convince you these things don't matter. Call first, make sure what they've got is exactly what you want, and then check it before you buy. Any good dealer selling a used Mac will guarantee it for between three months and one year.

Physical Checkout

Look for physical damage to the case, drives, mouse, or keyboard. Try the keyboard and mouse to make sure that everything responds as it should. Older keyboards have springs in the keys that can break or get sticky, and bad contacts can cause skipped or double letters. Open the mouse (see Chapter 14) and look at the condition of the metal rollers and the ball. If grime covers the rollers, you can clean them, but if the ball isn't smooth, you'll need to replace it.

Turn It On!

After the computer's been on for at least fifteen minutes, check the screen. The image should be steady and not flicker. If the image is slightly off center, it's no problem. But if it's unusually small or wobbly, it could be that part of the power supply (the flyback transformer) is about to die: a particularly expensive repair. Insert an unimportant data disk from another Mac to check the disk drives. If the unit has two drives, make sure both can read the same disk. If it has a hard drive (and we *don't* recommend buying a used hard drive) the only way to check it is to run a formatting program—which can erase all of the data.

Then, use your nose! Sniff around the case for a burnt or ozone smell, a sure sign of sick electronics. Don't worry about fan noise: the fan on early SEs is loud, but this is a characteristic of the breed.

Finding a Used Mac

Dealers of new machines can also be good sources for used ones, once you've convinced them they're not going to make a full-price sale. Ask for trade-ins or demo units. If something goes wrong with the machine, authorized dealers may be in the best position to honor any guarantees they've given. We've also received good deals on older models our local rental house wanted to upgrade. You can find similar deals at service bureaus, though they seldom have in-house repair facilities. A number of companies specialize in refurbishing used Macs and selling them with guarantees. Check the back of *MacWorld* and *MacUser* for their ads.

Many bulletin boards list systems and peripherals for sale. The service isn't responsible for deals you make with individuals, but it may be able to help you find independent experts to evaluate the machine. And don't forget your local newspaper: there are a lot of Macs out there, and a lot of folks who don't know any better way to sell one they're not using.

Mac by Mac, Down the Line

The prices here are street prices: average discounted new or used prices, as of Summer, 1992. Computer prices are volatile. Apple frequently adjusts list prices as the marketplace changes. When they introduce new models, they frequently lower the rest of their line. And used machines just keep on getting cheaper as they get older.

If you have access to Delphi or CompuServe, check for on-line listings from the Boston Computer Exchange (BoCoEx), a brokering service for all kinds of equipment. It compiles weekly averages for computers, just as the *Wall Street Journal* does for other commodities. You can also find BoCoEx in *MacWeek* and the *Boston Globe*, or call them at 1-800-BoCoExx (what else?).

There *are* bargains out there. If you're offered a machine for significantly less than this chapter or BoCoEx quotes, it isn't necessarily a lemon. Computers are a lot more consistent than cars. Check the machine and the guarantee, or ask your local user group or guru for an opinion.

All prices are for *minimum configurations*: the lowest amount of RAM and the smallest disk configuration shipped by Apple. Additional RAM usually adds about $35 per MB to used machines; used disks start at about $150 for 20 MB. We don't recommend used hard disks, since they're the part most likely to go bad with age or misuse. Dealers can install additional RAM and new hard drives in used Macs they sell, and it's frequently worth the extra price. If you do end up with a used disk, make *frequent* backups.

Mac 128K, 512K, 512KE

Don't buy these, unless they also come with exactly the software you want. Most current versions of programs won't work in these machines. Neither will modern double-sided disks. Hard disks are not practical with these machines, and new keyboards or mice might be impossible to find. Printer and modem ports require original cables or low-cost adapters. In 1984 and 1985, these were a good value at $2,500 or so. They haven't lost any capability, but people expect a lot more now. If all you need is a basic word processor or telecom terminal, they can be a bargain.

Processor: 68000, 8 MHz. RAM: a fraction of a megabyte. Price: $150 (for a 128K) to $300 (512KE).

Mac Plus

Still usable, and frequently a bargain if speed isn't an issue. The one-megabyte memory can be expanded by a technician. The Plus came with one double-sided internal floppy drive. It and all higher Mac models support modern SCSI accessories, including external hard disks. The Plus used the same non-standard mouse and keyboard as earlier machines, so replacement might be a problem. All but the most complicated new software will run happily in a Plus, though System 7 may have problems.

Processor: 68000, 8 MHz. RAM: 1 MB - 4 MB. Price $450.

Mac SE

A versatile workhorse, the SE was the first to use the ADB and modern connectors, as well as an expanded ROM chip to make operations faster. Some versions have a built-in hard disk and one floppy drive; others have two floppies. Older SEs usually have 800K floppies and a noisy fan; newer ones—the machine was current until 1991, when the Classic was introduced—have 1.4M SuperDrives and a slightly quieter fan.

Processor: 68000, 8 MHz. RAM: 1 MB - 4 MB. Price (no hard drive): $700.

Mac SE/30

It looks like an SE but the SE/30's more powerful chips, faster clock speed, and internal data paths make it the fastest compact Mac ever. It's slightly faster than the current IIsi, and it blows the Classic out of the water. It has one SuperDrive and one floppy. Apple discontinued the SE/30 in 1991, and most people who own one are still holding on to it. Still, you may be able to find a bargain on a used one.

Processor: 68000 with FPU. RAM: 1 MB - 8 MB. Price (20 MB drive): $1,700.

Mac Classic

Even Apple makes mistakes, and this was one of their three (okay, the others are the original Mac II and the Portable). This machine was intended as a low-cost, high-powered machine. Unfortunately, it worked exactly as well as the basic SE and lacked some of the SE's features such as a universal power supply, multiple ADB jacks, and optional configurations. People didn't want to pay new prices for old performance, so the Classic was discontinued after a year. Available only with one floppy and one hard drive.

Processor: 68000, 8 MHz. RAM: 1 MB - 4 MB. Price (20 MB drive): $800.

Classic II

At least Apple fixes its mistakes. This current version has a smarter CPU, faster speed, and more possible RAM than the original Classic. It can handle most tasks about twice as fast. Unfortunately, in the rush to upgrade the unpopular Classic, Apple didn't have time to completely redesign the machine. Its data path isn't as sophisticated as the older SE/30, so its performance isn't as good. Still, it's the only choice for those wanting a brand-new compact Mac.

Processor: 68030, 16 MHz. RAM: 2 MB - 10 MB. Price (new, 40 MB drive): $1,400.

Modular Macs

Prices for modular Macs (the LC, II, and Quadra families) do not include the monitor or video card. Used color monitors start at about $250, and new ones at about $475. Most Mac II models (except the IIci and IIsi) also need a separate video card for about the same price, so figure between $500–$900 to put a picture on one of them. Monitor and card prices can go sky-high, depending on features like size and accuracy.

Used modular Macs almost always include a keyboard. New ones don't—except for the LCII—so figure between $100–$150 extra depending on features and dealer discounts.

Mac II

When the II first appeared, using the then-new 68020 chip, it was a breakthrough. A lot were sold, and a lot ended up on the used market. We recommend avoiding them. Performance is not as good as a new LCII, even though it costs about the same. It can't handle high-density floppy disks without an expensive upgrade. And the '020 chip was used in only one other model, so future system software might not work efficiently with it. Its only advantage over the LCII is the expansion slots.

Processor: 68020, 16 MHz. RAM: 2 MB - 32 MB. Price (20 MB drive): $1,700.

LC

This was the other machine to use the 68020 chip and was discontinued for the same reason. Its performance is about the same as a Classic II, with the extra advantage of color—though not as versatile a color system as the Mac II series—and the ability to run an Apple IIe emulation card. There's a lot of Apple II software in schools, so this combination Mac/Apple II became popular with educators.

Processor: 68020, 16 MHz. RAM: 2 MB - 20 MB. Price (20 MB drive): $1,200.

LC II

Hooray for Apple! They plugged in a smarter chip and got a machine that runs only about 20% slower than a IIsi. Color capability is more limited than the IIsi, and it can't take expansion cards, but at least you're not waiting around for the processor. They kept the Apple IIe connection, making this a versatile new machine for schools and families.

Processor: 68030, 16 MHz. RAM: 4 MB - 10 MB. Price (new, 40 MB drive): $1,600.

IIx and IIcx

The **c** stands for compact. Except for the case size (and accordingly, the number of expansion slots) these two discontinued machines were virtually identical. The chip set and clock speed are about the same as the SE/30's, and performance is almost as good. On the other hand, these machines can run in color, and have slots for additional functions. You'll need a color or black-and-white video card, but that still leaves you with 2 plug-in slots on the IIcx and 5 slots on the IIx.

Processor: 68030 with 68882 FPU, 16 MHz. RAM: 1 MB - 8 MB. Price (40 MB drive): IIcx, $2,300; IIx, $2,700.

IIsi

This is the least powerful current modular Mac, but still quite respectable: a little faster than the LCII with the advantages of expandability. An optional adapter card adds an FPU and one expansion slot. Since the IIsi has built-in full color support (unlike the limited color of the LC series), the slot can be used for video capture or other functions. The extended data path means more RAM can be added.

Processor: 68030 (optional FPU), 20 MHz. RAM: 2 MB - 17 MB. Price new (40 MB drive): $2,000.

IIci

A fast clock, built-in FPU, and optional RAM cache make this as fast as the SE/30 in black-and-white, though using the built-in color support slows things down a little. There are three expansion slots, so you can add a separate video card and really speed things up.

Processor: 68030 with 68882 FPU, 25 MHz. RAM: 4 MB - 32 MB. Price new (40 MB drive): $3,300.

IIfx

This model is the fastest Mac II available. A built-in FPU, RAM cache for temporary data storage, and direct path between memory and SCSI hard disk make the IIfx's performance about three times as good as a IIsi. No video support, so you'll have to use one of the six slots for a separate video card.

Processor: 68030 with 68882 FPU, 40 MHz. RAM: 4 MB - 32 MB. Price new (40 MB drive): $3,900.

Quadra 700, 900, 950

The Quadras link the new 68040 processor chip to a new data structure, so even with a slower clock speed, the Quadra 950 works about 60% faster than a IIfx. The 700 has two expansion slots and the 950 has five. (The 900 was discontinued after a few months manufacture, with no particular comment from Apple.) All Quadras include built-in video support, including various levels of IBM and broadcast video monitors. If you're doing high-level graphics, photo retouching, or professional animation, these are the machines for you. They may be a little pricey for the rest of us.

Processor: 68040 with FPU, 25 MHz - 33 MHz. RAM: 4 MB - 64 MB. Price new (drive extra): $4,000 up.

Folding Macs

These are complete, with built-in hard drives, keyboards, and displays. Both new and used units generally include one rechargeable battery and a plug-in power supply.

Mac Portable

People used to say a lightweight, ergonomic, fully functional Macintosh was impossible. In late 1989, Apple proved them right: the Mac Portable featured a hard-to-see screen, a hard-to-type keyboard, and a a hard-to-reach trackball. At sixteen pounds, even its portability was questioned. Still, it *was* a Mac, and people with money to spend and a need to travel paid approximately $5,000 for the privilege. Now, slightly more than three years later, Portables are appearing on the used market for about one-quarter their original cost. If you need quasi-portability and want to save a few bucks, one of these used will give you the performance of a PowerBook 100 for considerably less money.

Processor: 68000 , 16 MHz. RAM: 2 MB - 9 MB. Price (40 MB drive): $1,300.

PowerBooks

Apple's response to the unpopularity of the Portable was a new series of lightweight computers—as little as five pounds—introduced in late 1991. While the keyboards are still too small for a touch-typist, the screens are larger and the more powerful PowerBooks are fully-respectable, high-speed Macs. All three units have ADB ports so you can use an external, full-size keyboard and mouse or trackball: highly recommended if you've got the room.

PowerBook 100

This smallest PowerBook is actually built to Apple's specification by Sony. The unit has a small, awkward trackball, hard-to-see screen, and comes without a floppy disk drive. It also feels flimsy. To transport data you can buy an external drive, or you can use a special cable that makes the whole PowerBook behave like a hard drive! Connect it to the SCSI port on another Mac, and it'll show up like a disk on the bigger unit's desktop.

Processor: 68000,16 MHz. RAM: 2 MB - 8 MB. Price new (20 MB drive): $2,000.

PowerBook 140

This more rugged PowerBook is about a pound heftier, and runs about as fast as an SE/30. It also has an internal SuperDrive and a sound input jack. The screen is the same as on the PowerBook 100, but the keyboard and trackball feel better. It's also made by Apple. Business travelers consider this one a favorite.

Processor: 68030 , 16 MHz. RAM: 4 MB - 8 MB. Price new (40 MB drive): $2,650.

PowerBook 170

The current top of the PowerBook line, with the same performance as the Mac IIci. The screen is much easier to see at all angles, making it the only portable Mac that can be used for group presentations at a conference table. Keyboard, drive, and trackball are the same as the PowerBook 140. Optional internal modems can send or receive faxes and communicate with bulletin boards.

Processor: 68030 with 68882 FPU, 25 MHz. RAM: 4 MB - 8 MB. Price new (40 MB drive): $3,600. Modem: about $275.

Power without the Book

A third-party supplier, Outbound Systems, has positioned their Notebook Series as direct competition for the PowerBook line. These use standard Apple chips for compatibility, but have more powerful processors, in a battery-powered package slightly smaller than the Apple's versions. Outbound dealers are harder to find than Apple ones (it's a *much* smaller company), but the machines are available from MacConnection, a respected mail-order house.

Authors' Choice

We don't find much difference between a good new machine and an equivalent good used one, other than such obvious characteristics as price and warranty. If you're going to use a computer for basic office or household tasks, you'll do equally well with a new Mac Classic II or a used SE with a new hard drive.

If your computer plans include occasional DTP, an LCII with a page-size monitor is the economical choice. If speed is important, make it a IIsi or used IIcx. More complicated data processing, including complex spreadsheets or databases, can be handled well by a new IIsi or a used SE/30.

If you're heavily into image manipulation, scientific computing, or sound processing, consider one of the powerhouses: the brand-new Quadras, or the slightly-older (but available new or used) IIfx. These cost the most, but you're paying for performance.

Obviously, travelers have different considerations. But most folks who buy *any* PowerBook end up wishing they'd sprung for the PowerBook 170 (or the third-party Outbound). One of these, with an external keyboard and third-party video adapter, can do double duty as a travelling and desktop machine.

In This Chapter

How to Hook Up Any Model Macintosh

•

Three Ways to Connect a Printer, and Which One You Should Use

•

Installing Hard Disks and Scanners

•

Building a Network of Your Own

Apple's computer "for the rest of us" wouldn't be much use if only a few of us could set it up. You can set up almost any Mac without tools, and with very few exceptions, the plugs will only fit into the proper jacks. This chapter describes how to set up any Mac equipment quickly and easily, including SCSI devices and AppleTalk networks.

16

You Gotta Have Connections

This chapter assumes two things: that you *aren't* an electrical engineer and that you *are* an intelligent, educated human being (as demonstrated by the fact you bought a Macintosh instead of any other personal computer). Too many technical book writers can't decide whether they're writing for MIT or Sesame Street and so do a bad job of both. This would be a mistake in a book about the Mac. If this is a computer "for the rest of us," it shouldn't be something only a few of us can hook up.

Can't Even Hook Up a VCR?

Even though the Macintosh is powerful, it's surprisingly easy to set up. Most of the connectors are unique. You can't accidentally plug the keyboard where the modem goes, because it just won't fit. (This doesn't always apply to older Macs. Apple started using their present connections with the SE. Very early models used the same plugs for the printer, modem, and mouse.)

There are just a few things you have to be careful about. Follow these rules whenever you connect a computer:

- Turn off the power before changing connectors. This isn't just for your safety. It's for the computer's safety, too.
- Don't force the connectors. Rotate them to find the proper orientation, and check to see if you're plugging them into the right socket. If they still don't go in easily, something is wrong.
- Use the clips or thumbscrews provided to keep connections tight. They may be necessary to shield your data from interference.
- Don't touch the connector pins. Static electricity can damage some components, and you don't want to bend the pins accidentally.
- Use a grounded (3-prong) outlet. You need a good ground for safety and for data reliability. If you have to use an extension cord, make sure it's the three-conductor kind that maintains the ground.

If you've got old-fashioned outlets, don't use a grounding adapter. Call an electrician instead. The Macintosh doesn't eat much electricity (about the same as a similarly sized television), so you probably won't need a separate circuit.

ImageWriters need an amp and a half while printing, and laser printers hog about six amps, but StyleWriters use less power than a rooming-house light bulb: 23 watts, maximum.

A Good Idea

After you unpack your Mac, save all the packing pieces. They're the only safe way to ship the unit, if you move or if it needs repairs. And for heaven's sake, send in the warranty cards once you're sure everything's working. Some of those cards entitle you to upgrades or free sample programs.

Basic Hookup

All the connections you'll need are on the back of the computer. The array of jacks and terminals may be daunting at first (see Figure 16.1), but things become fairly straightforward if you take them one at a time. Apple spent a long time making the Macintosh easy to install. Each connector has its own icon, and the icons tell you what should be connected where. Besides, most of the plugs just won't fit in the wrong hole.

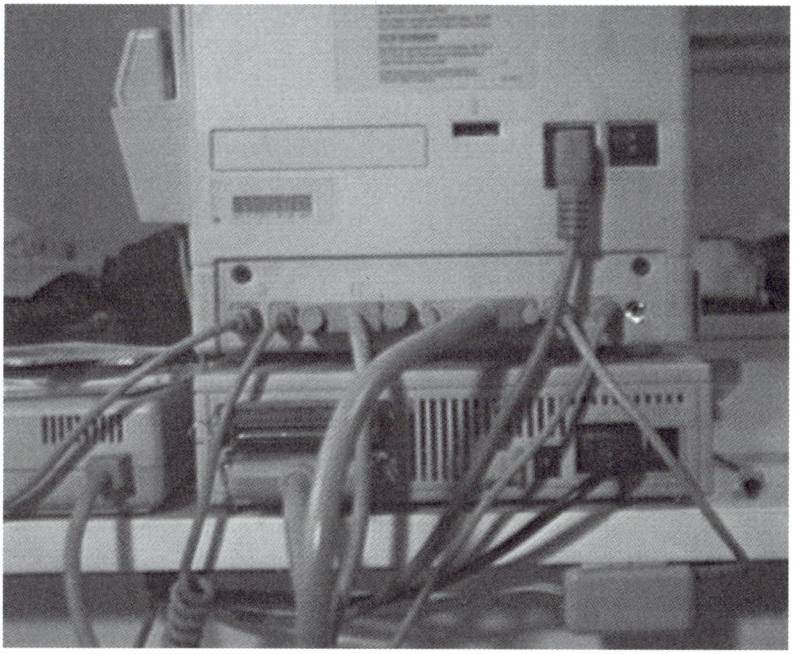

Figure 16.1

One of our SEs. You won't need all these wires, but in a few pages you'll know how to connect them.

Keyboard and Mouse: Newer Macs

In 1987, Macintosh started using the *Apple Desktop Bus* (also known as *ADB*). It doesn't matter if you've got a keyboard, a mouse, a trackball, or even a barcode reader—they all hook up the same. The ADB uses a small four-pin jack, like the one shown in Figure 16.2. Depending on the model, you'll have one or two of these jacks on the back of your machine.

Figure 16.2

The Apple Desktop Bus (ADB) connector and icon.

If you have two jacks on your Mac, use either or both. Or, you can form a *daisy chain* with the mouse plugged into the keyboard and the keyboard into the computer. (ADB jacks provide enough power for three input devices, so you shouldn't chain more than that on each one.) The Apple keyboard has two ADB jacks, as shown in Figure 16.3. So do most trackballs. You can use either jack or both.

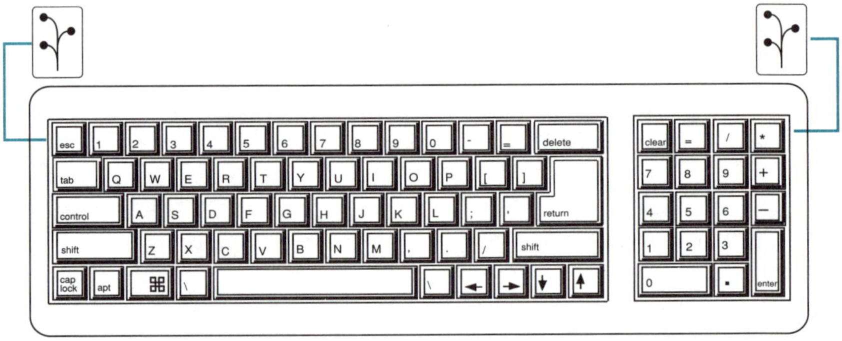

Figure 16.3

Keyboard ADB locations.

Connection Procedure

Apple's ADB cord (see Figure 16.4) is about three feet long, with a coiled section in the middle and two four-pin plugs. Other devices may have coilless cords. They work the same.

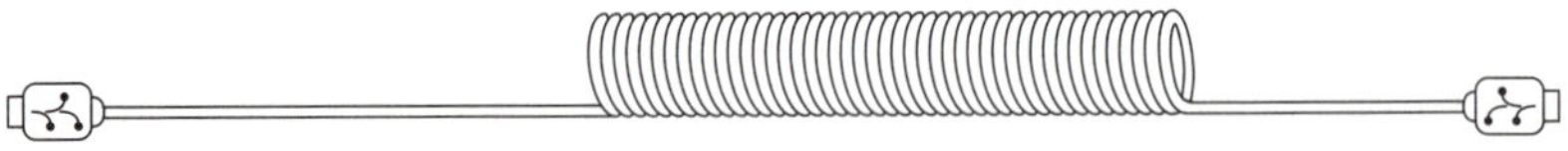

Figure 16.4

An ADB cord.

Plug one end of the cord into the computer. Plug the other end into the keyboard. It's up to you whether the coiled section is closer to keyboard or to computer. You might have to rotate the plugs to make them go in smoothly. On the Mac, the flat side of the plug faces up. On the keyboard, the flat side faces towards the ADB icon. Plug the mouse into the other ADB jack on the keyboard or a remaining ADB jack on your computer.

If your wiring looks like either of the diagrams in Figure 16.5, everything is properly connected. Flip the keyboard connections if you'd rather have the mouse on the left.

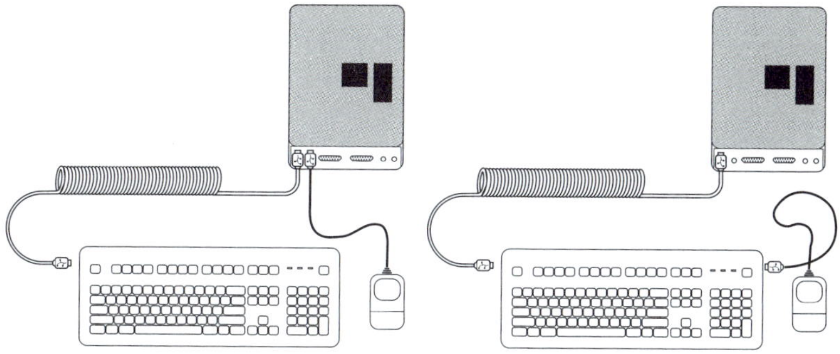

Figure 16.5

Desktop wiring. Reverse the setup if you're left handed, to put the mouse on the left.

Keyboard and Mouse: Mac Plus and Earlier

Early Mac designs had separate jacks for the keyboard and for the mouse. The mouse jack is on the left rear of the computer and has a mouse icon (see Figure 16.6). Plug the mouse's tail in and tighten both thumbscrews (ouch!).

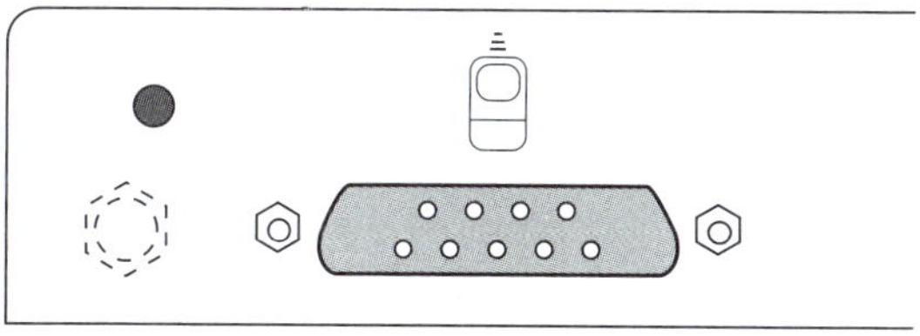

Figure 16.6

Mouse hole for the Mac Plus and earlier.

The keyboard cable looks and snaps in place like a standard telephone handset cord (but absolutely isn't; see Chapter 14). Snap one end into the bottom right front of the Plus or 512 and the other end into the back of the keyboard.

Any Other Components?

Plugging in the keyboard and mouse is enough to get a compact Macintosh ready for basic operations like video games. Chances are, you'll also want a printer, modem, local office network, or additional storage device. If you have a modular Mac, you'll *definitely* want a screen. Follow the appropriate instructions later in this chapter, before you connect the power.

Plug It In

The power input is next to the rear-panel power switch on all Macs, identified with a "~" (see Figure 16.7). Plug the power cord into the back of the Mac and the other end into the wall. To satisfy our lawyers, we should probably add some suitable warning here: "Hazardous voltages are present. Do not stick foreign objects including (but not limited to) fingers, ballpoint pens, or spaghetti into the socket."

The Macintosh SE and most newer machines automatically adjust to any standard wall current between 100 and 240 volts, 50 to 60 Hertz. Earlier models (and the lower-cost Classic) aren't so accommodating: they're built for specific voltage ranges. *Plugging an early Mac, or a Mac Classic, into the wrong power can cause permanent damage.* If you have any doubts, check the printed label near the power input jack.

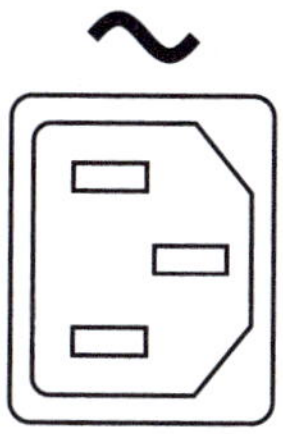

Figure 16.7

Power input jack and icon.

> A service technician easily can convert a Classic for use with European voltages.

Turn It On

Complete start-up instructions for various types of Macs are in Chapter 2. Or just play around. If the cables are properly connected, there's very little you can do to accidentally break a Mac.

Connecting the Monitor

The Mac II and LC series can support so many different kinds of color or monochrome video that the monitors are sold separately. Hookup details vary, but most are similar to the Apple monitors described in this section.

Macintosh LC, IIsi, IIci

These Macs have built-in monitor circuits connected to the jack on the back, shown in Figure 16.8. There's an identical jack on the back of most monitors (some have the cable permanently attached). Connect the thick monitor cable to the jacks, and tighten the thumbscrews.

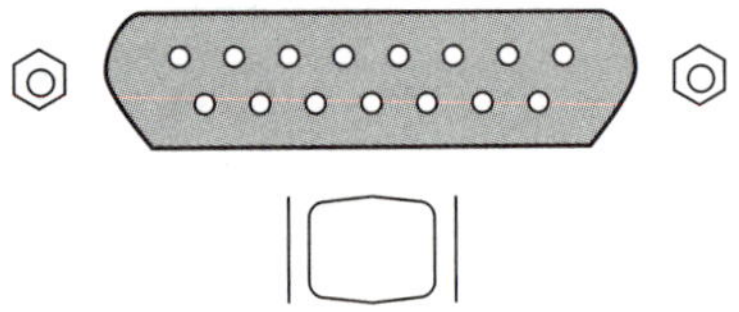

Figure 16.8

Video jack and icon.

Automatic Power Control

There's also a three-prong power connector on the back of most monitors, identical to the one in Figure 16.7. But the cord supplied with the monitor isn't what you'd expect. It has *two* computer-style connectors, one male and one female, instead of a wall plug. You plug the female end into its jack on the back of the computer, and leave the monitor turned on all the time. This way, the system controls the monitor power with its software. Check the manufacturers' instructions if you're using a very large monitor: the Mac can handle only a limited amount of power.

Other Mac II Models

More sophisticated Mac IIs frequently have specialized monitors, so Apple left the choice of video circuitry up the buyer. You'll have to buy a separate video card. There's none included with the machine. The card plugs into the chassis, with a video connector sticking out of a vertical slot on the rear. Follow the directions packed with the card and the following caution.

CAUTION: Computer cards are vulnerable to electric shock. Ordinary household static can seriously damage them. Leave the cards in their conductive packing material until you're ready to install them. When you do handle them, hold them by their edges. Don't rub them against Siamese cats.

If you don't see a video connector, you don't have a video board (or the one you have was seriously, improperly installed) and can't have video. Once the board is in place, connect it and the power cable as previously described.

Hooking Up a Printer

A wide range of printers easily connects to the Macintosh. This section discusses the most common types: ImageWriters, StyleWriters, SCSI laser printers (such as Apple's LaserWriter IISC), and PostScript laser printers (such as the LaserWriter IINT). Most printers from third-party suppliers work and are connected the same way as their Apple equivalents, but a few don't. Some may even require adapter cards or special interface boxes, so check before you buy.

ImageWriter and StyleWriter

This section applies to the ImageWriter, ImageWriter II, and StyleWriter—they're all wired the same. For a while, Apple also offered an AppleTalk ImageWriter. If you have one of these, connect it like a PostScript LaserWriter (described later).

StyleWriter, ImageWriter II, and Mac Plus or Later Computer

These machines have a round, eight-pin connector (on the left in Figure 16.9) similar to the ADB connector. On the computer, it's got a sort of ImageWriter icon. Plug either end of the cable into the computer, and the other end into the back of the printer. You might have to rotate the connectors before they'll go in.

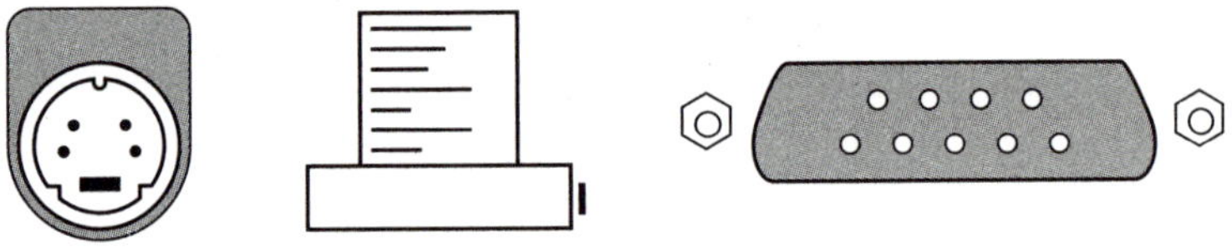

Figure 16.9

Printer jacks and icon. Newer Macs on the left; older ones on the right.

Original ImageWriter or Mac 512

The Mac 512 and 128 have a nine-pin rectangular connector (on the right in Figure 16.9) with the same printer icon. The ImageWriter has a 25-pin rectangular connector on the back. Obviously, the cable goes only one way. Don't forget to tighten the screws. (If you can't find an early-Mac to early-ImageWriter cable at your dealer, ask for a 9-pin to 25-pin modem cable.)

> **TIP:** You can extend the nine-pin end of an old-style printer cable with the nine-pin extension cords sold for video game joysticks.

Mixed Singles

There's no electrical difference between round and rectangular printer connectors. You can connect an ImageWriter II to an older Mac or an original ImageWriter to a Mac II. Ask a dealer for the proper adapter.

There is a slight difference between the printer and modem jacks on your computer. The modem jack—it's marked with an icon that looks like a telephone—is given priority by the Mac and should be saved for connections to the outside world. But if you've got two printers, you can certainly plug one into each jack.

There's a serious difference between the 25-pin jack on early ImageWriters and the identical 25-pin SCSI jack on the back of most Macs—that's probably why Apple changed the printer connector in later versions. Mixing up SCSI and printer circuits can damage both.

Laser Printers

Laser printers use a page-description language to describe the elements that make up the page as curves, lines, and shades. Depending on the type of setup you have, this description is transmitted through a cable to the printer, which translates the description into the tiny dots that make up graphics and type. Or, the Mac itself can translate the description into dots and send it over a special communications channel to the printer. The rest of this section describes these two printing methods.

The AppleTalk Standard

Most Apple and third-party laser printers use the PostScript printer language over the *AppleTalk* connection bus. In computer terms, a bus is a pathway between the computer and its associated devices, such as the printer on the AppleTalk bus, or the keyboard and mouse on the desktop bus. AppleTalk capability is built in to all Macs. You turn it on by selecting a LaserWriter (or any other AppleTalk device) in the Chooser. Figure 16.10 shows some of the possible choices. The icons with "feet" (such as AppleTalk ImageWriter and Public Folder) activate AppleTalk. Even if you're using a non-Apple PostScript printer, click the LaserWriter icon.

Macintosh computers send AppleTalk signals out the printer jack. Look for the connectors shown in Figure 16.9. The laser printer itself will have a similar connector, probably with an icon like the one shown in Figure 16.11.

Figure 16.10

A Chooser with lots of choices.

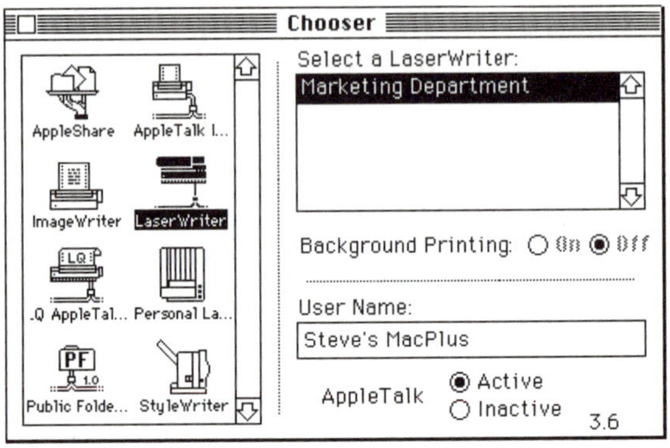

Figure 16.11

The AppleTalk icon.

ABC, NBC, CBS, and You

You can connect a single PostScript printer to a single computer using standard ImageWriter or StyleWriter techniques, and it'll probably work perfectly. But if you want to locate the printer further away than a standard eight-foot cable, or share it among computers, you'll need an AppleTalk *network*. This merely means adding special connector boxes to condition the signal, and then as much wire as you want. There's a whole section on building networks later in this chapter, but for a simple printer installation, you'll need just two of the boxes—one at the printer and one at the Mac—and some cable. You can add more devices to your network by extending the wire and adding more boxes.

Official Apple boxes and extension cable cost about $150. Third-party units like PhoneNET or TurboNet work just as well, hook up with ordinary modular telephone wires, and cost as little as $60 for an equivalent setup.

Get appropriate connector boxes that match the jacks on your computer or printer, plug them in, and connect the cable between them. If you're using a third-party system, you'll have to plug one of the terminating resistors they give you into each box. See "Network Connections," later in this chapter, for more details.

SCSI Printers

The *Small Computer Systems Interface (SCSI)* port first showed up on the Mac Plus, as a high-speed, versatile means of shuttling a lot of data to and from hard disks. (SCSI is pronounced "skuzzy," not "sexy.") General Computer Corporation—now GCC Technologies—realized SCSI could carry enough data to describe all the dots on a laser-printed page, eliminating the need for a separate computer in the printer and an expensive PostScript license. The concept broke a major price barrier, and Apple later appropriated the idea.

SCSI laser printing is *slow*, compared to PostScript. Your Mac has to describe and shoot out the SCSI port seven-and-a-half million little dots per page. On the other hand, it's faster than trying to describe an equivalent number of dots through the printer port to a StyleWriter.

SCSI Connections

Apple's LaserWriter SC and IISC and GCC's Personal LaserPrinter and PLP II all connect to the SCSI port on the back of your computer. While the SCSI standard calls for a 50-pin connector, Apple used a 25-pin jack on most Macs to save space. Look for a diamond-shaped icon, as shown in Figure 16.12.

To save even more space, PowerBook's SCSI jack is a miniature square connector with dozens of holes. You need a special PowerBook-to-standard-SCSI adapter (about $50) to use an external hard disk or SCSI printer with that model.

The cable supplied with the printer will probably have one 25-pin and one 50-pin connector. Locate the appropriate 50-pin connector on your printer, and plug away. Don't plug too *far* away, however. SCSI signals aren't designed to handle more than six meters of cable. Many users report problems after about three meters, or 10 feet. Most SCSI devices have two connectors wired identically. If you're using the printer with an external hard drive, scanner, or other SCSI device, just run a 50-pin to 50-pin SCSI cable from one to the next to create a daisy chain, as shown in Figure 16.13.

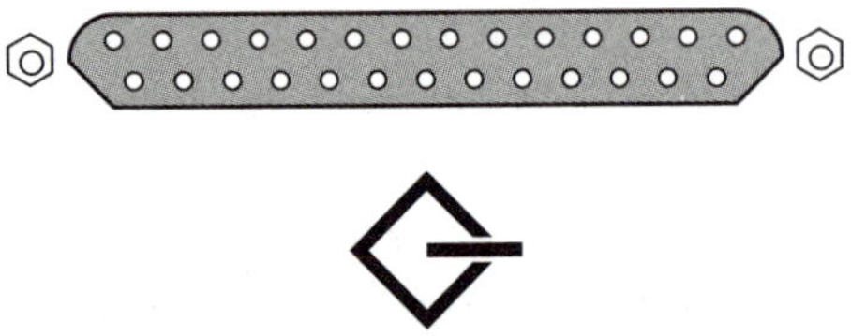

Figure 16.12
Mac SCSI connector and icon.

> **CAUTION:** Apple's SCSI port uses the same type of connector as the ImageWriter and most modems. It's electrically very different. Plugging SCSI and non-SCSI devices together will damage both.

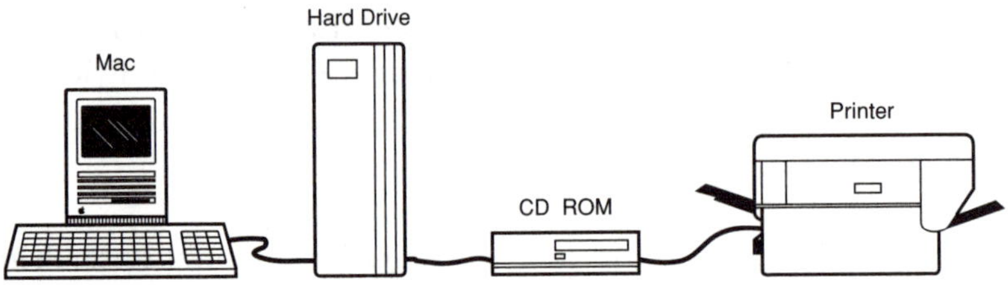

Figure 16.13
A SCSI Daisy Chain.

The Terminator

SCSI signals flash so quickly that the length of time it takes them to travel the wire becomes significant. Tiny data echoes can bounce from one end of the cable to the other, interfering with the precisely timed signal. *Terminators* act as dampers, to control these echoes. Unfortunately, too many dampers can muffle the signal and damage the chips that create it. You need exactly two terminators on a SCSI line: one at each end of the cable run. The one at the computer end is built into the Mac.

Most other SCSI devices don't have built-in termination and rely instead on an *external terminator*. It looks like a 50-pin plug and jack wired back-to-back and contains the resistors that do the damping (see Figure 16.14). This way, the user can hook up SCSI printers, scanners, and hard drives on the same line and plug the terminator into the last one. To use the external terminator, just insert it between the printer and the cable. If your printer has two SCSI connectors, you can put the cable on one and the terminator on the other.

Figure 16.14
An external SCSI terminator. Note the retaining clips.

If a device has an internal terminator, make sure it can be turned off or that the device is at the very end of the SCSI run. If an internally terminated SCSI device *has* to be in the middle of a run and the terminator can't be turned off, you'll probably have to modify it. This can be as simple as unplugging a resistor network but may require a technician: consult the manual.

Get in Line

You can have up to seven SCSI devices connected to a single computer. The system looks at a device's *priority number* when it's moving data back and forth. If any two devices have the same number, the whole system will probably crash.

The Macintosh itself is always device 7. If there's an Apple internal hard disk, it always has the number 0. You can assign any unused number to your printer or anything else on the SCSI line. Hardware that the Mac accesses more frequently (like an external hard disk) should have higher numbers.

Most SCSI devices have a small switch on them to set priority (check the manual because some have to be set in software). Never adjust the switch while any SCSI devices, including the computer, are turned on.

> Often the switch for setting priority will have more positions than the legitimate SCSI numbers 0 to 6, because stock switches are cheaper. Don't use the extra positions.

Printing with SCSI

These printers use their own software, instead of the LaserWriter printer driver supplied by Apple. Copy the *ChooserDocument* that came on the printer's disk into your *System* folder, then open Chooser and select the printer. You can now print in the normal way from any application. But be prepared to wait. As we said earlier, SCSI printing takes much longer than AppleTalk printing. (Some printers also come with *Spooler* software that lets the computer do some of the printing operations while you're running another program. Check the disk and manual.)

Data Storage

Hooking up an external data storage device—floppy or hard disk, tape drive, CD-ROM, or the like—is as easy as hooking up a printer. This section describes some of the possibilities.

External Floppy Disk Drives

If you've got an external floppy disk drive, plug it into the 19-pin floppy disk jack on the back of the computer. For some perverse reason, its icon (see Figure 16.15) doesn't look like a Macintosh disk. It's one of the obsolete cardboard disks the IBM PC used when the Mac was first introduced.

Figure 16.15

Disk drive icon. Why did they use an IBM disk?

Despite having the same connectors, a design change in some of the newer Macintosh models means these SuperDrive machines will not work with some third-party 800K external drives. Try before you buy.

To install a drive, just turn off the computer and plug it in. Be particularly careful of the connector pins. Some disk drive models are particularly vulnerable to static. Don't touch the contacts, and don't let them come into contact with static-making material (plastic bags, nylon carpets, Van de Graff generators). Position the drive on the side of the Mac *opposite* where the power cable goes in, to avoid possible magnetic interference. Also, place the drive alongside the computer (rather than on top of it) to avoid heat damage. This is essentially a "no brainer" with Apple drives, since the cable is too short to go anywhere else.

External Hard Disk Drives

While all of the newer Macs have an internal hard disk drive, many of the older ones don't. A hard drive is usually the first accessory people add to a Plus or dual-floppy SE, for more speed as well as additional storage capacity. You can add an external hard drive to any Mac, old or new, usually through the SCSI port. It's not recommended for very early Macs: the original and Mac 512 don't have SCSI ports, and their hard disks have to connect through the modem jack—losing most of the speed advantages.

SCSI considerations for hard drives are the same as those described earlier for printers. Give the drive a high priority number, and connect it close to the computer in a daisy chain. If it's the last (or only) item in the chain, terminate it just as you would a printer.

Hard Drive Software Setup

On a hard drive, you should set the *interleave value* to efficiently compensate for speed differences between the Macintosh processing chip and the drive itself. To do this, use the hard disk utility software supplied by the manufacturer. Check the software manual for instructions based on the model Mac you use.

Most hard drives come from the manufacturer already *formatted*, a process which makes the drive ready for data and locks out unreliable sectors. If a drive isn't formatted, the manufacturer will provide formatting software on a floppy disk. Once a drive is formatted, you can make it the startup device. Copy your *System* folder onto it, and restart the Mac (it may be necessary to "zap the PRAMs" first; see Chapter 14). If you have more than one hard drive, you'll have to select one as a Startup Device in the Control Panel.

Other SCSI Devices

Any Mac accessory that needs to move a lot of data in a hurry will probably connect to a SCSI daisy chain. Many users add backup storage (tape drives, removable hard disks) and CD-ROM players. For high-end publishing, you can add a graphics scanner. Professional audio editing systems often use the SCSI port to move massive amounts of digitized sound. In general, you just add the accessory to the chain, check terminators and priority numbers, and restart.

Daisy Chain Management

SCSI chains can be unreliable with too many devices connected, or if any of the devices on the chain aren't turned on. Switching the power of any device on or off while the rest of the chain is on can cause major problems. SCSI can also fail because of unpredictable conflicts between devices. But unpredictable as the conflicts are, they may be simple to resolve.

If a SCSI daisy chain isn't working properly, try the following steps:

- Turn off everything, disconnect all but one device, and restart the system. Verify that one device works.
- Turn off the power again, and add one device at a time until you isolate the problem.
- Try rearranging the daisy chain, giving the troublesome device a higher priority and different physical position. This will frequently cure the problem. You may have to try several rearrangements before you resolve the conflict.

Network Connections

AppleTalk lets you connect more than one computer to a single printer (or properly equipped modem, or other device), as well as share files and zip electronic mail between multiple Macs. File sharing and mail require additional software, but it isn't expensive. With a few accessories, you can also plug into networks of PCs and mainframes. (Properly speaking, AppleTalk is the data standard and LocalTalk is Apple's name for their connecting hardware, but the terms are used interchangeably.)

Give It a Name

Every message on an AppleTalk network has a specific *address*: a name given to each computer, printer, or other object on the network. The names are in ordinary English and usually describe the operator or location of the equipment. This way, AppleTalk conversations can happen simultaneously ("Steve's Mac" can talk to "Second Floor Printer," while "Marketing Department" is reading a database file from somewhere else). Setting up network addresses is simple.

> Well, AppleTalk can handle messages *almost* simultaneously. The network can really handle only one message at a time. But the delays are so slight users almost never notice them.

To give your computer an address, click Chooser and type a User Name in the box (see Figure 16.10). This is a misnomer. It's actually the computer's name, representing the Mac on the network, not something that changes with each operator.

To give your printer an address, use the *Namer* application that came on the printer's software disk. Figure 16.16 shows the *Namer.* It will find any AppleTalk printers operating on the network. Select one, and type a name for it. If you have only one printer, you can skip this step and use the name the manufacturer assigned. Other devices and network software may have other ways of assigning names. Check the manuals that came with the devices.

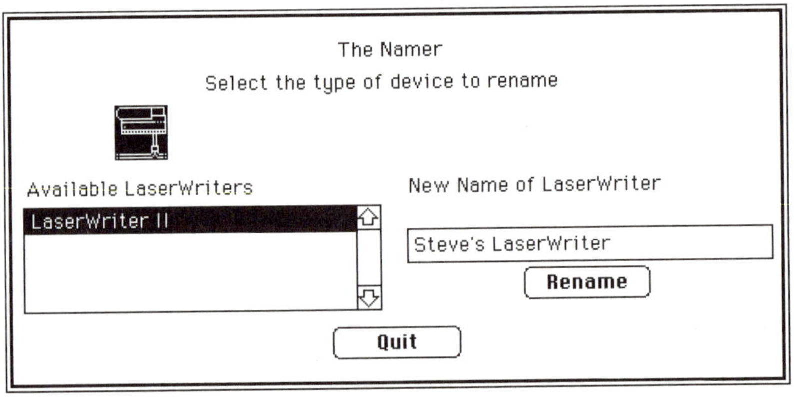

Figure 16.16
The Namer.

Network Hardware

A group of computers connected by one cable becomes a *Local Area Network* (or *LAN*). A LAN needn't be too local. Depending on the wiring, the individual devices on the network (or *nodes*) can be up to half a mile apart.

Each device on the network makes its own AppleTalk connection through a *connector box*. Each box has two jacks on it so you can form a daisy chain. Wire box A to box B, box B to box C, and so on. When you get to the end of the line, *stop*. Don't connect back to box A. A typical LAN configuration might look like Figure 16.17. The boxes and cables running from each piece of hardware form the AppleTalk "feet" that appear in the Chooser. The connection boxes also condition and terminate the signal and are necessary at both ends of the line.

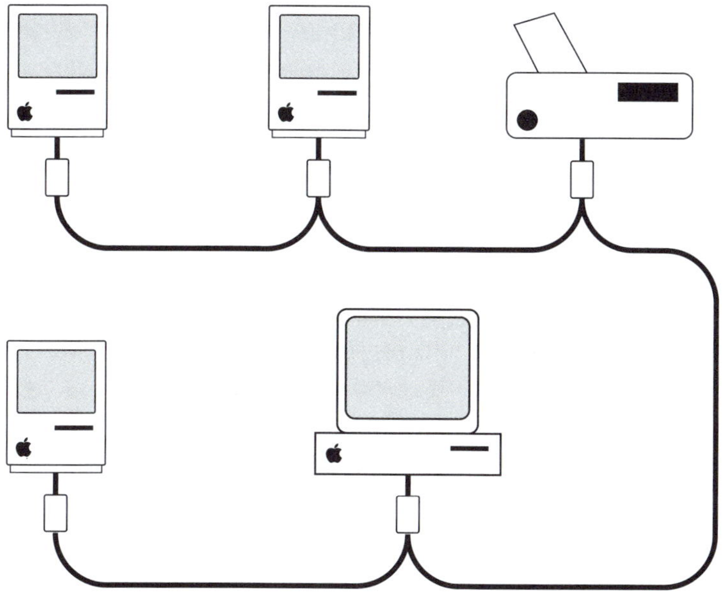

Figure 16.17

A simple AppleTalk network.

Apple's LocalTalk Hardware

Each node needs a LocalTalk connector box. Apple's connector boxes have a pigtail with either a round eight-pin or rectangular nine-pin plug. You have to get the right kind for each device on the network. (Most Apple equipment uses the eight-pin plug. Early Macs and some third-party equipment use the nine-pin version. Check your hardware before you buy.) Plug the connector box into the printer jack on your computer and the AppleTalk jack on other devices.

The connector box has two small jacks on it. A two-meter cable is supplied with the box. Plug it into one jack, run the wire as necessary, and plug the other end into one of the jacks on the next node's connector box. Repeat the process until the network is wired. Be careful while you're wiring. LocalTalk plugs like to fall out of their jacks.

If one two-meter cable isn't long enough, use the extension adapter supplied to link additional cables. Apple sells additional cables in 10- and 25-meter lengths. They also sell bulk LocalTalk wire so you can build your own cables. Be prepared to pay. Even in bulk, LocalTalk cables cost at least two dollars a foot.

Alternative Hardware

Instead of using official AppleTalk connector boxes and cables, you can get third-party connector boxes that use standard low-voltage wire. The cost savings are significant, their connectors are more reliable, and by using thicker wires, you can extend the network about three times farther than with LocalTalk cables.

Farallon Computing's PhoneNET system is the primary alternative system. The connector boxes are available with eight-pin, nine-pin, or 25-pin pigtails (for Lisas and Macintosh XLs). The boxes are much less expensive than Apple's and interconnect with ordinary modular telephone cables. You can even use the two extra conductors supplied in most telephone systems to run simultaneous voice and data through your existing wiring!

This system supports a number of different architectures besides the point-to-point daisy chain. You can have a single *backbone* network (see Figure 16.18) running through a building with computers and printers tapping into it wherever you want. Or you can have a *star* configuration (Figure 16.19) with multiple nodes all wired to a central junction point. You can also combine stars, backbones, and daisy chains in interesting and wondrous ways with the proper interfacing equipment. Each scheme has its advantages, discussed eloquently in Farallon's *PhoneNET Connector User's Guide.*

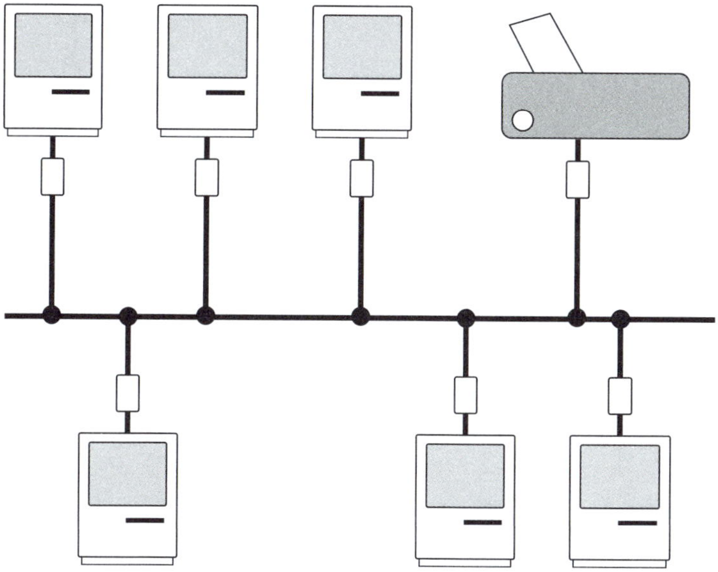

Figure 16.18

A backbone network.

Like SCSI lines, PhoneNET branches and daisy chains have to be terminated to dampen electrical echoes. Termination involves either bridging a small resistor across the wires or plugging in a modular telephone plug that has the resistor built in. Both types of termination come with the connector box along with complete instructions.

Farallon also makes a line of network controllers, adapters, and software so your PhoneNET can grow into a much more elaborate system, stretching between departments and buildings, and tying into existing mainframe networks. You can freely intermix other telephone wire network systems, including Nuvotech's TurboNet, with PhoneNET equipment.

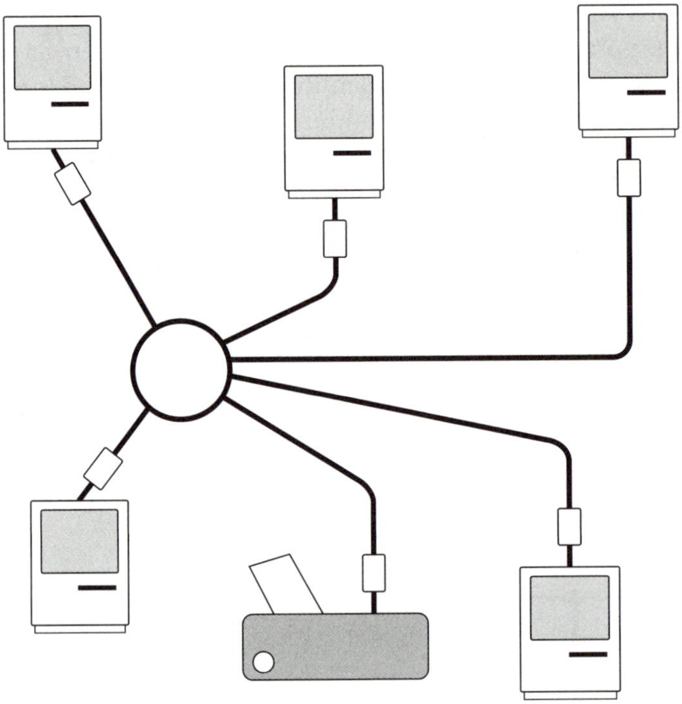

Figure 16.19
A star network.

Network Software

The basic communications between any number of Macintosh computers and a laser printer are taken care of by the system software. More elaborate software lets multiple computers share files, jointly access a database, and pass messages.

File Sharing

System 7 comes with built-in network capability, File Sharing. When it's activated, other System 7 users on your network can read—or change—files on your desktop from their own computers. You keep control, however, and can limit which files are accessible and to which users. To activate File Sharing, open the Sharing Setup control panel, as shown in Figure 16.20. When you want to make data (a file, a folder, or even a whole disk) available to other users, select it on the desktop and click Sharing... in the File menu. You'll see a dialog box like Figure 16.21, where you can specify who can get to your files and how much they can do to them. Once you've made a file available, its icon on your desktop will develop "feet" like the AppleTalk-equipped printers in Figure 16.10.

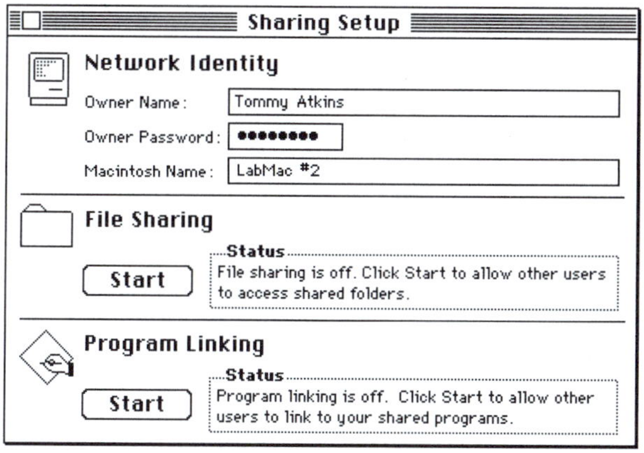

Figure 16.20

The Sharing Setup control panel in System 7.

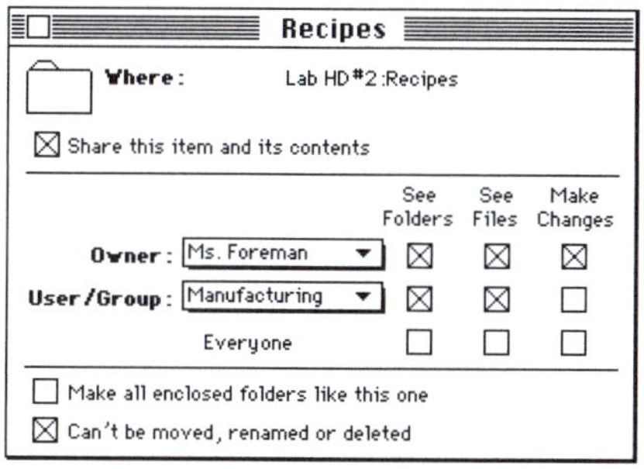

Figure 16.21

Controlling file access in System 7.

Public Folder

You can distribute files under System 6 (or in mixed 6- and 7-networks) using commercial network software, or with *Public Folder*. This is an incredibly helpful Chooser device, distributed free on some bulletin boards by Claris Corporation (at those prices, they don't guarantee support). Drop a copy into the system folder of every Mac in your network, and they'll be able to copy selected files. Figure 16.22 shows the *Public Folder* screen.

Figure 16.22

Public Folder.

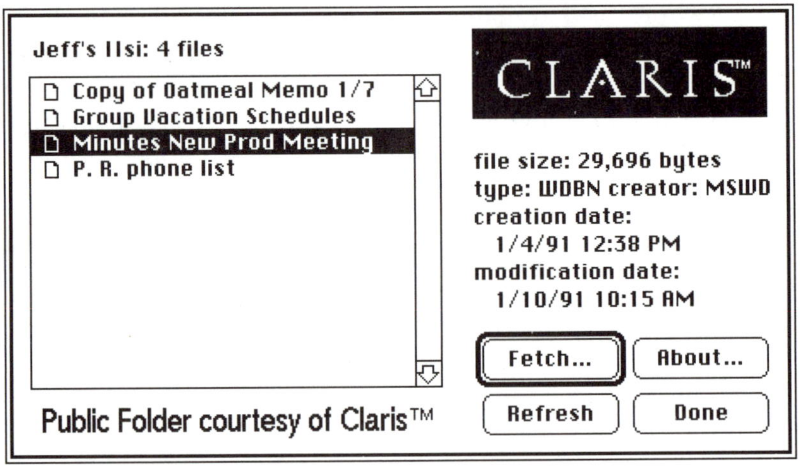

You make a file public by simply dragging it into a special folder on your desktop. Only files in this folder are accessible to other Macs. Everything else on your disk remains private. Users then select Public Folder in their Chooser, click on your network name, and grab a copy. Changes made to the copy won't affect your original: if other users update anything, they'll have to publish the changes in their public folders for you to copy.

Chat and Broadcast

These are shareware programs, distributed by user groups, that let you send messages from one AppleTalk Mac to another.

Commercial Network Software

TOPS, EasyShare, allShare, and other programs let you treat published files on a distant computer as if they were on your own hard drive. The distant computer becomes a *file server,* and depending on your access level (assigned by the server's human operator), you can read, modify, or delete files. Programs offer password protection, let multiple users open the same file at once, and can even offer files to properly equipped PCs.

Network software is a growing field, and prices and capabilities vary widely. Some programs (such as Claris' *FileMaker Pro* database) offer complete networking capabilities within the program itself. Additional software might not be necessary.

Network Management Programs

More elaborate networks with dedicated file servers (and dedicated human managers) often use special Macintosh software to analyze traffic patterns, check system response times, and predict the need for new branches. While any network that needs this kind of careful management is clearly beyond the scope of this First Book, it's comforting to know your basic AppleTalk wiring can grow this far without becoming obsolete.

A

Glossary for Non-Hackers*

*Including a definition of Hacker.

About... The first item on the Apple menu. If you click it while an application is running, it'll tell you the *version* number (and frequently how much *RAM* is available for additional documents). If you click it from the Finder, it'll tell you the system version number and total RAM.

Accelerator An expansion board accessory that makes the Mac run faster.

Active Window The open window, always the one on top with a highlighted *title bar.*

ADB See *Apple Desktop Bus.*

Alarm Clock A standard Mac *desk accessory* that tells you the time and date and can sound an alarm.

Alert box A box that appears on the screen to give you information or a warning.

Alias (System 7) A token for any file or folder on the desktop. When you open the alias, it acts as a shortcut to the original file.

Alpha testing Early testing of a program to search for *bugs.* There are usually plenty.

Apple Desktop Bus The connection for keyboards and mice on the Mac SE and later machines.

Apple key Another name for the *command* ⌘ or key.

Apple menu The first menu heading in any standard Mac application, identified by an symbol. This menu always contains DAs and frequently also contains About....

AppleTalk Apple's machine-to-machine networking standard. Commonly used to refer to the network hardware, as well.

Application software Properly, a program that accomplishes something for the user, as opposed to System software (which accomplishes something for the Application). It's a redundant term, because Application, Software, and Program are commonly used interchangeably.

Arrow keys On most Mac keyboards, the four keys with arrows on them. Use them to position the pointer, scroll down a list, or nudge a graphic.

Arrow pointer The basic shape the *pointer* takes; a tool used to select an item on the desktop or in a graphics program.

ASCII (ASK-key) American Standard Code for Information Interchange, with one-*byte* equivalents for every character and punctuation mark. For example, in ASCII "67-97-116" spells "Cat."

ASCII file A little file containing characters which any computer and most word processors can read. Also called a text file or ASCII text.

ASCII graphics Drawings made up of standard text characters that any computer can read, often used in telecommunications.

AT commands See *Hayes commands.*

Backup A copy of a program or document which you can use in place of the original. To *backup* is to make an identical copy.

Balloon Help (System 7) Comic-strip style text boxes used to explain system features.

BASIC An acronym for Beginners All-purpose Symbolic Instruction Code, a programming language largely obsolete on the Mac. HyperTalk's and White Knight's scripting language are very similar.

Baud The unit of measurement for data transmission speeds, approximately equal to one bit per second.

BBS (Bulletin Board System) A computer system maintained by an individual or computer user groups to share messages and software.

Beta testing Second-round debugging of a program. Beta versions may be posted on *BBS* as *shareware.*

Bézier curves Mathematically generated lines that can display non-uniform curves (as opposed to uniformly-curved arcs), frequently found in drawing programs.

Binary The base-2 numbering system that enables computers to express everything in terms of "on" or "off."

Bit The smallest possible single unit of information, either "on" (1) or "off" (0). Short for *B*inary dig*it.*

Bit-mapped font A typeface made up of dots and designed for use on dot matrix printers and the Mac screen. Also called an ImageWriter font.

Bitmap Any image described by bits or dots, including the Mac screen and ImageWriter printer output.

Bomb Any system malfunction that irrecoverably stops your program. Also, the *message* or *alert* box with a picture of a bomb in it, warning you that the system has been brought to its knees. The only cure for most bombs is a *boot.*

Boot To start the computer, loading its operating system and reorganizing its memory. From "bootstrapping," or "pulling oneself up by the bootstraps."

Box 1. An enclosed area on the Mac's screen with a message, such as a *dialog* box or an *alert* box. 2. Any of the various squares which control windows: *close* boxes, *scroll* boxes, and *zoom* boxes.

Buffer A space in the computer's memory for temporary data storage. A print buffer stores data until the printer is ready.

Bug A problem within a program which causes it to misbehave, *crash,* or even *bomb* the system. Comes from early computer terminology, when bugs ate the cloth insulation from the wiring.

Bundled software Marketing technique of including (usually) worthwhile software with another purchase. System, Finder, and HyperCard are bundled with new Macs. *Backup* programs are frequently bundled with hard disks. Some programs are frequently bundled together.

Button 1. An outlined area in a dialog box, which you click to choose a command. 2. The switch on top of the mouse, also called the mouse button.

Byte Eight *bits* of data, representing a decimal number between 0 and 255. Bytes frequently stand for individual characters in text.

Cache A section of *Random Access Memory* or *RAM,* which temporarily holds data on its way to or from a disk. Because RAM is faster than disks, caches make computer operations go faster.

CAD/CAM Computer Aided Design and Manufacturing (pronounced cad-cam).

Calculator A *DA* that works like a common, two-dollar calculator.

Cancel Stopping an activity. Cancel buttons appear in most dialog boxes, allowing you to change your mind before you permanently modify or print a file.

CD-ROM (Compact Disc, Read Only Memory) A system for optical storage and retrieval of information.

CDEV (SEA-dehv) The Control Panel device that is a utility program kept in the *system folder* and activated through an icon on the *Control Panel.*

Cell The basic unit of a spreadsheet containing a number, label, or formula.

Checkbox A button that works as a toggle. When you click it, an x appears in the box, and the activity it represents is "on." Clicking again removes the x and turns off the option.

Chooser A desk accessory used to select input and output devices, usually printers or network connections.

Chooser resources Files which display an icon in the Chooser window, usually *printer drivers* or *network resources.*

Click To position the mouse pointer over an icon, word, or object and press and release the mouse button once.

Clip art Pre-drawn artwork on disk or CD-ROM for use in your own documents or publications.

Clipboard Memory devoted to temporary storage of selected text or graphics. The Clipboard can hold one item at a time. Its contents disappear when you turn off the computer.

Close box A small box in the left corner of the title bar. Clicking here closes the document or removes its window from the screen.

Code Basic program instructions in a language the computer can read and understand.

Color wheel On color Macs, a segmented circle used to select one of a few million colors. Found in the Color CDEV and within many programs.

Command Anything you tell a computer to do. Commands are generally chosen by clicking on a menu or holding the command key simultaneously with one or two other keys.

Command key Also called the Apple key and the Cloverleaf key, because of the and ⌘ symbols engraved on it. Press it simultaneously with other keys to issue commands.

Control key Put on ADB keyboards, as a help to former IBM users who missed having one. It has no use except in telecommunications with non-Macintosh systems.

Control Panel A desk accessory that enables you to set the volume of sound, the speed of typing and clicking, and other system functions.

CPU (Central Processing Unit) The brains of the computer, from the days when computers consisted of more than one refrigerator-sized unit. Sometimes used to refer to the main processing chip or to the system unit in modular Macs.

Crash A condition of total computer failure, usually accompanied by a frozen screen and no response to the mouse or keyboard. A crash generally means that you must restart the system.

Curly Quotes The typesetters' kind of quote marks (“”) as opposed to the kind found on typewriters ("). Generate them automatically by selecting “smart quotes” in most word processors, or hitting Option-[.

Cursor Term sometimes applied to the pointer or text insertion point. See *Arrow keys.*

DA Desk Accessory.

Database A collection of organized information stored as a file, or the program used to create and organize the information.

Debug The process of finding errors in a program.

Default An action, command, or specification the computer will carry out unless you specify otherwise. For example, plain type (as opposed to **boldface** or *italic*) is the default style in most word processors.

Default button A button designated by a heavy border in a dialog box. The most likely or suggested action. You can choose it by clicking or by pressing the Return key.

Defragmenting Reorganizing a hard disk to make it store and retrieve data faster. You should do this periodically.

Delete key A key which erases characters from the insertion point in a word processor or deletes the whole selection in most programs.

Desk Accessories Small utility programs available under the Apple menu, which can be run while using another program.

Desktop The computer screen with no document windows open, or the basic working environment for the Macintosh. Also, a piece of furniture which ruins a *mouse* when it's dirty.

Dialog box A box that appears on the screen asking for information or actions from the user.

Digitize To convert an image or sound into a form usable by the computer.

Dimmed A menu choice or button that is grayed-out and disabled on the Mac screen.

Directory 1. A list of the contents of a disk; may appear as a collection of icons and folders. 2. A critical section of the disk's surface that steers the magnetic heads to data and program instructions.

Disk A magnetic storage medium holding information that the computer needs in order to function.

Document The file of data created by an application.

DOS (Disk Operating System) Every computer uses one, but the term generally refers to MS-DOS (used on IBM PCs and clones). Macintosh's DOS is usually called the *System* and *Finder.*

Dot matrix A printer that uses pins pressed against an inked ribbon to form images on the paper. ImageWriters are dot matrix printers.

Double-click To position the mouse pointer and press and release the mouse button twice in quick succession. Usually selects and opens a file.

Downloadable fonts PostScript or QuickDraw typefaces stored on a disk, which must be downloaded to the printer's memory before you can use the font.

Downloading Retrieving a file from one computer and storing it on another. The opposite of *uploading.*

DPI Dots per inch; a measure of the resolution of monitors, laser printers, and scanners.

Draft quality High-speed, low-resolution printing. An ImageWriter speeds up draft printing by using rough approximations of the screen fonts.

Drag To move something on the screen by positioning the pointer over it, holding the mouse button down, and rolling the mouse. Used to select groups of items or to move pictures or icons around the screen.

Draw program A graphics program which generates object-oriented graphics, treating elements as collections of lines and shapes instead of dots. Compare *paint program.*

Driver Software that tells the computer how to send screen or memory information to an outside device (usually a printer).

E-mail (Electronic mail) Personal messages exchanged via computer on BBS or an on-line service.

Edit menu In the Finder and most applications, the third menu from the left. Contains commands to cut, copy, and paste; may contain others, depending on the program.

Ellipsis The symbol (...) after a menu item indicating the item brings up a dialog box asking for more information.

Encapsulated PostScript (EPS) A graphics file format for finely-detailed pictures. Desktop publishing programs can manipulate this format.

F-key A Mac command accessed by pressing ⇧Shift-⌘ and a number. It has no relation to the function keys on extended keyboards.

Fat Bits A feature to edit graphics in a greatly magnified view.

Field In a database *record*, the area for a particular piece of data.

File Any collection of data on disk; an application or program.

File menu The second menu in all standard Mac applications. Contains commands for disk file and printer manipulation.

Find file Apple DA that locates files by name or partial name.

Finder The basic Macintosh program that creates the desktop and allows you to manage files and disks. Along with the System, it comprises the Mac's operating system.

Floppy disk A removable magnetic disk for data and program storage. Floppies for the Mac are housed in a plastic shell approximately 3.5"" square. Mac floppies do not flop or flex.

Folder A collection of documents or other folders, represented by a folder-shaped icon on the desktop. Roughly equivalent to MS-DOS's sub-directories, which we won't define here.

Font A set of numbers, letters, and symbols in a particular typeface, style, and size. The term also refers to the file that contains a *bit map* of those characters.

Font/DA mover A utility program used to install and remove fonts and desk accessories from the system.

Footprint The physical space the computer occupies on the surface where it sits. Compared to PCs, the Mac has a small footprint.

Fork Mac files are organized into two forks. The resource fork holds file instructions, and the data fork holds text, graphics, or numerical data. Other computers do not split their files into forks.

Form feed To advance the page to a specified position on a dot matrix printer.

Format 1. To design pages on a word processor. 2. To initialize a disk, checking its *sectors* and organizing a *directory*.

Freeware Public domain software for which no fee is requested.

Get Info window The window that appears when you select Get Info from the *desktop* File menu. It tells you the size of a selected file, when it was most recently modified, and where it is. You can also lock or unlock a file or disk in this window.

GIGO (Garbage In, Garbage Out) Programmers' disdainful term for errors caused by incorrect user input.

Graphic User Interface (GUI) A program design that lets the user click icons instead of typing text commands.

Hacker Person who enjoys computers and programming. Sometimes to the exclusion of job, family, eating, or sleeping.

Handshake A computer-to-computer message saying essentially, "Yes, I got that last instruction and am ready for the next."

Hard disk; hard drive; hard disk drive A rigid, usually non-removable magnetic disk and its housing and reading mechanism. A hard disk stores more information than a floppy disk and can be read more quickly.

Hardware Parts of a computer that have wires and electronics. Whatever is not software.

Hayes command set A standard collection of commands to control modems.

HFS (Hierarchical File System) A method of organizing data on a Mac disk, in which folders are active in list boxes as well as on the desktop. See also *MFS*.

Highlighting Indication that something has been selected, chosen, or is active.

Host A computer set up to accept *modem* calls from other computers.

Hot spot The working end of any pointer or graphics tool. The single dot where the action takes place.

I-beam pointer Pointer which indicates where the Mac will modify text; also called the *text tool.*

Icon A picture symbolizing, and linked to, a file or command.

Imagesetter A high-quality printer which can produce both graphics and type, frequently from PostScript files generated on a Mac.

ImageWriter A line of dot matrix printers made by Apple.

Import To load information created by one program into another.

Init (in-IT) Initialization program. Short program that subverts the Mac's working system upon startup, usually for some worthwhile purpose that Apple left out. Print spoolers and screen savers are typical INITs.

Initialize 1. To reset a program or device to its starting values. 2. To *format* a disk.

InkJet Printer Squeezes tiny drops of ink to create excellent images on a very limited range of paper stocks. Much slower than laser printers, but also much cheaper.

Integrated Application Program combining limited functions for word processing, database management, spreadsheet, and graphics (and sometimes including telecommunications or outlining). Also known as *Works.*

Interface A connection between two objects. Often short for user interface, the way a person gives commands to the computer.

Jaggies Kindergarten-block-like effect seen when bit-mapped characters are enlarged beyond their original size.

K (Kilobyte) A thousand bytes (actually 1,024 bytes) of data. Used as a measure of computer memory. (A Mac 512 has 512K of *RAM.*)

Kerning Closing up the space between two letters for better appearance.

Key combination (also called Keyboard equivalent) A fast way to issue a command without using mouse or menu, by pressing the ⌘ *key* and another key simultaneously. Key combinations are usually indicated next to the appropriate command on the menu.

Label (System 7) User-definable identification tags for desktop items. Files and folders can then be sorted by these labels.

LAN (Local Area Network) A system tying together several computers and one or more printers.

Laser font See *outline font.*

Laser printer A computer printer that creates images out of tiny dots of laser-generated light, reproducing them through a process similar to an office copier.

LaserWriter A line of laser printers manufactured by Apple.

Launching Starting an application.

List box Part of a dialog box with a long list of files to open or commands to execute.

LocalTalk Apple's cabling hardware standard for *LAN*; now usually included in the term *AppleTalk.*

Locking Preventing a disk or file from being accidentally changed. A locked disk is sometimes called write-protected.

Log on Connecting to a computer network or BBS.

Look and feel The style of a computer or program interface. Because all Mac programs share a similar look and feel, users can switch between them easily.

M (Megabyte or Meg) 1,024 kilobytes, roughly a million bytes.

Macro A command that quickly does something otherwise more complicated, such as typing a phrase or executing a string of other commands.

Marquee The flashing rectangle surrounding selected items, usually in *paint* programs.

Memory The place within the computer that stores information electronically. Usually refers strictly to *RAM,* but also includes the Mac's basic operating instructions, programmed in Read Only Memory at the factory.

Menu A list of commands. Choose a menu command by *clicking* on it with a mouse.

Menu bar The strip at the top of the Mac screen containing menu titles.

Message box A box that appears on the screen with information or warnings. Also called an alert box.

MFS (Macintosh File System) An early Macintosh desktop scheme that lets you put files into folders. The folders, unfortunately, weren't recognized by other programs. Superseded by *HFS.*

Modem (Modulate-demodulate) Essential telecommunications hardware, which converts digital data to voice-like frequencies the telephone system can handle.

Modifier key A key that modifies the effect of another key being pressed. Standard modifier keys are the Shift, Option, ⌘ Caps Lock, and Ctrl keys.

Monitor The screen on which a computer displays things. Compact Macs have a built-in monitor. Mac IIs use a separate monitor.

Mouse A device for moving any of various pointers on the Mac screen or selecting and dragging objects.

MultiFinder An Apple-supplied *INIT,* which enables several programs to be open at one time, in machines with sufficient memory.

Network Any collection of computers or peripherals wired together to share resources or information. Local Area Networks generally use high-speed cables within a single building. Other networks can use modems or digital telephone connections.

Node Any computer or other device connected to a network.

Object-oriented A programming technique that allows any screen element or typed phrase to carry program instructions. Macintosh *buttons* are objects.

Object-oriented graphic A collection of lines and shapes treated as a single unit by the program. Graphics created in a *draw* program, as opposed to *bit-mapped.*

OCR (Optical Character Recognition) Software, or software/hardware combinations, that can recognize *bit maps* of individual letters and convert them to *ASCII.*

Opening Double-clicking an icon of a folder to see what's in it, or double-clicking a document or application icon to start the program.

Outline font A font intended for use on a laser printer or Imagesetter. Rather than being made of dots like a bit-mapped font, it is an outline of each letter and can be scaled to any size without loss of quality. Frequently described in the PostScript language. Sometimes called a laser font.

Paint A graphics format for bit-mapped images; based on the original MacPaint.

Paint program A graphics program which generates low resolution (72 dpi) bit-mapped graphics in which each dot can be manipulated separately.

Palette A window of small icons representing the tools or graphic patterns available in a program.

Parking Locking the head of a disk drive so that neither it nor the disk will be harmed by vibration. Choosing Shut Down parks the head. Many newer hard disks park automatically when the power is removed.

Paste To put the contents of the Clipboard into a document.

Pasteboard In page layout programs, the temporary storage and work area outside the boundaries of the page.

PC (Personal Computer) Properly, any computer designed to be used by one person at a time. In modern usage, it refers specifically to small computers that are compatible with the IBM text-based standard.

PD (Public Domain) Refers to software distributed through bulletin boards and user groups. May be copyrighted and subject to *shareware* fees.

Peripheral A device that wasn't an original, integral part of the computer. A standard Mac mouse is not a peripheral; a trackball is. Common peripherals include printers, hard drives, and modems.

PICT (Pick't) A standard file format for object-oriented graphics.

Pixel (PICK-sill) A single dot. The individual units that make *bit-mapped* characters or graphics. Short for picture element.

Pointer The indicator which moves on the screen when you move the mouse.

Popup menu A list of options in a dialog box which stays hidden until you click on it.

Port Any data connection jack on a computer or peripheral.

PostScript Adobe's proprietary page description language, designed to relay instructions about fonts and *objects* to a printer.

PostScript font A typeface designed to work with PostScript; an *outline* font file in the PostScript format.

PowerBook Apple's line of portable, battery-powered Macs.

PRAM (Like a baby carriage) Parameter *RAM*, a portion of the Mac's memory used to store Control Panel settings and other user-specific information. A small battery keeps the PRAM from losing information when the computer is shut off.

Print buffer A hardware device that intercepts a print file and holds it in its own memory until the printer is ready to accept it, freeing up the computer for other things.

Print spooler An *INIT* which acts like a print buffer, but intercepts the print instructions within the system and directs them on hard disk. Usually requires *MultiFinder* to send the disk file to the printer while another program is running.

Printer driver (or Printer resource) A *Chooser* document that tells the Mac how to translate a file's text and graphics to a form a specific printer can use.

Program A group of instructions that tells a computer how to do something. Also called software. Talking about software programs, however, is like talking about an armchair chair, or a car automobile. Talking about Application software programs is just plain ridiculous.

Programmer's switch A piece of plastic which clips onto the side of compact Macs, touching an internal restart and program debugging switch.

Prompt A symbol on the screen, usually represented by >, !, or :, indicating that a computer is waiting to be told what to do. Found on mainframes, IBM PCs, and other old-fashioned machines. You may encounter these on telecommunications services.

Protocols A set of standard procedures controlling the way information is exchanged between computers.

Public Domain See *PD.*

Publish and Subscribe (System 7) System-level feature linking data between programs. If a chart or text is changed by the Publishing program, all copies of it in Subscribing programs will change to match.

QuickDraw Apple's built-in graphics software and the programming heart of the Macintosh *look and feel*: allows programs to draw or print lines and shapes much faster than on other small computers.

QuickDraw printer High quality (usually laser) printer that uses QuickDraw commands through the SCSI port, rather than PostScript.

QuickTime (System 7) System-level support to coordinate live video, animation, and sound in multi-media programs.

Quitting Leaving an application properly, and returning to the Finder or equivalent. Programs usually clean up files and do other housekeeping tasks upon quitting.

Radio buttons Groups of buttons shaped as small circles. Only one circle in the group can be filled, indicating that option has been selected. Named because they look and work like station-selecting buttons on a car radio.

RAM (Random Access Memory) Electronic data storage, much faster than disk storage. Also, unfortunately, *volatile:* power or program disruptions can destroy the data in RAM.

Ram Cache Area of computer memory devoted to temporary storage of hard-disk data. Lets the Macintosh system manage disk access better and run programs faster. Also ties up memory that could be used for other program purposes.

RDEV (ARE-dehv) A Chooser resource.

Read Me A file included on a new software disk, usually including last-minute instructions and program changes that couldn't be included in the manual.

Record In a database, a set of fields pertaining to one item.

Relational A database that can access or change information in one file based on user input to another file.

Resolution The spacing of dots on a page, or pixels on a screen, usually expressed in *DPI.* A higher resolution indicates finer-quality output. The Mac screen is 72 DPI. ImageWriter "Best" quality is 144 DPI. Most laser printers are 300 DPI.

Restart Rebooting from the disk without actually turning off the power. (Also known as *warm start* or *warm boot.*) Restarting loses anything that wasn't saved.

ROM (Read Only Memory) Part of the computer memory used for programs that are set at the factory. QuickDraw, and most of Mac's file and mouse interpreting routines, are stored in ROM.

Save Transfers data from memory to disk.

Save As... Command that lets you save a document under a different name or in a different location or format.

Scanner A device to convert images into digital form for use by a graphics program.

Scrapbook DA that stores a user library of text or graphic material.

Screen font Bit-mapped version of an *outline* font used to create the font on the computer screen.

Screen saver An INIT designed to prevent burnout of computer screens by blacking out the screen or putting up a moving pattern after a predetermined period of inactivity.

Screen shot A picture of the Macintosh screen saved as a Paint file or sent to the printer. From most programs press ⌘-Shift-3 to save a screen shot or ⌘-Shift-4 to print it.

Script A program or routine written by the user within a larger program such as HyperCard or White Knight.

Scroll arrow The arrows at either end of the scroll bar. Clicking them changes the window's view or moves a list up or down one line.

Scroll bar A rectangular bar that appears at right side or bottom of window if there's more to the display than can be seen at one time.

SCSI (Small Computer Systems Interface) A standard for hard disks and other devices that enables very rapid data transfer.

Serial port Either of the jacks on the back of the Mac labeled for the printer or modem. Serial means data is sent one bit at a time (as opposed to the parallel *SCSI* port). The ADB ports are also serial but are not commonly called that.

Service bureau A facility which rents time on a Mac and peripherals. Services vary but usually include 300 dpi laser printing, scanning, and imagesetting.

Shareware Public Domain software distributed on the honor system. Users are expected to send in modest shareware fees to compensate the author and support further development. Shareware is *not* free.

Shift-clicking Holding the ⇧Shift key while clicking the mouse button. Lets you select multiple objects or large amounts of text.

Shut Down A command on the Special menu in the Finder. It parks hard disk heads, ejects floppies, and prepares the Mac to be turned off. On newer Macs, it even turns off the power.

SIG (pronounced like Dr. Freud) A Special Interest Group within a larger *user group* or *BBS.*

SIMM (Single In-line Memory Module) Plug-in RAM chip arrays, used in many Mac models.

Startup disk The disk that contains the System and Finder software the Mac is currently running.

Startup screen A document you may create in a *paint* program to replace the Welcome to Macintosh screen.

Stationery A feature of many programs which allows you to create default documents with preset formatting.

Style A variation of a font, including **boldface**, *italic*, and other typographic niceties.

StyleWriter Apple's ink-jet printer.

Submenu A menu opened by selecting an item on a larger menu.

Subscribe See *Publish and Subscribe.*

Suitcase A file which stores fonts or DAs and is moved into the System file before use.

Sysop (System operator) Manager of a BBS or online service.

System 6, System 7 Radically different versions of basic operating software that controls how the Mac thinks. One of these systems must be in place before an application can be used.

System file The set of instructions which tells the Macintosh how to read and organize disks, how to open and create the Finder, and how to communicate with the user.

System folder A standard folder on the Mac desktop containing the *System* file and Finder. Depending on the user, it may also contain INITs, CDEVs, RDEVs, outline fonts, and temporary files put there by applications.

Teach text An application on the *System Tools* disk, which lets you read and print *Read Me* files.

Tear-off menu A menu or *palette* you can move around the screen like a window. Found in HyperCard and some graphics programs.

Text file An ASCII-only file, with no formatting codes or resource fork, that can be opened by most word processors.

Text tool See *I-beam pointer.*

TIFF (Tagged Image File Format) A standard graphics format for high resolution bit-mapped or scanned images.

Title bar Strip at the top of an open window containing its name. When the window is active, the title bar is highlighted with horizontal stripes and a close box.

Trash (Represented by a trash-can icon.) Lets you discard unwanted files.

Trojan horse A program that purports to do something useful, while it actually does something destructive or transmits a *virus.*

TrueType (System 7) Method for drawing smooth large-size fonts on the screen.

Undo A standard Mac command, which removes the effect of the last thing you did. You can undo text or graphic changes, but usually can't undo a save. See Chapter 4 for other limitations.

Uploading Sending a file from one computer to another over a network.

User group An affinity group of people who like a particular computer or application, trading information and rumors. Usually non-profit and independent of the manufacturer, frequently supported by a *BBS.*

Utilities Short programs that perform simple tasks, usually to support another program or as part of other programs.

Vaporware Exciting new computer programs supported by public relations and advertising but not by usable program code. Often the result of well-intentioned marketing types who just don't realize the product isn't ready to sell. Sometimes a fraudulent attempt to raise development money.

Version number A way of tracking changes made to software by the publisher, similar to edition numbers of a book.

Virtual Memory System feature that lets programs use the hard disk for their operations instead of faster but more expensive RAM memory.

Virus A section of program code that can copy itself to other programs without the user's consent. Often has destructive effects.

Warm See *reboot.*

Wetware Human beings. That part of a real-world computer system that isn't hardware or software. Often ignored by program developers and technical writers.

Window See *Active window.*

Wristwatch Shape the pointer assumes when the Mac is doing something that may take a long time. Some programs substitute a spinning beachball icon.

XCMD, XFCN Small programs added to HyperCard's resource fork to give the scripting language more power. The difference between XCMD (External Command) and XFCN (External Function) is strictly a question of what it does to data.

Zoom box Box to the right of the *title bar* on most windows enabling you to shrink and expand the window with a single click. Helpful when you have many layers of open windows.

I

Index

Symbols

A

B

C

D

G

H

I

J-K

L

M

N

O

P

Q

R

S

T

U

V

W

X-Z

Reader Feedback Card

Thank you for purchasing this book from SAMS FIRST BOOK series. Our intent with this series is to bring you timely, authoritative information that you can reference quickly and easily. You can help us by taking a minute to complete and return this card. We appreciate your comments and will use the information to better serve your needs.

1. Where did you purchase this book?

- ☐ Chain bookstore (Walden, B. Dalton)
- ☐ Independent bookstore
- ☐ Computer/Software store
- ☐ Direct mail
- ☐ Book club
- ☐ School bookstore
- ☐ Other ______________________________

2. Why did you choose this book? (Check as many as apply.)

- ☐ Price
- ☐ Author's reputation
- ☐ Quick and easy treatment of subject
- ☐ Appearance of book
- ☐ SAMS' reputation
- ☐ Only book available on subject

3. How do you use this book? (Check as many as apply.)

- ☐ As a supplement to the product manual
- ☐ In place of the product manual
- ☐ For self-instruction
- ☐ As a reference
- ☐ At home
- ☐ At work

4. Please rate this book in the categories below. G = Good; N = Needs improvement; U = Category is unimportant.

- ☐ Price
- ☐ Amount of information
- ☐ Examples
- ☐ Inside cover reference
- ☐ Table of contents
- ☐ Tips and cautions
- ☐ Length of book
- ☐ How can we improve this book? ______________________________
- ☐ ______________________________
- ☐ Appearance
- ☐ Accuracy
- ☐ Quick Steps
- ☐ Second color
- ☐ Index
- ☐ Illustrations

5. How many computer books do you normally buy in a year?

- ☐ 1–5
- ☐ 5–10
- ☐ More than 10
- ☐ I rarely purchase more than one book on a subject.
- ☐ I may purchase a beginning and an advanced book on the same subject.
- ☐ I may purchase several books on particular subjects.
- ☐ (such as ______________________________)

6. Have your purchased other SAMS or Hayden books in the past year? ______________

If yes, how many ______________________________

7. Would you purchase another book in the FIRST BOOK series? ______________

8. What are your primary areas of interest in business software? ______________

- [ ] Word processing (particularly ______________)
- [ ] Spreadsheet (particularly ______________)
- [ ] Database (particularly ______________)
- [ ] Graphics (particularly ______________)
- [ ] Personal finance/accounting (particularly ______________)
- [ ] Other (please specify ______________)

Other comments on this book or the SAMS' book line: ______________

____

Name ______________
Company ______________
Address ______________
City ______________ State ______________ Zip ______________
Daytime telephone number ______________
Title of this book ______________

Fold here

NO POSTAGE NECESSARY IF MAILED IN THE UNITED STATES

BUSINESS REPLY MAIL
FIRST CLASS PERMIT NO. 336 CARMEL, IN

POSTAGE WILL BE PAID BY ADDRESSEE

SAMS

11711 N. College Ave.
Suite 141
Carmel, IN 46032–9839